THE ORIGINS OF THE CHINESE NATION

In this major new study, Nicolas Tackett proposes that the Northern Song Dynasty (960–1127) witnessed both the maturation of an East Asian inter-state system and the emergence of a new worldview and sense of Chinese identity among educated elites. These developments together had sweeping repercussions for the course of Chinese history, while also demonstrating that there has existed in world history a viable alternative to the modern system of nation-states. Utilizing a wide array of historical, literary, and archaeological sources, chapters focus on diplomatic sociability, cosmopolitan travel, military strategy, border demarcation, ethnic consciousness, and the cultural geography of Northeast Asia. In this ground-breaking new approach to the history of the East Asian inter-state system, Tackett argues for a concrete example of a premodern nationalism, explores the development of this nationalism, and treats modern nationalism as just one iteration of a phenomenon with a much longer history.

NICOLAS TACKETT earned his BS from Stanford University (1998) and his PhD from Columbia University (2006). He has been at the University of California, Berkeley, since 2009, where he has taught undergraduate and graduate courses on a variety of topics, including "Imperial China and the World," "Precursors of Modern Nationalism," "Frontier History," and "History of Nationalism in Asia." Tackett's first book, *The Destruction of the Medieval Chinese Aristocracy*, received the American Historical Association's John Henry Breasted Prize in 2015. He was also the recipient of post-doctoral fellowships at Stanford University and the Getty Research Institute, and of an ACLS Digital Innovation Fellowship. He has given talks on four continents and in three languages on topics related to Tang-Song China.

D1453404

THE ORIGINS OF THE CHINESE NATION

Song China and the Forging of an East Asian World Order

NICOLAS TACKETT

University of California, Berkeley

CAMBRIDGE
UNIVERSITY PRESS

CAMBRIDGE
UNIVERSITY PRESS

University Printing House, Cambridge CB2 8BS, United Kingdom

One Liberty Plaza, 20th Floor, New York, NY 10006, USA

477 Williamstown Road, Port Melbourne, VIC 3207, Australia

314–321, 3rd Floor, Plot 3, Splendor Forum, Jasola District Centre,
New Delhi – 110025, India

79 Anson Road, #06-04/06, Singapore 079906

Cambridge University Press is part of the University of Cambridge.

It furthers the University's mission by disseminating knowledge in the pursuit of
education, learning, and research at the highest international levels of excellence.

www.cambridge.org
Information on this title: www.cambridge.org/9781107196773
DOI: 10.1017/9781108164917

First published 2017

Printed in the United States of America by Sheridan Books, Inc.

A catalog record for this publication is available from the British Library.

ISBN 978-1-107-19677-3 Hardback

ISBN 978-1-316-64748-6 Paperback

pour Zoe

Contents

Figures

Tables

Preface

It is hard to deny the formidable power of nationalism in modern times to shape the course of history. Historians and political theorists have responded with a proliferation of sophisticated studies exploring its development around the world since the nineteenth century. Fewer have addressed the question of nationalism's earlier history – a topic unfortunately tainted by partisans' own misleading claims about their nations' pasts. The present book is concerned with a form of Chinese nationalism that materialized at the court of Northern Song (960–1127) China. It seeks to describe this phenomenon and to explain its emergence, largely on the basis of the new inter-state dynamics of eleventh-century Northeast Asia. Many readers will strenuously object to my use of the terms "nation," "nationalism," and "national consciousness" when talking about the premodern period. Indeed, for those whose interests lie in the distinctiveness of Chinese society a millennium in the past, it may seem odd and unnecessary to seek out similarities with the modern world. But my approach is that of a comparative historian and social scientist. As such, while I strive to understand the unique cultural framework in which ideas circulated in eleventh-century China, I am simultaneously interested in recognizing commonalities shared by diverse human societies. Thus, in the chapters that follow, I will argue that modern nationalism and the complex of ideas that I refer to as Song "nationalism" are alternative iterations of a single phenomenon. Under what circumstances did this phenomenon emerge at certain times and in certain places? Why did a nationalism take form in the Song but not in the Tang? The present study attempts to answer just such questions.

The Origin of the Chinese Nation began as a seminar paper written in late 2002 on the subject of the Great Wall in the Song imaginary. I am greatly indebted to Bob Hymes for suggesting the topic. Since then, I have worked on the project in fits and starts. Between 2007 and 2009, during my tenures as postdoc at the Getty Research Institute (where

I benefited from workshops organized by Erich Gruen) and Stanford University, I wrote the core portions of Chapters 6 and 5 (in that order). I subsequently composed Chapter 3 during my first semester at Berkeley. Then, after a lengthy hiatus to complete a different book, I returned to the project in 2014. Much of Chapter 1 was written late that summer, during evenings spent on a leather couch encircled by jovial crowds of drinkers at the Berkeley Free House. The more methodical Chapter 4 was the product of structured time spent the following spring in cafes near Meizha Hutong, time made possible by an ACLS Fellowship, as well as by my mother-in-law Liu Bamei, who generously came to stay with us in Beijing to look after our infant daughter.

In the decade and a half spent on this project, my ideas were put to the test at conferences and talks held at the National University of Singapore, Stanford University, Minzu University, Leiden University, and Princeton University. In addition, I had a first opportunity to present the book in its entirety at the Écoles des hautes études en sciences sociales in Paris, in a series of four lectures delivered in spring 2015. For their invitations to present my research and for stimulating subsequent conversations, I heartily thank Al Dien, Huang Yijun, Hilde De Weerdt, Anna Shields, and Christian Lamouroux. I also benefited enormously from colleagues in the field and at Berkeley who took time to read and critique draft chapters, colleagues including Kerwin Klein, Yuri Slezkine, Tom Mullaney, Paul Smith, Maureen Miller, Peter Sahlins, Shao-yun Yang, and, most of all, Bob Hymes and Peter Bol, both of whom provided very extensive written commentaries to my entire manuscript. Over the years, I have had many, many inspiring conversations on the subject of my book, far too many to mention here. I recall particularly engaging and helpful discussions with David Johnson, Wen-hsin Yeh, Peter Zinoman (with whom I co-taught a graduate seminar on Asian nationalism), Geoff Koziol, Miranda Brown, my cousin (and a Roman historian) Jean-Jacques Aubert, Ye Wa, Victoria Frede-Montemayor, Carlos Noreña, Sarah Schneewind, James Vernon, Christian de Pee, Lu Yang, François Louis (my benchmate on a week-long Silkroad Foundation bus trip through Inner Mongolia), Naomi Standen, Li Hongbin, Nancy Steinhardt (with whom I quite fortuitously split a cab from Chaoyang, Liaoning, to Chaoyang, Beijing – roughly speaking, Xu Kangzong's route), Pierre Marsone, Mark Strange, and Jonathan Sheehan and Tom Laqueur (who offered their thoughts as I struggled on a bicycle up South Park and other steep hills). I extend my thanks as well to Lucy Rhymer, my editor at Cambridge University Press, who has enthusiastically supported this project, and to Robert Judkins.

Finally, I am infinitely grateful to my father (and a French historian) Timothy Tackett for taking the time on innumerable occasions and at moment's notice (often, moreover, as he was traveling in obscure corners of the world) to read and critique chapter drafts; to my wife Liu Kan for putting up with me and for sharing with me the invaluable intuition and insight of a rice farmer turned assembly-line worker turned cultural geographer; and to my daughter Zoe, who, with boundless energy, "strives to fly and stir, bringing light to old and tired eyes."

Notes on Supplementary Materials

1 Chinese characters were eliminated from this book to save on publication costs. For the reader's reference, the index includes Chinese characters for most person names. In addition, a PDF with the Chinese version of all translated text and a PDF of the original bibliography (containing Chinese characters) are both available on the author's website (www.ntackett.com).

2 Tangential comments in the footnotes were also eliminated to save on publication costs. Complete original footnotes (with Chinese characters, more detailed citation information, and additional random and extraneous observations) are also available on the author's website.

3 Also available on the author's website are the two databases described in Appendix B (a database of eleventh-century Northeast Asian tombs and a database of Northern Song diplomats and policymakers).

Map

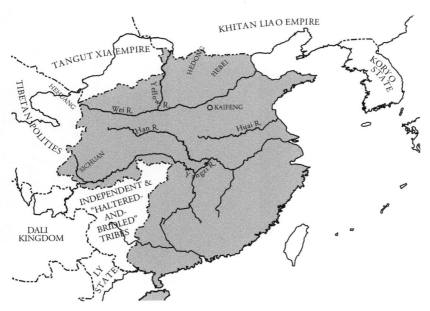

Map of Northern Song China

Introduction

During the eleventh century, men at the court of Song Dynasty China came to imagine in a new way the political entity to which they belonged. They started to articulate with far greater precision its spatial extent – which they now saw as bounded by natural topographic features as well as by the historical Great Wall – while simultaneously de-emphasizing an older theory of sovereignty premised on the idea of universal empire. They began to speak of a homogeneous cultural and ecological zone whose boundaries did not necessarily coincide with the political boundaries of the state. And they came to expect the allegiance of the people of this cultural zone – the "Han people" – including those living in neighboring states. These beliefs fueled the sentiment that the Song had the moral right to seize "former" territory that lay beyond the limits of its political control. Setting the stage for these new ideas was an East Asian inter-state system that reached a new degree of maturity under the Northern Song (960–1127). During an unprecedented one hundred years of peaceful coexistence with its northeastern neighbor, this dynasty became the first Chinese regime to interact with a steppe-based state according to the principles of diplomatic parity. For the first time in its history, China also embarked on a massive project to systematically demarcate its borders along multiple frontiers. The present study seeks to explore, contextualize, and explain these remarkable developments.

In fact, at the turn of the second millennium, China was in the midst of great changes affecting nearly all aspects of its society. In the period spanned by the Tang (618–907) and Song (960–1279) dynasties, a "medieval economic revolution" spurred expansions of the monetary system and of trade networks, as well as rapid commercialization and urbanization in several regions of the empire.[1] Simultaneously, the powerful aristocracy that had dominated society for much of the previous millennium vanished from the scene, replaced by a new elite defined on the basis of merit rather than blood.[2] In conjunction with these changes were innovations in Confucian thought – which now provided an ethical validation for this new elite – and in popular religion.[3] The period also saw the emergence of commercial printing, a concomitant enlargement of the literate population, and the expansion of the civil service examination system.[4] All of these transformations have been extensively studied by scholars. But whereas past scholarship has elucidated in substantial detail the economic, social, and cultural transition, little attention has been devoted to an equally remarkable change involving China's evolving sense of identity, changes set in motion in the context of an evolving inter-state system that would dominate East Asia until the nineteenth century.

In speaking of developments that amount, in essence, to the emergence of a "national consciousness" among Chinese sociopolitical elites, and in speaking of clearly demarcated borders and other phenomena typically associated with the post-Westphalian European state system, this book proposes to complicate entrenched narratives of modernity. The goal is not, however, to deny the significance of the Western/non-Western and modern/premodern dichotomies. Clearly, the globalization of the European state system in the nineteenth century transformed East Asia in radical ways. But it is important not to essentialize traditional Chinese society by treating it as static and unchanging. The emergence of a multi-state system in East Asia in the eleventh century had an equally profound impact on Chinese political culture. It spurred new ideas and a new worldview that together demonstrated that there has existed in world history a viable alternative to the modern system of nation-states, an alternative consisting of what I refer to as the "Chinese nation" and the "East Asian world order."

---

[1] Elvin, *Pattern of the Chinese Past*; Shiba, "Urbanization and the Development of Markets"; Shiba, *Commerce and Society*; Twitchett, "T'ang Market System"; Twitchett, "Merchant, Trade, and Government"; Skinner, "Introduction."

[2] Johnson, *Medieval Chinese Oligarchy*; Johnson, "Last Years of a Great Clan"; Ebrey, *Aristocratic Families*; Tackett, *Destruction*; Hartwell, "Demographic, Political, and Social Transformations," 405–25; Hymes, *Statesmen and Gentlemen*; Bol, *This Culture of Ours*, 32–75; Bossler, *Powerful Relations*.

[3] Bol, *This Culture of Ours*; Hansen, *Changing Gods*.

[4] Cherniack, "Book Culture"; Chaffee, *Thorny Gates*.

Premodern Nationalism and National Consciousness

Writing in 1887, the Qing poet and reformer Huang Zunxian (1848–1905) expressed a profound anxiety about how his country was known to others:

> Each country on earth, including England and France, is known to all by a single name. Only the Middle Kingdom lacks one. Tribesmen in the northwest refer to us as "Han"; islanders in the southeast refer to us as "Tang"; Japanese either call us "Tang" or "Nanjing," where "Nanjing" refers to the [capital of the] Ming Dynasty. But these all make use of a single dynasty's name; they are insufficient to encompass all of our history. Indians refer to us as "*Cīna*" or "*Shina*"; Japanese also refer to us as "*Shina*"; Englishmen refer to us as "*China*"; and French refer to us as "*Chine*." But these are all other countries' transliterations; they are not names we have used ourselves. Recently, when addressing foreigners, we have come to use the name *Zhonghua* ["Central Illustriousness"]. But our neighbors have denounced us for this, pointing out that all countries on earth see themselves as situated in the center, and, moreover, that treating ourselves as "illustrious" and others as "barbaric" constitutes no more than glorifying oneself in order to demean others.

After some further discussion of possible terminologies, Huang settled on the compound word *Huaxia* as the best name for his country. Although this term included the character for "illustrious" (*hua*), it made no explicit reference to centrality. Moreover, as Huang noted, it was a term that had long been used to refer to China as a transdynastic entity.[5]

This rather extensive linguistic exposition was not out of place in the context of the politics and intellectual climate of China at the turn of the twentieth century. Following a series of humiliating "unequal" treaties and a lopsided military defeat in 1895 at the hands of the Japanese Meiji state, many came to believe that only radical reform could save China. It was precisely in these years that an East Asian inter-state system long centered on China was finally abandoned to make way for the new world order based on a hegemonic Western European state system. Rather than sitting atop a hierarchy of subordinate political entities, China became, in the minds of educated elites, only one nation-state among many.[6] In the process, it embarked on a largely successful nation-building effort that would span much of the subsequent century, and would culminate

---

[5] Huang Zunxian, *Riben guozhi*, 49. Translation adapted from Liu, *Clash of Empires*, 76.

[6] Lydia Liu describes this transformation as "the invention of China"; Ge Zhaoguang writes of a shift from a world where China ruled "all under Heaven" (*tianxia*) to a world where China was only one of "a myriad states" (*wanguo*). See Liu, *Clash of Empires*; Ge Zhaoguang, *Zhongguo sixiang shi*, 2:440.

in the transformation of its massive population into a modern citizenry. Simultaneously, the Chinese state set out to define the component parts of its ethnically complex nation, classifying nearly every citizen into one of a fixed number of defined ethnic groups. By doing so, it unambiguously delineated who was part of the "Han" Chinese majority and who was not.[7]

Of course, modern national and ethnic identities necessarily emerge from a "negotiation" between the concerns of nation-builders and the "remembered historical narratives of community."[8] Indeed, Huang Zunxian's reflections were not without precedent. Eight centuries earlier, in the final years of the Northern Song, the writer and statesman Zhu Yu made similar observations:

> During the Han Dynasty [207 BCE – 221 CE], power and authority were extended to the northwest, so northwesterners refer to the Middle Kingdom as "Han." During the Tang Dynasty, power and authority were extended to the southeast, so the Man barbarians [living there] refer to the Middle Kingdom as "Tang." In the Chongning era [1102–07], various officials advised the throne that borderlanders customarily refer to the Middle Kingdom as "Tang" or "Han," that [these customs] have taken form in official documents, and that all such references should be changed to "Song," including cases like "Tang fashion" and "Han law." An imperial edict approved this measure. I personally think this was not appropriate; better to change such references to the word *Hua*. On all corners of the earth, there are none who do not submit to us; [the term *Hua*] maintains the distinction between the center [i.e., the Middle Kingdom] and the exterior world.[9]

Unlike Huang, Zhu was not anxious about the predicament of his country. He also embraced the notion of China's central position atop a hierarchy of states. But these differences aside, one sees striking similarities in the basic structures of their expositions. Like Huang, Zhu recognized that something called the "Middle Kingdom" had a history that transcended its component dynasties, yet, like Huang, Zhu also apparently felt a need for a different term to refer to this transdynastic entity. Zhu was also aware that his country was known by different names, and his references to northwesterners and southeasterners are nearly identical to those in Huang's comments. And both men ultimately settled on very similar names for China involving the character *hua*. Given that Zhu's

---

[7] Mullaney, *Coming to Terms with the Nation.*
[8] Duara, *Rescuing History*, 71.
[9] Zhu Yu, *Pingzhou ketan*, 35.

remarks survive in a well-known collection of observations and anecdotes, it is very likely that Huang had read them, and that he had them
in mind when writing his own thoughts on the topic centuries later.

The notion that there were important developments in the Song
regarding how Chinese came to view the political entity to which they
belonged has been raised in past scholarship. Some decades ago, Hoyt
Tillman and Rolf Trauzettel spoke of a "proto-nationalism" emerging
in the twelfth century that constituted the "first step towards Chinese
nationalism" and that resembled in many ways "German-inspired romantic nationalism."[10] In a more recent study, Ge Zhaoguang described the
initial appearance in the Song of a "China consciousness," which he saw
as a "distant precursor of contemporary nationalist thinking."[11] He took
note of the increased use of the term *Zhongguo* (the modern name for
"China") in Song-era texts, arguing that, whereas Tang political elites
believed they ruled over "all under Heaven," the Song saw itself as ruling
over a mere "state." A similar position has been taken by Deng Xiaonan,
who has asserted that there was a new tendency in Song political ideology
to "see ethnic, cultural, and political boundaries as one and the same."[12]
But despite the growing appreciation that radical new ideas about the
nature of China emerged during the Song, there has been little attempt to
synthesize these varied and – at times – impressionistic observations into a
coherent picture, nor to reflect on the possible origins of such ideas.

In speaking of "nationalism" or a "national consciousness" in the Song
Dynasty, it is important to distinguish clearly the situation existing in
Song China from the nationalist movements of the modern world. First,
the ideas under consideration here circulated essentially only among Song
intellectuals. By contrast, the new modes of nineteenth- and twentieth-
century consciousness affected large elements of the general citizenry.
Indeed, the mass movements of the twentieth century and the mobilization of great armies of willing recruits would have been inconceivable
until large segments of modern China's enormous population came to
see themselves as part of a single nation – through the expansion of mass
media and near universal education, and through concerted efforts of
propaganda. Even if literate elites in earlier times did conceive of such

---

[10] Tillman, "Proto-Nationalism"; Trauzettel, "Sung Patriotism."
[11] Ge Zhaoguang, "Zhongguo yishi."
[12] Deng Xiaonan, "Lun Wudai Songchu 'huhan.'" Dardess, "Did the Mongols Matter," 120–21,
argues that both the Song and the Ming sought only to rule over ethnic Chinese, having become
"uninterested in the conquest of frontier territory unless it already had a Chinese population or
appeared capable of sustaining one." See also Seo, "Toshi no seikatsu to bunka," 411–16.

a community – and there is ample indication that by the Song Dynasty they did – there is no evidence that the vast majority of the population concurred. This book, then, is not about mass consciousness, nor about state attempts to rally popular support, but rather about political ideals and notions of identity circulating among educated Chinese.

Second, the Song did not turn to principles of civic or ethnic national-ism in formulating a theory of government. There was no equivalent in Song China to the French Revolutionary idea of popular sovereignty, whereby a government existed legitimately only through the will of its people. Peter Bol has explored in some detail the impact of the eleventh- and twelfth-century Northeast Asian multi-state system on Chinese con-ceptions of empire.[13] During the Tang, imperial authority was thought to be universal, extending to the frontier tribal zone and beyond. By Song times, political universalism of this sort no longer seemed tenable. The solution, however, was not to reconceptualize the emperor as the ruler of a particular people – in the vein of modern nationalist thinking – but rather to envision his authority as now limited to the non-tribal "civilized" center. In other words, it was culture rather than ethnicity that defined the proper boundaries of the polity. To be sure, ethnic distinc-tions did exist in Song times, but, as Bol observes, they were not used as an "ideological foundation of state building."[14] From this perspective, the emperor was not the emperor of the Chinese. Armed with a mandate from Heaven, he was the ruler of the entire civilized world, including non-ethnic Chinese populations who may have migrated into imperial territory and become assimilated.

But if Song political ideals differed from those of contemporary times in critical ways, educated elites nevertheless shared something funda-mental with people of the present day, something that lies more in the realm of intuition and sentiment than of carefully reasoned ideology. Though popular sovereignty constitutes the ideological justification for twentieth-century nation-states, the cohesion of these nation-states ultimately depends less on a theory of governance than on the widely held *feeling* that the community and territory of the nation are "natural" and objectively real, with a history extending deep into the past. Thus, throughout recent times, nationalism has often been fueled by a crude nativism lurking beneath the surface of the carefully crafted ideals of nationalist intellectuals. It is for this reason that influential theorists of

[13] Bol, *Neo-Confucianism*, 10–15; Bol, "Geography and Culture."
[14] Bol, "Geography and Culture," 92.

nationalism like Ernest Gellner and Benedict Anderson have largely ignored ideology as a causative factor in the emergence of modern nationalism.[15] In the Song, though state ideology defined the empire on the basis of culture, policymakers invoked ethnicity as well, as we shall see in a later chapter. In dealing with the messy reality of frontier territories – for example, when struggling with how to make sense of an unwieldy mix of people of different cultures – they turned to ethnic categories that made intuitive sense to them as a practical tool of differentiation. It was the notion in these contexts that ethnic, cultural, and political boundaries ought to align that justifies referring to the Song worldview as a form of "nationalism," albeit one very different from its modern incarnation.

Scholars of nationalism have proposed two useful ways of relating the modern nation to the premodern world. One theory, represented by the writings of Anthony Smith, recognizes the modern nation-state as reflecting a radical break from the past, while also insisting that it was built upon pre-existing "ethnies." It was only by making use of ethnic categories already recognized by the masses of the population that it was possible to convince them to join the nationalist project.[16] Indeed, even historians who root the emergence of nationalism entirely within a narrative of modernity recognize pre-existing "potential nationalism" or "proto-nationalism" as historically significant.[17] But by emphasizing long-term continuities in "ethnies" and, simultaneously, radical distinctions between the modern and the premodern, Smith's approach says little about the fluidity of ethnic categories and how these categories evolved over time, nor does it do full justice to the complexity of the ideas circulating among educated elites in premodern times.

A second theory, proposed by social psychologists, argues that aggregation into groups constitutes a basic human survival mechanism, which provides security and safety, while simultaneously offering poorer members of lower status a means of basking in the prestige of their wealthier and more famous brethren. A natural human propensity toward group loyalties is said to explain national loyalties, but also other diverse social phenomena, from tribal aggregation on the Eurasian steppe to

---

[15] Gellner, *Nations and Nationalism*; B. Anderson, *Imagined Communities*.
[16] E.g., A. D. Smith, *Ethnic Origins of Nations*.
[17] Gellner, *Nations and Nationalism*, 42–48; Hobsbawm, *Nations and Nationalism*, esp. 75–77. Gellner notes that, as a result of its bureaucracy, premodern China "did display a certain kind of nationalism" (*Nations and Nationalism*, 16).

contemporary sports fandom.[18] Such a sociopolitical explanation, fundamentally ahistorical in its essence, may well explain why Chinese educated elites as early as the eleventh century were attracted to the idea of belonging to a vast empire-wide community. But it does not explain how the boundaries of the community came to be determined (both in terms of constituent people and constituent territories), nor why a new "national" consciousness emerged at a particular moment in time, nor how premodern group loyalties relate to the sorts of feelings of solidarity that one encounters in the contemporary world.

An alternative way of dealing with the premodern past and its relationship to the present, I propose, is to treat certain nineteenth- and twentieth-century phenomena as particular cultural manifestations of ideas and structures that might potentially emerge in any complex human society under the right conditions.[19] In reality, two factors often tied to the emergence of nationalism in the early modern West, general education (as distinct from specialized training) and commercial printing, already existed in China by the eleventh century.[20] Under such circumstances, one might expect the appearance of a new form of collective consciousness in Northern Song China as well. The relationship between the Song nation and the modern Chinese nation is, however, complex. Besides adhering to a very different ideology of political legitimacy, Northern Song Chinese differed from modern nationalists in how they defined the boundaries of their state. Contemporary China is conceived today to be a multiethnic state composed of fifty-six

---

[18] Druckman, "Nationalism, Patriotism, and Group Loyalty." Because national loyalties give prestige to people of low status, they can be far more alluring than class or other group solidarities. Unlike some social psychological theories of nationalism, Druckman's approach does not rely upon principles of evolutionary genetics. Cf. Gat, *Nations*, esp. 27–43.

[19] This approach to nationalism is similar to what Anthony Smith refers to as "recurrent perennialism" (see A. D. Smith, *Nation in History*, 40–41), though, like Reynolds, "Idea of the Nation," I see the nation as constructed and fluid, not rooted in pre-existing and unchanging "ethnies." Each new manifestation of a national consciousness involves a redefinition of the nation on new terms. Because nationalism is a recurrent phenomenon, it is meaningless to seek out a "prototype" nation upon which all other nations were modeled. Cf. Hastings, *Construction of Nationhood*; Greenfeld, *Nationalism*.

[20] On general education and nationalism, see Gellner, *Nations and Nationalism*, 29–34; on printing, see B. Anderson, *Imagined Communities*, esp. 37–46. Although Anderson speaks of "print-capitalism" in sixteenth-century Europe, some historians of capitalism prefer the term "commercial printing." One can think of the civil service examination curriculum as a form of general education insofar as it came to define the fundamental knowledge that all educated men were expected to have. See Hymes, *Statesmen and Gentlemen*, 32–33; Bol, "The Sung Examination System," 154–71. On the vitality of profit-driven commercial printing during the Northern Song, see Hymes, "Sung Society and Social Change," esp. 546–58.

"nationalities." Its "natural" territory extends deep into Central Asia. In its Song iteration, as will be clear in a later chapter, China was imagined to be a monoethnic nation that controlled neither Manchuria, nor the modern peripheral provinces of Guizhou, Yunnan, Tibet, and Xinjiang.

Clearly, one must approach the idea of the premodern nation with care. The nationview of the world – which sees all nations as modular replications of each other, all individuals as citizens of one of these nations, and all territory on earth as belonging exclusively and fundamentally to one nation and its people – has become engrained in the contemporary psyche. In order to legitimate modern claims over peoples and territories, the states ruling such nations produce myths of their own history, projecting their nationhood back into an antique past.[21] During the twentieth century, these myths have recurrently inspired devastating violence and warfare. But by taking the premodern nation seriously, it is possible to *denaturalize* the modern nation. One does so not by treating the premodern mindset as a sort of "proto-national" consciousness in the primitive stages of a long formative process, a notion that in fact accords well with national mythmaking. One does so rather by treating modern and premodern nations as distinct incarnations of a common phenomenon, defined by an alternative set of boundaries, and driven by a distinct set of contingent circumstances. The idea of a monoethnic nation described by Song Chinese certainly helps explain the uneasy place of non-Han nationalities within the People's Republic of China today. But it does very little to account for or to legitimate the complexities of contemporary China's ethnic policies and the expansiveness of its territorial claims.

The *Shidafu* Class and the Eleventh-Century "Imagined Community"

Why did a new sense of Chinese self-identity first blossom in the Northern Song? Two factors seem to have been particularly important. The first, explored here, involved internal structural and institutional changes within the Song state that spurred the development of a feeling of community among educated elites empire-wide. The second, explored at greater length later in the book, concerned contingent developments in the eleventh-century inter-state system that impacted how those elites

---

[21] Geary, *Myth of Nations*.

envisioned cultural and geographic boundaries. In the discussion that follows, it is useful to bear in mind the distinction between "national consciousness" (the powerful feeling of belonging to an "imagined community" of compatriots), "nationalist ideology" (the political principle that the boundaries of the state ought to correspond to the geographic extent of this community), and "nationalist movements" (political mobilizations that seek to implement the nationalist agenda, for example through military action or mass education).

Benedict Anderson's influential account of the emergence of nationalism is particularly useful here for understanding eleventh-century China, even though it treats the phenomenon as inherently "modern" in nature.[22] Most importantly, the mechanisms Anderson describes account for the development de novo of a new "subjectivity" and "mode of consciousness." The first instances of national consciousness – which, in his model, emerged in the Americas – were a consequence of sociological processes that were both unselfconscious and entirely self-contained. It was only in a second stage of development that the modular nation-state was reproduced around the world, as regimes and political organizers recognized its potential as a tool of mass mobilization. What I propose below is that the process by which Northern Song political elites came to imagine an empire-wide community shared striking similarities with Anderson's account of emergent national consciousness. Although my discussion undermines some fundamental elements of Anderson's account – most notably his implicit claim that nationalism was invented only once – in fact, the appearance of an analogous consciousness in premodern China as the result of similar sorts of mechanisms provides strong corroborating evidence for the explanatory power of Anderson's approach.

Anderson focuses on tracing the emergence of a very particular sort of "imagined community." Unlike a "real" community – the inhabitants of a village or the members of a tribe – in which most individuals know each other by name or face, the national community is one in which the vast majority of its members are anonymous strangers, who have never met and never will. It differs from other older notions of community – the religious ecumene and the dynastic realm – insofar as it is non-hierarchical and closed. Whereas universalist religions readily incorporated unbelievers into the fold, and populations of dynastic subjects could be transferred from one realm to another following a military invasion or a strategic royal marriage, in the modern nationview, individuals are "natural"-born

---

[22] B. Anderson, *Imagined Communities*.

into one and only one nationality. Their nationality cannot change, except by means of an onerous and exceptional process of naturalization.[23] In addition, whereas medieval society was hierarchical, such that greater solidarity existed between European nobles of different nationalities than between these upper social strata and their subject populations, all citizens of the nation-state are equal citizens. No imagined hierarchies exist to legitimate treating one as "more" of a citizen than another. Finally, the nation differs from other sorts of communities in its ability to arouse passionate commitment. Over the course of the twentieth century, tens of millions of people died willingly in great wars fought on behalf of these imagined communities of anonymous strangers.

A critical catalyst of the new mode of consciousness, according to Anderson, was commercial printing. Profit-driven printers, uninterested in limiting themselves to a Latin readership, promoted a new standardized vernacular language that replaced a vast array of regional dialects. Whereas a class schism had previously existed between a transnational educated elite communicating in Latin and the uneducated masses, new schisms developed between communities of readers in different linguistic zones. Mass-printed newspapers epitomized the power of print, contributing in two significant ways to the development of a new mode of consciousness. First, any given issue of the news periodical juxtaposed otherwise unrelated events that shared only the commonality of happening simultaneously in time. Key to the idea of the nation was a recognition that anonymous strangers might at any given moment be involved in a multitude of unrelated pursuits – "steady, anonymous, simultaneous activity" – even while remaining linked to each other as fellow nationals.[24] Second, newspapers were themselves read in the thousands or even tens of thousands, as part of a mass ceremony. Reading the same headlines in the morning at the kitchen table alongside countless other anonymous compatriots sitting at their own kitchen tables at nearly the same moment contributed to a feeling of intimacy with the people of one's nation, a sentiment of being "all in it together." This feeling of closeness was critical for spurring individuals to sacrifice their lives on the battlefield on behalf of their imagined brethren. Trade embargoes on printed material and other cross-border trade restrictions further reinforced a sense of national community by segregating communities of readers by administrative boundaries rather than according to larger linguistic zones.[25]

---

[23] Sahlins, *Unnaturally French*.
[24] B. Anderson, *Imagined Communities*, 26.
[25] Ibid., 54. It is partly for this reason that, after independence from Spain, the new nation-states of Latin America maintained colonial-era administrative boundaries.

Another catalyst of national consciousness in Anderson's model was the emergence of professional bureaucracies. These bureaucracies did not merely reproduce older, aristocratic hierarchies. Instead, they were staffed by functionaries recruited broadly from an ever larger educated population, the effect of which was to create a sense of human interchangeability that would be at the heart of national thinking. These bureaucrats, whose careers as "creole" elites were limited to the territorial extent of single colonial provinces, participated in common "pilgrimages" to the provincial capital from "remote and otherwise unrelated localities," and also followed similar peregrinations to appointments at various posts under provincial administrative control.[26] The strong feelings of community shared by these functionaries as a result of their common experiences became the foundation of a new sentiment of national consciousness. Nineteenth-century national movements were thus the product of deeply rooted feelings regarding the natural extent of one's political community, as engendered by the print industry and the state bureaucracy.

In Northern Song China, although the process by which a national identity emerged differed in many of its details, certain basic elements were very similar. As in the case of Anderson's model, the intuitive sense that the "imagined" political community was "natural" was not the product of a carefully crafted theory of government, but rather the unselfconscious outcome of particular sociological processes. In addition, the development of a new mode of consciousness in eleventh-century China came on the heels of a similar triad of phenomena: the breakdown of older "aristocratic" social hierarchies, the blossoming of commercial printing, and the greater professionalization of the bureaucracy along more meritocratic principles – reflected in the Northern Song case in the greatly expanded use of the civil service examination. Moreover, the new Northern Song "national" consciousness emerged among a political elite in many ways not unlike the "creole" elites who, in Anderson's model, played a particularly critical role in the initial appearance of national thinking.[27]

The first of the triad of causative factors was the radical transformation of the sociopolitical elite between the Tang and the Song. Until the

---

[26] According to Anderson, because the political careers of "creole" elites were confined by law to the boundaries of the colonial provinces they inhabited, independent nation-states defined by old colonial provincial boundaries seemed "natural" to them, and not merely an administrative convenience.

[27] According to Anderson, early nationalist elites "were hard put to it not to make a show of 'inviting in' (if only to the pantry) their oppressed compatriots," and thereby "consciously redefined these populations into fellow-nationals." Ibid., 50, 81.

very end of the Tang, political power was dominated by a circumscribed group of families, who intermarried with each other and who resided overwhelmingly in the two capital cities of Chang'an and Luoyang. These families constituted a "bureaucratic aristocracy" insofar as they served in office generation after generation, and their long-term presence in the upper bureaucracy provided them with immense social and political prestige. However, this social class was largely annihilated at the turn of the tenth century through a series of violent wars and rebellions, and with it disappeared an "aristocratic ethos" that emphasized the blood line and accumulated achievements of one's ancestors.[28] By the Northern Song Dynasty, success in the civil service examination became the pre-eminent marker of sociopolitical prestige, and under the Southern Song (1127–1279), an education in the examination curriculum (irrespective of one's success on the exams) came to define the social elite. The rise to prominence of the exams was bolstered by a new, more meritocratic culture, as represented by the popularity during the period of "rags-to-riches" tales.[29] Although Song society was by no means egalitarian – indeed, elites in any "meritocratic" society always find ways to seize advantages for their kin – educated Chinese no longer imagined their society in terms of permanently entrenched social hierarchies.

Alongside the destruction of the medieval aristocracy and its associated ideology was a radical reconfiguration of the geography of political power. The Tang sociopolitical elite was overwhelmingly concentrated in the capital region – whether in one of the two capital cities or in the Capital Corridor linking the two nearby metropolises. Men from these families were rotated among provincial positions all over the empire, but they maintained their residences in the capital zone and continued to participate in a capital-centric social network. In essence, the capital maintained a colonial relationship with the vast imperial periphery and the subaltern provincial elites. Under the Northern Song, however, the dominant political elite originated in numerous population centers around the empire. Although an upper bureaucratic class reconstituted itself by the mid-eleventh century, and began once more to aggregate in the capital region, the Song capital of Kaifeng was never as dominant as Chang'an and Luoyang under the Tang. In conjunction with the rapid expansion of the educated population over the course of the dynasty, political power became increasingly decentralized, such that, by the

[28] Tackett, *Destruction*, esp. 241–42; Tackett, "Wan Tang Hebei ren."
[29] Hymes, *Statesmen and Gentlemen*, 29–34; Bossler, *Powerful Relations*, 17–18.

Southern Song, the families that produced the most powerful central government officials were evenly distributed across all the most densely populated regions of China. Thus, a fairly homogeneous community of elites came to exist scattered throughout the empire.[30]

By the mid to late eleventh century, moreover, this community of educated elites had become self-conscious of its own identity, as clearly documented by the expanded usage of the term *shidafu* (sometimes translated as "literati") to refer to their positions in society.[31] In the political discourse of the era, members of the *shidafu* generally portrayed themselves as bound together by horizontal rather than vertical or hierarchical bonds.[32] This new sense of collective identity was partly the product of the spread of printing, in conjunction with the much more extensive use of the civil service examinations and of an empire-wide system of government schools for the recruitment of a professional bureaucracy. A national market for printed books and a national educational curriculum together ensured that the *shidafu* were immersed in a common textual tradition – including not only classical scholarship, but also the more recently published poetry and prose of their peers. As important as was the spread of printing itself in explaining the emergence of an imagined horizontal community of brethren was the *perception* that classical scholarship was now universally available to all. "Printed editions of these works are abundant, and officials and commoners alike have them in their homes," asserted one early eleventh-century official.[33]

Educated elites partook in numerous other common experiences. Those serving in office made regular "pilgrimages" to the capital for periodic reassignments. They also dutifully visited many of the celebrated cultural landmarks around the empire during their travels to and from provincial appointments; and they wrote poems about those sites with the conscious knowledge that many among their peers had visited the same sites, and had written similar lines of verse.[34] The majority among the *shidafu* who never managed to secure a post in the bureaucracy – the inevitable result of an increasingly competitive examination in light of

---

[30] For the classic description of the "localist turn," see Hymes, *Statesmen and Gentlemen*; for an analysis of the impact of the localist turn on the geographic distribution of political elites, see Tackett, "Imperial Elites."

[31] Tackett, "Transformation," 177, n.201.

[32] Hymes, "Sung Society," 631–37.

[33] Egan, "To Count Grains of Sand," 33. I thank Joseph Passman for drawing my attention to this quote.

[34] Zhang Cong, *Transformative Journeys*, esp. 154–206.

an ever growing educated population – spent decades immersed in the examination curriculum, driven onward by the knowledge that, even if they failed the exams, their education was itself a marker of status. By the turn of the twelfth century, some 200,000 students were enrolled in prefectural and county schools, and nearly 80,000 candidates regularly attempted the prefectural exams, held across the empire on a triennial basis.[35] During their daily toils at their writing desks, and during the ceremonies associated with examinations that many were destined to fail, these young men could seek solace in the knowledge that countless other anonymous strangers just like themselves, from "remote and otherwise unrelated localities" around the empire, were simultaneously engaged in the same tribulations. This experience of community, evident in a burgeoning anecdotal literature bemoaning the challenges and hardships of the examination life, helped establish a sentiment of solidarity among educated strangers empire-wide, a feeling of being "all in it together."[36]

To be sure, *shidafu* consciousness did not inevitably lead to a "national" consciousness. The emergence of this class introduced a schism between educated/cultured people and uneducated/uncultured people. In subsequent centuries, during periods of non-Chinese rule, the *shidafu* might well incorporate individuals of non-Chinese background. Like the European aristocracy, it had the potential to become a transnational community of people of high status. But there is little evidence that the *shidafu* of the Song Dynasty ever conceived themselves to be transnational in this way. To the contrary, *shidafu* consciousness in the Song contributed to the development of a national consciousness in two ways. First, as in the case of colonial bureaucrats and the educated reading public in Anderson's model, the horizontal, empire-wide community of *shidafu* spurred the development of a new mode of consciousness that made it possible to think of anonymous strangers anywhere in the empire as one's brethren. Second, because of the new meritocratic ethos positing that even a peasant's son might someday rise to high office, it was not difficult conceptually to translate *shidafu* consciousness into a broader vision of an empire-wide community that included even the peasantry.

If the implication here is that a new mode of consciousness emerged in the Song that was not unlike the national consciousness described by Anderson and other scholars of modern nationalism, one must still account for how this consciousness came to spur a Song nationalist

---

[35] Chaffee, *Thorny Gates*, 34–35.
[36] Ibid., 157–81; Hymes, *Statesmen and Gentlemen*, 29–32.

ideology and nationalist *movement*. More specifically, how did the collective consciousness of Song educated elites acquire an ethnic dimension? Why did Song Chinese come to insist that the political boundaries of the state ought to align with the geographic extent of the Han ethnoculture? And what spurred a political movement to recover "former" territories that had never been under Song control? Much of this book will deal precisely with this set of questions. To better understand the context for China's evolving place in the world, however, we first turn to an overview of the eleventh-century East Asian inter-state system.

The East Asian World Order

Throughout the period under consideration here, Song China coexisted with several other important East Asian powers (see map, p. xix), though not all were of equal concern to Song policymakers. Contact with states in Korea, Japan, and maritime Southeast Asia was generally limited to trade (often under the guise of tribute missions), although, due to its shared border with the Khitan Liao empire – to be examined in some detail below – the Koryō Kingdom in Korea would come to play an important ancillary role in Song–Liao relations. To the south, the two most significant states, the Kingdom of Dali (937–1253) in Yunnan and the Ly Dynasty (1009–1225) in Vietnam, remained separated from China by a buffer region inhabited by autonomous tribes. During the Song, Chinese colonists spread relentlessly southward, recurrently provoking armed opposition from tribal groups in their path. Some of these tribes were held under a "haltered-and-bridled" system, whereby in exchange for maintaining their de facto independence their chiefs accepted Chinese bureaucratic titles and other symbols of subordination to the Chinese throne.[37] Contact with Dali, however, was restricted to an important trade that supplied horses for Song China's northern campaigns.[38] Military confrontations with Vietnam broke out only after the destruction of one of the intervening tribal regimes in the late eleventh century.[39] In sum, due to the relatively limited scale of direct political interaction or military confrontation, the southern and maritime frontiers were never the main focus of attention at the Song court.

[37] Von Glahn, *Country of Streams and Grottoes*; Von Glahn, "Conquest of Hunan"; An Guolou, *Songchao zhoubian minzu*, 54–62.
[38] Yang Bin, *Between Winds and Clouds*, chap. 3, paras. 59–69.
[39] J. Anderson, "Treacherous Factions."

By contrast, the steppe-based regimes on the northern and northwestern frontiers were understood to be an immediate threat to the Song's very existence. In the words of one mid-eleventh-century statesman, in response to a policy question from the emperor regarding unrest in the south, "How are these trifles worth exhausting imperial power and intruding on the emperor's concerns?'. . . The most significant border issues lie in the west and the north!"[40] Indeed, in the 1120s, the Jurchens, precursors to the Manchus of the Qing Dynasty, would sweep down from Manchuria to conquer the whole of North China, forcing the Song court to flee southward and establish a new regime – the Southern Song – based beyond the Yangzi River. In the next century, the Mongols descended from the Eurasian steppe, first destroying the Jin Dynasty (1113–1234) of the Jurchens, and then overrunning the Song four decades later. But long before the Jurchens and Mongols arrived on the scene, China already faced two major steppe powers.

To the northwest were the Tanguts and their state of Xi (Western) Xia (982–1227). In the early decades of the Song Dynasty, the court paid little attention to this state, which was generally seen as posing no substantial military threat. A peace agreement in 1006 ushered in three decades of good relations. By the 1030s, however, the Xia Kingdom had expanded significantly, mostly by seizing territories further west from various Uighur and Tibetan tribes and chieftaincies. The first significant war with China broke out in 1038, when the Tangut ruler had gained enough confidence to proclaim himself emperor, thereby undermining the symbolic superiority of the Chinese monarch. During the subsequent years of warfare, the Tangut regime amply demonstrated its military might. After a temporary peace treaty in 1044, hostilities broke out again two decades later following repeated Tangut incursions – exacerbated by the military adventurism of Song frontier commanders, and the simultaneous disintegration of Song China's Tibetan client state based in Hehuang (in modern-day Qinghai). Thereafter, the Song emperor Shenzong (r. 1067–85), guided by his hawkish advisors, embarked on a series of large-scale military campaigns. Over the next sixty years, under Shenzong and his successors, this irredentist agenda fueled repeated wars, leading to crippling losses of men and resources on both sides. Nevertheless, by the 1120s, Song China had managed to

[40] QSW 38:24.

capture large swathes of Tangut territory, while simultaneously annexing Hehuang.[41]

The Northern Song's most formidable neighbor, however, was undoubtedly the Liao empire (916–1122), established by nomadic Khitans in the early tenth century. Even before the founding of the Song, during the Later Jin Dynasty (936–47), the Liao had obtained sixteen prefectures in northern Hebei and Hedong that had been traditionally under the control of Chinese regimes. The result was an unusual geopolitical situation, whereby the Song–Liao border cut directly across the North China Plain. Song China's second emperor, Taizong (r. 976–98), twice attempted to recapture this territory – in 979 and again in 986 – but both military campaigns failed miserably. The next two decades saw nearly continuous border skirmishes, culminating in a massive Liao invasion in 1004 that brought Khitan troops to within a hundred miles of the Song capital of Kaifeng. The Khitan invasion was halted only after the Song emperor Zhenzong (r. 998–1023) personally led his troops into battle. At this point, realizing that their army was precariously over-extended, the Khitans agreed to a peace settlement. Thus, in January 1005, Zhenzong and his Liao counterpart exchanged oath letters at Chanyuan on the northern banks of the Yellow River.[42] Thereafter, there were two significant confrontations, first in 1042, when the Khitans took advantage of the Song–Xia war to claim ten counties in Hebei that they had controlled prior to the founding of the Song Dynasty; and second in the mid-1070s, when the Song and Liao courts had a heated disagreement over the proper course of the border in Hedong to the west. But both disputes were resolved diplomatically. Peaceful relations broke down only in the late 1110s when Song China embarked on a misguided alliance with the Jurchens against the Liao, an alliance that went sour and led both to the fall of the Khitan state and to the Song's loss of all of North China.

Two important consequences of the Chanyuan peace are worth stressing. First, the many years of diplomatic exchanges, spanning the eleventh century and lasting over a hundred years, spurred a new form of cosmopolitanism, whereby Song political elites acquired firsthand experiences traveling into the steppe and socializing with Liao diplomats. Second, the

---

[41] For more on Song–Xia relations, see Dunnell, "Hsi Hsia," esp. 168–97; P. J. Smith, "Irredentism as Political Capital"; P. J. Smith, "Crisis in the Literati State"; Lamouroux, "Militaires et bureaucrates"; Li Huarui, *Song Xia guanxi shi*.

[42] For a good summary of Song–Liao relations up until the Oath of Chanyuan, see Lau and Huang, "Founding and Consolidation of the Sung Dynasty," 247–51, 262–70.

unusual geopolitical configuration of the Song–Liao border brought a large ethnically Han population under the control of the Liao state. These Han people were recruited in large numbers to staff the Liao civil administration at all levels, even as the Liao state sought actively to preserve the sharp ethnic divide between them and the Liao Khitans. The significant presence of ethnic Chinese in influential governmental positions undoubtedly contributed to Liao's unique relationship with Song China.

The century of peace between Song and Liao also played a critical role in the evolution of the structures and norms of traditional Chinese diplomacy. An especially influential thesis, put forward three decades ago in a volume edited by Morris Rossabi, emphasized the pragmatism and innovation evident in Song China's relationship with Liao. According to Rossabi, the diplomatic parity that existed between the two states – whereby the monarchs of both Song and Liao recognized each other as an "emperor" equal in status – discredited once and for all the notion of a "Chinese world order," formulated by John King Fairbank, an interpretation holding that external regimes could interact with China only on China's terms, by accepting their subordination and offering regular tribute to the Chinese ruler. To the extent that Song–Liao relations took on certain characteristics of the post-eighteenth-century European state system, Rossabi's thesis seems to underline yet another area in which Song China was ahead of its time.[43]

It is possible to expand on the implications of Song–Liao diplomacy by exploring the cultural dimensions of inter-state systems. The contemporary world order does not, of course, constitute the only legitimate mode of inter-state relations. One might argue that a maximally rational system of inter-state relations is any system in which all participants generally agree to a single set of rules.[44] These rules may well develop over time as different regimes, perhaps with very different linguistic and cultural backgrounds, are compelled to find ways to coexist. Prior to the arrival in East Asia of large numbers of Europeans,[45] those East Asian

---

[43] Rossabi (ed.), *China Among Equals*; Fairbank (ed.), *Chinese World Order*.

[44] Though such an ideal-type inter-state system is stable in the sense that all participants agree to the rules, stability did not preclude the possibility of war. Throughout the late imperial period, Chinese regimes fought wars with their neighbors to the north and to the south. The violent conquests of Yunnan, Guizhou, and other parts of the south should not be treated as "internal" conflicts – as a nationalist might insist – but rather as wars of conquest against established neighboring polities.

[45] The earliest Europeans arriving in East Asia were willing to integrate into the East Asian inter-state system. Thus, e.g., when the Portuguese reached Southeast Asia, they agreed to receive the tribute that the Malaysian sultan had once sent to China. See Santos Alves, "Voix de la prophétie," 43.

regimes that came into frequent contact with one another had already developed their own set of arrangements for inter-state interactions, arrangements that I refer to here as the "East Asian world order." Such an understanding differs from Fairbank's original thesis. First, it does not assume that China had exclusive control over how the inter-state system developed. Second, it does not consider inter-state dynamics to have been fixed and unchanging. As is true of the modern world order, the East Asian world order was a constantly evolving system, developing at the interface between the political cultures of several coexisting East Asian states.[46] Indeed, as we shall see below, Song foreign relations contained elements of earlier inter-state dynamics, even as they would also include important new developments.

How then can one characterize the East Asian world order as it existed by the beginning of the Song period? In the first place, it was clearly hierarchical. Not surprisingly, the hierarchy in question generally reflected the relative political and military might of the various constituent states. It was made explicit in the language of diplomatic correspondence, in the titles given to envoys, in the "appointment" edicts sent to the rulers of subordinate states, in the choice of whose calendar was used in dating documents, and, of course, in the symbolic tribute offered by smaller states to their larger neighbors. Because it was largely expressed symbolically, hierarchy did not preclude pragmatic negotiations between nominally unequal regimes. In fact, in some sense, it expanded the flexibility of diplomacy, allowing one state to accept a putative subordination as a concession for some other gain that it might consider more valuable. In general, it was unusual for any two states to acknowledge equality, but the Song–Liao example makes it clear that parity was not impossible. Though tributary states were expected to subordinate themselves to only one other state, instances of "multiple sovereignty" – whereby one small regime simultaneously offered tribute to and recognized the suzerainty of more than one larger neighboring state – were probably quite common.[47]

In the second place, communication between regimes within the East Asian inter-state system was generally embodied in formal missives

---

[46] On the role of non-Chinese regimes in defining East Asian diplomatic practices during the Tang, see Skaff, *Sui-Tang China*; Wang Zhenping, *Tang China in Multi-Polar Asia*.

[47] For a discussion of "multiple sovereignty" in Southeast Asia, where it seems to have been a common practice, see Thongchai, *Siam Mapped*, 81–94. A comparison of Tibetan and Chinese chronicles reveals that, already in the eighth century, the Yunnan-based state of Nanzhao simultaneously accepted the suzerainty of both the Tang and Tibet (unbeknownst to the Chinese). See Backus, *Nan-chao Kingdom*, 40–45.

written in classical Chinese, dispatched to the court of a neighboring state via an ambassador and his retinue. With no tradition of permanent diplomatic representation, premodern East Asian regimes relied on traveling embassies for inter-state communication. Ambassadors were dispatched to neighboring states bearing "state letters" or other types of diplomatic correspondence,[48] along with a large number of valuable gifts.[49] These embassies did not stay abroad long, returning home soon after delivery of the letter. Thus, there were no ambassadors based permanently or semi-permanently at foreign capitals. A variety of additional protocols developed over time, including, for example, restrictions on the sending of envoys whose given name violated the "taboo" name of the host country's ruler.[50]

The Chanyuan Oath seems to have spurred further developments in this East Asian inter-state system. The oath letters exchanged between the Song and Liao emperors provided the language used in subsequent inter-state agreements, notably between the Song and the Jin, and between the Song and the Xia.[51] There is also evidence that, in the century after Chanyuan, agreements between states were increasingly seen both as contractual in nature and as built upon an accumulation of precedents. As we shall see in Chapter 3, it was only in the late eleventh century that the Song central government began insisting upon the consistent archiving of all past agreements. These archives provided the late Northern Song government with what one might call "archival authority." After convincing its neighbors to accept the principle that countries should abide by past agreements, the Song regime began to benefit directly from the relative comprehensiveness of its own archives. Its ability to produce agreements from a past generation helped it maintain a degree of hegemony on the world stage.

In addition, the large number of embassy missions traveling between Song and Liao over the course of the eleventh and early twelfth centuries – described in Chapter 1 – brought about the routinization of procedures

---

[48] Franke, "Sung Embassies," 119–21. In fact, the term "state letter" (*guoshu* or *guoxin*) was only used for Song–Liao correspondence; "edict" or "decree" was used in the case of letters sent to Koryŏ and the Xia, which were not treated by the Song as diplomatic equals.

[49] Ibid., 130–31.

[50] E.g., the powerful Song minister Sima Guang (1019–86) could not serve as ambassador to Liao because his given name coincided with part of the name of the second Liao emperor, Yelü Deguang. See QSW 55:123.

[51] Franke, "Sung Embassies," 119. E.g., the oaths with Liao, Jin, and Xia all included nearly verbatim clauses regarding the repatriation of cross-border fugitives. See XCB 58.1299; Yuwen Maozhao, *Da Jinguo zhi jiaozheng*, 37.527–28; XCB 80.2022.

governing how foreign ambassadors were accompanied from the border to the capital, how they were received at court, the seating arrangements at diplomatic banquets, and the type and number of gifts exchanged.[52] One can contrast this routinization with the much more ad hoc diplomatic ceremonies of earlier times, such as the late eighth-century oath ceremony between Tibet and Tang China.[53]

During the same period, several East Asian regimes seemed to move toward a common model for legitimating rulership, evident in the circulation and widespread influence of certain specific texts. Although the "Confucian" classics remained popular throughout East Asia, new works on political philosophy gained currency in the eleventh century, notably the early eighth-century *Zhenguan zhengyao* (The Essentials of Government of the Zhenguan Era). Perhaps deemed more practical and up-to-date, this text – which provided advice on statecraft in the form of dialogues between the early Tang emperor Taizong (r. 626–49) and his ministers – became influential at the Khitan, Tangut, Koryŏ, Jurchen, and Mongol courts.[54]

Finally, as discussed in some detail in Chapter 3, the Song–Liao border demarcation prompted by the Chanyuan Oath led to a systematization of techniques for designating inter-state boundaries. Clearly, for the demarcation to be effective, the frontier had to be marked onto the landscape in a way that was recognizable by neighboring populations. The fact that a particular combination of trenches and tumuli was used to indicate both the Song–Liao and the Song–Xia frontiers suggests that the populations of multiple states had come to accept and recognize this particular means of territorial demarcation.

How did the eleventh-century multi-state system influence the emerging Chinese sense of self? In response to this question, most historians of the period focus on the combined military threat of the Tanguts and the

---

[52] For descriptions of proper ritual protocols for the reception of envoys and of the choreography of diplomatic visits to the Song and Liao courts, see SS 119.2804–10, 328.10565; Li Xinchuan, *Jianyan yilai chaoye zaji*, vol. 1, 3.97–98; Ye Longli, *Qidan guo zhi*, 21.200–03; QSW 27:104–06; QSW 50:228–37.

[53] To sanctify the oath, the Tibetans and Chinese had initially agreed to sacrifice an ox and a horse, respectively. But the Chinese representative had second thoughts "as Chinese cannot farm without oxen, and Tibetans cannot travel without horses." He proposed sacrificing sheep, pigs, and dogs in their stead. His Tibetan counterpart agreed to the idea, but no pigs were available, so the diplomats had once more to change plans. Eventually, the Tibetans settled on a ram, and the Chinese on a sheep and a dog. See JTS 196b.5247.

[54] Franke and Twitchett, "Introduction," 33, 34; Franke, "Chinese Historiography," 20, 21, 22; Bol, "Seeking Common Ground," 503; Lee, *Sourcebook*, 1:273–74.

Khitans, which are said to have compelled the Song Chinese to reimagine their place in the world. But the annals of Chinese history are filled with instances of great nomadic confederations developing on the Eurasian steppe, threatening China's existence, and even – on occasion – invading the Chinese heartland.[55] The mere existence of powerful neighbors on the frontiers, then, is insufficient to explain developments that date specifically to the eleventh century. Moreover, Northern Song policymakers were not nearly as concerned about the threat of a northern invasion as has sometimes been imagined, a point explored in some detail in Chapter 1. As we shall see, the impact on Chinese mentalities of the new East Asian world order of the eleventh century was complex. The military threat from the north did play a role in forcing Song statesmen to reassess the limits of imperial power, but so did the formal recognition of a second emperor – the ruler of Liao – within that world order. Perhaps even more significant, I will argue, was the diplomatic "cosmopolitanism" emerging in the era, a cosmopolitanism that involved both new forms of sociability and new travel experiences to lands beyond the frontier.

Sources and Methodological Issues

The present book seeks to identify the conceptualizations and underlying assumptions shared by sociopolitical elites of the Northern Song. But how does one document and reconstruct the culture of those elites? In fact, partly because of the rapid expansion of woodblock printing in this era, a wealth of Northern Song source materials survives, many of which are now available in digitized and searchable form. In contrast to earlier periods, court chronicles are remarkably rich. The modern punctuated edition of the most extensive of these chronicles includes over 11,000 pages dealing with the eleventh century alone. A variety of additional documents survives in the collected works of individual authors. The recently published *Quan Song wen* (Complete Song Prose), which incorporates texts from hundreds of extant collected works, preserves some 40,000 pages of Northern Song material. Other literary sources can convey additional perspectives on how elites viewed their world, including embassy travelogues, annotated maps, and geographic gazetteers. And because of the important place of poetry in the social life of educated Chinese, the well over 10,000 extant Northern Song poems

---

[55] For a history of sino-steppe encounters over the *longue durée*, see Barfield, *Perilous Frontier*.

provide us with additional valuable insight into the worldview of the sociopolitical elite. Finally, abundant archaeological material dating to the eleventh century also survives. In particular, a great number of tombs have been excavated in recent decades, many of which have been analyzed and incorporated into the database exploited in Chapter 5. Grave goods, tomb architecture, and tomb murals are particularly useful for the comparison of Northeast Asian mortuary cultures and of Song and Liao representations of ethnicity.

Of course, all such historical sources pose certain methodological problems. Appendix A describes some of the issues concerning archaeological data. Policy-related documents can present complex interpretive problems in that they were composed in a particular rhetorical style – a type of "bureaucratese" – designed primarily to win over other officials to the positions being argued. It is often difficult to ascertain why an individual chose to take a specific position and to what extent that position was ultimately shaped by the intricate factional politics of the era. However, whatever an author's specific stance, one can assume that his policy arguments reflected a perceptive understanding of the cultural values and assumptions of his social milieu. Thus, by identifying the emerging tropes and modes of reasoning that were mobilized, it is possible to reconstruct the rationales that the authors believed would be accepted as the most persuasive and legitimate by others.

However, it is important to emphasize that the ideas and policy positions circulating among the political elites of the period were never systematized into a unique and coherent vision. The Chinese political elite was large, complex, and rarely if ever of one mind. A single individual did not always come to a clear resolution when struggling to make sense of the complexity of the world. Moreover, because such elites were well read in a broad range of classical and historical scholarship, they frequently revived and repeated much older ideas, even as new and altogether contradictory ideas came to the fore. Cultural change can be detected less by the disappearance of older concepts and formulations than by the emergence of new ideas that came to exist side by side with the old.

Finally, one must be aware of how both censorship and self-censorship in succeeding generations may have affected discourse dealing with foreigners and inter-state relations. Under the Northern Song, court fears of offending the Khitans led to an explicit policy forbidding the use of derogatory language in certain specific contexts, such as in Song–Liao inter-state communiqués and toasts delivered during diplomatic banquets.[56] Under the later Mongol Yuan and Manchu Qing dynasties, printed editions of Northern Song works were sometimes abridged and cleansed to avoid offending the ruling elite.[57] The most famous and far-reaching instance of such censorship involved the "literary inquisition" of the mid-1770s, during the compilation by the Qing court of the *Siku quanshu* (Complete Library of the Four Treasuries) – a vast compendium of nearly 3,500 books from earlier dynasties, including hundreds of Song-era titles. Due to Manchu sensitivities, the editors systematically replaced language thought to denigrate or demean Khitans and Jurchens, both of whom were seen as progenitors of the Manchus themselves.[58] A particularly colorful example involves an 1128 appeal encouraging the Song emperor to return to the north in the wake of the Jurchen invasion. The author insisted that the ethnic Chinese population of the North China Plain would cheer on the Song armies – "even children a mere three feet in height would fervently wave their arms to encourage us." In the earlier Ming edition of this text, however, the passage went even further, claiming that the population of the North China Plain so despised the Jurchens that they yearned to cut off their heads and eat their flesh. Presumably so as not to give any ideas to the Chinese under Manchu rule, the *Siku quanshu* edition carefully excised this allusion to the cannibalistic treatment of an ethnic other.[59]

Book Overview

The primary goal of this book is to document and explain the rise of a new sense of Chinese identity under the Song and to link its emergence to the far-reaching effects of the particular geopolitical configuration of the post-Chanyuan era. The approach taken here is multidimensional. To some extent the chapters represent a series of distinct essays, approaching the issue from different perspectives, political and cultural, as well as military and diplomatic, with a particular focus on the inter-state dynamics

---

[56] Tao Jing-shen, "Barbarians or Northerners," 69–70; Sima Guang, *Sushui jiwen*, fulu, 1.332.

[57] Jay, "Memoirs and Official Accounts," 599–604; Jay, *Change in Dynasties*, 71–78.

[58] E.g., in a memorial by Qiang Zhi (1023–76) included in the compendium *Lidai mingchen zouyi*, two references to Khitans as "caitiffs" in a Ming version of the text are eliminated from the *Siku quanshu* version through subtle changes in grammar. All references to Khitans as "Tartars" (*huren*) are changed to "people of Liao" (*Liaoren*) or to "tribesmen" (*zhubu*); and one reference to "Tartar horses" (*huma*) is changed to "enemy horses" (*dima*). See QSW 66:29–30; *Yingyin wenyuan ge siku quanshu*, vol. 442, 344.8b–10a.

[59] QSW 129:350; *Yingyin wenyuan ge siku quanshu*, vol. 325, 15.21b.

of the eleventh century. By stressing both context and contingency, the book explores the possibility of a kind of "total history" of the origins of a national consciousness among Chinese elites.

The book is divided into two parts, each composed of three chapters. The first part, entitled "Political Space," deals with inter-state dynamics in the century following the Chanyuan Oath. Chapter 1 introduces the eleventh-century "cosmopolitans" whose impact on the Song worldview was so influential. These men who traveled on embassies to Liao or hosted their Liao counterparts at the Song court not only enjoyed opportunities to socialize with Khitans and Liao Chinese, they were also able to observe firsthand the physical and cultural geography of Northeast Asia. As it turns out, over half of the most important policymakers at court had traveled on such embassy missions earlier in their careers. Their cosmopolitan experiences had, I argue, an immediate impact both on fundamental policy decisions of the era and on how the Chinese sociopolitical elite came to view their world. The chapter focuses in particular on how cosmopolitan sociability humanized Song China's northern neighbors, while also serving to sustain the remarkably durable Song–Liao peace of the post-Chanyuan period. Chapter 2 then shifts to the issue of military defense, focusing in particular on the system of perimeter defense on the northern frontier that sharply distinguished the Song from its predecessor, the Tang. The linearizing of the military frontier in part reflected new ideas about the nature and limitations of the Chinese state. It also established a cultural context for one of the great border demarcation projects of premodern times, described in detail in Chapter 3. These bilateral borders – largely the product of an unusually activist central government – had the unintended consequence of implying a new notion of bounded sovereignty at odds with the older ideals of universal empire.

The second part of the book, entitled "Cultural Space," focuses on key eleventh-century developments in how China was conceptualized by sociopolitical elites. Chapter 4 explores with some care the component elements of the new Chinese self-identity. It pays particular attention to Northern Song ways of imagining Han ethnicity, ethnic solidarity, and Chinese territory, which together provided a conceptual framework that would fuel revanchist movements in the Song Dynasty and would have an enduring influence in later periods. The next two chapters seek to explain the emergence of this new idea of the nation. Chapter 5 demonstrates the degree to which Liao ethnic policy helped maintain a sharp cultural divide between a Liao Chinese cultural zone – situated south of the Yan Mountains of northern Hebei – and a steppe cultural zone lying to the north. Chapter 6 examines once more the ambassadors to Liao, first introduced in Chapter 1. But rather than focusing on diplomatic sociability, it takes into account the traveler's gaze. While on their journeys to the fringes of the Eurasian Steppe, Song diplomats experienced firsthand the dramatic topography of northern Hebei, the remains of the historical Great Wall, and the stark cultural divide between the North China Plain and the Eurasian steppe, experiences they shared with others through their travel prose and poetry. The empirical knowledge these envoys gained spurred a new belief that China possessed natural borders that did not coincide with the existing Song–Liao political border. Within these borders lay a remarkably homogeneous "sinic space." Although the Tang Dynasty is sometimes also portrayed as a "cosmopolitan" era due to the presence of foreigners in large numbers at the Tang capital, Song cosmopolitanism, I will suggest, was far more significant in its transformative impact on the worldview of Chinese educated elites.

PART I

Political Space

Diplomacy and Cosmopolitan Sociability

On the fourteenth day of the fifth month of the year 1067, three days after crossing the Baigou River, which marked the border between the Song state and the Khitan Liao empire to its north, the Song ambassador Chen Xiang (1017–80) arrived in the outskirts of Yanjing, the Liao Southern Capital (at the site of modern-day Beijing).[1] There, he was hosted at a dinner in his honor by the deputy metropolitan governor, a man by the name of Han Jin. Chen had met the man three years earlier in Song territory, and had been his host at a similar banquet. Both remembered their previous meeting and exchanged pleasantries. After toasting each other during dinner with a total of nine rounds of wine, the evening concluded with an exchange of a set number of prescribed gifts. The following day, Chen and his entourage were invited to another banquet, in which they were served thirteen rounds of wine. During one toast, their host – this time, the Liao state finance commissioner Liu Yun – praised the many years of peace between the two states, describing them as "just like one family." Chen responded in kind – "Since antiquity, there has never been a friendship like the one between our two courts!" Chen was then offered more wine. Though he insisted he was a light drinker, Liu explained that he and no less than a dozen of his relatives had previously traveled to Song China on embassies. On this note, Chen could not politely turn down the offer, and all the banquet's participants drank to the brim. At the conclusion of the banquet, Chen presented his host with gifts he had brought from the Song capital, "in accordance with precedent."

As the present chapter will demonstrate, Chen Xiang's experience during his sixty-eight days in Liao territory was in no way uncommon. By the second half of the eleventh century, the inter-state system that developed in the years following the Song–Liao Peace of Chanyuan of 1005 had

---

[1] The scene that follows is described in Chen Xiang's extant embassy report. See QSW 50:230–31. For an English translation of the entire report, see D. C. Wright, *Ambassadors Records*, 63–88.

reached a certain degree of maturity, with a well-defined set of protocols and precedents, all agreed upon by the Song and the Liao. Beneath the façade of such strict protocols, there flourished a cosmopolitan sociability, in which hundreds of the most influential political and cultural elites from both the Song and the Liao came to know each other well. They entertained each other at countless banquets, drinking vast quantities of wine in the process. In some sense, the "unprecedented friendship" between Liao and Song – a refrain repeated frequently in documents dating to the eleventh and early twelfth centuries – was also reflected in the social relations between individual diplomats of the two states.

Numerous historians have previously studied China's foreign relations during the eleventh century.[2] In their work, they have described the institutions supporting the diplomatic activity, compiled lists of the men serving in embassies, assessed the degree to which Song–Liao relations adhered to the characteristics of the modern world state system, and struggled to integrate into nationalist historical narratives a system whereby Chinese regimes seemed to offer "humiliating" regular "tribute" to their non-Chinese neighbors. Here, I seek to explore a somewhat different set of questions. I focus on the experiences of the Song diplomats themselves, describing in considerable detail the impressive volume of social interactions between them and their Liao counterparts. This intense sociability, I will suggest, was an important element in the sustained peace between the Song and its northern neighbor. It also helps explain certain broader cultural trends, including newly emergent ideas among Chinese political and cultural elites regarding China's place in the world.

Song Cosmopolitans

During the century following the Oath of Chanyuan, both Song and Liao sent multiple embassies annually to each other's court, to carry official New Year's wishes, as well as to convey birthday greetings to the other state's emperor, empress, and empress dowager. Additional ad hoc embassies were undertaken to express condolence upon the death of a Chinese or Khitan emperor, or to announce the ascension of a new ruler.[3] As we shall see, many of the most influential statesmen of the age participated in these

---

[2] Probably the most influential works in English are Rossabi (ed.), *China Among Equals*; Tao, *Two Sons of Heaven*. The literature in Chinese is too abundant to list here.

[3] For a list of twelve types of embassies, see Nie Chongqi, "Song Liao jiaopin kao," 5; Ang, "Sung-Liao Diplomacy," 102–04; D. C. Wright, *From War to Diplomatic Parity*, 103–07.

diplomatic exchanges. In this sense, the eleventh century was an exceptionally cosmopolitan era. A later chapter will examine the travel experiences themselves, focusing on how Song travelers made sense of alien landscapes and cultures. Here, I focus on a different component of eleventh-century cosmopolitanism – the social interactions between diplomats.

Song embassies to Liao consisted of large parties of some one hundred individuals. Accompanying the ambassador and the deputy ambassador – the former a civilian bureaucrat and the latter generally a military man – one could find soldiers, grooms, carrier coolies, clerks, scribes, interpreters, cooks, and riding instructors.[4] Although somewhat less is known about the reciprocal Liao missions to their southern neighbor, it is clear that they were led by politically prominent officials, with a Khitan serving as ambassador and a Liao official of Han ethnicity serving as his deputy.[5] At the border, embassies traveling in either direction were greeted by escorts, who accompanied the ambassadors and their retinues throughout their stay. These escorts included "welcoming commissioners," who guided the envoys from the border to the capital; "hospitality commissioners," in charge of envoys while at the imperial court; and "parting commissioners," who escorted the diplomats back to the border on their trips home.[6] Like the ambassadors, the escorts tended to be relatively high-ranking civilian officials. Given the frequency of Song–Liao embassies and the numbers of people in the ambassadors' and escorts' retinues, it is clear that post-Chanyuan diplomacy provided opportunities for large numbers of Song and Liao officials to interact with each other at a personal level.

To get a better sense of the political prominence of the people involved in embassy missions, one can compare reconstructed lists of Song diplomats to the list of men who served in the four most powerful policymaking positions, advising the emperor on a near daily basis: the chief ministers, deputy chief ministers, commissioners of military affairs, and deputy commissioners of military affairs.[7] In total, 618 individual Song men are

[4] Ang, "Sung-Liao Diplomacy," 104–12; Franke, "Sung Embassies," 123–24; Nie Chongqi, "Song Liao jiaopin kao," 6.

[5] Liao ambassadors were all surnamed Yelü or Xiao, implying they all came from the Khitan imperial or consort clans, whereas deputy ambassadors had Chinese surnames. For a complete list of Liao ambassadors, see tables appended to Nie Chongqi, "Song Liao jiaopin kao."

[6] Ang, "Sung-Liao Diplomacy," 130. These three titles – which implied a degree of respect for the incoming ambassadors – were only used for escorts receiving embassies from Liao (or, rarely, from Koryŏ). Diplomats from other neighboring states were received and sent off by "guidance commissioners," and hosted in the capital by "surveillance commissioners."

[7] The discussion that follows is based on a database of Northern Song diplomats and top policymakers described in Appendix B.

Table 1.1 *Service by Song diplomats in top policymaking positions (1005–1120)*[a]

Diplomatic appointment	Number serving in top policy positions[b]	
Ambassador	79/360	(21%)
Deputy ambassador	1/320	(0%)
Parting commissioner	6/24	(25%)
Hospitality commissioner	19/43	(44%)
Welcoming commissioner	10/45	(22%)

[a] See Appendix B for description of database used for this and subsequent tables.
[b] Top policy positions include chief minister, deputy chief minister, commissioner of military affairs, and deputy commissioner of military affairs.

known to have served at least once as ambassador or deputy ambassador to Liao in the period 1005 to 1120. But whereas the list of ambassadors and their deputies is fairly complete through the year 1100 (the final year covered by the most comprehensive extant chronicle of the Northern Song), only a small percentage of the Song escorts of Liao diplomats have been identified in extant sources.

The majority of these Song diplomats were mid-ranking civilian officials, although many would later rise to the highest positions in government. Melvin Ang calculated that 60 percent of Northern Song ambassadors to Liao attained policy positions during the course of their careers.[8] Moreover, as indicated in Table 1.1, over 20 percent of the diplomats – excluding the deputy ambassadors, who, as military men, were not promoted within the civilian bureaucracy – would eventually serve in one of the four powerful posts listed above. Much the same was true of the escorts, with a particularly high percentage of hospitality commissioners eventually attaining top posts.[9] Indeed, both the Song and Liao courts seem commonly to have appointed escorts who were equal in prestige to the incoming ambassadors. Thus, for example, when the

[8] Ang, "Sung-Liao Diplomacy," 154. Ang provides a list of "policy positions" at 237–38. Besides titles identifying chief ministers and deputy chief ministers (1–13 in Ang's list) and commissioners and deputy commissioners of military affairs (21–25), Ang also includes notaries of the Bureau of Military Affairs, as well as academicians, drafting officials, censors, and remonstrators.
[9] Service as hospitality commissioner was possibly the most prestigious diplomatic assignment as it did not require leaving the capital.

Table 1.2 *Average ages of Song diplomats and top policymakers (at time of first appointment)* *(1005–1120)*

Appointment	Age[a]	n
DIPLOMATS		
Ambassador	51.3	316
Deputy ambassador	47.6	113
Welcoming commissioner	47.9	38
Hospitality commissioner	51.1	37
Parting commissioner	50.4	20
All diplomats	50.3	524
TOP POLICYMAKERS		
Chief minister	60.2	66
Deputy chief minister	56.3	121
Commissioner of military affairs	57.9	62
Deputy commissioner of military affairs	56.1	80
All top policymakers	57.4	329

[a] Age (calculated in *sui*) determined using data from October 2013 edition of the Chinese Biographical Database (CBDB). When birth year unknown, it was approximated by subtracting 59 from CBDB "index year."

distinguished Song statesman Ouyang Xiu (1007–72) arrived at the Liao court in 1055, he was escorted by one of the Liao chief ministers, as well as by several other eminent court officials.[10]

Because the contention here is that diplomatic experience influenced political culture, it is important to note that men served as diplomats prior to serving in policy positions. This fact is already clear if one compares the relative ages of diplomats and of top policymakers (Table 1.2). The typical ambassador or escort was in his late forties or early fifties,

[10] *Ouyang Xiu quan ji*, 6:2696; Sima Guang, *Sushui jiwen*, fulu, 1.334; Wang Pizhi, *Shengshui yantan lu*, 2.15.

Table 1.3 *Period between diplomatic service and service in a top policymaking position (by diplomatic appointment) (1005–1120)*

Diplomatic appointment	Average period (in years)	Minimum period (in years)	n
Ambassador	12.9	1	180
Welcoming commissioner	17.2	1	19
Hospitality commissioner	8.6	0	42
Parting commissioner	19.2	9	9

Table 1.4 *Period between diplomatic service and service in a top policymaking position (by policy position) (1005–1120)*

Policy position	Average period (in years)	Minimum period (in years)	n
Chief minister	16.7	2	62
Deputy chief minister	11.2	0	88
Commissioner of military affairs	15.4	2	43
Deputy commissioner of military affairs	8.7	1	59

whereas the typical chief minister or commissioner of military affairs was in his late fifties. One can also assess the length of time between diplomatic service and service in a top policymaking position for all those individuals who served in both types of office (Tables 1.3 and 1.4). On average, men served as diplomats ten or more years prior to serving in top policy positions, and there are no cases of men serving as diplomats after serving in such positions (see "minimum period" in Tables 1.3 and 1.4).[11]

---

[11] The only individual serving as diplomat and top policymaker in the same year was Lü Dafang (1027–97), who was hospitality commissioner in the first month of 1086, then promoted two months later to deputy chief minister. See XCB 366.8794, 366.8903; SS 340.10841–42.

As a result of the high rate of promotion of diplomats into policy positions, between two-fifths and one half of the commissioners and deputy commissioners of military affairs, and over half of chief and deputy chief ministers had served previously as ambassador to Liao (column one of Table 1.5). In the case of the chief ministers, one obtains an even higher proportion if one takes into account the lengths of tenures in office (column two) – in other words, assessing the chance that at any given moment a sitting chief minister had prior diplomatic experience. The figures are higher yet if one examines specifically those men known to have served as escorts for Liao envoys (column three). Because only a small fraction of the escorts have been identified, one can estimate that these proportions would be even greater if we possessed the complete list (column four). It seems likely, moreover, that some of the top officials without experience as an ambassador or escort would have served as embassy clerks or scribes – positions whose holders are rarely identified.[12] What is clear is that a majority of the most powerful statesmen of the Northern Song – men who had an inordinate influence both on the formulation of state policy and, through their political networks, on the evolution of political culture at court – had firsthand experience traveling to the Liao capital and/or welcoming Liao ambassadors in the Song capital.

What, then, did such diplomatic experience entail? Song embassies were not brief two- or three-day events. Song ambassadors traveled long distances, whether to one of the Liao capitals, or to wherever the mobile Khitan court was currently encamped. Chen Xiang, for example, spent sixty-eight days in Liao territory during his 1067 embassy.[13] Typically, Song envoys spent several days at the Liao court – either in a Liao capital city, or at an encampment on the Inner Mongolian steppe. There, they visited the emperor, empress, and empress dowager, paying their respect to each in person. Then, in the presence of the emperor, they participated in a variety of activities, including archery contests, drinking games, and evening banquets.[14] Liao envoys would have had similar experiences in Kaifeng, though with much less direct contact

---

[12] E.g., although Su Song's 1077 trip to Liao is well known because he served as ambassador, his earlier trip in 1068 is known only from a sequence of poems found in his collected works. See Su Song, *Su Weigong wenji*, 1:160–68.

[13] QSW 50:228–37.

[14] For accounts of two Song envoys who proved able marksmen despite no training in archery, see QSW 111:132; QSW 135:55. For the description of an unusual drinking game involving music and ice fishing, see XCB 177.4281; Liu Zhi, *Zhongsu ji*, 475.

Table 1.5 *Past diplomatic service of top policymakers (1015–1105)*[a]

Policy position	Served previously as ambassador (by officeholder)		Served previously as ambassador (by years in service[b] in policy position)		Served as escort or ambassador (by years in service[b] in policy position) (min. estimate)[c]		Served as escort or ambassador (by years in service[b] in policy position) (max. estimate)[c]	
Chief minister	29/54	(53%)	94/154	(61%)	102/154	(66%)	127/154	(82%)
Deputy chief minister	61/96	(63%)	145/210	(69%)	158/210	(75%)	196/210	(93%)
Commissioner of military affairs	22/53	(41%)	48/120	(40%)	57/120	(48%)	65/120	(54%)
Deputy commissioner of military affairs	38/71	(53%)	77/152	(51%)	83/152	(55%)	104/152	(68%)

[a] The dates 1015 to 1105 were selected on an empirical basis: the percentage of policymakers with diplomatic experience changed relatively little during this period of time. As embassies to Liao were infrequent prior to the Chanyuan Oath, few policymakers had diplomatic experience prior to the year 1015. Because few ambassadors have been identified after the year 1100 (the last year covered by the most detailed chronicle of the Northern Song), it is not possible to determine with the same degree of accuracy a policymaker's past diplomatic service after approximately 1105.

[b] Years in service in a policy position was calculated by subtracting the start year from the end year of service, except in the case of appointments that began and ended within the same year, in which case the years in service was assumed to be 0.5.

[c] Although the reconstructed list of ambassadors and deputy ambassadors is nearly comprehensive for the period 1005 to 1100, very few escorts have been identified. The "minimum estimate" of top policymakers who previously served as ambassador or escort only takes into account escorts who have been identified based on documentary sources. The "maximum estimate" assumes that the number of top policymakers who served previously as ambassador and/or escort is 35 percent larger than the number known only to have served as ambassador (a rough estimate derived from the fact that, of 27 escorts known to have later served in policy positions, only 20 are known also to have served as ambassador).

with the Chinese emperor.[15] But it was not at court that Song and Liao diplomats passed the longest time together. Most of the weeks in foreign territory were spent on the road. Ambassadors and their escorts invariably had numerous opportunities to chat while traveling abreast on their horses.[16] Perhaps the most important context for social interaction was the banquets to which – as Chen Xiang's report makes amply clear – Song envoys were treated virtually every night by their escorts or by other prominent local officials.[17] Liao envoys were likewise invited to sumptuous feasts of wine, fish, and assorted meats at nearly every rest stop during their travels through Song territory.[18]

These social exchanges would, moreover, have been conducted in a common dialect of Chinese. Most ethnic Chinese in the service of the Liao state came from Yan in northern Hebei, the most populous portion of the Sixteen Prefectures. A significant component of the early Song elite – including civilian bureaucrats, military officials, and the imperial clan, itself – had family origins in Hebei or neighboring Hedong, such that the culture of Hebei had a measurable impact on early Song metropolitan culture.[19] The inordinate representation of individuals from Yan and its surrounding regions in both Song and Liao officialdom would undoubtedly have facilitated the use of a dialect of North Chinese as a *lingua franca*.[20] Although it is possible that some of the ethnic Khitans among the Liao diplomats required interpreters, it is clear that many Khitans could speak Chinese. One account of a Song embassy at the Liao court notes the moment when the Khitan emperor turned to his advisors and began to speak in the "Tartar language," suggesting that the emperor had previously been communicating in Chinese.[21]

---

[15] E.g., though Song envoys regularly met with the Khitan empress dowager, a Liao envoy was informed by his escort that even high-ranking Song ministers had never laid eyes on the Song empress dowager during her regency (because as a woman she attended court hidden behind a curtain). See SS 286.9630. On another occasion, Song censors were aghast at the presumptuousness of the Song envoy Han Zong, who, during a banquet, had dared exchange toasts with the Liao emperor himself. See XCB 163.3919; SS 315.10300; *Zhang Fangping ji*, 697; QSW 41:171.

[16] See, e.g., Xiang Nan (ed.), *Liaodai shike wenbian*, 646, which suggests that the Liao escort Wang Shiru had lengthy scholarly conversations with his charge, the Song ambassador, while "on the road to the [next] post station."

[17] QSW 50:228–37. In addition, the envoy Lu Zhen (957–1014) noted in his embassy report that banquets were held "wherever envoys arrive." See Jiang Shaoyu, *Songchao shishi leiyuan*, 77.1016.

[18] QSW 25:368.

[19] Tackett, "Wan Tang Hebei ren."

[20] The influence of the language of Yan on Song Chinese explains why a dictionary composed by a tenth-century monk from Yan was found to be without errors in its phonetic glosses – to the surprise of many Song literati. See Shen Gua, *Mengxi bitan*, 15.132 (#264).

[21] QSW 71:317.

To be sure, at the court audiences and banquets, the interactions between Song and Liao officials were governed by strict rules and conventions. Chen Xiang seems to have been particularly concerned with matters of protocol; his terse report focuses largely on the choreography of the nightly banquets – the seating arrangement of the various dignitaries, the predetermined number of toasts exchanged, and the number and types of gift offered.[22] The descriptions of embassies in eleventh-century funerary biographies – which typically seek to portray their subjects as ideal Confucian ministers – also often focus on matters of protocol. In 1079, Zhang Zao apparently rebuked his charge, the Liao Ambassador, for requesting an elaborate reception while the Song court was still mourning the emperor's mother.[23] So too Fan Bailu (1030–94), who, while on a mission to Liao in 1085, reprimanded a Liao official for asking about the health of the Song empress dowager – then serving as regent – and not about the health of her son, the young emperor.[24]

As representatives of their respective states, envoys also often had to answer to competing agendas. Accounts in Song sources sometimes portray encounters between Song and Liao officials as a battle of wits between wily diplomats, each seeking to uncover the other's secrets. When Lü Dafang (1027–97) served as hospitality commissioner in Kaifeng, he found his Khitan charge to be a crafty man, who tried repeatedly to steer their conversations toward confidential Song court affairs. But Lü let him know he was on to his tactics with a well-timed witty retort.[25] Liang Qian (990–1059) once hosted a Liao ambassador for a night while serving as chief civilian administrator of the border prefecture of Xiongzhou. He managed to get the envoy to reveal the contents of the state letter, and sent this bit of intelligence to the throne post haste. Liang's biographer specifically praised him for his diligence and shrewdness in this instance. The Liao envoy, however, strongly criticized Liang for reporting what he believed to have been a private conversation. The Song court apparently agreed, and Liang was reassigned elsewhere.[26]

The Liao envoy's surprise in this case suggests that many exchanges between Song and Liao envoys during their travels together involved

[22] QSW 50:228–37.

[23] QSW 82:61–62.

[24] QSW 99:38. For other accounts in funerary biographies of Song officials reprimanding their Liao counterparts for lapses in protocol, see QSW 75:261; *Zhang Fangping ji*, 604; Su Song, *Su Weigong wenji*, 2:920.

[25] SS 340.10841; Zhou Hui, *Qingbo zazhi jiaozhu*, 4.159.

[26] Liu Zhi, *Zhongsu ji*, 273; XCB 138.3326.

conversations of a more casual nature. Indeed, despite the importance of protocol and the need to defend one's state's interests, abundant anecdotal evidence indicates that Liao and Song diplomats were not always on the clock. Chen Xiang's report makes it clear that ambassadors might drink abundantly during their travels. During his 68 days on the road, he was offered a total of 375 rounds of wine at 50 formal banquet events, all the while finding it altogether challenging to refuse one more toast.[27] While on a 1054–55 New Year's embassy to Kaifeng, the Liao Chinese Feng Jianshan sought to fend off yet another toast from the welcoming commissioner by insisting that "one should urge another to drink only up to his capacity."[28] But even if a banquet participant drank merely to his "capacity," it seems unlikely that he did not loosen up a bit by the end of the evening.

Though Song sources rarely reveal details about the final hours of embassy banquets (one might imagine that many participants wisely avoided admitting in their written reports late-night breaches of protocol), a few extant anecdotes allude to some of the excesses. Fang Xie (992–1055) drank so much during a 1042 embassy to Liao that the much amused Khitan ruler named a wine vessel after him.[29] Three decades earlier, while escorting a Liao envoy in 1014, Sun Mian "got drunk to the point of losing all sense of propriety."[30] Liang Qian, by contrast, seems to have been exceptional in his spartan austerity. When hosting a Liao embassy at the border on the first night of their mission, "nobody dared carouse" in his presence. However, as soon as the Liao ambassador and his retinue were transferred to the charge of the less severe welcoming commissioner, "that very evening the lot of them fell into great wantonness."[31] The most colorful case of rowdy banqueting involved Wang Gongchen (1012–85), who was later impeached by the notorious censor Zhao Bian (1008–84). In 1054, while on his second mission to Liao, Wang and his retinue attended a banquet in his honor. There, he and three companions purportedly ignored the prearranged seating arrangement in order to intermingle more freely with their Khitan hosts. They then "fell into a drunken frenzy that lasted deep into the night, during which time they caused a shameful commotion, at times

[27] QSW 50:228–37.
[28] Fan Zhen, *Dongzhai jishi*, buyi, 47; Jiang Shaoyu, *Songchao shishi leiyuan*, 78.1019.
[29] Wei Tai, *Dongxuan bilu*, 15.171; Jiang Shaoyu, *Songchao shishi leiyuan*, 78.1018.
[30] XCB 83.1897.
[31] Liu Zhi, *Zhongsu ji*, 273.

clasping the caitiff [i.e., Liao] officials' hands, at times slapping the Tartars [i.e., Liao officials] on the shoulders, at times composing mocking lines of verse, at times speaking in the crude language of the street." Fortunately for Song–Liao relations, the Liao officials were far less disturbed than Zhao by Wang's behavior. Indeed, they had so enjoyed the Song diplomat's *joie de vivre* that they dubbed him "Jolly Wang" and "Wang-May-He-Live-Forever."[32]

Of course, not all banquets devolved into bouts of unrestrained merriment. But, even when they were more restrained, the consumption of wine as part of the exchange of toasts might have prompted more frank conversations between diplomats. One example, discussed in more detail below, involves the lengthy tête-à-têtes between the Song official Fu Bi (1004–83) and the Liao officials Xiao Ying and Liu Liufu, who arrived in Kaifeng in 1042 at the height of a particularly severe diplomatic row. The Liao envoys "first came to appreciate [Fu's] sincerity" after a clever repartee whereby Fu convinced the two to partake in one more round of wine.[33] There are other accounts of cordial exchanges between diplomats that may also have been facilitated by the consumption of alcohol. In 1057, when the Song envoy Zhang Bian (992–1077) traveled to Liao, his escort was a Khitan named Xiao Aozhi, whose father had died battling Song armies on the eve of the Peace of Chanyuan. Xiao struggled to avoid bearing a grudge against the Chinese. "Our two courts are on friendly terms; our oaths [exchanged at Chanyuan] are [as firm as] the mountains and the rivers," he said to Zhang according to one account. "We should not let minor grievances shake up the great faith [our courts have in each other]." The two men conversed together at great length during their time together, "exhausting what was on their minds." Zhang came to hold the Khitan Xiao in great esteem. It surely bode well for the maintenance of good relations between Song and Liao when the open-minded Xiao later became chief minister of the Liao state.[34] A decade later, in 1067, when the Liao envoys Xiao Linya and Yang Xinggong (j.s. 1050) arrived in Kaifeng, the Song court was initially nervous, as an embassy the previous year had not gone smoothly. This time, their escort in the capital was a Song official named Teng Yuanfa (1020–90),

---

[32] For three documents issued by Zhao Bian regarding Wang Gongchen's mission, see QSW 41:170–73.

[33] QSW 71:315. In Su Shi's terse summary of their conversation, he notes simply that "[Fu Bi] spoke to them frankly, and did not treat them like barbarians." See *Su Shi wenji*, 2:526.

[34] Ye Longli, *Qidan guo zhi*, 15.158.

who "spoke with them frankly," politely asking them in some detail about their families. Yang, in particular, was delighted by his treatment in Kaifeng, and consequently did not once bring up the previous year's events. Greatly relieved by the news, the Song emperor promoted Teng to higher office.[35] Though certain accounts of Song and Liao embassies – including Chen Xiang's report – dwelt on issues of protocol and ritual propriety, in fact the lengthy periods of travel together provided ample opportunities for Song and Liao political elites to engage with each other in a much more casual manner.

Some of the best evidence of the relaxed nature of their conversations is reflected in the various tidbits of information on Liao customs gathered by the more curious of the ambassadors. Yu Jing (1000–64) started his description of Khitan customs by explaining that, while on three separate embassies to Liao (in the mid-1040s), he had interrogated a gamut of Liao subjects, from the escorts accompanying him to various soldiers and clerks he encountered. "While among the barbarians," he wrote, "we are not suspicious of each other, so when I inquired about [their] customs, I obtained detailed responses."[36] There are numerous other indications of the curiosity of Song envoys and their casual efforts to learn more about Khitan practices. In one anecdote, a Liao ambassador asked his Song escort about the etymology of the name of a minor office in the escort's entourage.[37] On another occasion, a Liao envoy explained to his Song escort that the word *nabo* – used to refer to camp sites in Liao territory – was Khitan slang for "temporary residence." Another Liao diplomat informed his Song counterpart that the "yellow sheep" referred to in a Liao poem described a type of sheep whose meat is less muttony in flavor.[38] Then there was the Liao official who told his Song charge about a group of pastoral nomadic vegetarians whose intestines were tough enough to offer protection from arrow shots.[39] And there is the one who discussed the Khitan practice of invigorating a horse by extracting its liver.[40] When Liu Chang (1019–68) went to Liao in 1055, his

---

[35] *Su Shi wenji*, 2:461–62. See also SS 332.10674. Note also the example of Zhang Fangping (1007–91), who, in the mid-1070s, was selected to host a Liao embassy because, as an elder statesman and in contrast with newer bureaucratic recruits, he possessed the gravitas to "speak more frankly" with the foreign dignitaries. See *Zhang Fangping ji*, 810.

[36] QSW 27:104.

[37] Zhao Lingzhi, *Houqing lu*, 105.

[38] *Quan Liao shi hua*, 58, 78–79.

[39] Jiang Shaoyu, *Songchao shishi leiyuan*, 78.1019.

[40] Ye Longli, *Qidan guo zhi*, 25.241. The Liao official admitted, however, that only one or two horses in ten survived the dangerous surgical procedure.

escort asked him about a tiger-eating beast with a horse's head supposedly encountered in the Yan Mountains. Liu was able to identify it by name, citing classical scholarship as evidence.[41] Finally, there is the case of the Liao Chinese Wang Shiru (c.1046–c.1107), whose funerary biography, discovered by archaeologists in the 1950s, provides rare insight into the Liao as opposed to the Song perspective on post-Chanyuan diplomacy. According to the biography, Wang's learning greatly impressed the Song envoy Qian Xie (1034–97), on mission to Liao in the year 1080. While on the road, the two were said to have discussed a wide range of topics, from classical scholarship to astronomy, divination, medicine, geography, and the occult.[42] Indeed, Song and Liao officials did far more than negotiate on behalf of their respective states. They spoke to each other casually on a wide variety of topics, from the scholarly and the serious to the far more trivial.

An additional indicator of the degree of sociability between bureaucrats involves one of the most characteristic practices of Chinese elite society, the social composition of verse. In Song China of the eleventh century, no banquet or other gathering of educated men was complete without extemporaneous poetry-writing. Several anecdotes confirm that such literary games were also practiced by ambassadors and their hosts during diplomatic missions.[43] The poetry composed by envoys in the presence of the emperor tended, it seems, to celebrate the many years of peaceful relations. Zhao Gai (996–1083) wrote a poem entitled "Our Sworn Oath is [Firm] like the Mountains and Rivers," which the delighted Liao emperor had inscribed on a fan that he kept on his person.[44] Yu Jing, ambassador to Liao in 1044 and 1045, likewise wrote on the theme of peace and friendship, and as a demonstration of his literary virtuosity, he managed to integrate Khitan words into his Chinese poem.[45] In the corpus of extant Song verse, one also finds two poems by Song Xiang (996–1066) commemorating the Khitan ambassador's attendance at a banquet in the capital, and one by Wang Gui, written on the eve of his departure from the Liao court and dedicated to his escort, the Khitan hospitality commissioner Yelü Fang.[46] Diao Yue (j.s. 1030), who, like Yu Jing, also

---

[41] QSW 69:209; SS 319.10384.
[42] Xiang Nan (ed.), *Liaodai shike wenbian*, 646.
[43] For a few examples, see Tao Jing-shen, *Song Liao guanxi shi yanjiu*, 194–95; Tao, *Two Sons of Heaven*, 22–23.
[44] QSW 53:328.
[45] Ye Longli, *Qidan guo zhi*, 24.232–33; Jiang Shaoyu, *Songchao shishi leiyuan*, 39.513–14.
[46] QSS 4:2220; QSS 9:5970.

incorporated Khitan words into his poem, described exotic Khitan curiosities in four lines of verse probably presented to the host of the banquet, a Liao official mentioned in the first line.[47] Not all social poetry was so tame, however. "Jolly" Wang Gongchen, who had so shocked the Song censors, apparently wrote several lewd poems inspired by the eighth-century femme fatale Yang Guifei, followed later by a couplet implying most presumptuously (albeit probably accurately) that the Liao emperor was enjoying the drunken revelry at the banquet.[48] Although few embassy poems survive – these were the sorts of literary trifles not deemed worthy of inclusion in a man's collected writings – it is significant that the Song court felt it necessary, in 1042, to issue an edict strictly limiting the composition of poetry by envoys on diplomatic missions.[49]

To be sure, there was diplomatic activity between the Song and other Northeast Asian states over the course of the eleventh century. Though there is far less extant source material, much of this diplomacy appears to have followed a very similar pattern. Thus, for example, there is evidence of the social exchange of poetry between Koryŏ and Liao diplomats,[50] Koryŏ and Song diplomats,[51] as well as Liao and Japanese diplomats.[52] But given the number of embassies exchanged between Song and Liao, the number of influential political elites who served as ambassadors, and the amount of time men from Song and Liao spent together engaged in a variety of social practices revolving around drinking and banqueting, it is clear that Song–Liao diplomacy was unique. As a result of their relationship with officials of the Khitan state, Song Chinese of the eleventh century enjoyed a sort of cosmopolitan sociability that was unusual in premodern times. It is worth, then, considering in more detail the repercussions of this situation on the cultural history of eleventh-century China.

Cross-Border Circulation of Ethnic Categories

One apparent impact of Song–Liao diplomatic sociability was on conceptions of ethnicity among Chinese educated elites. Not only did Song envoys have opportunities to learn more about the Liao and their customs, there is also evidence that they came to share certain analytical

[47] Shen Gua, *Mengxi bitan*, 25.212 (#463).
[48] QSW 41:171–72.
[49] XCB 135.3219.
[50] *Quan Liao shi hua*, 70.
[51] Ibid., 124–27; QSW 111:133; Su Song, *Su Weigong wenji*, 1:151.
[52] *Quan Liao shi hua*, 223–24.

categories used in the Liao understanding of ethnic identity. There can be no doubt – as we shall see in a later chapter – that the Liao enforced ethnic policies that served to maintain a sharp distinction between populations of Khitans and populations of ethnic Han living within their empire. What is striking is that over the course of the eleventh century Song and Liao elites came to represent ethnicity in very similar ways.

In his study of Khitan tomb murals, Robert Rorex found that the manner in which Khitans and Khitan culture were depicted on their tomb walls was strikingly similar to how they were presented in contemporaneous Song court paintings. The paintings examined all included scenes of Khitan daily life. Of particular interest were the camel-drawn yurt carriages, the distinct hairstyles of the Khitan men, and their distinctive costumes, composed of round-collared robes with narrow sleeves, held at the waist by a belt, with trousers beneath the robe tucked into felt boots. Also of note were the representations of kitchens, and of meat cooking in tripod cauldrons. All of these elements were nearly identical in appearance in both Song paintings and Liao murals.[53]

Rorex underlined such similarities both as a means of dating Song court paintings, and to assess the accuracy of the depictions of Khitan culture. Yet one can also treat the paintings not as accurate snapshots of Khitan daily life, but rather as staged representations. The elements of Khitan culture that the artists (or those commissioning the paintings) chose to highlight constituted the elements the artists themselves deemed most characteristic of Khitan society. Comparing several Northern Song court paintings (Figure 1.1) with scenes from Liao tomb murals (Figure 1.2), certain elements are found to recur. Painters both at the Song capital and in Liao territory apparently shared a sense of how one ought to depict Khitan daily life. One needed to include a large tent, a camel-driven yurt cart, and men wearing Khitan hairstyles and costumes. Another motif appearing in multiple depictions was the Khitan cooking scene, featuring one or more cauldrons from which protruded large cuts of meat.[54] The frequent recurrence of all these elements suggests that they had become visual markers of ethnic identity for both the Song and the Liao.

[53] Rorex, "Some Liao Tomb Murals."
[54] For examples in Liao tomb murals of camel-driven yurt carts and cauldrons of meat resembling those appearing in Song court paintings, see "Aohan qi Lama gou Liaodai bihua mu," 93–94; "Aohan qi Qijia Liao mu," 51; "Aohan qi Yangshan 1–3 hao Liaomu," 20–21, 25–26, 29–30; Dai and Lei, "Shuozhou Liaodai bihua mu," 21; "Kulun qi di wu, liu hao Liao mu," 40; Liu and He, "Hebei Zhuolu xian Liaodai bihua mu," pl. 8; Shao Guotian, "Aohan qi Baitazi Liao mu," pl. 11; Shao Guotian, *Aohan wenwu jinghua*, 242; Wang and Chen, *Kulun Liaodai bihua mu*, 29–30, 44; Xiang Chunsong, "Liaoning Zhaowuda diqu faxian de Liao mu," 30, pl. 8; *Xuanhua Liao mu*, 293, pl. 226.

Figure 1.1 Three depictions of Khitan daily life in Song court paintings
Line drawings based on scenes from *Lady Wenji's Return to China* at Boston Museum of
Fine Arts (top, lower left) and National Palace Museum (lower right).

There is an interesting parallel, moreover, between the predilection to include such cooking scenes in depictions of Khitan daily life, and the performance of ethnicity at diplomatic banquets. Though most descriptions of such banquets emphasize the wine-drinking, a surviving fragment of Lu Zhen's embassy report, written shortly after the Peace of Chanyuan, describes the food served at a dinner held near the Liao Southern Capital:

> Ornate wooden bowls brimmed with caitiff food. First came camel gruel, served with a ladle. There was boiled bear fat, mutton, pork, pheasant, and rabbit, and there was dried beef, venison, pigeon, duck, bear, and tanuki, all of which was cut into square chunks and strewn onto a large platter. Two Tartar youths wearing clean clothing, each with napkins and holding a knife and spoon, cut all of the various meats for the Han envoys to eat.[55]

---

[55] Jiang Shaoyu, *Songchao shishi leiyuan*, 77.1011.

Figure 1.2 Three depictions of Khitan daily life in Liao tomb murals from Inner Mongolia
Line drawings adapted from Wang and Chen, *Kulun Liaodai bihua mu*, 29–30; "Aohan qi
Yangshan 1–3 hao Liaomu," 20; "Aohan qi Lama gou Liaodai bihua mu," 93–94.

The Liao Southern Capital (modern Beijing) was situated in the region
of Yan – that portion of the North China Plain under Liao control. As
we shall see in a later chapter, the population of this region was almost
entirely Han, not Khitan. Yet the banquet featured stereotypic Khitan
food – large cuts of boiled meat – that feature so prominently in Song
and Liao paintings. Moreover, as if to accentuate the ethnocultural
divide, pages were assigned to cut the meat into smaller pieces, necessary
so that the Song Chinese envoys could eat with chopsticks (as was
the Chinese custom) rather than with their hands (as was the Khitan
custom). In this manner, the act of eating at the banquet involved a
performance of one of the key ethnic distinctions later incorporated into
both Song and Liao scenes of Khitan daily life. Earlier tenth-century
Chinese depictions of Khitan daily life seem not to have emphasized
either the cooking scenes or the yurt carts.[56] By contrast, Lu Zhen's
description suggests that Khitans were already distinguishing ethnic

[56] Leung, "Felt Yurts Neatly Arrayed."

eating practices at diplomatic banquets immediately after the Chanyuan treaty. It seems plausible, then, that the way Liao diplomats encoded the Khitan–Chinese divide in their endless embassy banquets helped stimulate the development of a common cross-border sense of how to understand ethnicity, a common understanding leading to similar visual representations of ethnic difference.[57]

Celebrating Peace on the Steppe Frontier

Besides creating new avenues of knowledge circulation, the cosmopolitan sociability of Song and Liao political and cultural elites also played a role in encouraging mutual trust among policymakers of the two courts and by this means in discouraging hawkish irredentism. For centuries, the Oath of Chanyuan has been treated by Chinese historians as one of the great humiliations of their past. The peace agreement required annual payments from Song to Liao. In addition, Song China permanently gave up its claim to the "Sixteen Prefectures of Yan and Yun." Already by the Southern Song, the Sixteen Prefectures had become a rallying cry for Chinese patriots, as we shall see in Chapter 4. But during most of the Northern Song itself, the court showed little interest in a war with the Liao. To be sure, prior to the Chanyuan agreement, in the final decades of the tenth century, the second Song emperor Taizong led two armies into Yan. After Chanyuan, however, it was only in 1115, 110 years later, that the most notorious of the war advocates – including notably the eunuch Tong Guan (1054–1126) – began a concerted effort to convince Emperor Huizong (r. 1100–25) to ally with the Jurchens against the Khitans. Though they ultimately succeeded in winning the emperor to their cause, they faced vigorous opposition from a sizable number of court officials.[58] By and large the military expansionism of the eleventh century, embarked upon at great financial and human cost, was directed toward the Tangut and Tibetan territories in the northwest, as well as the tribal regions in the southwest, not toward

---

[57] Food continued to play a similar role in diplomatic banquets after the Jurchen invasion. See Zhou Hui, *Beiyuan lu*, 1. One does not know whether these standardized representations of ethnicity were understood by Song Chinese, Liao and Jin Chinese, Liao Khitans, and Jurchens in the same way. Song Chinese viewed eating with chopsticks as a mark of civilization, whereas Khitans and Jurchens perhaps saw the Chinese use of chopsticks as evidence of effete decadence.

[58] Ebrey, *Emperor Huizong*, 379–85.

the Khitan-controlled lands in the northeast.[59] Tao Jing-shen, Paul Smith, and others have previously described the eleventh-century court's commitment to their peace with Liao.[60] Here, I would like first to establish the relative influences of doves and hawks at court in the post-Chanyuan century, then to convey the fervor and zeal of those advocating peace, and, finally, to demonstrate a link between the peace movement and diplomatic sociability.

To be sure, over the course of the century after the Chanyuan peace agreement, one does encounter individuals pushing for an invasion of Yan. It is important, however, to place these hawks in perspective. Table 1.6 presents a sample of essays, policy proposals, speeches, and poems dating to the period between 1005 and 1114 that advocate for or against the conquest of Yan. Hawkish positions were most prevalent around the year 1042 and in the mid-1070s – precisely at the time that significant diplomatic confrontations with Liao provoked widespread frustration and concern at the Song court. At the time they advocated war, hawks were on average nearly fifteen years younger in age than those pushing for peace (37.4 vs. 51.9 years old). They also tended to be men who held less sway at court, both in that they spent less time in policy positions over the course of their careers (1.6 years of service on average vs. 3.6 years), and in that their policymaking service generally occurred much later in their careers (Table 1.6, column 6). The commitment to peace at court was maintained even as the Song political elite came almost universally to see Yan as properly Chinese – and, therefore, Song – territory. Thus, it was not uncommon for doves to express the hope that one day the Song would take possession of Yan, but it would do so only after the Liao state had collapsed, perhaps due to an internal rebellion. It was only younger officials with less political influence who openly advocated war.

Zhang Fangping (1007–91) constitutes a good case example. His collected writings include a short piece he wrote in 1030 in honor of a friend heading off to serve on the northern frontier. In it, Zhang explicitly articulated the hope that his friend might play a role in recovering the lost prefectures, thereby "cleansing the Central Plains [i.e., China]

---

[59] P. J. Smith, "Irredentism as Political Capital"; Lamouroux, "Militaires et bureaucrates." By my count, nearly two thirds (34/54) of Northern Song prose pieces (in vols. 1–140 of QSW) mentioning "former lands" – that is, land that would have been the target of an irredentist agenda – refer to the Tibeto-Tangut frontier. Only one third refer to Yan (and generally not in the context of advocating war with Liao).

[60] Tao, *Two Sons of Heaven*, 68–78; P. J. Smith, "Shen-tsung's Reign," 464–65.

Table 1.6 *Authors of select post-Chanyuan essays, policy proposals, memorials, and poems advocating for or against the conquest of Yan (1005–1114)*[a]

Date	Name	Reference	Years as top policymaker		Age[c]
			(Entire career)[b]	(Prior or concurrent)[b]	
HAWKS (Advocates for reconquest of Yan)					
	Zhang Fangping	QSS 6:3874–75	0.5		
	Hua Zhen	QSW 123:87–89	0	0	
	Liu Zhi	QSS 12:7972	5.5		
1028(?)	Xia Song	QSW 17:54–55	7.5	6	44
1030	Zhang Fangping	QSW 38:5–6	0.5	0	24
1042	Liu Chang	QSW 59:251–52	0	0	24
c.1045(?)	Su Xun	QSW 43:61–65	0	0	37
1060	Guo Zi	XCB 191.4622–24	0	0	
1072	Lü Tao	QSW 73:304–08	0	0	42
1073	Feng Shan	QSW 78:261–67	0	0	46
1074	Yang Wenguang	XCB 258.6288	0	0	60[d]
c.1075	Chao Buzhi	QSW 125:321–36	0	0	23
c.1075(?)	Li Qingchen	QSW 78:393–95	8	0	44
c.1078	Qin Guan	QSW 123:333–34	0	0	30
		Average:	1.6	0.5	37.4
DOVES (Advocates against reconquest of Yan)					
	Song Qi	QSW 24:335–39	0	0	
	Li Fu	QSS 19:12436	0	0	
	Zhang Lei	QSW 128:33–35	0	0	
	Bi Zhongyou	QSW 111:79–80	0	0	
c.1007	Xia Song	QSW 17:53–54, 193–94	7.5	0	23
1041	Zhang Fangping	QSW 37:35	0.5	0	35

(Continued)

Table 1.6 *(Cont.)*

Date	Name	Reference	Years as top policymaker		Age[c]
			(Entire career)[b]	(Prior or concurrent)[b]	
*c.*1041	Yin Zhu	QSW 27:301–03	0	0	41
*c.*1043	Fan Zhongyan	QSW 18:152–59	2.5	0	55
1044	Zhang Fangping	XCB 150.3657–58; QSW 37:95–96	0.5	0	38
1044	Fu Bi	XCB 150.3638–55, 151.3674–76, 153.3729–31	10.5	2	41
1045	Han Qi	XCB 154.3737–39; QSW 39:220–22	13	2	38
*c.*1045	Fan Zhongyan	QSW 18:303–05	2.5	2.5	57
*c.*1049	Song Xiang	QSW 20:398–401	10	6	53
1052	Bao Zheng	QSW 26:40–41	1	0	54
1055	Song Qi	QSW 24:340–52	0	0	58
1055	Ouyang Xiu	QSS 6:3630	7	0	49
1063	Wang Anshi	QSS 10:6510	6	0	43
1065	Sima Guang	XCB 206.5008–10	1.5	0	47
1065	Hu Su	QSW 22:44, 46–47; SS 318.10368	5	5	70
*c.*1067	Zheng Xie	QSW 68:48–49	0	0	46
*c.*1070	Qiang Zhi	QSW 66:29–30	0	0	49
1072	Wen Yanbo	XCB 238.5787, 238.5790–92	19	15	67
1072	Wang Anshi	XCB 238.5787, 238.5790–92	6	5	52
1075	Zhang Fangping	XCB 259.6320–21	0.5	0.5	69
1075	Han Qi	XCB 262.6386–91	13	13	68
1076	Wen Yanbo	QSW 30:223–25	19	15	71
1078	Huang Tingjian	QSS 17:11472	0	0	34
1083	Su Song	QSW 61:340–42	3	0	64

Table 1.6 *(Cont.)*

Date	Name	Reference	Years as top policymaker		Age[c]
			(Entire career)[b]	(Prior or concurrent)[b]	
1084	Bi Zhongyou	QSS 18:11899–900	0	0	38
1085	Sima Guang	XCB 363.8689–91	1.5	0	67
1086	Lü Tao	QSW 73:241–44	0	0	56
*c.*1089	Bi Zhongyou	QSW 110:243–44	0	0	43
*c.*1089	Su Che	QSW 94:360–61	3	0	51
1093	Lü Tao	QSW 73:180	0	0	63
*c.*1100	Su Che	QSW 96:28–29	3	3	62
*c.*1100	Chao Yuezhi	QSW 129:401–18, 130:250–51	0	0	42
1101	Ren Boyu	QSW 108:230–33	0	0	55
1114	Hong Zhongfu	QSW 119:127–29	0	0	66
		Average:	3.6	1.8	51.9

[a] This table was compiled by performing a keyword search in QSW (vols. 1–140, i.e., roughly representing the Northern Song), QSS, XCB, SHY, SS, and SCBM. Search terms included references to "Yan" (燕薊, etc.), "former lands" (故地, etc.) "cleansing [national] shame" (雪恥, etc.), and "peace" (通好, etc.). Of the resulting texts, only those explicitly advocating for or against the conquest of Yan were included. Men arguing that there might be an opportunity to retake Yan at some undefined time in the future (after the Liao regime had collapsed on its own) were considered to be "doves." The end date of 1114 represents the year before a coalition of hawks began a concerted effort to convince the emperor and the court to ally with the Jurchens against the Khitans.

[b] Years in service in a policy position calculated by subtracting start year from end year of service, except in case of appointments that began and ended within the same year, in which case years in service was assumed to be 0.5. "Entire career" tabulates all service in a top policy position over the course of individual's career; "prior or concurrent" only tabulates length of service in appointments beginning before date of essay, policy proposal, memorial, or poem in question.

[c] Age (calculated in *sui*) determined in most cases using data from October 2013 edition of Chinese Biographical Database (CBDB). When birth year unknown, it was approximated by subtracting 59 from CBDB "index year."

[d] SS identifies Yang Wenguang as the son of Yang Yanzhao; in estimating his age, I treat him as a grandson instead, on the basis of the dates in which he served in particular offices. Note that the early dramaturgic work *The Generals of the Yang Family* also identifies Wenguang as the grandson of Yanzhao.

of a century of humiliation."[61] At the time, he was twenty-four years old; he would not pass the *jinshi* civil service exams and embark on his bureaucratic career until four years later. By 1041, however, he had become a vigorous proponent of peace with Liao.[62] At this point, he was an established bureaucrat on the verge later that year of a prestigious appointment to the Remonstrance Bureau, which would give him the authority to critique court policy. There is also the case of Qin Guan (1049–1100). Though no warmonger by the time he entered office in the mid-1080s, he admitted to an acquaintance that, as a young man in the late 1070s, he had yearned to gain fame by spearheading a reconquest both of Yan and of some of the Tangut lands.[63] Finally, there is the example of Guo Zi, who seems to have been a bit of an eccentric. After earning a *jinshi* degree, he made the unusual decision to pursue a career in the military bureaucracy, where he was unlikely ever to attain a policy position. In 1060, he presented the court with unsolicited battle plans for seizing Yan that recommended the use of 4,500 specialized lances and war chariots, devices that he himself had designed.[64] There are various explanations for this correlation between youthfulness, lack of political influence, and a hawkish stance regarding relations with Liao. Among them is the possibility that political maturity acquired through the course of a career in the bureaucracy – not to mention during diplomatic encounters with Liao envoys – tempered the views of young warmongers.[65]

One last important conclusion to draw from Table 1.6 concerns the major factional divide of the late eleventh century, a divide pitting the supporters and opponents of chief minister Wang Anshi (1021–86) and his New Policies – a series of fundamental reforms intended to strengthen the state's financial base. Traditional historians have sought to blame Wang for the downfall of the Northern Song, partly on the grounds that he purportedly inspired the hawks of the late 1110s. From this perspective, Wang is seen as having pushed for an aggressive foreign policy that culminated ultimately in the Song annexation of Yan in 1122, followed soon after by the debacle against the Jurchens.[66] There is no doubt that

---

[61] *Zhang Fangping ji*, 561–62 [QSW 38:5]. For the convenience of readers, this and subsequent notes provide the QSW reference in brackets when referring to texts included in Table 1.6.

[62] *Zhang Fangping ji*, 263 [QSW 37:35].

[63] QSW 123:333.

[64] XCB 191.4622–24; SS 326.10531–32.

[65] In addition, pro-peace partisans, once entrenched at court, may have consciously sought to keep hawks out of policy positions.

[66] For a review and critique of the traditional perspective, see Tao, *Two Sons of Heaven*, 68–78.

Wang was a fervent supporter of military expansionism in the northwest, and can indeed be blamed for setting in motion events that would lead, in the decades after his death, to the seizure by the Song of Tibetan and Tangut lands.[67] Moreover, Wang Anshi's political opponents were nearly unanimous in condemning the northwestern campaigns, condemnations that often incorporated a broader critique of all of the reforms associated with the New Policies.[68] That being said, Wang Anshi and his followers did not advocate war with Liao. In fact, as of the 1070s, those few hawks pushing for an invasion of Yan – men like Lü Tao (1031–1107), Feng Shan (j.s. 1057), Chao Buzhi (1053–1110), and Qin Guan – tended to be Wang's political opponents.[69] By and large, advocates of peace with Liao spanned the factional divide.

One particularly striking element of political discourse in the late eleventh century – evident in the texts included in Table 1.6 – was the explicit celebration of peace for its own sake. A lengthy articulation of this proposition worth examining in more detail comes from the late Northern Song statesman Su Che (1039–1112), who sought to explain "what is meant by the advantages of ceding Yan":

> After Emperor Zhenzong personally led the Six Armies and vanquished the caitiffs at Chanyuan, he recognized that they hoped to avoid more hostilities, and so enticed them with gold and silks. The caitiffs joyfully obeyed the command, sending envoys annually in order to maintain peace between the neighbors. It has now been over a century since the people on the northern frontier have seen the weapons of war. This is something that was not experienced even in the heydays of the Han and Tang dynasties. In the past, barbarians have come and gone; there was always some tribe out there hostile to the Middle Kingdom. Emperor Wen of the Han handled them with marriage alliances, which only made the Xiongnu [tribesmen] more arrogant by the day. Emperor Wu [of the Han] controlled them with his military might, but the Central Plains [of China] became each day more impoverished . . . The generosity with which our court treats [the Khitans] today does not exceed that of Emperor Wen of Han, yet the caitiffs have been tamed. Thus, we recognize here the advantages of the Later Jin ceding Yan and Ji. If a bear or tiger pounces on a man, it will back off if it is given an ox. Ever since the Khitans came to

---

[67] P. J. Smith, "Irredentism as Political Capital"; Lamouroux, "Militaires et bureaucrates."

[68] E.g., *Su Shi wenji*, 2:737; XCB 363.8689–90; QSW 78:266–67.

[69] Indeed, among the doves opposed to the New Policies, some even criticized Wang and his political allies for indulging the Khitans during diplomatic negotiations. See, e.g., XCB 238.5791–92, 381.9283. For more on Wang's opposition in the early 1070s to war with Liao, see Tietze, "Liao-Sung Border Conflict," 130–31.

occupy all of Yan, they have appropriated its agricultural riches, and have seized its treasures and its population. They overtax their people, while depleting their northern territories, and then supplement all of this with the generous goods our court gives to them. This is what Jia Yi called the "five baits"; we have made full use [of this strategy]. Though their customs are to wear felts and drink milk, yet now they partake of fine silks, sweet wines, teas, and citrus fruits, such that their hearts of beasts have become drunk with satisfaction. So they bow their heads and submit to our treaty, and learn to practice the [correct] rituals and rites.[70]

Su's argument began and ended with language intended to play down the notion that peace with Liao was a humiliation. It was the Khitans and not the Chinese, according to Su, who had begged for peace at Chanyuan. Subsequently, like any tributary vassal, the Khitans "obeyed" the emperor's "command" by sending envoys annually. In fact, such face-saving rhetoric was common throughout the post-Chanyuan period. Others described Song's relationship to Liao as a paternalistic "haltered-and-bridled" (*jimi*) arrangement (not unlike Song's relationship with southwestern tribal chiefs), in which Song "cherished those from afar [i.e., the Khitans] with the civilizing sway of its culture."[71] By Su's times, it was even possible to claim the success of this civilizing mission. Su brings up the "five baits" theory of the Han Dynasty scholar Jia Yi (200–168 BCE) to imply that the annual payments to the Khitans had lured them into embracing civilization. No longer were they as insatiable and unpredictable as wild beasts. Now they interacted with others according to fundamental principles – the rites – created by the sages of antiquity to maintain order in society.[72] In the words of one of Su's contemporaries, this transformation had been so successful that the Liao ruler now sighed reverently at the mention of former Song emperors, so moved was he by the compassionate grace they had shown him.[73]

Amid this chauvinistic rhetoric – which was, of course, not new to Chinese political culture – Su made a much more striking point. In praising the century of peace, he described it not merely as an accomplishment, but as something unprecedented in China's history. Earlier in the dynasty, one found Fan Zhongyan (989–1052) arguing that the Chanyuan peace

[70] *Su Che ji*, 3:1012–13 [QSW 96:28].
[71] QSW 22:44; QSW 111:80; *Zhang Fangping ji*, 561–62 [QSW 38:5]. For more claims that it was the Khitans who had begged for peace at Chanyuan, see QSW 17:53–54; QSW 27:302.
[72] For other references to the "five baits" in discussing Song–Liao relations, see QSW 20:399; QSW 24:343; QSW 30:223. On the "five baits policy" under the Han, see Barfield, *Perilous Frontier*, 51–52.
[73] QSW 129:407.

put the Song emperors on a par with such venerated figures as Emperor Wen (r. 180–157 BCE) of the Han.[74] By the middle of the eleventh century, however, it became common to speak of the peace with Liao as something that neither of the two great dynasties of the past – the Han and the Tang – had managed to realize, something, therefore, that the Song emperor and his court might consider one of their utmost triumphs. As early as 1041, Zhang Fangping, then serving as prefectural supervisor in South China, submitted a lengthy ten-point policy recommendation on frontier defense, in which he described the unusual nature of the Song–Liao relationship on precisely such grounds: "The friendly relations between us and the Khitans have now lasted over thirty years; beginning with the Han Dynasty, it has never been possible to make peace with the barbarians and then to adhere strictly to the treaty for as long as this."[75] In the mid-1060s, Hu Su (996–1067) made a similar observation:

> Ever since [the Chanyuan Oath], the frontiers have not experienced the dusty stampedes [of cavalry attacks], and village elders have not had to respond to the alarms of war . . . In the century since our dynasty's founding, we have had peaceful relations for sixty years. This is something past dynasties have not enjoyed.[76]

A decade later, in the midst of a diplomatic confrontation over the demarcation of the Song–Liao border, the official Wen Yanbo (1006–97) stressed much the same point:

> After the court of Zhenzong established peaceful relations with [the Khitans], the populace has enjoyed a respite [from war] for nearly eighty years . . . When considering the successive dynasties of the past, there have never been peaceful relations between the Middle Kingdom and the barbarians that have lasted for such a long period of time.[77]

And a few years after that, in 1083, Su Song (1020–1101) explained in the preface to his compilation of Song–Liao diplomatic correspondence:

> When I consider the ways in which past dynasties guarded against [the people of] the northern deserts . . . it is only our dynasty that has implemented superior policies. Year after year for [now] seven decades, our frontier defenses have met with no calamities; the annual payments and diplomatic correspondence have elicited ever more respectful interactions. Travel [near the border] is unhindered; frontier cities can shut their gates

---

[74] QSW 18:304.
[75] *Zhang Fangping ji*, 263 [QSW 37:35].
[76] QSW 22:46.
[77] QSW 30:223.

late at night; and the local common people can grow old and die without seeing the weapons of war.[78]

Even in the final years of the Northern Song, policymakers continued to invoke the unprecedented duration of the peace with the Liao. In 1118, Zheng Juzhong (1059–1123) argued against an alliance with the Jurchens on just such grounds:

> As of today, we have entered a second century in which soldiers do not see the weapons of war, and peasants are not burdened with corvée obligations. Although the Han and the Tang made peace with the barbarians, [what they did] never matched the policies of our Song Dynasty.[79]

At about the same time and in the same spirit, the official Yuwen Xuzhong (1079–1146) reminded the court that, over the course of a long century of peace, there had been only minor disputes over territory or etiquette, disputes that had always been resolved diplomatically:

> The peace between the Middle Kingdom and the Khitans has now lasted over a hundred years. During this time, the [Khitans] sometimes behaved greedily, but they never demanded more than the ten counties of Guannan; during this time, they sometimes behaved haughtily, but they never did more than shirk a few ritual protocols in the presence of the Middle Kingdom's ambassadors.[80]

Yuwen proceeded presciently to warn that relations with the Jurchens were very unlikely to be so easy.

Of course, one must take care to distinguish this celebration of peace from modern pacifism. The sort of chauvinistic rhetoric that we see in Su Che's essay was common even among doves at court.[81] Moreover, even some who opposed an all-out war with Liao were still in favor of taking a tough stance against the Khitans. In 1072, for example, Wen Yanbo – whom we saw above praising the eighty years of peaceful relations – insisted that the Song should respond in kind to the harassment of the frontier by Khitan cavalrymen.[82] And nearly everybody agreed that the court could not permit the frontier defenses to deteriorate. Men like Zhang Fangping and Hu Su, even as they praised the unprecedented nature of the peace with Liao, insisted that the court remain vigilant.[83]

---

[78] Su Song, *Su Weigong wenji*, 2:1005 [QSW 61:342].
[79] SCBM Zhengxuan, 1.5.
[80] Yue Ke, *Tingshi*, 103; SS 371.11526–27.
[81] Tao, *Two Sons of Heaven*, 34–52.
[82] XCB 238.5791.
[83] *Zhang Fangping ji*, 263 [QSW 37:35]; QSW 22:46–47.

Some felt that the peace was doomed to break down in the end, a particular concern in the years leading up to the renegotiation of the oath in 1042, as well as during the border negotiations of the 1070s. It was also always understood that a hawkish emperor might one day ascend the Liao throne.[84] Finally, it was not unusual even among those advocating against war with Liao to hold open the possibility that, at some point in the future, Song China might regain control of Yan. Perhaps the people of Yan would rebel against the Khitans and welcome in Song troops; perhaps the Liao empire would collapse as a result of conflict with another neighboring state; or perhaps the Khitans would themselves initiate a war with Song, giving the Chinese no choice but to invade.[85] Despite these variant positions, the doves at court all shared in common the view that Yan was not worth a war. In the words of one contemporary writing in the mid-1070s:

> Everywhere today things are calm; the frontier never raises the alarm. And so, though some may feel indignation and resentment when looking north [at Yan], or they may debate the advantages and disadvantages [of particular policies], government officials and local literati alike are all unwilling in this time of great peace to provoke an incident for the sake of the great merit [of leading a reconquest]. It is only for this reason that some of the Middle Kingdom's lands – possessions of the former kings – have not yet been recovered.[86]

To renege on the Chanyuan Oath would be to throw away a long-cultivated relationship that had secured on the sino-steppe frontier a peace that was unprecedented in China's history.

How does one explain the strong cross-factional support among Northern Song policymakers for preserving peace with the Khitans for over a century? Given the increased sense over the course of the eleventh century that Yan was properly Chinese territory – a point explored in Chapter 4 – why did revanchism not play a greater role in decision-making at court? Advocates for peace put forward numerous arguments. One set of arguments was based on simple pragmatism. The Khitans possessed a formidable army that had already marched across the North China Plain to the vicinity of the Chinese capital region on three occasions – in 936 and 947 (prior to the founding of the Song) and again in 1004.[87] If the founding emperors with their battle-hardened armies had

---

[84] E.g., QSW 24:351; QSW 108:232–33.
[85] QSW 66:29–30; XCB 154.3738; QSW 18:159; QSW 24:349–50.
[86] QSW 125:321–22.
[87] QSW 18:157.

failed to take Yan, few believed this territory could be seized, especially after decades of peace had, it was widely acknowledged, rendered the Song's northern armies weak and unprepared.[88] As late as 1114, the military commissioner of one of the northern prefectures was so convinced that the Song could never defeat the Khitans in battle that he declared in a report to the court that "if the emperor's advisors insist upon reoccupying the former territories of Yan and Yun, even were it to mean I would die ten thousand deaths, I would not dare obey the imperial edict."[89] Meanwhile, doves also took into account financial considerations. In particular, it was well understood that the annual payments to Liao represented only a tiny fraction of the costs of a war.[90] Among pragmatic concerns, doves also pointed to the religious sanction built into the Chanyuan Oath. The Oath – which included the declaration that an emperor violating its terms "shall no longer remain on the throne" – was sworn before the Altars of Heaven and Earth and before the shrine to the imperial ancestors. In the late 1110s, when seeking desperately to discourage Huizong from violating the peace accord, the chief minister Zheng Juzhong (1059–1123) insisted that "if today His Majesty is lured into abandoning the treaty in order to recover Yan, I fear the wrath of Heaven."[91] In fact, as later Southern Song historical commentators would observe, as they mourned the loss of the north, the wrath of Heaven on the Song was indeed severe.[92]

Besides such pragmatic concerns, the peace agenda was further bolstered by the growing importance in Northern Song political culture of respecting the precedent established by earlier emperors of the dynasty.[93] Indeed, it was specifically on these grounds – namely, that one should "abide by the norms of the [former] emperors Zhenzong and Renzong" – that, in the mid-1060s, the deputy director of military affairs Hu Su sought to advise the newly enthroned emperor Yingzong (r. 1063–67). Although Hu recognized that "today among court officials, there are those who feel humiliated that Yan lies outside the realm," he advised

---

[88] For expressions of concern over military preparedness dating to the 1040s through the 1110s, see QSW 18:95; XCB 142.3414; QSW 22:46–47; QSW 26:40; QSW 111:80; QSW 119:127–28.

[89] SCBM Zhengxuan, 19.180.

[90] E.g., according to Fu Bi, the payment to Liao amounted to a mere 1 or 2 percent of the cost of armed conflict. See XCB 150.3640.

[91] SCBM Zhengxuan, 1.5. Earlier, in 1076, Wen Yanbo urged the Song emperor to hold fast to the treaty on the grounds that Heaven would assist Song if Liao were to attack first. See QSW 30:223–24.

[92] E.g., Zhuang Chuo, *Ji le bian*, 2.45.

[93] Deng and Lamouroux, "Ancestors Family Instructions."

the new emperor to continue to "choose good generals to defend the frontier, select able officials for diplomacy, externally adhere firmly to the peace, and internally bolster border defenses."[94] Yingzong's successor, Shenzong, seems to have been particularly intent on learning from his predecessors. In 1075, he asked one of his advisors to identify the greatest of the early Song rulers. The advisor responded that Taizu and Zhenzong (the first and third emperors) were greater than Taizong (the second), because they sought to establish peace with their neighbors, whereas Taizong provoked over two decades of warfare after seizing Hedong and twice attempting to take Yan.[95] Three months later, Shenzong expressed frustration with the negotiations with Liao over the Hedong border, but insisted, nevertheless, that he would treat the Khitans with forbearance "out of respect for the peace oath of my imperial ancestors."[96] Through the end of the eleventh century, it was common for doves to underline the fact that the Chanyuan Oath had been the accomplishment of earlier Song emperors.[97]

Officials at the Northern Song court also brought up ethical concerns. According to the basic tenets of Chinese political philosophy, any legitimate monarch claiming Heaven's Mandate to rule had the responsibility to keep his people content and well fed, while not burdening them with warfare and excessive taxation. Good governance was far more important than territorial ambitions. Emperor Zhenzong set the example when, a mere two years after Chanyuan, one of his advisors proposed that he send an army to take Yan, in order to "brush away the humiliation." Zhenzong responded, "The people of Hebei have only just now been spared the misfortunes of war; how could I do such a thing?"[98] This basic principle was oft repeated in policy recommendations throughout the dynasty. In 1071, Su Shi noted that "certainly it might be called an accomplishment to seize Lingwu to the west and to seize Yan to the north, but the long-term survival of the state does not depend on this."[99] Instead, Su pushed the emperor to focus on remedying the impact of the bureaucracy on

---

[94] QSW 22:44.

[95] XCB 259.6320–21.

[96] XCB 262.6386.

[97] After Shenzong's reign, imperial precedent was invoked by hawks, who argued – on the basis of a "policy of carrying on the past [emperor's] will" (or "policy of carrying on" for short) – that military expansionism was necessary to fulfill the ambitions of both Taizong and Shenzong.

[98] Su Che, *Longchuan biezhi*, 1:72; XCB 67.1506. The notion that Zhenzong had condescended to peace with the Khitans for the benefit of his people was a common refrain later in the dynasty. See, e.g., QSW 18:157; XCB 262.6386–87.

[99] QSW 86:224.

society (meaning, from Su's perspective, dismantling Wang Anshi's New Policies). Bi Zhongyou (1047–1121) made a similar point later in the century, by means of a particularly appropriate analogy. The decision on whether or not to go to war with Liao, according to Bi, was analogous to the decision a statesman might make on whether or not to engage others in a heated court debate. The statesman needed to consider whether or not he was right in his argument, whether or not there would be political repercussions for his family and descendants, and whether or not he had prepared sufficiently the main points of his argument. In a similar fashion, prior to embarking on a military campaign against the Khitans, the Song court needed to consider whether or not the cause was right, whether or not the population was happy and supportive of the monarch, and whether or not state funds were sufficient.[100] As late as 1121, on the eve of the first military expedition into Liao territory in well over a century, the official Li Qiu (d. 1151) invoked one last time this political ideal in arguing against a war with Liao: "Today we have inherited an era of Great Peace; the populace has had the good fortune of never witnessing warfare. Even if we were never to obtain this land of Yan and Yun, what would China really be lacking?"[101]

Obviously, many of these arguments in favor of peace with Liao could have been deployed just as well to oppose war with the Tanguts. Why was there sufficient political support for war in the northwest but not for war in the northeast? Moreover, given their roots in traditional Chinese thinking, many of these arguments could also have been used to push a peace agenda during other periods of military expansionism – during the early Tang or the early Ming, for example. In fact, throughout the imperial period, there existed a dovish rhetoric that bureaucrats and courtiers could deploy to push for peace. But they did not always do so. It is, of course, difficult to distinguish the root cause driving a particular political agenda from the plethora of justifications used to buttress it. However, given the unprecedented nature of the post-Chanyuan peace, it is clear one should pay particular attention to factors unique to the eleventh century. It is my contention in the discussion that follows that the intensive social relations that had developed between Song and Liao officials constituted one of the key factors explaining the dominance of the doves at court.

Given the scope of their social interactions during repeated diplomatic missions, and their participation together in typical pastimes of

---

[100] QSW 111:80.
[101] SS 377.11654.

the Chinese elite – from banqueting to poetry – Song and Liao officials appear at times to have come to see each other as belonging to a common community of educated men. The great Song literatus Su Shi certainly seems to have thought so. In 1088, in a clever ploy to get Su to drink one more cup at a banquet, an ambassador from Liao cited two lines of Su's published verse celebrating the consumption of wine. His ego stoked, Su initially feigned surprise – "the caitiffs [i.e., Liao officials], too, enjoy my poetry!" Later, he concluded, "I myself have observed their assembled officials; there are many Chinese *shidafu* among them."[102] Over the course of the eleventh century, *shidafu* became the most common term of self-identification used by the new class of educated elites that emerged in the wake of the demise of the medieval aristocracy. For a man as eminent as Su Shi to recognize fellow *shidafu* among officials of the Khitan regime was remarkable.

Educated elites among the Liao populations of Chinese descent likely also identified with this community of *shidafu*, though it is more difficult to find unambiguous evidence. When reading Chen Xiang's embassy report, one is struck by the number of times a Liao official asked the envoys for news of another Song official. Thus, for example, the Liao state finance commissioner Liu Yun inquired about Lü Gongbi (1007–73) and Hu Su, whom he had met on his trip to Kaifeng; and the Liao revenue commissioner Zhao Wei asked about Cai Xiang (1012–67), who had hosted him on his trip to the south.[103] Liao literati inhabiting the predominantly Chinese region of Yan seem also to have been fascinated with the writings of famous Song writers. Despite strict embargoes on the exportation of published books from Song to Liao, the works of the most famous Song writers seem to have been available in Khitan territory.[104] A few Song envoys also boasted having encountered in their travels to Liao one of their own or their friends' published poems.[105] And, in an epitaph that Su Shi composed for Fan Zhen (1008–88), we learn that Fan's writings were appreciated by Khitans (as well as Koreans).[106] Regardless of the accuracy of such boasts, the suggestion that being cited

---

[102] *Su Shi wenji*, 1:288, 5:2154.

[103] QSW 50:228–37. See esp. entries for the 11th, 13th, 15th, and 25th days of the 5th month; and the 2nd, 11th, 18th, and 20th days of the 6th month. Similarly, according to Sima Guang, Liao officials had once asked a Song envoy for news about him. See Sima Guang, *Sushui jiwen*, fulu, 2.354.

[104] *Su Che ji*, 2:747. For more on cross-border book embargoes during the Song period, see De Weerdt, "What did Su Che See?"

[105] E.g., Wang Pizhi, *Shengshui yantan lu*, 2.15, 7.89–90.

[106] *Su Shi wenji*, 2:442. The text is ambiguous on whether "Khitan" here refers to Liao Chinese.

by Liao officials was something to be proud of implies that the Song authors of these accounts believed them to possess a *shidafu's* tastes and ability to recognize quality writing. Needless to say, the idea that Song and Liao Chinese belonged to a common community of *shidafu* may have reinforced the notion that Yan and its ethnically Han population ought to be controlled by Song China – an issue I bring up again in Chapter 4. But it could also bolster the mutual trust between Song and Liao diplomats, thereby in the long run helping to preserve friendly relations between the two states.

Diplomatic sociability seems also to have helped reinforce the discourse celebrating the unprecedented nature of the Chanyuan peace. We have previously seen evidence suggesting that the choreography of diplomatic banquets created and propagated shared ethnic categories. Banquets also offered countless opportunities to praise the Chanyuan peace. Surviving examples of diplomatic banquet poetry suggest they revolved around the theme of harmonious relations between the two neighbors.[107] The same can be said of many of the polite exchanges between diplomats. The trite language of greetings and of other expressions of courtesy tended to celebrate the many years of peace. One example concerns Lu Zhen's (957–1014) mission to Liao in 1009, just a few years after Chanyuan. As Lu's embassy report recounts, during a banquet that followed an archery contest at the Liao court, the Khitan host, a certain Yelü Ying, urged his Song counterparts to drink from a particularly large wine vessel with the proclamation, "May friendship between our two courts last millions of years!"[108] An account also exists of the Song official Zhang Baosun (1015–85), who chanced to participate in a farewell banquet for a passing Liao envoy while he was serving in a prefecture not far from the Liao border. At the banquet, the envoy invoked the unachieved ideal of many a dynasty (and many a millenarian popular revolt): "The concord between our two courts has lasted a long time, such that we travel back and forth like members of a single family – this surely is the Great Peace!"[109] One finds another example in Chen Xiang's embassy report, which, as we recall, paid particularly close attention to proper banquet protocol. Soon after crossing into Liao territory, the Liao Chinese host at one of the banquets urged Chen to drink another toast on the grounds that "the peace between our two courts has

[107] QSS 4:2220–21; Ye Longli, *Qidan guo zhi*, 24.232–33.
[108] Jiang Shaoyu, *Songchao shishi leiyuan*, 77.1014.
[109] QSW 98:329.

already lasted many years; the ambassadors (and their deputies) and their escorts (and their deputies) look upon each other as one family."[110] The similarity between the language of embassy banquet toasts and the language of Song policy debates celebrating the unprecedented nature of the Song–Liao peace is surely no coincidence. Simply put, the repeated use of such language in the trite ritualized language of diplomatic exchange – especially given that the participating diplomats included many of the most influential court elites – played a role in ingraining a particular pro-peace discourse within Song political culture.

It is possible to reconstruct in somewhat more concrete terms the link between diplomatic sociability and the growing trust between Song and Liao policymakers with a case example. The three extant funerary biographies of the mid-eleventh-century chief minister Fu Bi, probably composed on the basis of both official records and Fu's private papers, record in some detail his conversations in 1042 with the Liao officials Liu Liufu and Xiao Ying, as well as with the Liao emperor.[111] Previously, we have seen how Fu first gained the trust of the two Liao envoys at a banquet held while en route to Kaifeng. Xiao subsequently confided to Fu, forthrightly identifying the mutual suspicions that had provoked the diplomatic crisis of the moment – that is, the Song fear that the Khitans were planning an alliance with the Tanguts, and the Khitan fear that the Song troop buildup on the Tangut frontier might be used to attack Liao instead. Fu Bi added that mutual suspicion allowed "treacherous people to achieve their goal of creating a rift." Xiao then concluded that, "in the future, when our two courts dispatch ambassadors, we should select these men with care; ambassadors [should] make transparent the wishes of our two rulers, in order to dispel their suspicions."[112]

In the next few months, Fu Bi went on two consecutive embassies to Liao. Most historians have focused on the results of the negotiations. In exchange for an increase in Song's annual payment to Liao, Fu was able to convince the Liao court to withdraw its claim to ten counties still under Song control. More interesting for the present discussion was how his lengthy conversations with Liu Liufu and the Khitan emperor prompted him to have great confidence in his own understanding of the Liao agenda. Fu's conversations with the emperor and his minister lasted

---

[110] QSW 50:230–31.
[111] For relevant passages in the three biographies, see QSW 49:229–33; *Su Shi wenji*, 2:526–28, 530–32; QSW 71:314–21.
[112] QSW 71:315.

several days; they talked at court, but also while hunting together on horseback. As the lengthy summary transcripts of their discussions make clear, Fu Bi and his Liao interlocutors came to trust each other and to believe that they understood each other's agendas and motivations. By 1043, now back at court, Fu submitted a letter to the throne confidently asserting his expertise:

> I have recently served as ambassador to the Khitans. I have met those officials in charge of their state policy whom Han envoys have never before met. I have discussed [those topics] that envoys from the two courts have formerly held as taboo. For this reason, I have achieved a detailed understanding of the situation.[113]

The following year, when Liao amassed troops on its western frontier with the Tanguts, Fu Bi convinced the Song emperor that this troop buildup was not a threat to Song by means of a detailed, nine-point analysis. So confident was he in his own judgment that he went on to proclaim that, if the Khitans did attack Song, then "I will have deceived my emperor and bungled state affairs."[114] It should be noted that Fu's trust in the Liao court's good faith did have its limits. He knew there was always the risk of a rift provoked by "treacherous men." Thus, even while expressing certainty that Liao had no plans to attack Song in the near future, he was also adamant that Song should not neglect its northern defenses. But despite his cautious attitude about the durability of Song–Liao relations in the long term, it is clear that, at the time, there existed a sense of mutual trust between certain Song officials and the Liao court, and that this mutual trust was the product of a sociability rooted in the diplomatic encounters.

Fu Bi's diplomacy represented a breakthrough in Song–Liao relations, both in the sense that he successfully renegotiated the peace agreement, and in the sense that he seems to have spurred a new sense of mutual trust between certain Song officials and the Liao court, and – perhaps more importantly – a new faith in the efficacy of the diplomatic process. Although the Khitans had massed troops on the border in early 1042, and many at the time thought war was inevitable, a mere two years later one official observed that all had now been forgotten, such that the northern defenses had already fallen into neglect.[115] By the mid-1060s,

---

[113] XCB 140.3360–61; QSW 71:320.
[114] *Su Shi wenji*, 2:531–32; QSW 71:321.
[115] QSW 46:351–52. By 1076, Wen Yanbo would refer to the 1042 confrontation as a "mere trifle." See QSW 30:223.

Hu Su – who had served as ambassador to Liao in 1048 and 1057 and on at least two other occasions as a diplomatic escort – expressed a complete confidence in diplomacy. In response to news of minor border incursions, he was adamant that "diplomatic missives are sufficient to handle this; why would we rush to raise troops?"[116] Zheng Xie (1022–72), who had accompanied a mission to Liao a few years earlier, was similarly forceful in insisting that the Song not overreact to rumors that the Khitans had coercively conscripted Song borderlanders. He was confident that the Liao state "acted in accordance with what is right or wrong," leading him to ask rhetorically, "Given that there are currently no rifts [between us], why would they rush to plot a southward invasion [i.e., into Song territory]?" Zheng went on to imply that the true culprits in the matter were likely rogue strongmen acting without the Khitan emperor's consent.[117] A few years later, Han Qi (1008–75), who had served as ambassador to Liao in 1038 and as escort in both 1038 and 1059, in warning court officials not to overreact during the Hedong border negotiations of the mid-1070s, reminded them that the Khitans had as many reasons to be suspicious of the Song as the Song had reasons to be suspicious of the Khitans.[118]

Confidence among Song officials in the Chanyuan Oath and in the good faith of the Liao court was on display in a particularly interesting way in 1072. At the time, the chief minister Wang Anshi was at the height of his power, and was largely preoccupied with the implementation of his New Policies. In the fourth month of the year, the civilian administrator of one of the border prefectures, a certain Zhang Liyi, began dispatching reports to the throne about Khitan incursions across the Baigou River.[119] Some at court felt it was necessary to respond forcefully with Song troops, while simultaneously reinforcing military defenses in Hebei, even at the expense of violating the Chanyuan Oath (which explicitly forbade the construction along the border of new fortifications). Wang Anshi objected vigorously. He was probably driven partly by a desire to conserve state resources, in order to ensure the successful implementation of his agenda. But the grounds on which he actually voiced his objections are noteworthy. First, he expressed

---

[116] QSW 22:44.
[117] QSW 68:49.
[118] XCB 262.6387–88.
[119] For detailed accounts of these reports and the court's response, see XCB 232.5638–242.5801 *passim*.

a complete faith in the treaty system, insisting that the initial response ought to involve diplomacy. When Zhang Liyi requested permission for a pre-emptive raid on the Liao side in order to discourage the Khitans from building defensive works in Song territory, Wang bluntly called into question the very possibility that Khitans might encroach upon Song territory in that way. He then insisted, "If we wait until they [actually] build fortifications within [our territory], then we can handle the matter with an exchange of diplomatic communiques."[120]

Wang's second argument is perhaps even more interesting. Probably on the basis of his own private channels of intelligence, he argued vigorously that it was in fact Zhang Liyi and other men he referred to contemptuously as "minor border officials" who were to blame. It was they who were antagonizing the Khitans, and then sending misleading reports to the court. If Song's own border officials were not to be trusted, in whom did Wang suggest one might place greater faith? "The Khitan emperor has been on the throne already twenty years," he observed in court. "His disposition is known; he is certainly not one to turn to war without any regard to reason and good sense." A few days later, he repeated the same point: "The Khitan emperor has been on the throne some twenty years. Examining his past actions, [it is clear] he would certainly not provoke an incident for no reason."[121] In essence, by the early 1070s, undoubtedly as a result of the abundant contact between Song and Liao political elites, it was possible for policymakers at the Song court to have more faith in their Liao counterparts than in their own subordinate provincial officials.

Su Che provides a final example of an increasing Song confidence in Liao court officials by the late eleventh century. Although Su is often portrayed as one of Wang's political opponents, insofar as he objected to the New Policies, his view of the Liao court and its officials was in line with that of Wang. Shortly after his 1089 mission to Liao, he reported his views to the Song court:

> The emperor of the Northern Court [i.e., Liao] appears to be over sixty years old, yet he remains vigorous and healthy; his appetite has not yet begun to decline. Having been on the throne so long, he has quite a good understanding of what is to [Liao's] advantage. [Liao's] friendship with our court has lasted many years, such that tribal and Han people enjoy tranquil existences, all living together in harmony, with no desire for war. Moreover, [the emperor's] grandson, the Prince of Yan, is young and

---

[120] XCB 236.5725.
[121] XCB 236.5734–35, 236.5751.

fragile. In one of the past years, powerful Khitan courtiers had his father executed. Thus, he has been seeking revenge, and looks for support from Chinese and from our court to consolidate his position. North of the border [i.e., in Liao territory], even commoners speak of this. After I crossed the border with my retinue [while on a diplomatic mission], I witnessed [Liao's] wise, old officials . . . all speaking of our [two courts'] friendship, with a deep sigh, as something unprecedented since antiquity. They also related to me that the emperor of the Northern Court treats those in charge of southern [i.e., Song] envoys very generously. One of the reception officials was [promoted to] deputy Hanlin commissioner even before we reached the Great Tent [of the Liao emperor] . . . Everybody said it was in recognition of his work receiving the southern envoy. From this, we can see that, as long as the emperor of the Northern Court remains healthy, we can be certain our northern frontier [with Liao] will remain free of incidents. [The problem] is only that his grandson, the Prince of Yan, is mediocre and weak in spirit, undignified in appearance, and [so] does not live up to his grandfather. Though his heart may seem to turn to China, we do not yet know whether or not, after he attains [the throne], he will be able to suppress the conflict between tribal and Han people, and secure his position.[122]

In this account, Su Che communicates his confidence in the good faith of the Liao court in part by emphasizing the deep sighs of the wise Liao officials when they speak of the Song–Liao alliance, an alliance then over eighty years old. Undoubtedly, it was as a result of his own experience as envoy to Liao that he came to perceive his counterparts as wise and forthright. To be sure, like Fu Bi, Su Che remained cautious about the future; the vagaries of imperial succession, much like the actions of Fu Bi's "treacherous men," could create rifts in the Chanyuan alliance. But overall, Su Che seemed to hold great faith in the commitment of his counterparts at the Liao court to the Oath of Chanyuan and in the efficacy of diplomacy as a means to solve disagreements.

Of course, one must not overlook the existence of what one might call the dark side of cosmopolitan sociability. Nightly banqueting, often fueled by large volumes of alcohol, did not exclusively foster friendship and good will between participants. Grudges and hatreds of various sorts could also emerge from such intense social encounters. In the early years of the twelfth century, for example, a certain Lin Shu traveled to Liao on an embassy. Due to a perceived slight involving a literary pun, he got into an argument with his escort. It is significant, however, that he was

---

[122] *Su Che ji*, 2:748–49.

subsequently demoted, after high ministers at the Liao court reported him to their counterparts.[123] Clearly, the Song court considered Lin's behavior to be atypical and unacceptable. A few other such cases led to similar downgrades. In 1041, when Liu Hang (995–1060) got up rudely to leave a banquet hosted by his Liao escort, the Song court demoted him upon his return home.[124] And when Wu Kui (1011–68) and Guo Kui (1022–88) refused to exchange respectful greetings with Liao court officials during their 1054 mission, and then turned down the honored seats at a Liao court audience, all the while maintaining a confrontational attitude, the Liao court reported their behavior to the Song court, which proceeded to punish both men.[125]

The most fateful of the grudges emerging from a diplomatic mission involved the eunuch Tong Guan (1054–1126), a man who had gained great power during the latter years of the reign of Emperor Huizong. As a result of an inopportune decision by the emperor, he was dispatched as ambassador in 1111 to convey the Song court's birthday greetings to the Liao emperor. As a eunuch, he lacked the status of the great literati officials usually sent on such missions. His very presence at the Liao court was deemed insulting, and he was humiliated publicly on various occasions during his time there. From the perspective of the mid-twelfth-century Southern Song historians, the grudge he bore as a result initiated the chain of events that led both to the destruction of the Liao state and to Song China's loss of North China.[126] Before returning home, Tong Guan identified disgruntled Liao Chinese officials who were willing to defect. With the help of these defectors, and a few other minor frontier officials, he then lobbied the Song emperor and a few other imperial advisors – notably Wang Fu (1079–1126) and, perhaps, Cai Jing (1047–1126) – to enter into the fateful alliance with the Jurchens. Tong Guan's example in some sense confirms the importance of sociability for preserving Song–Liao relations; when sociability broke down, disaster struck. But it is important to remember that even in the late 1110s – as reports made it increasingly clear that the Liao empire was collapsing in the face of the Jurchen onslaught – Tong Guan had considerable difficulty convincing policymakers to support a conquest of Liao.[127] Several decades

[123] Zhao Yanwei, *Yunlu manchao*, 10.165.
[124] SS 285.9606.
[125] QSW 98:340.
[126] Li Xinchuan, *Jianyan yilai xinian yaolu*, 1.2.
[127] Ebrey, *Emperor Huizong*, 379–85.

later, the Southern Song scholar and official Lu You (1125–1210) noted what he believed to be a final bit of irony:

> Initially, in the Yuanfeng era [1078–86], Cai Jing went on embassy to the caitiffs [i.e., Liao]. He was escorted by [Li] Yan; their friendship was quite profound. By the time of the Chongning era [1102–07], both were in charge of their respective states [as chief ministers]. With the exchange of each embassy, they asked about each other's good health. Yet, in the end, the two men were the foundations of the downfall of their states. How strange![128]

If Patricia Ebrey is correct in positing that Cai Jing was ambivalent at best about taking Yan, then the irony is quite easily resolved.[129] His friendship with Liao officials may indeed have kept him from backing wholeheartedly the war faction. In any case, the very fact that a Chinese official of the next generation believed that Cai's relationship to Li ought to have helped preserve the peace says much about how political elites of the period experienced and understood the impact of diplomatic sociability.

Conclusion

The Oath of Chanyuan put into place an embassy system with far-reaching consequences for Chinese political culture. Chapter 6 will discuss in some detail another result of this system – how the ambassadors' journeys gave them a new perspective on the physical and cultural geography of the frontier. In the present chapter, however, I have focused on the impact of the sociability created between Song and Liao officials. As a result of the several missions traveling between the Song and Liao courts every year, a substantial proportion of the most influential men at the Song court – notably the policymakers in the Council of State and the Bureau of Military Affairs – had opportunities to meet their counterparts at the Liao court and to welcome them in turn at the Song court in Kaifeng. These men enjoyed a sort of cosmopolitan experience unusual in the Chinese imperial period. Whereas neighboring states under past dynasties had sent envoys on a regular basis to offer tribute to the Chinese throne, Chinese officials had only on rare occasions left court to travel beyond the frontier. Moreover, there is no evidence of close social interactions between Chinese court ministers of past dynasties and

[128] Lu You, *Jiashi jiuwen*, 1.191–92.
[129] Ebrey, *Emperor Huizong*, 523–25.

incoming foreign envoys. The fact that Song diplomats represented the pinnacle of China's political elite meant that their diplomatic experiences could play a pivotal role both in defining state policy and in molding Chinese political culture. Even the minority of top policymakers who had never served as ambassadors or diplomatic escorts were likely influenced by this evolving political culture through conversations with colleagues.

As we have seen, this sociability was closely tied to the nightly banqueting that took place during the several weeks that envoys spent in foreign territory. But it was also the product of other activities, such as hunts on horseback, archery contests, or poetry composition. Although heavy consumption of alcohol at the banquets occasionally led to arguments and rude behavior, it also permitted open and forthright conversations. As a result of these intense social interactions, men from Song and Liao could exchange knowledge and even share elements of each other's worldviews, notably in their manner of imagining the Khitan–Chinese ethnic boundary, a boundary that – as we shall see in Chapter 5 – was created and reinforced through Liao ethnic policies.

Eleventh-century cosmopolitan sociability also quite predictably enhanced mutual trust between the Song and Liao courts. There is clear evidence, in fact, that the policymakers at the Song court sometimes had more faith in their counterparts among the Liao than in Song's own provincial officials. Sentiments of this sort undoubtedly help explain the little interest that Song court officials had in pushing for a reconquest of Yan, even if many saw Yan as Chinese territory that the Song ought in theory to control. To be sure, it is likely that the strongest feelings of camaraderie developed between Song officials and people of Han ethnicity at the Liao court. These men after all shared a common vernacular based on the Hebei dialect of Chinese. However, in the examples of sociability described in this chapter, one also encounters men of purely Khitan extraction, men like Xiao Ying, Yelü Fang, and Yelü Ying. Though Liao Chinese may have greatly facilitated Song–Liao diplomatic sociability, Liao Khitans did participate in it as well.

In analyzing the mechanics of Song–Liao diplomacy in the eleventh century, Tao Jing-shen has noted similarities with diplomatic practices between Chinese states both during the Five Dynasties and during the much earlier Warring States period.[130] Others have drawn a comparison

---

[130] Tao, *Two Sons of Heaven*, 5–8.

with inter-state relations as they developed in the early modern West. One should be careful, however, not to take such analogies too far. Rival Chinese diplomats during the tenth-century interregnum would have seen each other as common descendants of the Tang Dynasty; during the Warring States period, they saw each other as members of a single Zhou ecumene. Similarly, in Europe, representatives at the diplomatic congresses of the eighteenth and early nineteenth centuries – congresses that came to exemplify the Western European state system – were largely aristocrats and other social and political elites belonging self-consciously to a transnational salon culture and Republic of Letters.[131]

Song–Liao relations were different. Most critically, Song legitimacy from the very beginning depended on its claim to have accomplished its reunification project.[132] In Song political rhetoric, it was necessary for the territories under the control of the Khitan regime to be conceptualized as lying beyond the pale of civilization, and therefore not properly under the control of the legitimate Chinese Son of Heaven. It was for this reason that a large proportion of Song documents persisted in referring to Khitans in derogatory terms. Moreover, although there was clear recognition among Song educated elites of the distinction between Liao Chinese and Liao Khitans, it was, in fact, not uncommon to refer to all subjects of the Liao state, including ethnic Han people, by the term Khitan. In this context, what is fascinating and significant is that there were, nevertheless, moments when Song political elites conceived of Liao officials as civilized men – at times even as members of the community of *shidafu*. A possible implication was that the distinction between China and the world beyond was no longer a distinction between civilization and barbarism, but rather an ethnic distinction between civilized Chinese and potentially civilized Others.

---

[131] Vick, *Congress of Vienna*, 112–52.
[132] See Chapter 4.

2

Military Defense of the Northern Frontier

If we are fully to understand the inter-state system of the eleventh century and how China's place in this system was imagined, it is essential to look beyond diplomacy alone and broach the issue of how the Song's frontiers were defended. In the past decade, there has been a resurgence of interest in Song military history, as scholars have come to reject the sentiment of earlier historians that the Song military was weak and therefore not worthy of serious study.[1] In this chapter, I build on this new scholarship, focusing in particular on the first half of the eleventh century, in the decades immediately following the Chanyuan Oath. By then, the Khitans had demonstrated their military might, and many Song court officials remained very concerned about an invasion from the north. Meanwhile, in the 1030s, the Song began to face a new challenge from the Tanguts on the northwestern frontier. As detailed in this chapter, in response to these twin threats, the Northern Song expended great resources establishing linear military fortifications – composed of trenches and other man-made barriers – along large sections of its frontier with the Liao and the Xia. These defenses then fell into disuse in the late eleventh century, as the court became more confident of its enduring peace with Liao, and as it simultaneously embarked on a campaign of military expansion into Tangut Xia territory.

A telling overview of historical approaches to frontier strategy appears in the fourth of five policy questions composed by deputy chief minister Wang Anli (1034–95) for the 1082 civil service examination:

> The barbarians have always been a threat to the Middle Kingdom; it has always been so . . . Today, we would like you to evaluate the suitability of various approaches [to dealing with them] in order to seek out the most

---

[1] Important recent scholarship in English on Song military history includes P. J. Smith, "Irredentism as Political Capital"; P. J. Smith, "Shuihu zhuan"; Wyatt, *Battlefronts Real and Imagined*; Lorge, *Reunification of China*; Alyagon, "Inked."

appropriate one. If one examines this according to the paths already followed, then [one finds that] the ancient ways of defending against the
barbarians were limited to either ordering generals to attack them, building a Great Wall to cut them off, or offering them gold and silk in order
to establish friendly relations . . . [The mid-Han general] Yan You believed
there were no perfect plans in ancient times: the Zhou had an average
plan; the Han had a poor plan; and the Qin had no plan at all . . . That
being the case, after examining the events of the past while taking into
consideration what is appropriate for the present day, what is the most
effective plan that we can implement in order to extend our prestige to
the barbarians of the four directions while strengthening the Middle
Kingdom's interior?[2]

At the heart of this examination question was a problem that numerous
past Chinese regimes had faced: how to deal with the cavalry armies of
the pastoral nomads of the Eurasian steppe. Indeed, all dynasties based in
North China faced a number of similar geographic circumstances, involving both terrain and cultural ecology. The first part of this chapter explores
these parameters. But despite these fixed constraints, policymakers in
different historical eras nevertheless approached frontier defense in very
different ways, as Wang Anli makes clear in his examination question.
Whereas the Northern Song in the first half of the eleventh century established a perimeter defense, its predecessor the Tang had depended on a
network of allied client regimes.[3] How does one account for a particular
Northern Song approach to the northern frontier?

One answer to this question lies, of course, in the contingency of
geopolitical circumstances. The Khitans possessed an army more formidable than any the Tang Dynasty had ever faced. Moreover, as discussed below, the fact that the Song–Liao border cut directly across the
North China Plain created particular challenges for military planners.
But strategic decision-making during the Song was influenced not just
by the practical realities of geopolitics. Also significant were broader
cultural trends, which played an important role in defining policy
priorities. More specifically, a new Song worldview and understanding of empire helped to define the perceived natural limits of Chinese
military power.

---

[2] QSW 83:71.
[3] Skaff, "Straddling Steppe and Sown." As late as the mid-ninth century, the Tang court continued to
expend military and political capital managing its relations with allied tribes and maintaining its
hegemony on the steppe. See, e.g., Drompp, *Tang China*.

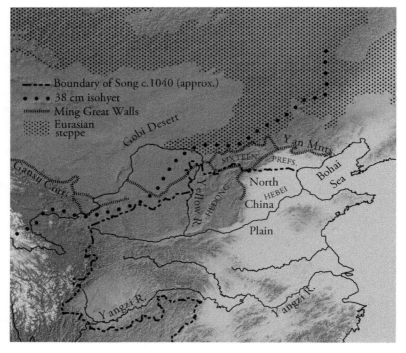

Figure 2.1 Physical geography of Northeast Asia

Geographic Constraints

Before considering more directly the question of Chinese and, more specifically, Northern Song military policy, it is important to consider the implications of the physical geography of East Asia (Figures 2.1 and 2.2). Three features of the natural environment were of particular relevance to the question of frontier defense. The first was the natural limits of pre-industrial agriculture. All Chinese regimes were agricultural regimes; their primary activities revolved around the management and taxation of agrarian populations. The administrative infrastructure inherited by consecutive dynasties was designed to extract resources from farmland, and to tap farming populations for soldiers and conscript laborers. Though by Song times the Chinese had developed advanced technologies for the administration of arable zones, it was rarely cost-effective to control lands

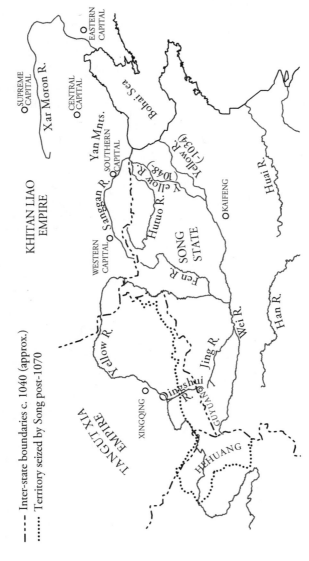

Figure 2.2 The Northern Song's northern frontier

---- Inter-state boundaries c. 1040 (approx.)
...... Territory seized by Song post-1070

unamenable to cultivation. For this reason, the south was always a zone of expansion for Chinese civilization. There, moist and warm weather permitted cultivation after a significant initial investment of labor to fell forests and drain or polder marshlands.[4] To the north and northwest, by contrast, the spread of crop farming was limited by the cold, dry climate of Inner Asia. In regions receiving less than 38 centimeters of rain per year, where non-oasis agriculture is difficult if not impossible, it remained particularly costly in premodern times to extend the administrative infrastructure and to supply military garrisons.[5] It is not a coincidence that, to this day, the vast majority of the Chinese population resides in "China Proper" in the eastern half of the People's Republic of China, a region lying entirely south and east of the 38-centimeter precipitation isohyet.

The second relevant feature of East Asian physical geography was the presence to the north of the great Eurasian steppe. This vast band of pastureland extending from Eastern Mongolia to Eastern Europe lay beyond the limits of non-oasis agriculture, but could support grasses that thrived under colder and more arid conditions and, consequently, could support pastoral nomadic economies. Indeed, the divide between the steppe and the sown was as much a dramatic cultural frontier as an ecological frontier.[6] Steppe nomads maintained great herds of horses, and all children learned to ride at a very young age. Although it would have been possible in principle to raise horses in the Chinese agricultural zone to the south, fiscal imperatives always favored agriculture, which produced significantly more calories per unit area than animal husbandry.[7] Consequently, in China, procuring sufficient war horses and men capable of riding them was a long-standing problem.[8] Most Chinese regimes could field effective cavalry armies only by recruiting allies or non-Han soldiers. Though rival polities based in the surrounding pastoral zones might threaten the frontier with cavalry raids, the Eurasian steppe to the

[4] On the south as an "indefinite horizon of potential further expansion," see Lattimore, "Frontier in History," 475–77; on the transformation by Chinese settlers of the landscape of South China over a period of several thousand years, see Elvin, *Retreat of the Elephants*, 9–39.

[5] Skaff, "Straddling Steppe and Sown," 242–62; Perdue, *China Marches West*, 38–40. For a very detailed study of provisioning troops on the Northern Song's northwestern frontier, see Cheng Long, *Bei Song xibei zhanqu*.

[6] Barfield, *Perilous Frontier*, 1–31.

[7] Bulliet, *Hunters, Herders, and Hamburgers*, 18.

[8] As Song Qi observed, "The Middle Kingdom has few horses; moreover, the people do not learn to ride." See QSW 23:258. On horse breeding and trading under the Tang, Song, and Ming, respectively, see Skaff, "Straddling Steppe and Sown," 178–207; P. J. Smith, *Taxing Heaven's Storehouse*, 13–47; Perdue, *China Marches West*, 68–72.

north posed by far the greatest of such threats. A steppe leader who succeeded in consolidating multiple tribes into a single confederation could
have at his disposal an army of horsemen far larger than any that might
be fielded by pastoral populations based in Tibet or Yunnan in the southwest. Such steppe cavalries did not usually have the numbers to establish a
permanent foothold in China Proper, but their periodic raids could wreak
havoc in the frontier zone. As administrators commonly observed, "there
is no best strategy for defending against the northern barbarians."

The third geographic parameter affecting military strategy concerned
the significant physiographic barriers separating Chinese territory from
zones under pastoral nomadic control. The most striking of these natural
obstructions consisted of the Yan Mountains that marked off the northern extremity of the North China Plain. Controlling the strategic passes
through these mountains was important for defending the vast flatlands
extending from modern-day Beijing in the north down to the Yangzi
River a thousand kilometers to the south. The Yellow River constituted
a secondary obstacle that could block access to the Song capital city of
Kaifeng, but it did nothing to protect the Hebei plains to its north. West
of the North China Plain, the terrain was more rugged. Of critical concern here was the defense of agriculturally rich river valleys, especially
those leading south and east toward the Chinese interior. The imposing Hengshan range of central Hedong was particularly strategic, as it
separates the Sanggan River (then under Liao control) from the Fen and
Hutuo Rivers, both of which flowed deep into Song territory. It was for
this reason that the Northern Qi had erected an "Inner" Great Wall in
these mountains, as would the Ming a millennium later. The dramatic
multiple layers of rammed-earth fortifications at Yanmen Pass remain to
this day a testament to the impulse of Ming-era military planners. Song
China also clung tenaciously to its strategic position in these mountains.
During a border dispute in 1074–75, when the Liao sought to renegoti-
ate the course of the border to its advantage, the Song expended great
effort to retain possession of Mount Huangwei, a promontory over-
looking the Hutuo River watershed. Occupying this massif would have
allowed the Liao army to control the pass they had used to invade North
China in 936.[9]

One finds numerous examples of ways in which administrators and
military planners from different Chinese dynasties dealt in similar

---

[9] Tackett, "Great Wall," 125–26.

ways with the particular configuration of East Asia's physical geography. As a result of the natural limits of the agricultural zone, the major dynasties usually controlled all of "China Proper," but not necessarily territories further afield. Thus, Manchuria in the northeast and the Tarim Basin of modern-day Xinjiang Province in the far west were only occasionally under Chinese control. It is surely no coincidence that long stretches of the Ming Dynasty Great Wall traced roughly speaking the course of the 38-centimeter isohyet (Figure 2.1). Moreover, as in the case of the Hengshan range, other segments of the Ming Wall followed natural lines of defense exploited by earlier dynasties. The Song–Liao border in many locations ran alongside the Great Wall of the Northern Qi, while in some places the Song–Xia border closely followed the frontier wall built by the Qin Kingdom of the Warring States period.[10] The site of modern-day Guyuan, in southern Ningxia Province, was of particular value. It constituted a strategic forward base, obstructing passage through the mountain passes separating the valley of the Qingshui River (known as the Hulu River during the Song), which streamed north toward the steppe, from the upper reaches of the Jing River, which flowed southeastward toward the Wei River and the Chinese heartland. As Li Feng has observed in his study of the Western Zhou, the upper Jing river valley was a primary entry point for foreign invaders during many periods of Chinese history. Numerous fortifications dating to the Western Zhou and the Warring States have been found just north of Guyuan.[11] This region is also littered with Northern Song-era forts, whose rammed-earth walls rise to this day above the surrounding corn fields.[12] There was one region, however, in which the Song did not benefit from the natural borders that had protected earlier dynasties. Because it controlled neither the region of Yan nor the Yan Mountains to the north, the entire North China Plain lay open to a Khitan cavalry attack, a vulnerability that, as we shall see, preoccupied many court officials and military planners throughout the eleventh and early twelfth centuries.

[10] Ibid., 125–27.

[11] Li Feng, *Landscape and Power*, 35–40, 52. Today, the G70 freeway connects Guyuan to the Upper Jing river valley.

[12] The remains of several Song fortresses just north of Guyuan appear as orange ovals on *Zhongguo wenwu ditu ji (Ningxia)*, 128–29. Two of these, Sanchuan and Gaoping, are identifiable on Google or Bing satellite maps at the following latitude-longitude coordinates: 36.125265N, 106.250609E; and 36.081780N, 106.175989E.

Historical Approaches to Defending the Northern Frontier

Besides facing a number of ecological and physiographic constraints, Song court officials were also influenced by their understanding of how frontier defense had been managed by earlier dynasties. As a result of their educations, Chinese statesmen were all well versed in historical scholarship and commonly invoked historical precedent during policy debates. In fact, history provided them with a range of possible options when devising military strategy, as articulated in a memorial of 989 by Zhang Ji (933–96). The similarities between this memorial and Wang Anli's 1082 examination question are revealing of the role of historical precedent as a source of inspiration for Song policymakers:

> The northern barbarians are a peril to the Middle Kingdom; since antiquity it has been so. Ever since the Xia and the Shang dynasties, their ferocity and cruelty has only multiplied. All of the techniques for defending against them are contained within the historical records. Some [past dynasties] have crossed the frontier to engage in fierce battle; some have established good relations through dynastic marriages; some have won over certain tribes to divide up their strength; and some have sought to swear oaths of peace in order to fix their intentions. Among this diversity of schemes, not one has been fully successful. All that really works, in brief, is to train soldiers, accumulate grain provisions, divide up the garrisons along the frontier, then defend the line when [the barbarians] arrive, and hold back from pursuing them when they leave.[13]

It is worth elaborating on the diversity of strategies listed here by Zhang Ji.

The first option – "crossing the frontier to engage in fierce battle" – referred to the sort of military expansionism made famous by Emperor Wu of the Han Dynasty. Coming to the throne after several decades of relative peace with the nomadic steppe confederation of the Xiongnu, Emperor Wu's approach reflected a dramatic shift in policy. Beginning in 129 BCE and over the course of the next three decades, he sent out armies far to the north and northwest, first expelling the Xiongnu from the Ordos region (under the great bend of the Yellow River), then taking the Gansu Corridor, and finally establishing garrisons in the major oases of the Tarim Basin in the far west.[14] A few hundred years later, during the first century of Tang rule, Taizong and his successors followed a similar pattern, beginning with a great victory in 630 over the Turks, who were then based in Mongolia. In subsequent decades, Tang armies

---

[13] XCB 30.666.
[14] Yü Ying-Shih, "Han Foreign Relations," 389–91, 405–11.

re-established Chinese garrisons around the Tarim Basin.[15] Though the
Song Dynasty was never able to project military power so far from the
agricultural zone, subsequent Chinese regimes turned to equally aggressive military policies. In the late fourteenth and early fifteenth centuries,
for example, the Ming Dynasty would embark on over a half dozen
major military expeditions deep into the Mongolian steppe, in the hope
of eliminating the surviving remnants of the Mongol Yuan regime.[16]
Given the success of their armies, expansionistic regimes of this sort
did not need to rely upon frontier walls for their defense. Neither the
Tang nor the early Ming concerned themselves with building a Great
Wall. Instead, mobile armies were garrisoned in a chain of walled cities –
including the celebrated Tang "Surrender-Here Cities" and the "eight
outer garrisons" of the early Ming. From these positions, they could
rapidly respond in force to any enemy attack.[17]

The second approach mentioned by Zhang Ji involved the policy
known as *heqin*, a policy that also had origins in Han relations with the
Xiongnu. At its core was a series of dynastic marriages, whereby Chinese
princesses (or palace ladies) were married off to consecutive Xiongnu
confederation leaders. The most famous of Han-era women dispatched
to the steppe as a bride was the palace lady Wang Zhaojun, who became
a stock literary figure in later times, helping to preserve the *heqin* system
in historical memory. Though historians generally focus on the marriages
alone, the original *heqin* policy of the Han Dynasty also involved regular
"gifts" sent by the court to the Xiongnu. In addition, the Han agreed to
treat the steppe confederation as a "brotherly state."[18] Similar practices
were sometimes followed under the Tang, which in the course of the
dynasty established matrimonial unions with the Turks, the Tibetans, and
the Uighurs.[19] Though the Song Dynasty never itself sent princesses to
the Khitans, some policymakers of the post-Chanyuan period used the
term *heqin* to describe Song–Liao relations, presumably because the two
respective emperors referred to each other using terms of kinship, and
because the Song sent regular "gifts" to the Liao.

A third approach mentioned by Zhang Ji was a classic divide-and-
conquer strategy, involving the manipulation of steppe politics by means

---

[15] Wechsler, "T'ai-tsung the Consolidator," 220–28.
[16] Waldron, *Great Wall*, 72–79.
[17] For the Tang case, see Skaff, "Straddling Steppe and Sown," 216–71; for the Ming case,
see Waldron, *Great Wall*, 76.
[18] Yü Ying-Shih, "Han Foreign Relations," 386–89.
[19] Pan Yihong, "Marriage Alliances."

of selective alliances. Both Emperor Wu of the Han and Tang Taizong, for example, employed this strategy: Emperor Wu joining forces with the Southern Xiongnu, and Taizong with the Bilgä Qaghan. So successful was the Tang emperor Taizong at manipulating the politics of the steppe that he ultimately convinced numerous chiefs to recognize him as the "Heavenly Qaghan" – that is, to treat him as the de facto leader of a steppe confederation.[20] The Song court, by contrast, was never particularly successful in establishing client regimes on its frontier.[21] One might also include within Zhang's third category of strategies the use by Chinese regimes of steppe military commanders, along with their subordinate troops. The "foreign generals" (*fanjiang*) of the Tang were men of this sort, who came from Tibet or the Eurasian steppe, and contributed their expertise in cavalry warfare to the Tang cause. Hundreds of years later, the Ming court would also call up tribesmen from Guizhou in the southwest to fight the Japanese invader Hideyoshi on the Korean peninsula.[22] As we shall see, the Song made use of Tibetan fighters, though only on a limited scale in the northwestern theater.

As for Zhang Ji's fourth approach – "swearing oaths of peace" – one should note that he was writing more than a decade before the Chanyuan agreement. Later in the dynasty, the Chanyuan Oath would become a new model for good relations with the steppe. Zhang Ji seems to have believed, however, that oaths were even less reliable than dynastic marriages. The series of sworn agreements between the Tang empire and the Tibetan Kingdom constituted a case in point. In the late eighth and early ninth centuries, the Tang engaged in a series of shaky treaties with the Tibetans. The Qingshui Treaty of 783, for example, was followed a mere three years later by a major Tibetan invasion. During the ensuing peace talks in 786 at Pingliang, where another oath was to be sworn, the Tibetans kidnapped and killed several of the Tang negotiators. Although the two parties reached a new peace agreement in 809, hostilities continued for most of the next decade. It was only beginning in the 820s that China and Tibet were able briefly to coexist peacefully.[23]

Zhang Ji's preferred solution for managing relations with the steppe was to establish a military cordon that was well supplied and well

[20] Yü Ying-Shih, "Han Foreign Relations," 403–05; Wechsler, "T'ai-tsung the Consolidator," 222.
[21] Song policymakers also on occasion considered divide-and-conquer strategies, such as when they tried to instigate a feud between the Tanguts and the Tibetan tribes in the 1040s. See QSW 37:36–37.
[22] Herman, *Amid the Clouds and Mist*, 164–65.
[23] Twitchett, "Tibet in Tang's Grand Strategy," 152–76.

defended, and beyond which Chinese troops were forbidden to go even if in pursuit of the enemy. Elsewhere, Zhang elaborated that the military cordon should take advantage of natural physiographic boundaries.[24] The importance of such military lines will be discussed in more detail below. Needless to say, military lines of this sort were not unlike the Great Walls of past dynasties as a type of defensive strategy. One should note that Zhang Ji did not, himself, draw this obvious analogy. To understand why neither Zhang nor later Song policy advisors advocated building an actual border wall, one must explore the Great Wall's position in historical memory.

What one refers to as the Great Wall today consists in fact of multiple lines of fortifications on China's northern frontier constructed over a two thousand year period. The most extensive walls were built during the late Warring States period, during the Qin and early Han, during the sixth and early seventh centuries, and – nearly a millennium later – during the mid to late Ming Dynasty. Since these walls were conceived as defensive structures, those from successive dynasties often followed nearly identical courses along strategic mountain ridges. But others, notably those of the Qin and Han, were built in multiple layers, extending hundreds of kilometers beyond the limits of China Proper. Such walls seem to have served an offensive purpose, supporting forward military positions for continued operations against the tribes of the Eurasian steppe. Because no Great Wall was built for nearly a millennium after the fall of the Sui Dynasty, only remnants of these fortifications survived into the eleventh century, most of which lay beyond the borders of the Song state.[25]

But if by Song times the physical walls were mere artifacts of the remote past, the Great Wall nevertheless retained a powerful presence in historical memory, usually – prior to the Southern Song – as a vehicle for criticizing tyrannical government. The First Emperor of Qin had purportedly driven tens of thousands of labor conscripts to their deaths in the construction of lengthy border walls spanning the desolate wilds of the northern frontier. The fact that the Qin and, much later, the Sui had both collapsed from internal rebellions shortly after major wall-building projects helped to enshrine the Great Wall as a cautionary symbol of the disastrous consequences of burdening the populace with excessive tax and labor obligations. By the tenth century, this representation of the

---

[24] XCB 31.701.
[25] For an overview of Song firsthand encounters with the Great Wall, see Tackett, "Great Wall," 109–20.

Wall had made its way into popular literature in the form of the famous tale of Meng Jiangnü, who discovers the bones of her husband, a conscript laborer, buried beneath it.[26] During the Northern Song, some of the most influential policymakers at court invoked the Wall in this vein. According to a line of verse in a poem by Wang Anshi, "half the people of Qin died beneath the Great Wall."[27] And, in one memorial to the throne, Wang's political rival Su Che (1039–1112) invoked the Wall metaphorically to condemn a plan for a massive labor project to shift the course of the Yellow River.[28]

In one common variation of this line of criticism, the defensive value of the Great Wall was said to be inferior to that of a talented general. The premise was that, by selecting able generals, it was not necessary to exploit the labor of the populace. Having witnessed firsthand the collapse of the Sui Dynasty, Tang Taizong praised his frontier general Li Ji (594–669) on just such grounds:

> Emperor Yang [of the Sui] did not wield men to defend the border; instead, he made the Middle Kingdom labor to build the Great Wall to protect against the caitiffs. Now, I use [Li] Ji to defend Bing [i.e., Hedong], and the Turks do not dare move south. He is far more worthy than a Great Wall![29]

By Song times, verse and prose alike commonly praised generals by comparing them to the Wall. There were references to military men who were "impressive as the Great Wall," "mighty as the Great Wall," "reliable as the Great Wall," or "a Great Wall for the country."[30] Though these expressions of praise did not deny the potential efficacy of such a structure for military defense, they suggested that employing men of talent was preferable to burdening the populace with the construction of a long frontier wall.

Given the cultural meaning of the Great Wall by Song times, it is unsurprising that the dynasty never seriously entertained the possibility of embarking on a similar construction. Early in the dynasty, Song Taizong was explicit on this question, proclaiming in a 989 edict that "constructing a Great Wall" would merely "project weakness," and would constitute a policy that "will be laughed at by later generations."[31] A 999 memorial

[26] Idema, *Meng Jiangnü*, 10–14.
[27] Wang Anshi, *Wang Jing Gong shizhu bujian*, 6.113.
[28] *Su Che ji*, 2:737.
[29] XTS 93.3818–19; JTS 67.2486.
[30] E.g., QSW 2:108; QSW 8:168; QSW 17:52; QSW 26:211.
[31] SHY *bing* 27.3.

from a court official reiterated the idea that the Qin Wall had become the butt of jokes: "As for the Qin's construction of the Great Wall, after which the common people rose up in rebellion . . . this satisfied the desires of one era, but became the laughingstock for a myriad generations."[32] But although the Song was adamantly opposed to harnessing corvée labor to build a Great Wall, the dynasty did, as we shall see, construct a system of perimeter defense on a similar scale.

"The Cavalry's Advantage is on Flat Plains"

The construction of linear frontier barriers under the Song was the product of both geopolitical circumstance and new ideas concerning the distinctive nature of China and Chinese regimes.[33] One significant problem faced by the Song but not the Tang was the presence on the eastern Eurasian steppe of a powerful, centralized state. The Tang had confronted a series of Mongolia-based Turkish and Uighur confederations, but could take advantage of their loose structures to acquire tribal allies through a divide-and-conquer strategy. Through these clients, the Tang was able to project its power onto the steppe. During the Northern Song, by contrast, the Khitans maintained a firm hold over both the steppe and the Sixteen Prefectures. Under these circumstances it was, practically speaking, impossible for the Song to secure client tribes.

Moreover, Liao control of the Sixteen Prefectures produced an additional geopolitical problem, because it meant that the Song–Liao border cut directly across the North China Plain (Figure 2.1). This northeastern border region – as flat as a "straw mat" in the words of Song Qi (998–1061) – would provoke perpetual anxiety, and consequently shaped military policy in ways that would ultimately affect decision-making across the northern frontier.[34] Numerous early Song policymakers brought up the fact that there existed no natural barriers that could hamper an invasion from the north. In his 989 memorial, for example, Zhang Ji elaborated at length on the military value of the Yan Mountains:

> That which the Middle Kingdom relies upon are strategic barriers, and nothing more. In the far north, there are layers upon layers of difficult terrain, with remote mountains and deep valleys extending for myriad miles. This must be how Heaven and Earth have sought to separate Hua

---

[32] XCB 44.931.
[33] The following discussion elaborates upon Tackett, "Great Wall," 124–33.
[34] QSW 24:343.

[i.e., the Middle Kingdom] from the barbarians, and to divide the inner from the outer.

Steppe nomads had always feared crossing the passes through these mountains, Zhang explained, even at the height of their power under the Xiongnu and, much later, the Turkish confederation:

> Some would attack the frontier passes, but, in the end, none ever sought to flaunt their forces in the Central Plains by crossing the frontier defenses, and – barking and braying like dogs and sheep – charging southward toward Luoyang and the Yellow River. They feared that Han [i.e., Chinese] soldiers would entrench themselves at the strategic passes, thereby blocking off a retreat.

What upset the geopolitical balance, according to Zhang, was the Later Jin's cession of the Sixteen Prefectures to the Khitans:

> East of Feihu, as for the rugged passes crossing through multiple ranges of mountains – the great barriers of the northern frontier – all are in the hands of the Khitans. Southward from Yan, the land is flat for hundreds of miles, devoid of any notable mountains or great rivers that might serve as obstacles . . . It is for this reason that we have lost the advantages of favorable terrain, thereby causing harm to the Middle Kingdom.[35]

Numerous of Zhang's contemporaries expressed similar concerns. By the turn of the eleventh century, the Khitans had already invaded numerous times. In 947, not long before the founding of the Song, they had even managed to seize and briefly to occupy Kaifeng. As one Song courtier reminded the emperor, "These [recent invasions] are all recorded in the histories."[36] The danger seemed all the more severe after 1004, when a Liao army once again charged south across the North China Plain, reaching the banks of the Yellow River.

Even after the Chanyuan Oath, sworn the following year in 1005, Chinese policymakers continued for decades to worry about the strategic vulnerability of Hebei.[37] In a lengthy speech at court in 1044, not long after completing his embassy missions to Liao, Fu Bi (1004–83) reiterated the point:

> I humbly submit that Hebei Circuit is the foundation of all under Heaven. Formerly, before losing the land of Yan, the passes of Songting, Gubei, and Juyong [in the Yan Mountains] served as strategic strongholds for the

[35] XCB 30.667.
[36] XCB 46.999.
[37] E.g., QSW 17:54–55; *Ouyang xiu quan ji*, 3:875–76; QSW 26:42; WJZY, part 1, 16.2b.

Central Plains, holding back the Xiongnu, who dared not cross south.
Kings and emperors through the ages paid great attention to the defense [of
these passes], without ever neglecting them. Since the founding emperor
of the [Later] Jin abandoned the land of Yan, all the strategic passes of the
north have belonged to the Khitans. When the Khitan [armies] arrive, there
are no barriers that remain.[38]

New concerns emerged after the Yellow River broke through its banks in
1048. As a result, the main channel swerved to the north, emptying into
the Baigou River on the Song–Liao border. Most of its waters, however,
spread across northeastern Hebei, forming a broad, shallow delta that
rendered the mighty river of little use for defensive purposes.[39] According
to Hu Su (996–1067), who served as deputy commissioner of Military
Affairs in the mid-1060s:

> The topography in Hebei lacks strategic sites for its defense. South of
> Xiong and Mo, the land is flat for hundreds of miles . . . Ever since the
> Yellow River breached its dikes at Shanghu, and ceased following the old
> Henglong channel, the waters of Hebei have spread all over, such that we
> have lost the Middle Kingdom's great riverine barrier, and can no longer
> keep out northern horsemen. In the dead of winter, when the waters
> freeze, armored cavalry can cross over. If the northerners were ever to send
> crack riders into the wastelands of Cang and Jing [in Song territory], they
> could charge south and wreak havoc in Jingdong [just east of the capital].[40]

In referring to the Yellow River as a "great riverine barrier," Hu Su clearly
had in mind the 1004 invasion, when the Yellow River had served as the
final obstacle preventing the main Khitan army from reaching the walls
of the Song capital at Kaifeng.[41]

Concerns about the loss of natural barriers were made all the more
acute by what was considered to be an inherent asymmetry between
steppe nomadic and ethnic Chinese armies. In the words of an important mid-eleventh-century military manual, "The cavalry's advantage is
on flat plains; the Middle Kingdom, with its many foot soldiers, benefits
from strategic barriers."[42] Whereas horses could easily outflank infantry
positions in an open field, they lost this advantage when forced to cross

---

[38] XCB 153.3729.
[39] On the policy implications of the Yellow River's change of course, see Lamouroux, "From the
Yellow River to the Huai."
[40] QSW 22:47.
[41] Hu Su explicitly brings up the 1004 invasion in a second memorial probably written on the same
occasion. See QSW 22:43. On the strategic implications of the 1048 breach, see QSW 24:346;
Lamouroux, "From the Yellow River to the Huai," 561–62.
[42] WJZY, part 1, 16.28a.

through narrow mountain passes. In later decades, Song policymakers frequently reiterated the idea that steppe nomadic cavalry troops had a significant advantage over Chinese soldiers in open plains.[43] It is important, however, to recognize the ideological facet of these concerns. Military strategists of earlier dynasties had of course understood that infantry armies on the fringes of the steppe should remain in fortified garrisons when possible, and avoid facing off against steppe horsemen in the open.[44] Yet during its rule, the Tang regime made very effective use of its own cavalry armies, which were sent on occasion deep into Central Asia to the west and the steppe to the north. These armies consisted in large part of non-Han fighters, serving either under the command of their own tribal leaders or, more commonly, integrated into the Tang imperial army. There were also soldiers and generals of mixed Chinese-Särbi ancestry, who were trained in a variety of equestrian pursuits. The game of polo, for example, was a popular pastime among military men and certain court elites during the Tang.[45] In fact, the Song also incorporated cavalry units into its armies, especially on the northwestern frontier.[46] Thus, the persistent, essentializing claim made by Song policymakers that it was in China's nature to field infantry armies and that only steppe-based regimes could amass cavalry armies was inaccurate. It reflected a new Song way of imagining "China" (described in more detail in Chapter 4) that involved drawing a sharper distinction between it and steppe polities to the north. Whereas the Tang had been a multinational empire that enlisted subject tribes to raise horses and help fight its wars of conquest, the Song saw itself as a Han state with armies manned by people who were culturally and ethnically Chinese.

Song Military Lines

Faced with this perceived military asymmetry between Chinese and steppe armies, the Song court opted to construct linear obstacles that stretched across vast distances. As early as 989, Taizong – adamant that

---

[43] E.g., QSW 17:54, 68:49, 120:269, 132:152. Cf. XCB 469.11212, which argues that rugged terrain in the northwest did not slow Tangut cavalrymen, who "galloped over mountains and dales as if stomping on flat ground."

[44] E.g., Drompp, *Tang China*, 240–41.

[45] Skaff, "Straddling Steppe and Sown," 274–91; Liu, "Polo and Cultural Change." The pre-An Lushan Tang (unlike the Song) controlled important pasturelands in the northwest, notably Region VI (Hexi-Gansu Corridor) on Paul Smith's map of East Asian pasturelands. See P. J. Smith, *Taxing Heaven's Storehouse*, 25.

[46] For statistics and useful maps showing the placement of Song cavalry units, see Cheng Long, *Bei Song xibei zhanqu*, 87–91.

the Song should never build a Great Wall – sought instead to establish a line of defense involving a system of palisades backed by self-supporting military colonies. "This will obstruct the barbarian horses, while greatly benefiting our infantry troops," he explained.[47] In fact, the court ultimately embarked on a much more ambitious project. Beginning in the 990s, 18,000 soldiers set to work constructing a complex hydraulic defense system along the entire Hebei frontier.[48] Rivers were dammed and redirected to form a network of pools and marshes that were "not deep enough for boats to pass, and not shallow enough to cross on foot."[49] The entire defensive system occupied a band dozens of kilometers wide, protecting the border from the Hengshan range in the west to the Bohai Sea in the east. To supply troops stationed there with food, poldered fields were established in the midst of the pools and marshes. Because it was not possible to extend the hydraulic system into higher elevations, a second type of defensive barrier had to be devised. Thus, some 3 million trees were planted in the hills of western Hebei, forming a dense palisade with tree trunks close enough together to block incoming horses. These defensive lines were then reinforced with a variety of horse traps, including a type of *cheval-de-frise* known as "deer antlers," consisting of wooden spikes planted into the ground.[50]

Through the middle of the eleventh century, the Hebei defenses appear to have been effective, and were the subject of great praise. As Ouyang Xiu observed, in a text dating probably to the 1030s:

> The Khitans have extended their control over the hills of You [i.e., the Yan Mountains], and so have cut off the impediment of Gubei [Pass]. Back and forth, entire armies have invaded, crossing the Changshan range, and stomping over the region of Wei [in southern Hebei]. As a consequence of the Chanyuan campaign [of 1004], their horses drank from the Yellow River, and the populace [of Hebei] could no longer eke out a living. This came to pass not because the northern caitiffs [i.e., the Khitans] are brave and flourishing, but because we have lost our strategic strongholds. Nowadays, since there are no mountains or hills to serve as natural barriers, what we rely upon is simply the embankments that channel the flow of the rivers, consolidating accumulated waters to form a terrain of strategic waterways, within which crack troops are garrisoned at critical locations.[51]

[47] SHY *bing* 27.3.
[48] WJZY, part 1, 16.26a–27b; SS 95.2358–63; Yan Qinheng, "Bei Song dui Liao tangdai sheshi"; Lin Ruihan, "Bei Song zhi bianfang," 199–205.
[49] XCB 112.2608.
[50] WJZY, part 1, 16.27a.
[51] *Ouyang Xiu quan ji*, 3:875–76. Translation adapted from Tackett, "Great Wall," 130.

A few years later and soon after his embassy mission to Liao, Zhang Fangping (1007–91) spoke of the importance of the hydraulic defenses in similar terms:

> I went on a mission recently, and saw the waterworks on the northern border, vast like rivers and lakes, with a depth such that neither boats nor carts can cross over. It must occupy two thirds of the northern frontier. The caitiffs appear to be reluctant in their hearts. They look southward, but hesitate to advance, as if knowledge [of these defenses] has given them a fright.[52]

By the second half of the eleventh century, however, the hydraulic defenses seem no longer to have been maintained properly. After the Yellow River changed its course in 1048 (Figure 2.2), extensive flooding across Hebei severely damaged the weirs channeling the waters into the defensive pools. Attempts to repair them were unsuccessful.[53] By the 1070s, the still usable components of the waterworks had silted up. Though the court sent inspectors to assess the problem, no substantive efforts were made to dredge the channels and pools.[54] Moreover, the system set up to monitor and maintain proper water depths had also broken down, making the pools as ineffective in summer as they were when they froze over in winter. As one official declared at court in 1072, "water is sometimes present and sometimes not, such that one can wade across it in summer; when a deep freeze occurs in winter, [the hydraulic defenses] are tantamount to a flat plain."[55] One critic of the system compared the excavation of water channels after the loss of the Yan mountain passes to the plight of a rich family that – in the face of robbers who have already breached the walls – decides to dig a ditch in front of the threshold to the house, a ditch the bandits shrug off with a laugh.[56] The hydraulic defenses were allowed to decline in part, as we shall see in the next chapter, because of the Song court's desire to increase the productivity of farmland on the frontier. The court was undoubtedly also lulled into complacency by the long peace with the Khitans. But there were always some policymakers who advocated re-establishing these defenses. One civil service examination policy question, dating to the turn of the twelfth century, praised the hydraulic defenses in their heyday, before posing a telling question: "As of the present

[52] QSW 37:98–99.
[53] Sima Guang, *Sushui jiwen*, 4.73–74.
[54] QSW 98:92.
[55] XCB 235.5707.
[56] QSW 78:394.

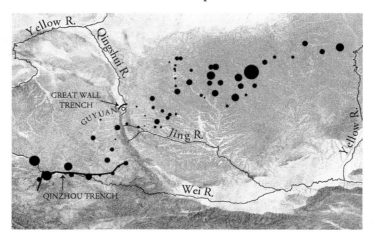

Figure 2.3 The northwestern theater (showing trenches and "Western soldiers")
Course of Qinzhou trench reconstructed from textual sources; course of Great
Wall trench adheres to the known course of the Warring States Great Wall. Circle area
proportional to the number of tribal "western" fighters and their horses, based on
SS 191.4752–55, with data for Huanzhou estimated based on the number of tribes listed.
Topographic layer provided by MapSurfer.net.

year, the old regulations governing the water depths have long since been
abandoned; moreover, [the system] was wrecked by the waters of the Yellow
River. What should we do to return [the system] to its former state?"[57]

Outside the Hebei region, the Song did not face the same threat of a
massive cavalry invasion like the one of 1004. The Hengshan range of
central Hedong constituted a particularly effective barrier.[58] The rugged
terrain even further west on the Tangut border, though less formidable
than the Hengshan range, was still much less amenable than the North
China Plain to a cavalry attack. Nevertheless, in the first decades of the
eleventh century, the Song constructed linear military fortifications along
several stretches of the Sino-Tangut frontier, with the primary goal of
securing the agricultural flatlands in critical river valleys (Figure 2.3).
Most substantial was the system of trenches excavated under the direction
of Cao Wei (973–1030). Cao was the son of Cao Bin (931–99), one

---

[57] QSW 130:251.
[58] For this reason, Daizhou, situated just south of this mountain range, was apparently one of the
best-defended sites on the northern frontier. See *Ouyang Xiu quan ji*, 5:1742.

of the most important generals of the early Song.[59] Like many children of prominent military men, he had been given a classical education, even though he began his career in military positions under his father's command. At the age of nineteen, through his father's recommendation, he was put in charge of the northwestern prefecture of Weizhou.[60] Over the subsequent thirty years, he would serve in key administrative posts all over the northwest. During the course of his career, he acquired a reputation for his grasp of strategy, once impressing the emperor with a map he produced of the northwest theater. It was in this context that he set to work designing a system of linear defenses "sufficient to block the caitiffs," consisting of a continuous trench at least five meters in width and depth that skirted around terrain too rugged to excavate.[61]

Cao Wei built the first of his trenches in Zhenrong (modern-day Guyuan) in 1005. This site on the Qingshui River was critical, as we have seen, because it controlled access to the passes leading to the upper Jing river valley and the Chinese interior. The Qingshui Valley, however, is one of the broadest river valleys in the northwest, making it tricky to defend. As Cao explained to the Song court, "the open country surrounding the military command is broad and flat; it is convenient for cavalry warfare, and not to the Middle Kingdom's advantage." To remedy this problem, he proposed to dig a trench across the entire valley, running "along the old Great Wall" – that is, in this case, the Qin wall of the Warring States period.[62] This military line, referred to as the "Great Wall Trench," was probably fifteen to twenty kilometers in length, and was defended by militias composed of locals. In 1018, the trench was apparently extended eastward into the mountains.[63] Meanwhile, a series of new fortified stockades was erected a few kilometers beyond the trench. In order to defend these stockades, a second "new trench" was excavated a dozen or so kilometers north of the original one. Subsequently, because

---

[59] For a biography of Cao Wei, see SS 258.8984–89.

[60] Thus, from Weizhou, he was transferred to Zhenrong in 1004, Binzhou in 1007, back to Weizhou in 1010, and on to Qinzhou in 1015.

[61] XCB 109.2534; SS 258.8988. Ten years after Cao's death, the Bureau of Military Affairs proposed requiring all frontier administrative units to dig trenches that took advantage of the terrain in similar ways. See XCB 127.3021.

[62] XCB 60.1337. Some sort of trench already existed north of the Qin Great Wall in 1002, before Cao Wei's arrival in Zhenrong. This trench may not have extended across the full breadth of the valley. See XCB 52.1149–50.

[63] XCB 91.2100.

the "new trench" extended into the forested mountains, it in turn needed to be defended by yet another line of stockades.[64]

In 1016, Cao Wei built an even longer trench in the vicinity of Qinzhou. This trench began about 130 kilometers south of Zhenrong, and extended west for some 200 kilometers, parallel to a string of fortresses on the upper Wei River. Cao had plank bridges constructed at each of the forts to control passage over the trench.[65] One immediate goal of this military line was to defend the surrounding agricultural zone. As Cao observed, "Previously, along the border [here], there has been no trench, such that Tangut tribesmen raid frequently."[66] Besides offering security to farmers of the region, the trench also had broader strategic objectives. Protecting the upper reaches of the Wei River was vital for stopping raiders from accessing the vast agricultural lands of the lower Wei river valley, site of numerous imperial capital cities of past Chinese dynasties.

Aside from the military trenches near Zhenrong and Qinzhou, there are references in the historical records to several similar excavations, about which fewer details survive. In 1009, Cao Wei began to dig a trench near Huanzhou, northeast of Zhenrong. Though the court asked him to halt the project, there are, nevertheless, references to a "border trench" in the vicinity of Huanzhou in a work dating to 1045.[67] There are also allusions to similar defensive lines excavated at "strategic points" on the Zhenrong and Yuanzhou frontier around the year 1002, built under the direction of the eunuch Qin Han (952–1015), and in Yuanzhou in 1018 and 1023. Finally, whereas all of the trenches mentioned so far were situated on the Sino-Tangut frontier, there was apparently also a trench excavated in 1041 on the Song–Liao border, in the vicinity of Kelan in the Hedong uplands. It, too, was built for the purpose of "blocking barbarian horses" at a site where the "terrain is flat and broad."[68]

Unlike remnants of the Great Wall, built either of stone or of rammed earth (which could be as hard as cement), the military trenches were apparently much less resilient to the effects of time and erosion; none of them are visible today. Nevertheless, circumstantial evidence suggests that

[64] QSW 38:329; SHY *bing* 4.2. For reference to two additional forts in the region that lay "beyond the border trench," see WJZY 18.22a–b.

[65] XCB 86.1982, 87.1992; SHY *bing* 27.19. For approximate locations of the forts, see Tan Qixiang, *Zhongguo lishi ditu ji*, 6:20–21, row 4, cols. 5–7. For references to the nearby "border trench" and to "Tangut territory beyond the trench," see WJZY, part 1, 18.26b, 27b, 29a.

[66] XCB 86.1982.

[67] XCB 71.1599; WJZY, part 1, 18.12b, 13a.

[68] XCB 60.1337, 92.2118, 101.2332, 133.3173.

they could be highly effective in preventing cross-border troop movements. The one near Zhenrong was probably the most formidable, measuring 15–20 meters in both width and depth. So deep was it that one Tangut incursion was initiated only after the raiders had managed to "fill in the long trench." A more dramatic illustration of its efficacy occurred at the expense of a Song army. In 1042, in the notorious "Dingchuan defeat," Song troops became trapped on the wrong side of the Zhenrong trench after a Tangut army had destroyed the wooden bridge that spanned it. Unable to escape, 10,000 Song troops were annihilated in one of the worst debacles of the Sino-Tangut wars.[69] Finally, it is telling that, in 1009, the Song court halted the excavation of the trench near Qingzhou upon the request of the Tangut ruler. Apparently, the trench was sufficiently daunting to prevent Tangut traders from crossing to the other side.[70]

It is notable that the Great Walls of earlier eras were left to decay during the Song, even as trenches were excavated alongside their ruins. The decision to lay trenches stemmed at least in part from how the historical Great Walls were remembered by policymakers at court. Ironically, trenches required an input of labor probably comparable to some earlier border walls.[71] Thus, Qin Han's trenches in Zhenrong and Yuanzhou were apparently excavated by a large force of 300,000 men toiling for more than a year.[72] But trenches remained more politically palatable because, in the eleventh century, they were not associated with imperial tyranny and misrule.

Militias and Tribesmen in the Northwest

There are virtually no references to military trenches on the northwestern frontier after the 1040s.[73] Instead, especially in the Shaanxi administrative circuits, local militias played an increasingly critical role in bolstering the Northern Song's perimeter defense. In the terminology of military historians, these fighters constituted a form of defense-in-depth, helping

---

[69] Tackett, "Great Wall," 127–28.

[70] XCB 71.1599.

[71] The distinction between a "trench" and a "wall" can be ambiguous because digging a linear trench can produce a parallel ridge (composed of the excavated soil) resembling an earthen wall, as in the case of the Jin Dynasty "border trench" on the Inner Mongolia–Heilongjiang border. I thank Pierre Marsone for alerting me to this point.

[72] XCB 60.1338; SS 466.13613.

[73] To draw this conclusion, I searched systematically for the characters 塹 and 壕 (terms frequently used to refer to military trenches) in XCB, SHY, SS, WJZY, and the first 140 volumes of QSW.

to slow down or fend off enemy incursions across a broad band of frontier territory. Song contemporaries, however, referred to the panoply of militias as a "hedge" or a "screen." Like the Great Wall or other linear fortifications, once established, they protected the Chinese interior without requiring the constant attention of the central government.

Among the hodgepodge of local armed groups helping to defend the Shaanxi frontier were both ethnic Chinese militiamen and non-Han tribesmen. The most significant among the first group were units referred to as "archers."[74] As one late Northern Song official observed, "Shaanxi relies on archers to serve as a hedge for the state."[75] The Shaanxi "archers" gained particular prominence because of the role they played in confronting Tangut horsemen, especially once they began to replace army regulars, large numbers of whom died in battle beginning in the 1040s.[76] As bow-wielding foot soldiers, they held an advantage over light cavalry whenever they occupied fortified positions. Recruited locally, they were "familiar with the hidden paths crossing the frontier, understood the Tangut language, and could withstand the bitter cold" – unlike soldiers of the imperial armies, who for most of the eleventh century served in frontier garrisons only for brief three-year stints. Since they were also granted frontier land to cultivate, "archers" required neither food provisions nor weaponry from the state – a particular advantage in the eyes of the central government.[77]

Perhaps of even greater significance than the Chinese militiamen were the Tibetan and Tangut tribesmen allied with the Chinese state, referred to in Song sources as "assimilated [lit., "cooked"] households" or "subordinate households." For reasons undoubtedly rooted in intertribal politics, these groups had surrendered to the Song at various points throughout the dynasty. Many simply turned over their tribal lands to the Song and continued to reside in place. Others migrated into Song territory, resettling at sites near Song frontier forts or walled cities. By the 1040s, tribal fighters – called "Western soldiers" – and their horses were registered by Song officials at the Song fort with which they were affiliated. These men

---

[74] For a brief overview of the complex assortment of ethnic Chinese militias – which included "righteous braves" in Hebei and Shaanxi, "local men" in Sichuan, "stalwarts" in the far south, and "lancemen" in the southeast – see SS 190.4706. To fill these units, the state conscripted a proportion of the able-bodied men from local families. By far the greatest numbers of such units were on the Liao and Xia frontiers.

[75] SS 190.4724. For a 1093 memorial referring to the Shaanxi "archers" as a "hedge," see QSW 72:105.

[76] SS 190.4706.

[77] SS 258.8985. For a similar observation by Sima Guang, see XCB 204.4948–49.

maintained the right to name their own chiefs, who were rewarded by the Song court with Chinese military titles.[78] Though some tribes apparently turned to agriculture, most probably persisted as mobile herders, remaining culturally more akin to the Tanguts and Tibetans.[79] Their cultural affinities with rivals of the Song provoked recurrent fears they might be lured away by the other side.[80] Indeed, there are cases of entire tribes departing from one day to the next after a fallout with Song authorities. Because of this risk, considerable care was taken to avoid antagonizing them.[81]

The military value to the Song of tribal militias derived above all from the large numbers of horses and skilled horsemen they provided. Though they may have been settled in the general vicinity of Song fortresses primarily for their own protection,[82] most seem to have established their encampments at some distance out of town in order to maintain a degree of autonomy.[83] From these positions, the tribesmen on multiple occasions helped fend off Tangut raiders.[84] Often, they acted under the command of Chinese generals. Indeed, by the 1040s, Song military commanders led them repeatedly into battle alongside both "archers" and regular troops.[85] But in other cases, they appear to have acted autonomously, fighting off enemy horsemen who attempted to cross their grazing lands.[86]

One can get a general sense of the geographic distribution of the "Western soldiers" from an extant 1067 list of troop strengths in four administrative circuits spanning much of the Sino-Tangut border.[87] This list identifies the number of tribal soldiers and horses affiliated with each of sixty-four different Song fortified positions. By mapping this data

[78] Kim, *Sōdai no seihoku*, 160–85; An Guolou, *Songchao zhoubian minzu*, 67–78. I translate *fanbing* here as "Western soldier," and *fanjiang* below as "foreign general." The word *fan* (蕃) had multiple connotations in the Northern Song. Often, it referred to tribal populations on any frontier. More frequently, it was used as an ethnonym designating either Tibetans or Tanguts (residing on the Song's western frontier). Thus, "*Fan* language" and "*Fan* script" refer to either Tibetan or Tangut.

[79] On "assimilated households" engaged in agriculture, see XCB 154.6436; on "assimilated households" as culturally akin to Tibetans or Tanguts, see XCB 35.768, 139.3341.

[80] E.g., XCB 51.1112, 88.2011.

[81] In one case, a Song official sent out to inspect the allied tribes near Qinzhou was ordered to "receive their written complaints" and "not to allow suspicions to give rise to a rift." See SS 191.4752.

[82] For examples of Song armies intervening to defend "assimilated households," see XCB 89.2048, 95.2178–79.

[83] For examples of "assimilated households" encamped a few kilometers away from Song forts, see WJZY, part 1, 18.12b, 22b, 26b, 28b.

[84] E.g., XCB 49.1074, 57.1251.

[85] XCB 139.3352, 144.3486, 149.3599, 214.5196.

[86] E.g., XCB 54.1184, 54.1188, 59.1318, 81.1840, 81.1842.

[87] SS 191.4752–55.

(Figure 2.3), it becomes evident that tribal fighters were stationed at positions along a broad swathe of the Sino-Tangut frontier. Though there is no extant data for the eastern section of the frontier (in northwestern Hedong), anecdotal evidence confirms the existence of "subordinate households" here as well.[88] According to Figure 2.3, there were no tribesmen in the Qingshui valley, an agricultural region probably populated primarily by Han peasants. However, there were "Western soldiers" affiliated with nearly all of the fortresses along the Qinzhou trench further south. In total, over 100,000 tribal fighters were positioned in the northwest theater, with over 30,000 registered war horses at their disposal.[89] By comparison, in the same region, the Song commanded no more than 137,500 imperial troops and 30,000 "archers."[90]

The map in Figure 2.3 locates the "Western soldiers" at the sites of the forts to which they were affiliated. In fact, they would have been distributed over a fairly broad zone surrounding the forts. The extent of this dispersal is conveyed in a 1086 description by Han Qi of a portion of the Qinzhou frontier north of two specific Song fortresses:

> North of Yongning and Anyuan, extending outward contiguously for fifty to a hundred kilometers, everywhere one finds assimilated households of western tribesmen. Among them are some who have not received supplementary titles of office [from the Song court], whose fighters and horses are not subject to government oversight, and who are consequently known as "unassimilated households." They live interspersed with the assimilated households and, together with them, form a hedge.[91]

In the reference to a "hedge," one recognizes the same language used to describe the frontier "archers." Given the fact that the allied tribes were positioned in a broad zone across the entire Song–Xia frontier, it is not surprising that they were conceived of as a military line. Xia Song used similar language, referring to "the tribal households along the border" as a "hedge," and Sima Guang called them "the Middle Kingdom's hedge." So, too, Zhang Fangping, who described the allied tribes as a frontier "screen."[92]

---

[88] XCB 132.3144; SS 191.4750.

[89] The figure of 100,000 fighters (and 30,000 horses) can be derived from two sources: WJZY, part 1, 18.2a, 8a, 15a, 25a; SS 191.4752–55.

[90] The figure of 137,500 imperial troops is an estimate based on the fact that 275 battalions were stationed in Shaanxi. See McGrath, "Military and Regional Administration," 171. In principle, there were no more than 500 men per battalion. For the figure of 30,000 "archers," see WJZY, part 1, 18.2a, 8a, 15a, 25a. Data for Qingzhou (unfortunately excluded from this source) can be estimated based on the number of military units.

[91] QSW 39:236.

[92] QSW 17:59, 37:108, 55:116. For other references to these units as a "hedge" or "screen," see SS 187.4569, 191.4750; XCB 131.3111, 132.3144, 469.11212; QSW 108:305.

The northwestern theater was unusual in its reliance on non-Han fighters. Indeed, the fourteenth-century editors of the Song dynastic history note the trouble they had properly classifying "Western soldiers" in their overview of Song military organization.[93] Outside of the northwest, non-Han militias seem only to have existed in Sichuan and the southwest. Included were the "grotto men" of the southwestern tribal region (a region known as the "land of streams and grottoes").[94] But these units seem to have been formed comparatively late in the dynasty, in the 1050s. Moreover, unlike the "Western soldiers," they were subordinate to the "haltered-and-bridled prefectures" of the southwest, where the Song did not maintain military garrisons and so had no operational control over local fighters. By contrast, the "assimilated households" of the northwest not only resided in the vicinities of Song forts, but were also often outnumbered by the combined forces of the imperial army and the local "archers." In addition, tribal fighters affiliated with any given fort were typically divided into several different tribal "surnames," suggesting that there was no single tribal hierarchy that might have served as the basis for organized resistance against the Song state.[95]

A comparison of Tang and Song uses of non-Han soldiers is useful here. The Tang was famous for its reliance on military men of steppe or Tibetan origins, including both common soldiers and commanders. The best known of these were the "foreign generals," to whom Ouyang Xiu devoted an entire chapter in his history of the Tang Dynasty.[96] Comparatively speaking, the Song used non-Han military men on a much smaller scale.[97] Kim Sŏnggyu points to two important institutional developments between the Tang and the late Northern Song with regard to the use of non-Han military personnel. One type of "foreign general" appears to have disappeared entirely in post-Tang times – those who relocated to the Chinese interior, where they were integrated into the regular military hierarchy and assimilated into Chinese society. Another type remained on the frontier in control of tribal armies, much like the fighters from tribal units of Northern Song times.[98]

---

[93] SS 187.4569.
[94] On "grotto men," see SS 191.4746–49; An Guolou, *Songchao zhoubian minzu*, 79–85. On southwestern frontier society during the Song, see von Glahn, *Country of Streams and Grottoes*; von Glahn, "Conquest of Hunan."
[95] Kim, *Sōdai no seihoku*, 174–75.
[96] XTS 110.4111–30.
[97] Chen Feng, *Bei Song wujiang qunti*, 70.
[98] Kim, *Sōdai no seihoku*, 195–212.

A second development occurred during Shenzong's reign in the late eleventh century, when – in response to a broad reorganization of the frontier military, in conjunction with practical concerns arising from the Song occupation of Tibetan lands in Hehuang – the Song began relying to a greater degree on "Western soldiers," even apparently integrating them with Han soldiers into common military units.[99] Unlike in the Tang, however, these non-Han soldiers always served at home locally; they were never brought into the Chinese interior or assigned to fight on other fronts. Moreover, it is clear that not everybody at court was happy about troop integration. As Li Xian argued in a 1083 memorial:

> Han and "western" infantry and cavalry troops have been haphazardly combined into one army. This has already today caused quite a bit of harm, to say nothing of what would happen when they go to war. Since Han and Tibetans speak mutually unintelligible languages, when the troops are garrisoned, it has gotten to the point that mealtime has become inconvenient.[100]

Indeed, as will be clear in the next chapter, the Song preferred when possible to keep populations on the frontier segregated along ethnic lines.

The difference between Tang and Song treatment of non-Han troops makes sense in the context of a new Song ideology of empire. Kim Sŏnggyu has proposed that the "foreign generals" serving at the Tang court were sometimes thought of as equivalent to the sons of the rulers of tributary states, held as "hostages" at Chang'an during the very same period.[101] Both phenomena reflected the Tang's vision of itself as a world empire. As we will see in a later chapter, the Song had a rather different sense of self-identity – seeing itself not as a universal empire, but rather as a culturally and ethnically Han state. It is not surprising then that neither "grotto men" nor "Western soldiers" served away from their homes in the regular Song army. The new Chinese identity of the Song affected the historical record as well, thereby accentuating the appearance of difference between the compositions of Tang and Song military forces. Deng Xiaonan has argued that the Song imperial clan and many of the founding generals of the dynasty were of mixed Turkish-Chinese or Xi-Chinese ancestry, but that their mixed heritage is concealed in most source material. Unlike Tang emperors and military commanders, whose mixed ethnic ancestries are readily apparent in the historical record,

[99] Ibid., esp. 217–44.
[100] XCB 338.8141–42.
[101] Kim, Sōdai no seihoku, 202–04.

Song sources were produced by men who were themselves convinced that the Song empire was properly an ethnically Han regime.[102] In order for policymakers and court historians alike to transform Song China into a Han state, it was necessary both to homogenize the population of the interior by effacing the non-Han backgrounds of the regime founders, and also simultaneously to clarify ethnic boundaries on the frontier by segregating Han and non-Han populations.

Conclusion

This chapter has sought to contribute to a burgeoning scholarship on Song military history as part of the book's broader goal to explore how contingent circumstances of the eleventh century impacted China's place in the world – both real and perceived. Despite the century of peace with the Liao, the Northern Song court remained concerned throughout much of the first half of the dynasty that the Khitans might mount a cavalry invasion similar to the one of 1004. Simultaneously, on the northwestern frontier, the Tanguts would pose a second substantial threat by the 1030s. In response, the Song embarked in the first half of the eleventh century on a massive campaign to construct linear barriers across a vast swathe of the frontier, barriers that included a network of pools and canals in the northeast, and a combination of tree palisades and deep trenches further to the west. These man-made constructions were then bolstered by a heterogeneous assortment of allied tribesmen, local militiamen, and troops of the regular army, who were positioned in a broad zone along the frontier.

Historians have long treated the Song as militarily weak, especially in contrast to the Tang. But one need not conclude that the Song approach to frontier defense represented the foreign policy of a militarily feeble regime. The transformation in the late first century CE of Rome's "grand strategy," as described in Edward Luttwak's classic study, offers a useful point of comparison. Prior to the first century, Rome, like the Tang, depended for its frontier defense on client states, driven into submission by their fear of Roman military might. Later, while still at the height of its power, Rome transformed itself from a "hegemonic empire" to a "territorial empire," establishing a perimeter defense in the process.[103]

---

[102] Deng Xiaonan, "Lun Wudai Song chu 'huhan.'" See also Kim, *Sōdai no seihoku*, 204–06.

[103] Luttwak, *Grand Strategy*. For useful diagrams contrasting "hegemonic" and "territorial" empires, see 20–21.

Similarly, the Song did not turn to a perimeter defense out of weakness. Policymakers were responding in part to the new geopolitical circumstances of the tenth and eleventh centuries. Already by the founding of the Song in 960, the Khitans had a mightier army than any the Tang ever had to face. Moreover, in light of effective Liao political centralization, it was not possible to establish client regimes through a divide-and-conquer strategy. These problems were compounded by the fact that the Song–Liao border traversed the Hebei plains, leaving no natural obstacles to block a cavalry attack.

But strategic thinking is governed as much by trends in political culture as by particular geographic and military parameters. In the Roman example, the decision to provide greater security to the imperial periphery was – according to Luttwak – spurred by the development in the first century CE of "a much broader and altogether more benevolent conception of empire" that accompanied the process of Romanization on the imperial periphery.[104] So, too, the Northern Song approach to frontier defense reflected particular trends in how Chinese statesmen conceptualized their state. Because they came to think of their dynasty as a culturally and ethnically Han state (and not a universal empire in the Tang fashion) – a shift in worldview examined in detail in Chapter 4 – Song policymakers made little effort to incorporate Tibetan horsemen into the regular army (as had done the Tang), and simultaneously underestimated the efficacy of their own ethnic Han cavalry forces. They based strategic decisions on a perceived stark distinction between steppe armies of nomadic horsemen on the one hand and the "foot soldiers" of the "Middle Kingdom" on the other. In the end, a conjunction of geopolitical circumstances and particularities of Song political culture drove the dynasty's approach to its steppe frontier.

Given the attention paid by the Song court itself to its relations with its northern neighbors, this chapter has focused on the Song–Liao and Song–Xia borders. During the same period of time, there were no attempts to establish on Song China's southwestern and southern frontiers a system of perimeter defense of the sort established in the north. These differences in military strategy on different frontiers exemplify what Matthew Mosca has termed a "frontier policy" – in opposition to a

---

[104] Thus, as people across imperial territory adopted the culture of Roman Italy and ultimately acquired the rights of Roman citizens, "the frontiers were efficiently developed to defend the growing prosperity of all, and not merely of the privileged [at the imperial center]." See ibid., 5.

Table 2.1 *Sites of previous service of Northern Song prefects*[a]

Site of appointment as prefect	Site of previous appointment as prefect					n
	Northeast[b]	Northwest	Sichuan	Southwest	Interior	
Northeast	9%	19%	3%	15%	53%	228
Northwest	3%	**48%**	5%	11%	32%	1040
Sichuan	5%	16%	11%	15%	53%	252
Southwest	2%	7%	2%	**35%**	53%	902
Interior	2%	9%	3%	14%	**72%**	4388

[a] Source of data: Chinese Biographical Database (CBDB) (October 2013 version). "Northeast" = Hebei and Hedong; "Northwest" = region north and west of the Wei River, plus region north and west of Xingyuan; "Sichuan" = Sichuan Basin plus Yangzi river valley west of Jiangling; "Southwest" = region south of the Yangzi and west of 115°E longitude plus Jiangling; "Interior" = all other regions.
[b] Most data on prefectural appointments in the northeast is missing from CBDB.

"foreign policy" (or, to use Luttwak's terminology, a "grand strategy").[105] Rather than maintaining a consistent approach to dealing with all of its neighbors on the basis of a panoramic understanding of China's place in the world, the Song court treated each frontier as conceptually distinct, developing a particular set of policies and strategies for each theater. The difference in how military strategists approached the northeastern theater in contrast to the northwest and the south was partly due to the divergent circumstances on the ground, which required an alternative set of solutions. But the distinctiveness of the different strategies was accentuated by the tendency for those in charge of military affairs in one particular theater to specialize in that region alone.

Tables 2.1 and 2.2 provide a rough measure of the degree of regional specialization of military planners, indicating where prefects and military circuit intendants in four regions had previously served in office. Prefects were the men in charge of local military units, planning strategy in conjunction with military circuit intendants (who themselves all held concurrent appointments as heads of one of their subordinate prefectures). To be sure, the tables reveal that the court made an effort to rotate its officials

[105] Mosca, *From Frontier Policy to Foreign Policy.*

Table 2.2 *Sites of previous frontier service of Northern Song military intendants*[a]

Site of appointment as intendant	Site of previous appointment as intendant				n
	Northeast	Northwest	Sichuan	Southwest	
Northeast	38%	44%	10%	8%	240
Northwest	21%	**63%**	7%	9%	246
Sichuan	34%	44%	10%	11%	61
Southwest	29%	26%	6%	**40%**	35

[a] Source of data: Wu Tingxie, *Bei Song jingfu nianbiao*. For definitions of regions, see notes to Table 2.1.

all over the empire. But in certain key regions – notably the northwestern and southwestern frontiers – the court tended to appoint men with prior experience serving in the theater in question, especially by comparison with appointment patterns in the interior (last row of Table 2.1). Regional specialization of this sort helps explain the development of particular regional strategies of military defense. It was because Cao Wei was appointed to multiple posts in the northwest that he was able to replicate in several circuits the system of military trenches that he had devised.[106]

The next chapter will shift from frontier defense to the question of border demarcation. The hydraulic defenses in Hebei were all constructed in the first thirty or forty years of the eleventh century. Subsequently, they would be neglected and fall into disrepair, as the Song became increasingly confident there would be no war with the Khitans. Around the same time, in the middle of the eleventh century, military planners ceased digging defensive lines in the northwest, which presumably had become irrelevant once Song armies began to seize lands under Tibetan and Tangut control. By mid-century, the court was far more interested in simply demarcating its political borders and far less in defending these borders. On the basis of a careful study of late eleventh-century border demarcation, the next chapter will examine an alternative way of defining the limits of Chinese control and explore how a new vision of an activist central government promoted a more panoramic "foreign policy."

[106] Xiong Ben's (1026–91) career in southern Sichuan and then on the Sino-Vietnamese frontier provides another interesting example, as he appears to have established militias of "local men" on both frontiers. See SS 191.4741, 191.4745.

3

Bilateral Boundaries

In 1041, reports arrived at the Song court that a pair of Liao farmers, named Nie Zaiyou and Su Zhi, had crossed the border near Daizhou in Hedong to cultivate land several kilometers within Song territory. A few years later, Ninghua Military Prefecture announced a similar case of encroachment by another "northern agriculturalist" named Du Sirong. For the sake of maintaining peace, the Song court initially ordered the Daizhou authorities to shift the border stones further south.[1] More than three decades later, however, these incidents re-emerged as an issue in the context of the Song–Liao border negotiations of the mid-1070s. During these negotiations, opposing diplomats fell into a lengthy and heated wrangling over which state had territorial claim to the fields of these three farmers.[2] Whereas the Song had initially been almost nonchalant about giving up individual tracts of land, the late eleventh-century court seemed much more concerned about these and other small strips of frontier territory.

As it turns out, the court's increasing fixation over the precise course of the border in Daizhou was part of a broader phenomenon. During the final three decades of the eleventh century, Song China embarked on an unprecedented and sustained project to mark its borders on multiple frontiers, a project described in detail below. In the process, the state expended significant time and energy conscripting laborers and then micromanaging the laying of ditches and other lines of demarcation all along China's vast borderlands. Although undoubtedly inspired by a mentality that spurred the linearization of frontier fortifications, described in the previous chapter, these lines of demarcation were fundamentally different from military trenches and other border defenses. In particular, the boundary

---

[1] For the best overview of these incidents, see XCB 184.4462; SHY *fanyi* 2.18. See also XCB 132.3123, 134.3205; SHY *bing* 27.27, *fanyi* 2.12.
[2] XCB 265.6499, 265.6507–08, 265.6510–12.

lines of the late eleventh century involved bilateral decision-making and, as such, reflected the division between two sovereign zones. In narratives of early modern Europe, territorial sovereignty of this type has been tied to a particular international system that emerged in the centuries following the 1648 Peace of Westphalia. As I shall argue, such narratives have little applicability in the case of China. Nevertheless, border demarcation in the late Northern Song can be historicized; the processes leading to the demarcation project made perfect sense in the context not only of geopolitical particularities, but also of eleventh-century trends culminating in the radically new vision of an activist state proposed by Wang Anshi, the most influential statesman of the late Northern Song. After they were established, the boundary lines took on a life of their own, influencing developments in notions of Chinese identity.

Eleventh-Century Border Demarcation Projects

In the eleventh century, especially the late eleventh century, the Song court was involved to an unprecedented extent in both border *delimitation* – whereby policymakers at court working with maps determined roughly speaking where the border should run – and border *demarcation* – whereby the course of the border was marked directly onto the physical landscape with a fence, border stones, or by some other means. Under the Tang, China's northern border had been neither delimited nor demarcated in this way; the state had constructed fortresses in strategic locations, but had not necessarily sought to control the contiguous stretches of land in between.[3] In the southwest, a border between Tang China and Tibet was established and re-established on several occasions in the eighth and ninth centuries. This border, however, seems to have been limited in scope and to have involved delimitation in a few locations rather than comprehensive demarcation.[4] The situation under the Song, then, was fundamentally different. The Liao–Song border has elsewhere been described as a "genuine international frontier in the modern sense."[5] However, the Liao–Song border was not unique; it was rather part and parcel of a broader policy involving Song China's approach to its frontiers with multiple neighbors.

---

[3] Tackett, "Great Wall," 121–22.
[4] Pan Yihong, "Sino-Tibetan Treaties," 116–61.
[5] Twitchett and Tietze, "The Liao," 110.

Following the Peace of Chanyuan of 1005, the course of the Chinese-Khitan border remained remarkably stable until the Jurchen conquest of North China in the 1120s, despite the renegotiation of the peace agreement in the 1040s, and a fairly serious border dispute in the 1070s. In Hebei, much of the border was set along the Baigou River, which ran across the North China Plain about 100 kilometers south of what is today downtown Beijing. In Hedong further west, the border roughly followed the crest of the mountains separating the Hutuo and Kelan river valleys from the Sanggan river valley. Initially, earthen embankments, as well as older structures that included the remnants of a 500-year-old Great Wall built in the Northern Qi Dynasty (a stretch of which appears on the dust jacket of this book), served to mark the border.[6] These lines of demarcation seem to have rapidly fallen into neglect. By the 1070s, Song and Liao court representatives sent out into the field were unable even to locate one particular stretch of embankment.[7] Already in the 1040s, ambiguities in the course of the border north of Daizhou led to incursions by Liao farmers such as those mentioned above, incursions that spurred the Song government to dispatch men to mark the border with stones and a ditch.[8] Border tensions increased over the next decades, reaching a crisis point in 1074. The two years of border negotiations that followed are documented in minute detail in extant court records, and have been described most recently by Christian Lamouroux.[9] Traditional Chinese scholarship dealing with these negotiations has tended to revolve around the long-term significance of the "700 li" of territory transferred at this time to the Khitans, partly because this territorial transfer was at the crux of one of the more sustained attacks on Wang Anshi and his followers during the regency of Dowager Empress Xuanren (r. 1085–93).[10] More pertinent to the present discussion, however, is that these negotiations culminated in a far more extensive and systematic border demarcation project, whereby men were sent out across the entire length of the Hedong border to

[6] Tackett, "Great Wall," 113–16.
[7] XCB 256.6254.
[8] XCB 174.4194; SHY *fanyi* 2.18.
[9] Lamouroux, "Geography and Politics." See also Tietze, "Liao-Sung Border Conflict."
[10] Later historians, notably Li Tao (who was no friend of the New Policies) probably exaggerated the size of this stretch of territory. The chief border negotiator at the time, Han Zhen, was not criticized at court for giving up these "700 li" until a decade after the fact, in early 1086, as part of an aggressive campaign to remove Han and other reformists from prominent ministerships. See XCB 366.8810, 369.8901, 371.8988–89.

"dig ditches and erect mounds."[11] The demarcation project was largely concluded by 1076.[12]

The history of border demarcation between Song China and the Tangut Xia Kingdom seems to have followed a nearly identical pattern, beginning with an exchange of oath letters in 1006 and a renegotiation of these oaths during the Qingli era (1041–48).[13] As with the Song–Liao border, demarcation seems to have been limited and unsystematic prior to the reign of Shenzong.[14] The period of most active border demarcation began in the 1070s. In the final month of 1071, the court appointed an official to delineate the border with Suizhou, which the Song had recently acquired from the Xia though military action. Simultaneously, the court dispatched officials to each of the circuits neighboring the Xia Kingdom to take charge of erecting mounds and digging ditches along the border, a project that itself implied that there was as of then no systematic and continuous, demarcated border.[15] In the following year, however, the Tanguts – justifiably suspicious that the Song planned to seize territory elsewhere along its frontier – complained that only the Suizhou border had been properly demarcated.[16] A series of Chinese-Tangut wars over the next three decades led to substantial territorial adjustments (Figure 2.2), resulting in new rounds of border negotiations that stretched out well into the last decade of the eleventh century.[17] Thus, the border was demarcated at Yanzhou in 1090,[18] at Lanzhou in 1095,[19] and at Huizhou

[11] E.g., XCB 266.6526, 267.6541–42. The character for "mound" (堠) can mean either "dirt mound" (封堠) or "beacon platform" (烽堠). See Yang Rui, *Xi Xia dili yanjiu*, 69–70. It is clear, however, that when in conjunction with the digging of a ditch, reference is to a mound. See, e.g., XCB 226.5515, 228.5547.

[12] By Emperor Shenzong's own account, border demarcation was complete by the fourth month of 1076. See XCB 274.6718. Nevertheless, some ditch digging was still reported along the Hedong border as late as 1082. See XCB 322.7760.

[13] XCB 64.1428, 152.3706–07; SS 466.13619. For a detailed study of Song–Xia border demarcation, see Kim, *Sōdai no seihoku*, 47–158.

[14] On demarcation with a ditch in the vicinity of several stockades in Huanqing Circuit in 1046, see XCB 158.3828; SHY *fangyu* 20.13; on demarcation with stones and mounds in Linzhou and Fuzhou in 1057, see XCB 185.4470, 186.4489.

[15] XCB 228.5547. Three months earlier, the emperor had already announced to the Xia that the Song intended to do just this. See XCB 226.5515. For a tomb epitaph confirming that demarcation with earthen mounds was organized near Suizhou at this time, see QSW 112:271.

[16] XCB 229.5578.

[17] On territorial change along the Song–Xia border during the reigns of Shenzong and his successors, see Yang Rui, *Xi Xia dili yanjiu*, 39–58; on the Song–Tangut wars under Shenzong and Zhezong, see P. J. Smith, "Shen-tsung's Reign," 464–78; Levine, "Che-tsung's Reign," 505–09, 548–51.

[18] XCB 437.10546, 445.10717–18.

[19] SHY *fangyu* 20.19.

in 1099.[20] In many of these western regions, details of the border were first worked out carefully in the vicinities of Song fortified cities, where mounds and ditches might curve around the city at a fixed distance of twenty *li*. The border then followed a straight line along the line of sight connecting one city to the next.[21] The final result was a demarcated border that ran the full length of the Song–Xia frontier, "crossing the four circuits from Fuyan [in the east], through Huanqing, Jingyuan, and Xihe [in the west]."[22]

In the very same decades of most active border demarcation with Xia and Liao, the Song court was involved in similar projects along its southern frontier. Unfortunately, extant historical records preserve far fewer details than for the north. It is clear, nonetheless, that the court sent envoys in 1078 and 1084 to demarcate the border with the Ly regime, based in what is now northern Vietnam.[23] In addition, although its overall extent is not clear, Richard von Glahn has gathered evidence pointing to the existence of "forbidden hills" – a sort of no-man's-land – that "demarcated the border between Han and native territories" in southern Sichuan.[24] Although it is not clear when this neutral zone was established, mounds were used to demarcate at least one section of the border during the Zhiping (1064–67) era, while the future chief minister Lü Dafang was serving in Qingcheng County (just west of Chengdu in Sichuan).[25] It is plausible that additional sections were established in conjunction with the creation of a state garrison network that "demarcated the edge of the frontier," a garrison network that emerged in conjunction with the implementation of Wang Anshi's New Policies in the 1070s and early 1080s.[26] Song China's approaches to both its northern and southern borders thus seem to have followed parallel chronological trajectories, culminating with a sharp increase in the 1070s in border demarcation activity.

Three aspects of these developments are particularly noteworthy. First, it is clear that late Northern Song border demarcation was far more labor-intensive and involved a greater degree of government resources than in earlier times. Pre-Song regimes were quite likely content to

---

[20] XCB 514.12221.
[21] For good descriptions of this border delineation process in the vicinity of Saimen (near Suizhou), see XCB 437.10546, 437.10550, 439.10581, 439.10588.
[22] XCB 446.10735.
[23] XCB 287.7011, 300.7311, 349.8372–74; SHY *fanyi* 4.37; SS 16.312; J. Anderson, *Rebel Den*, 144–46.
[24] Von Glahn, *Country of Streams and Grottoes*, 6.
[25] SHY *bing* 29.41, *fangyu* 12.8.
[26] Von Glahn, *Country of Streams and Grottoes*, 166.

delineate their frontiers when necessary only along critical stretches of the border and only by exploiting pre-existing features, such as mountain ranges, rivers, and Great Wall remains. The late Northern Song state, by contrast, greatly expanded the scope of these projects, devoting more resources to demarcation and recruiting what must have been vast teams of manual laborers, in order to erect the markers that designated the exact course of the border along much of, if not the entire, northern frontier and a portion of the southern frontier.

Second and more striking, it was the Song central government, rather than local authorities, that was most actively engaged in this enterprise. At times, decisions regarding the precise course of the border were worked out on site by high-ranking officials dispatched from Kaifeng to the frontier; at other times, decisions were made at court itself on the basis of maps produced by these officials. Maps and documents held in the imperial archives apparently provided the central government with the tools necessary for overseeing and micromanaging the frontier regions under its control. Cartography went hand in hand with the demarcation process. Maps were first produced, sometimes in full color, to assist the court in its deliberations.[27] Then, armed with these documents for reference, Song representatives went to the border to negotiate with their foreign counterparts.[28] These men then produced additional maps depicting fortifications and topographic features, in conjunction with their final reports to court detailing the conclusions of the negotiations.[29]

These maps held in the central archives – along with other archived documents relating to past border agreements – not only allowed the central government to guide and keep itself up to date on the minutiae of the border agreements, they were also critical in providing the Song state with what one might call "archival authority." The Song archives seem to have been more comprehensive than those of the Liao or the Xia; thus, the Song court could sometimes dictate the direction of border negotiations by bringing up the precedent of past agreements. For instance, before

---

[27] Prior to border negotiations with the Tanguts, authorities in Lanzhou "drew in color a map" of local terrain for the court's reference. Later, at court, Lü Dafang "unfolded a map to discuss border demarcation." See XCB 452.10844, 462.11043.

[28] E.g., in 1046, a map of Fengzhou was forwarded to court to help strategize the placement of the border; this map was subsequently used during negotiations with the Tanguts. See XCB 159.3847; SHY *fangyu* 21.12–13. In 1081, Huang Lian (1034–92) sent a "Map of the Twelve Stockades" of Daizhou along with his recommendations concerning the Hedong border. This (or a similar) map was then used during negotiations. See XCB 317.7675–76, 322.7760. In some cases, additional maps were sent to update the court during talks. See XCB 266.6526, 432.10426.

[29] E.g., XCB, 186.4489, 193.4679–80, 282.6918.

going off to negotiate with the Khitans on the course of the border in Hedong, Han Zhen (1019–97) examined archival maps and documents assembled for him by the Bureau of Military Affairs, with the goal of acquiring the background knowledge needed to "get the Northern Court [i.e. Liao] to understand the whole picture."[30] Han would later insist that all Song border officials be required promptly to transmit to court copies of all communiqués with foreign representatives, thereby ensuring that new appointees to frontier assignments had access to the documents instructing them in the "whole picture."[31] In another case, during a disagreement between Xia and Song as to the proper course of the border, the Song representative Zhao Xie (1027–91) was able to produce a letter from the former Tangut ruler Li Deming to bolster the Chinese claim. As a result, "the caitiff envoy, stunned and unable to respond, withdrew his claim."[32] The late Northern Song state fully recognized the importance of maps and archival material both for effective state oversight of foreign policy and for gaining an edge in inter-state negotiations. Any deficiencies in these documents or in archival preservation were deemed unacceptable. In one instance, Emperor Shenzong became furious at an official who had "inspected the frontier, [but then] drew a map that was unclear."[33] And Han Qi complained when officials were unable to locate critical past correspondence between Song and Liao.[34]

Third, in the 1070s, the Song court appears to have begun to move away from reliance on unsystematic, ad hoc approaches to demarcation in favor of a standardized process. Earlier in the dynasty, the border was marked with an assortment of border stones, pre-existing structures, and natural features. But by mid-century, the court began to adopt a more uniform strategy. In the 1050s, for example, Song used stones to mark stretches of border with both Liao and Xia.[35] Finally, in the 1070s, the court began consistently to employ a standardized combination of mounds and ditches to mark the entire Song–Xia frontier, as well as

---

[30] XCB 252.6176.

[31] XCB 302.7346.

[32] SS 290.9724. There are other examples. In 1056, to demonstrate that the Liao farmers Nie Zaiyou and Su Zhi had encroached on Song territory, the court ordered its envoy to show a "Map of the Hedong Border" to the Liao representative to explain the "whole picture." See SHY *fanyi* 2.18; XCB 184.4462. In 1074, after disagreeing on where negotiators should sit, the Song side produced a state letter establishing a precedent for their proposed seating protocol. As a result, the two Liao representatives "did not dare contest" the point any further. See XCB 256.6253.

[33] XCB 262.6373.

[34] Sima Guang, *Sushui jiwen*, 11.205.

[35] SHY *fanyi* 2.18; XCB 185.4469–71.

the Hedong portion of the frontier with Liao. So common was it to use mounds and ditches in this way that they came to constitute a sort of international "language of demarcation" – that is, they acquired a transcultural significance like a red traffic light in today's world, understood by all as indicating that one should stop and not cross.[36]

Simultaneously, the process for determining where to set lines of demarcation increasingly relied on precedents initially developed in other regions. In 1089 and 1090, for example, both Yanzhou and Lanzhou implemented the so-called "Suizhou model," patterned – as suggested by its name – on the border established two decades earlier (in 1072) further east in Suizhou.[37] The Suizhou model, which involved a 10 *li* non-tilling zone on either side of the border, seems itself to have been developed in imitation of the "Kelan model," implemented by Ouyang Xiu in the mid-1040s at a single location along the Song–Liao border and similarly involving a 10-*li* zone off-limits to cultivation.[38] The standardization of the methods of demarcation was accompanied by what may have been a deliberate attempt to develop a corps of bureaucrats with specialized expertise. There are references to a "Bureau of Demarcation" established in Hedong in the mid-1070s that may have served to routinize elements of the demarcation process.[39] Officials with border demarcation experience were sometimes sent elsewhere to embark on similar projects. Zhang Muzhi (fl. 1070s) worked on marking the frontier first in Huanqing in 1071, then in Fuyan in 1072.[40] Zhao Xie (1027–91) was involved in establishing the border with the Tanguts in 1072, with Vietnam in 1078, and then again with the Tanguts in 1090.[41]

Much has been made by historians of the differences in how the Song dealt with the Liao on the one hand, and with the Xia on the other. Indeed, if one focuses on rhetoric or diplomatic protocol, one finds that the Song treated the Liao as an equal, but the Xia as a subordinate. Letters between Song and Liao were called "state letters," but those between Song and Xia were entitled "memorials" (from Xia) and "edicts" (from Song). In these letters, the Xia emperor referred to himself as the Song emperor's

---

[36] In the Song, mounds were also erected to keep locals from encroaching on designated state pastureland. See XCB 82.1869. Mounds may have been efficacious in keeping people out because they resembled tumuli erected above tombs in Chinese cemeteries.

[37] XCB 434.10471, 437.10546, 445.10717–18, 452.10844–50.

[38] SHY *shihuo* 2.3, *shihuo* 63.73.

[39] XCB 266.6537, 267.6541, 269.6582, 269.6584, 270.6627, 278.6798, 283.6937.

[40] XCB 233.5652.

[41] XCB 237.5777, 300.7311, 437.10546.

"servant."[42] But this diplomatic rhetoric – which in essence involved jockeying for position within an East Asian world order based on hierarchical relationships – should be carefully distinguished from other more pragmatic facets of inter-state relationships. By focusing rather on the process of boundary demarcation, one finds striking similarities underlying the Song's interactions not only with the Liao and the Xia, but even with China's southern neighbors. In Chapter 2, I proposed that, in the first half of the century, Song China turned to different defensive military strategies on each of its frontiers, treating each theater as a discrete problem to solve. By contrast, the fact that the court was involved in near simultaneous demarcation projects on three frontiers in the 1070s suggests that, by the time of the Wang Anshi regime, Song policymakers had come to operate and make decisions on the basis of a more coherent and panoramic understanding of China's place within a larger world.

This more coherent vision undoubtedly had an impact on the development of the East Asian inter-state system. The consistency of Song China's foreign policy on multiple frontiers would have helped ensure that multiple neighboring states, even those of very different cultural backgrounds, came to accept certain common frameworks and sets of rules. Previously, we saw how the Song oath letters with the Xia and with the Jin were both modeled on the Chanyuan accord, suggesting a common blueprint for inter-state relations. The implementation of a coherent border policy, involving a consistent "language of demarcation," meant that borderland populations in far corners of East Asia, from Yunnan in the south to Tibet in the west and Manchuria in the northeast, had necessarily to acquire a common understanding of a line of mounds across the landscape. Moreover, it appears that Song China had managed to establish the prestige of state archives. Diplomats from neighboring states accepted the authority of archived documents when determining long-forgotten details from inter-state agreements of past generations.

Bounding Sovereignty

In order to understand the novelty of the eleventh-century border demarcation project, it is worth addressing here what on first impression may seem to constitute similar large-scale endeavors: the Great Walls built by numerous earlier Chinese regimes, as well as the linear military defenses

---

[42] Dunnell, "Significant Peripheries," 335–36; Wang Gungwu, "Rhetoric of a Lesser Empire," 55; Li Huarui, *Song Xia guanxi shi*, 344–60.

constructed in the first half of the eleventh century. Border demarcation in the Northern Song was something fundamentally new in three
important ways. First, the demarcated borders, unlike the Great Walls
and other military lines, did not serve a military function. In Hebei, the
Baigou River formally marked the Song–Liao border. Yet, as described
in Chapter 2, this river was deemed insufficient as a defensive position.
Deeply concerned that a Liao cavalry attack could outflank Song infantry positions, the Song established an extensive network of canals and
other hydraulic fortifications that, together with a tree palisade, extended
across a broad zone south of the river. In Hedong, though the mountains
separating Song from Liao served a strategic function from a military perspective, the actual border line was initially demarcated for quite lengthy
stretches with remnants of the Northern Qi Great Wall, built five hundred years earlier and already in a state of significant disrepair. Needless
to say, these remains would not have effectively hindered enemy troop
movement.

Further west, along the Song–Xia frontier, defensive trenches were
excavated, in some cases following the 1,500-year-old Warring States
Qin Great Wall. These trenches were intended to block cavalry movement in a region of the frontier devoid of mountains or of other strategic
topographic features.[43] But these defensive trenches, generally dating
to the early eleventh century, should not be confused with the border
demarcation ditches established later in the century. Demarcation ditches
were generally ineffective as tools of military defense. Those laid in the
mid-1050s in response to the repeated encroachments by Liao farmers
near Daizhou served primarily as physical markers on the landscape,
indicating the site of the border to the local inhabitants.[44] Thus, in 1071,
when the court dispatched officials to four circuits bordering on the Xia
in order to "clearly establish mounds and border ditches," the goal was to
communicate "clearly" the precise location of the border to frontier residents, who may otherwise have had little awareness of its precise course.[45]
By the very end of the eleventh century, some stretches of the Song–Xia
border were demarcated with mounds alone, rather than with the standard mound-ditch combination, demonstrating once again that, unlike
the Great Wall and other linear defensive fortifications, the demarcated

[43] Tackett, "Great Wall," 126–28.
[44] XCB 174.4194, 184.4462.
[45] XCB 228.5547.

border served as a visual indicator rather than as a military tool. Mounds continued to serve as indicators of borders in subsequent dynasties.[46]

Second, and perhaps more importantly, unlike the construction of the Great Wall and other military fortifications, border demarcation was a bilateral activity. Representatives of both states met at the frontier to negotiate the course of the border. In 1071, when Emperor Shenzong proposed establishing the border with Xia "unilaterally," Wang Anshi argued emphatically that this would be a mistake. If the Tanguts were not consulted, they might rise up in revolt in order to reclaim land they felt they had lost.[47] Bilateral demarcation seems to have become the norm in later decades. In 1089 and again in 1091, during a brief rapprochement with the Tanguts, court edicts dispatched to Xia called for the two sides to "jointly establish the border" of the land recently annexed by Song.[48] Bilateralism was also at the heart of Liao–Song border negotiations. Christian Lamouroux and Klaus Tietze have described in considerable detail the negotiations over the Hedong border, held on site in the 1070s.[49] Perhaps equally interesting was the border demarcation organized near Daizhou in 1082, for which fairly detailed records also survive. According to Emperor Shenzong's instructions, the officials directly managing the laying of the ditch were to adhere to the extent possible to a map of the region vetted by the court, but not before they first "waited for the northerners to come to discuss" the matter.[50] In terms of manpower, although the Hedong military intendancy believed that 500 conscripts would be required, the hope was that both Song and Liao would contribute equal numbers of laborers.[51] The demarcated border near Daizhou was, in principle at least, the product of bilateral decision-making and a bilateral organization of manpower.

Third, as a consequence of their bilateral nature, one can think of the demarcated borders of eleventh-century North Asia as double-sided, unlike the Great Wall and other lines of military defense. When border walls were built, it was not necessarily assumed that a neighboring state would employ the same wall to serve as its own boundary. Indeed, as is almost always the case for defensive structures, the Great Walls were often

---

[46] For example, in the Qing dynasty, mounds referred to as "earth cows" were used in Taiwan to restrict the spread of Chinese into aboriginal lands. See Meskill, *Chinese Pioneer Family*, 36, 51.

[47] XCB 229.5579.

[48] XCB 429.10370, 445.10718.

[49] Lamouroux, "Geography and Politics"; Tietze, "Liao-Sung Border Conflict."

[50] XCB 322.7760.

[51] XCB 323.7781.

situated well within the notional territories of the state they served to defend.[52] For example, the Great Wall of the Warring States Qi Kingdom ran a course that lay consistently to the north of its southern neighbors, the states of Song, Chu, and Lu.[53] Lying between the Qi Wall and the military fortifications of Song, Chu, and Lu would have been a no-man's-land over which no state sought necessarily to exert political control. In the case of the much later Northern Qi and Ming Great Walls, the Hedong portions of these fortifications consisted of an "Inner" Wall north of the Hutuo River and an "Outer" Wall north of the Sanggan River. Needless to say, with an outer line of defense dozens of miles further north, the Inner Great Wall was in no way conceptualized as marking the extremity of the regime's territory.

In contrast to these Great Walls, eleventh-century border lines marked the bounds of two states rather than just one. As the Song emperor Zhezong explained in a 1099 edict sent to the Tangut ruler Qianshun:

> I have already commanded the military intendancies of all circuits to order all places reached by our patrols clearly to establish the border, and to prevent fort and stockade commanders from sending out soldiers across the border unless the Westerners have violated the border [first]; you too should admonish chieftains along the border to forbid violations of the border.[54]

In other words, the border was designed to restrict equally the movements of residents on either side; moreover, the political authorities on both sides were responsible for enforcing these restrictions.

As a boundary shared by two states, bilateral borders reflected a trend toward an alternative notion of sovereignty. A comparison with Europe is useful here. Territorial sovereignty and border demarcation have played important roles in accounts of the European historical trajectory toward modernity. These narratives derive from the fact that, at some point in the early modern period, there was a fundamental transformation in the structure of political authority. The earlier period was dominated by "jurisdictional" sovereignty, whereby authority derived from an accumulation of titles and rights over subordinates rather than the acquisition of a circumscribed territorial space. Sovereignty was exercised in multiple domains (juridical, ecclesiastical, military, fiscal), domains whose boundaries did

---

[52] On defenses in Hebei that "lay well within the notional boundaries" of the regime in question, see Standen, "(Re)Constructing the Frontiers of Tenth-Century North China," 64–65.

[53] Tan Qixiang, *Zhongguo lishi ditu ji*, 1:34.

[54] XCB 515.12240; SHY *bing* 8.35.

not necessarily coincide. In some parts of Western Europe – such as in Alsace and the southwestern German states – authority derived from a complex heterarchy of ecclesiastical and secular seigneuries and independent towns that was "unmappable" in the sense that its component spaces were too heterogeneous to make meaningful linear representations of borders on paper. Defining sovereignty in jurisdictional terms meant that a state's central government had little or no incentive to embark on border demarcation projects. In the two centuries following the Peace of Westphalia, however, the modern system of nation-states came into being, a system involving a new territorial notion of sovereignty in which sovereign powers (be they kings or republican institutions) had supreme authority over homogeneous geographically defined territories. Because territorial sovereignty and border demarcation became possible and desirable in the European context only in conjunction with the disappearance of the last vestiges of feudalism, their development was intimately tied to post-Westphalian Europe and the emergence of the modern world.[55]

By contrast, in China, the principle of jurisdictional sovereignty – if it ever existed at all – would have disappeared no later than the mid-Western Han period, over a millennium prior to the founding of the Song Dynasty. By the Song period, the homogeneity of the Chinese bureaucratic system ensured that legal rights and privileges were consistent throughout the empire. Moreover, for most of the imperial period, the sphere of political influence of the Chinese state was defined in terms of the territory under its administrative control rather than in terms of juridical rights over subordinate entities. In the Tang and pre-Tang, implementation of the equal field system meant that the state was directly involved in the redistribution of land; even after the fiscal reforms of the late eighth century, the state depended as an important source of income on a land-based tax that, practically speaking, required updating land surveys on a regular basis. Given such circumstances, it makes little sense to imagine border demarcation in China as a distinct mark of "modernity."

Nevertheless, border demarcation in eleventh-century China did reflect an important shift in notions of sovereignty. The shift in this case was from unbounded to bounded sovereignty, rather than from jurisdictional to territorial sovereignty. From its inception at the founding of the Qin Dynasty in 221 BCE, Chinese imperial sovereignty was – ideally at least – universal and, as such, unbounded. It was in this regard that the emperor

---

[55] Sahlins, *Boundaries*, 28–29, 53–59; Nordman, *Frontières de France*, esp. 131–49, 295–307, 511–27.

transcended the kings of the former Warring States, whose authority was limited to a single domain. This model of imperial rulership went hand in hand with the conception of the emperor as "Son of Heaven," with the claim by some Tang emperors to the title of "Heavenly Qaghan," and with the tendency in many historical periods to organize foreign relations in the context of a tributary system. In line with this model, diagrams of the cosmos – discussed in the next chapter – were produced that divided space into a series of either five or nine concentric squares representing the diminishing influence of the emperor's moral sway as one distanced oneself from the imperial center. The prevailing conception of the Great Wall accorded well with this model. Rather than constituting the absolute limits of China, the Wall was one of several lines of division separating one level of civilization from the next level of increasing barbarity.[56]

In the context of this model, the bounded sovereignty of the late Northern Song emperors was fundamentally different. The demarcated borders of the eleventh century meant that one moved from one sovereign region to an entirely different one simply by crossing what may have seemed to some locals to be an arbitrarily erected line of dirt mounds. The bilateral nature of the demarcated border meant that the authority of the Tangut and Khitan rulers over their own lands was indistinguishable from the authority of the Chinese emperor over China. Neighboring states had equal responsibilities to enforce the inviolability of the border by preventing their own people from crossing over to the other side. All parties were expected equally to honor past agreements preserved in state archives.[57] In other words, rather than deriving sovereign authority over territory through the will of Heaven, the Song emperor and the rulers of neighboring states worked out border disputes as individuals might work out land disputes on the basis of existing land contracts.[58]

[56] It is plausible that the concentric square model explains why some of the Warring States walls, esp. the walls of the states of Wei and Chu, were square-like in their overall layouts. See Tan Qixiang, *Zhongguo lishi ditu ji*, 1:33–34.

[57] Wang Gungwu, "Rhetoric of a Lesser Empire," 48–49, has identified a "rhetoric of contractual relations" in Tang diplomatic documents that he associates with an "external" language used with foreigners when chauvinistic rhetoric was inappropriate. During the Song, contractual rhetoric was utilized in "internal" court discussions as well. Thus, Hu Su argued for Song China's rights to a frontier territory on the grounds that documents proved it had been offered to Song by Tibetan tribes two decades earlier; and Su Che argued it was "crooked" to annex Tangut territory seized by the Song military. See QSW 22:45; XCB 381.9280; SS 339.10832–33.

[58] Europeans also utilized the language of individual property rights to speak of national territory. *Uti possidetis ita possideatis* ("that which you possess, you continue to possess"), frequently invoked during territorial disputes, was derived from Roman property law. Similarly, the English claim to

State Activism and the Frontier

China's eleventh-century border demarcation project was also tied to contemporaneous debates regarding the proper role of the state in society. The state might have defined the border on the basis of pre-existing natural features; and it might have delegated the handling of the nitty-gritty details to local authorities. In reality, however, the central government expended substantial economic and labor resources to establish a clearly defined border of mounds and ditches between China and its neighbors. The most fervent border demarcation activity occurred in the 1040s and then again in the 1070s and subsequent decades. It is probably not a coincidence that these activities coincided with periods of ideological commitment by the emperor and the court to a more activist state – that is, the period of the Qingli Reforms, followed by the eras during which Wang Anshi and his successors implemented the New Policies.

Historians typically link the New Policies and state activism to an expansionist frontier policy. Wang Anshi convinced Emperor Shenzong to support his program by arguing that a powerful state was a precursor to the recapture of land once under Tang control. Increasing the state's wealth was necessary for building a stronger military, which was itself a tool of territorial expansion.[59] Linking an expansionist foreign policy to bounded sovereignty is perhaps counter-intuitive. However, a survey of arguments made at court suggests that centralization and the strengthening of the state were very much at the heart of both the border demarcation project and the heightened sensitivity to issues of territorial sovereignty. The demarcation efforts of the late eleventh century can be thought of as consisting of a two-stage process that together involved the gradual elimination of ambiguously defined borderlands. First, in the mid-eleventh century, the state showed renewed interest in expanding agricultural productivity on the frontier, in order to enlarge the tax base. Second, the diminished size of the buffer zones separating Song from its northern neighbors spurred the state subsequently to construct mounds and ditches along the entire frontier, largely as a means of controlling its own population of borderlanders.

The most detailed surviving accounts of court proposals to cultivate frontier land involve the Song–Liao border. Even though this border was

---

territories based on the principle of "first settlement" seems to have derived from English property law. See Seed, *Ceremonies of Possession*, 16–40.

[59] P. J. Smith, "Shen-tsung's Reign," 464–65.

set by treaty in the early eleventh century, vast swathes of the frontier remained inaccessible to Chinese farmers for the next several decades. In Hebei, the border was highly militarized, with large zones dedicated to garrisoned troops, pasturage for a strikingly inefficient horsebreeding program, and hydraulic defenses consisting of a broad network of man-made pools and rivers. In 1049, Bao Zheng (999–1062), then serving as vice commissioner of the Census Bureau, addressed the court twice to lament the fact that 1.5 million *mu* of some of the best land in Hebei was set aside to maintain a herd of only 5,000–6,000 horses. In another address composed the same year, he further complained that "the fertile land along the border has been entirely converted into pools and embankments, [such that] no tax revenue . . . is coming in." According to Bao, nearly half of the arable land in Song-controlled Hebei either was flooded for defensive purposes or was devoted to pastureland.[60] Bao encouraged the court to slash or eliminate the horsebreeding program. Others at court argued that the Hebei hydraulic defenses could be effectively replaced with a simple tree palisade, sufficient on its own to obstruct a surprise Liao cavalry attack.[61] Both arguments were based on the notion that reducing the scope of bloated frontier military installations would expand the tax base of cultivated land.[62]

In Hedong to the west, it was the broad, demilitarized "forbidden zone," rather than military fortifications per se, that became a primary issue at court. The Hedong "forbidden zone" had originally been established by the Song general Pan Mei (921–87) in the first decades of the dynasty. In order to protect border populations from constant harassment by Liao troops, Pan forcibly evacuated residents from a broad zone across the entire breadth of Hedong.[63] In 1045, Ouyang Xiu, who had gone to Hedong to investigate the frontier region, asked the court for permission to resettle this land. Partly, he was concerned about encroaching Liao farmers, the very ones mentioned at the beginning of this chapter. But he was also interested in this land as a potential source of tax revenue. According to his calculations, settling the forbidden land across the entire Hedong border would open up 2–3 million *mu* of land, which would produce 3–5 million piculs of grain annually.[64]

[60] QSW 26:33–35; XCB 166.3991–94, 166.3997.

[61] SS 95.2362; XCB 235.5707.

[62] In subsequent decades, opponents of the New Policies like Lü Tao and Shen Gua argued against dismantling the hydraulic defenses, partly on the grounds that the amount of land converted to military use had been exaggerated. See QSW 73:180; Shen Gua, *Mengxi bitan*, 13.117–18 (#236).

[63] XCB 178.4316–17.

[64] *Ouyang Xiu quan ji*, 5:1762–63; XCB 154.3748–49; SHY *bing* 27.35–36.

With the fervent support of Fan Zhongyan, Ouyang's plan was implemented first on a small scale in the forbidden land north of Kelan Military Prefecture. The zone less than ten *li* from the border remained a restricted zone; elsewhere, the state recruited 2,000 households to farm and serve as militia "archers." Although the tax revenue from this land amounted to several tens of thousands of bushels per year, the Hedong military intendant Ming Hao (d. 1048) blocked the further implementation of Ouyang's plan in other regions of Hedong. Ten years later, however, Han Qi resurrected the idea. Like his predecessor, Han was concerned about encroaching Liao farmers. He was also interested in finding new ways to raise revenue and supply frontier garrisons. In 1055, he asked the court for permission to implement Ouyang's "Kelan model" in two other regions of Hedong: Daizhou and Ninghua. With the support of Fu Bi, another prominent minister at court, Han was able to recruit 4,000 households to farm 960,000 additional *mu* of land.[65]

These mid-eleventh-century movements to expand the agricultural productivity of the northern borderlands – under the direction of Ouyang Xiu, Fan Zhongyan, Han Qi, Fu Bi, and other men closely tied to the short-lived Qingli Reforms – were ultimately driven by Northern Song centralization efforts. New sources of revenue were needed both to supply frontier armies and to finance an expanding state. Consequently, the state played an active role in allocating new farmland, and recruiting and relocating farmers to the border regions. Simultaneously, ministers at court were increasingly sensitive to the possibility that Liao agriculturalists might poach on potential sources of revenue by trespassing onto Song territory. The ultimate effect of this mid-century drive was to diminish greatly the scope of the broad militarized (or demilitarized) zone separating Song from Liao. It was in the context of the resulting situation, with Song borderlanders now in much closer proximity to Liao farmers and, later, to Tangut herders, that the late Northern Song court embarked on its unprecedented border demarcation project.

Reining in the Borderlanders

Borderlanders everywhere constitute a challenge to a state's centralization efforts. As Owen Lattimore observed long ago, "border populations on both sides of a frontier" often constitute "a joint community that is functionally recognizable though not institutionally defined" and

[65] XCB 178.4316–17; SS 190.4712–13.

whose "ambivalent loyalties" are frequently "conspicuous and historically important."[66] Michiel Baud and Willem van Schendel have imagined a similar model, of "borderland elites" defending "border interests," while participating in a "'creole' or syncretic border culture."[67] In other words, both frontier *culture* and frontier *interests* are often at odds with the cultures and interests of the two states straddling the frontier region. Indeed, at multiple times in China's history, frontier cultures emerged where "bravado . . . and physical strength" were preferred to the "refined gentry politics" that marked elite society in core regions.[68] Richard von Glahn's description of "local magnates" on the Sichuanese frontier in the Song Dynasty and Johanna Menzel Meskill's account of "local strongmen" on the Taiwanese frontier in the Qing Dynasty feature precisely such cultures of bravado.[69] At the same time, because of the general undesirability of frontier appointments, border officials were not infrequently selected from among the dregs of officialdom.[70] Their rapaciousness and incompetence at times drove Chinese inhabitants of the frontier away from the reaches of the state. Perhaps most famous of all were the transfrontiersmen of the late Ming who eventually allied themselves with the emerging Manchu state. Although Chinese in origin, their interests in trade (or "smuggling") and their predilections for a more martial lifestyle led them, it has been argued, to feel greater affinity toward non-Chinese tribesmen.[71]

In the Northern Song, one observes very similar tensions between borderlanders and the state. Central government interests frequently conflicted with the needs of northern frontier families. Accounts exist of the widespread havoc caused by the Song armies stationed in northern Hebei, who forced countless farmers off their lands.[72] To make matters worse, newly enacted laws banned local inhabitants from felling

[66] Lattimore, "Frontier in History," 470.

[67] Baud and van Schendel, "Towards a Comparative History of Borderlands." For an example of a borderland where smuggling constituted a significant part of the local economy, see Sahlins, *Boundaries*, 140.

[68] Zelin, "Rise and Fall of the Fu-Rong Salt-Yard Elite," 99. Although Zelin is more interested in portraying the Fu-Rong elite as a commercial or industrial elite, the Fu-Rong region (close to the region examined in Richard von Glahn's study of the Sichuanese frontier) can also be thought of as a peripheral or border region.

[69] Von Glahn, *Country of Streams and Grottoes*; Meskill, *Chinese Pioneer Family*. Although Meskill ties the Lins' bravado culture to a "southern heroic tradition," I suspect it was the product of frontier conditions.

[70] Meskill, *Chinese Pioneer Family*, 31.

[71] Wakeman, *Great Enterprise*, esp. 41–45; Iwai, "China's Frontier Society."

[72] E.g., QSW 26:33.

trees in the nearby forests, trees that the state hoped would obstruct a Liao cavalry attack. The result, as noted by one Hebei official, was that "borderlanders suddenly lost their livelihoods."[73] To add insult to injury, the Hebei hydraulic defenses sometimes flooded the ancestral cemeteries of local villagers.[74] Embargoes on cross-border trade would have additionally impacted these populations. The Song state – as was true of Chinese regimes in other eras – sought to restrict inter-state commerce to select border markets, which authorities could then shut down when necessary to punish steppe regimes. Such a policy made sense to the state as part of a grand strategy, a strategy that would, however, have been of little interest to petty merchants engaged in cross-border trade.

Divergent interests between borderlanders and the central government were nowhere more obvious than in their frequent violations of restrictions on inter-state travel. Locals living on both the Liao and Song sides crossed over without permission for a variety of reasons. They crossed to farm, to fetch water, even to gamble or find brides.[75] In Hebei, officials struggled to prevent locals from fishing in the Baigou River that marked the Song–Liao border.[76] Elsewhere, accusations abounded that locals on both sides crossed to collect firewood.[77] The sometimes arbitrary or careless nature of demarcation often eliminated pre-existing communication routes, spurring additional violations of the border. In one particular case, a Song investigation prompted by a formal Liao protest found footprints demonstrating that, indeed, Song soldiers stationed nearby frequently used an older road that cut into Liao territory.[78] The Song state was perhaps least successful in its attempts to restrict cross-border commerce. Violations of trade restrictions were frequent and widespread.[79] Although court debates typically portrayed trade as something China engaged in merely to appease its northern neighbors, it is clear that Chinese frontier families were willing participants in such activities.

---

[73] XCB 166.3996.

[74] SS 95.2360; XCB 117.2761. Flooding of cemeteries reportedly prompted acts of vandalism against critical dikes.

[75] Encroachments by Liao and Xia farmers on Song territory are discussed elsewhere in this chapter; on encroachment by Song farmers on Xia territory, see XCB 290.7093. On Liao individuals crossing the Hedong border to fetch water, see XCB 513.12206–07, 514.12211–12; SHY *bing* 28.44. On cross-border gambling, see SHY *xingfa* 4.5; XCB 77.1762. On crossing the border to kidnap brides, see XCB 60.1334–35.

[76] XCB 193.4671–72.

[77] E.g., XCB 205.4969.

[78] XCB 311.7534, 319.7705–06.

[79] E.g., XCB 341.8214, 364.8725; SHY *shihuo* 38.33, *xingfa* 2.4, *bing* 27.7.

Borderlanders on both sides benefited from inter-state trade, whether or not it was legal.

Endemic tensions between the state and the frontier came to the fore when borderlanders directly threatened state stability. Prior to peace treaties and the demarcation of a border, the people inhabiting the frontier region between two empires might pit the two states against each other through a stratagem of shifting alliances, with the ultimate goal of preserving their own autonomy. At the same time, men deemed outlaws from the perspective of the center might flee from one state to the other in order to evade their pursuers. Clearly demarcated and well-policed borders serve to diminish the authority of these actors. Thus, in eighteenth- and nineteenth-century North America, peace agreements between European powers and the United States led to a "transborder collusion among nation-states to curb the mobility and autonomy of borderlanders" – in this case, the multiethnic Indian confederacies that had once served as useful buffers between rival empires.[80] Similarly, early Sino-Russian and Franco-Spanish border treaties included clauses requiring the repatriation of cross-border fugitives. It was in the interest of both neighboring powers to eliminate the freedom of movement of tribal chiefs, as well as of "thieves, assassins, and deserters," who took advantage of neighboring sovereign zones to evade capture.[81] The Song followed a similar pattern. Naomi Standen has argued that the Peace of Chanyuan represented the culmination of the central government's struggle to eliminate semi-autonomous northern governors who, by shifting allegiances between Song and Liao, had flourished to the detriment of both states.[82] Indeed, an important clause of the Chanyuan agreement required that "if there are bandits and robbers who abscond and flee, neither side shall allow them to seek asylum."[83] Similar clauses requiring the repatriation of cross-border fugitives were incorporated not only in the earliest Xia–Song oath letters, but also in the letters that Song exchanged with Jin in 1123.[84]

Perhaps even more threatening to the state than autonomously minded borderlanders were those among them whose activities antagonized neighboring regimes, creating a volatile situation that might rapidly escalate into a full-blown war. In the eighteenth century, the Qing state

[80] Adelman and Aron, "From Borderlands to Borders," 838.
[81] Perdue, "Boundaries, Maps, and Movement"; Perdue, *China Marches West*, esp. 161–73; Sahlins, *Boundaries*, 89–90.
[82] Standen, *Unbounded Loyalty*, 25; Tackett, "Great Wall," 134–35.
[83] XCB 58.1299.
[84] See note 51 of Introduction.

looked upon ethnically Han frontiersmen in Hainan and Taiwan alike as ne'er-do-wells with a penchant for picking fights with the natives. As a result, the Qing expended considerable energy trying to prevent Chinese from encroaching on native lands.[85] The Song state faced – or imagined it faced – precisely such risks both to the north and to the south. On the Sichuanese frontier in the south, Han homesteaders regularly encroached on the territories of native tribes, provoking violent responses. In one case, in the words of Von Glahn, "five years of turbulence that began in 1078 and claimed thousands of lives can be traced back to a street quarrel over a meal of fish and bamboo shoots."[86] Fears of a similar war on the northern frontier constantly occupied policymakers at court. Even very minor border violations were seen as the "sprouts" of "border strife."[87] On some occasions, the court issued specific instructions to combat such problems. In 1086, Hedong Circuit authorities received an edict asking them to "command those in charge of fortified cities and stockades along the border to keep frontier households and patrols on mission under control; from now on, nobody should trespass across the border without cause."[88] A decade earlier, in 1074, following a rash of reports that Han soldiers had killed tribal allies, passing them off as enemy soldiers in order to claim rewards, the court was forced to tattoo the ears of the allied tribesmen to identify them as friendlies.[89]

But such instructions did not necessarily help much when the prime culprits antagonizing neighboring populations were the border officials themselves. The prefect of Xiongzhou on the Hebei border with Liao was blamed for provoking the Khitans in the mid-1040s, nearly leading to war.[90] A half century later, in 1090, the movement spearheaded by the anti-New Policies partisan Su Che against the annexation of Tangut land revolved around the notion that greedy officials had driven China into an unnecessary conflict to capture what Su portrayed as an insignificant stretch of land: "High ministers have been drawn to small gains; they peered at the profitable fields of the Xia state, and coveted them without end." According to Su, although Dowager Empress Xuanren's regency brought change at court (by forcing out the followers of Wang Anshi),

[85] Csete, "Ethnicity, Conflict, and the State," esp. 233, 249; Meskill, *Chinese Pioneer Family*, 36.
[86] Von Glahn, *Country of Streams and Grottoes*, 89, 106.
[87] QSW 22:47.
[88] XCB 370.8956.
[89] XCB 251.6133.
[90] QSW 22:44. The prefect in question apparently encouraged local fishermen to enter the forbidden waters of the Baigou River that marked the Song–Liao border.

the officials in the field remained no less dangerous: "Since the Yuanyou era, the court has not instigated a border incident; all [incidents] have arisen from the machinations of former border officials, who have repeatedly killed allied tribesmen . . . and plundered their wealth." The inevitable border conflicts were all, thus, the result of the "perfidious scheming of border officials."[91]

Two general approaches were employed to rein in borderlanders and rogue officials. The first involved the clear demarcation of the border, an approach that was fostered by both Wang Anshi and Emperor Shenzong. Wang's support of clear borders was already evident in a speech he delivered at court in 1071 that sought to account for the recent military debacle at Luowucheng near Suide.[92] According to Wang, "Suide has not delineated its border, so the Tanguts are naturally unwilling to demobilize their troops."[93] Wang elaborated on his position later that year. In response to the assertion that it was in fact rogue border officials that initiated conflicts, not the lack of clear borders, Wang retorted: "Incidents of encroachment often arise from a border that is unclear; if we want to prevent [our own] border officials from encroaching on the others, we need first to make the border clear."[94] In other words, border demarcation was a means by which the central government could rein in its own frontier officials. Interestingly, it was in the course of the same discussion that Wang Anshi convinced the emperor that it was unwise to demarcate the border unilaterally. The Tanguts had to be consulted in this process. Apparently, Wang was more suspicious of his own border officials than of representatives of the neighboring states. For Wang, an important benefit of border demarcation involved the assertion of central authority over both populations and administrators operating on the periphery.

The second approach designed to rein in borderlanders and rogue officials was to establish a no-man's-land between the neighboring states. Such a buffer zone would minimize the cross-border interactions that might lead to skirmishes. A fixed "dual non-tilling zone" – whereby territory ten *li* on either side of the border was demilitarized and designated as off-limits to cultivation and herding – would, by the end of the eleventh century, go hand-in-hand with the demarcation of clearly defined

---

[91] XCB 452.10849–50.
[92] For more on the Luowucheng debacle, see P. J. Smith, "Shen-tsung's Reign," 469–70.
[93] XCB 221.5388. There was also an element of partisan politics at work: by means of this comment, Wang sought to protect his political ally Li Fugui from punishment for the military debacle at the expense of another military commander, Chong E.
[94] XCB 229.5578.

borders. Initially, however, this approach of using a zone off-limits to farmers appears to have been seen as an alternative to Wang Anshi's plan. Of five officials appointed in the twelfth month of 1071 to oversee demarcation in provinces bordering on Tangut territory, two men – Fan Yu (d. *c.*1096) and Lü Dazhong (d.a. 1096) – declined to go, submitting instead lengthy and impassioned arguments in opposition to the entire project. Both men made similar arguments, though Fan's argument reveals most clearly the crux of the disagreement.

Fan began by enumerating four reasons why replacing the "dual non-tilling zone" with a demarcated linear border was bound to fail:

1. I once went to the border and enquired into the so-called "dual non-tilling zone." Tens of *li* at its widest, several *li* at its narrowest, the designated land serves as a barrier, [allowing] the Hua [i.e., Chinese] and the barbarians to live separately, and agriculture and animal husbandry to be practiced without coming into contact, thus leading to the cessation of conflict. Depending now instead on separation [merely] by means of a trench and tumuli will lead the residents of the adjoining territories to trespass on each other, thus transforming what is now stable into a dangerous situation.

2. I have found out that, along the former borders of the five circuits, ever since skirmishes broke out, borderlanders have taken advantage of this opportunity to encroach and farm, [leading to a situation like] the interlocking of dog's teeth, with some Qiang [under Chinese suzerainty] occupying fields within the territory of the *rong* [i.e., Tanguts]. If we now demarcate the border, we will have abandoned [this zone], [since] the fallow land on the frontier is not the Middle Kingdom's territory. But if we now demarcate the border within [this fallow land], then we will have seized it. If we abandon what was formerly ours, then we will begin to lose the hearts of our people; if we take what is not ours, then the *rong* people will instigate a conflict.

3. I have also heard that the *rong* and *di* barbarians are shameless in their endless deceits; they covet benefits without taking notice of righteousness. Now I hear that they have offered us land while harboring resentment, such that when our envoys approach the territory, they were still hiding there and would not go, and such that when there emerged a dispute over land, we put up with it without a fuss. What will come of this? If we arrive [at the border] in a lone cart, there will be no way for us to deal with a betrayal; if we come with armed troops, there will be no way to instill trust.

4. East from Linzhou and Fengzhou, west to Qinzhou and Weizhou, the land spans 1,500 to 1,600 *li*. Even a ditch only a foot wide and deep [would require] a total of 500 to 600 man-days of labor. [This project] will cause years of corvée duty for men on both sides of the border. No sooner will the bitterness of war have come to an end that the labor of the scoops and spades will begin anew.[95]

Fan Yu's argument, then, constituted a critique of the notion that the central government could successfully play an active role on the frontier. His second point implied that the state did not properly understand the complexities of border society; the state might draw a straight border line when in fact only a jagged line (shaped like interlocking dog's teeth) could properly reflect the distribution of farmers from the two states. His third point suggested that Fan was far more skeptical than Wang of the trust-worthiness of the Tanguts; by contrast, nowhere did Fan reveal that he shared Wang Anshi's suspicions of Chinese border officials. Finally, Fan's fourth point mirrored many of the later criticisms of the New Policies regarding their predilection for large-scale state-organized labor projects.

Following these four points, Fan brought up one more reason that he claimed superseded the four aforementioned points in significance. This last reason is particularly revealing because of its reference to the Nine Zones of Submission of the concentric squares model of the cosmos:

> I have also heard that in the Zhou system the Grand Minister over the Masses established trenches and tumuli in the states and fiefdoms; as for the Nine Zones of Submission, the Director of Regions did no more than distinguish these [without marking their divisions with trenches or tumuli]. When Masters of Hospitality took charge of [receiving] trib-ute, the outer frontier states did not participate in this. [The way] the Sage Kings treated the barbarians consisted of praising the good [among them] and pitying the incompetent; they believed that reprimanding them with-out ever amending the regulations, rewards, and punishments [to take into account their different situations] was a deficient notion. Now to impose on the barbarians the system of digging trenches to mark borders, this was not the intention of the ancient kings.[96]

Fan purposefully refers to demarcation as the "trench-tumuli system" – a term used at no other time during court discussions on demarcation during the eleventh century – in order to draw a parallel between the mounds and ditches of Northern Song demarcation and the system of

[95] XCB 228.5548.
[96] XCB 228.5548–49.

demarcation alluded to in the *Rites of Zhou*, a classical text describing the ideal society put into place by the ancient sage kings of the early Zhou Dynasty.[97] Unfortunately for Fan, the clumsy use of classical precedent provided Wang Anshi with rich fodder for a rebuttal:

> [Fan] Yu says that the *Rites of Zhou* only established trenches and tumuli in the Central States [i.e., in the interior] and that there were none in the territories adjoining the barbarians. Well I say to Yu: As for establishing trenches and tumuli in the heart of the Middle Kingdom and not establishing them in the territories adjoining the barbarians, how does this make any sense?[98]

But Fan's last point is important because it reflected an unease with certain implications of bilateralism and bounded sovereignty. Rather than imagining the Chinese state as a component of a larger world system, where a logic that applied to China might also apply to the Tangut state, Fan clung to an older vision of China's place in the world derived from the concentric squares model. China's way of organizing society was thus unique; even border demarcation – a product of the civilizing influences of the great culture heroes of antiquity – was a phenomenon that only made sense well within the bounds of the Chinese ecumene.

It would be simplistic, however, to try to fit this particular debate between border demarcation and the establishment of a no-man's-land within the reformist–conservative paradigm by which the political world of the late Northern Song is commonly understood. Fan Yu himself was later remembered as a partisan of Wang Anshi, especially after post-Yuanyou reformers praised him for his strenuous protests against relinquishing territory captured from the Tanguts in the early 1080s.[99] Both approaches to stabilizing the border were absorbed into late eleventh-century foreign policy discourse. In 1077, after Liao complained that Song troops had violated their territory and destroyed the home and fields of a certain Liu Man'er, the Song emperor observed that "if we do not . . . rapidly establish the line of demarcation, then after showing forbearance for some time, there will again be a violent incident."[100] A decade and a half later, Fan Bailu (1030–94), then vice director of the Secretariat, asserted that "when the border is not set, then skirmishes and raids

---

[97] For the use of the term "trench-tumuli" in a Qing reprint of a Song edition of the *Rites of Zhou*, see *Zhou li zhushu fu jiaokan ji*, 10.2a (p.149), 10.16a (p.156).

[98] XCB 228.5551.

[99] For more on the debates at court regarding the relinquishment to Xia of four stockades in the Hengshan highlands, see Levine, "Che-tsung's Reign," 506–08.

[100] XCB 285.6989.

will necessarily occur without pause."[101] And, as noted above, Emperor Zhezong insisted in 1099 to his Tangut counterpart Qianshun on the need to "clearly establish the border"; indeed, that same year, Huizhou was ordered by the court to "clearly establish the border mounds."[102]

But whereas emperors and ministers of the final decades of the eleventh century recognized the importance of laying a clear border with China's neighbors, these same policymakers simultaneously insisted on the need for a no-man's-land. The widespread implementation of the "Suizhou" and "Kelan" models represented just such a compromise, combining Wang Anshi's demarcated border of mounds and ditches with an intervening demilitarized buffer zone. Even the Tanguts insisted on the importance of the Suizhou system which, by "separating Han [people] from Westerners [i.e., Tanguts] into inner and outer, will eliminate incidents of conflict," though Xia eventually mutually agreed with Song to reduce the "dual non-tilling land" on either side of the border to a mere five *li* in breadth.[103] The late Northern Song's centrally organized drive to demarcate its borders was, in this sense, the product of consensus rather than of dissension.

But although the development of these two approaches to stabilizing the border did not ultimately reflect the ideological differences between New Policies proponents and their opponents, it did very much reflect developments in understandings of the role of the state. Unlike later political thinkers, those of the Northern Song state still believed that "government, or more particularly the imperial court, was the place from which the world could be made well again, or at least made better."[104] The same environment in which the New Policies could plausibly emerge produced a drive toward court-organized demarcation. The Northern Song vision of the state spurred state-organized colonization of the border regions, the micromanaging of the precise course of the border, and decisions to dispatch thousands of laborers to dig hundreds of miles of ditches.

Boundaries and Eleventh-Century Chinese Identity

The marking of boundaries necessarily involves defining the limits of one's realm. In the process of making decisions regarding where to lay

---

[101] XCB 479.11411.
[102] XCB 514.12221, 515.12230.
[103] XCB 445.10717, 449.10786. On the translation here of the word *fan* as "westerner," see Chapter 2, note 78.
[104] Schirokauer and Hymes, "Introduction," 12.

down the border and physically define China, policymakers at court sometimes revealed their underlying assumptions on the nature of the state and culture to which they belonged. In the next chapter, I deal with principles underlying territorial claims; here I focus more narrowly on border delimitation and demarcation. On this matter, two key factors appear to have guided policymakers: cultural ecology and ethnicity. Fan Yu, in the memorial quoted above, implied just such an understanding of the nature of the border. According to Fan, the Song–Xia border allowed "Hua people and barbarians to live separately, and agriculture and animal husbandry to be practiced without coming into contact." In other words, it constituted a division not only between Chinese and Tanguts, but also between farmers and pastoralists. Because Tanguts themselves engaged in farming along the border zone, however, ethnicity was usually the more important determinant. Indeed, ethnic segregation was enshrined early on in diplomatic agreements between Xia and Song. In 1044 – the fourth year of the Qingli era – an exchange of oath letters between the rulers of the two states specified that, in regions where Han people and Tanguts both resided, they should "mark the midpoint between Westerners and Han people as the border."[105] In subsequent discussions at court, policymakers reiterated on multiple occasions this principle of ethnic segregation. Thus, in 1072, Emperor Shenzong issued an edict to Huanqing Circuit asking the authorities there when negotiating with the Tanguts to "fix the border according to the places where one sees Han people and Westerners now residing and [respectively] plowing or herding."[106] A decade and a half later, in 1089, during another round of border demarcation, the Chinese court reminded the men sent out to negotiate that "when establishing the border, one should accord with the Qingli oath letter, and set it in between where Han people and where Westerners reside."[107] The following year, in the midst of a policy debate, a memorial from the Bureau of Military Affairs reiterated this principle:

> When originally agreeing to demarcate the border . . . the mounds that were erected served as a border to separate Han people from Westerners. As for the land on the inner side of the mounds, this was to be defended by Han people; as for the land beyond the mounds, this was to be occupied by the Xia state.[108]

[105] XCB 152.3706. Cf. *Song da zhaoling ji*, 233.908.
[106] XCB 231.5610. For a similar edict regarding the frontier closer to Suizhou, see XCB 226.5515.
[107] XCB 432.10426.
[108] XCB 437.10546.

And the year after that, Su Che had occasion to bring up this point yet again: "The court has recently renegotiated the border with Xia. If we want to make use of the old Qingli model, we should fix it between where Han people and where Westerners reside. This principle is the most straightforward."[109] In fact, the court was well aware that there was not always a clear geographic dividing line between Han and non-Han populations – all the more so given the Song court's reliance on "Western soldiers," as described in the previous chapter. Indeed, accounts of the northwestern, Sichuanese, and southwestern frontiers mention complex zones of interspersed settlements of different ethnic groups (Table 3.1).[110] It is important to note, however, that this intermingling of ethnic populations was generally portrayed as a problematic obstacle to an ideal of clear ethnic segregation. The various terms referring to interspersed populations usually included the character za, a term with negative connotations that implies confusion and disorder. Part of the problem from the perspective of Chinese administrators had undoubtedly to do with linguistic barriers.[111] But it was also understood that, in frontier regions, it was "not possible to govern all in accordance with Hua [i.e. Chinese] law."[112] Mid and late imperial Chinese regimes commonly turned to a form of legal pluralism in these regions, allowing each ethnic group to be governed according to its own customary laws.[113] The resulting administrative confusion contributed to the sense that societies with intermixed populations were not ideal, that they were "difficult to govern."[114] Though the interspersing of populations was understood to exist in the borderlands, drawing a demarcated border between them remained attractive as a way of bringing institutional and legal clarity to the frontier.

But whereas it may have been still possible to envision as an ideal a neat ethnocultural boundary between the Xia and the Song states, the Liao–Song border was far more problematic. The bulk of the residents of Liao-controlled Hedong and Hebei were ethnic Chinese agriculturalists.

---

[109] XCB 460.10999.

[110] In most cases, neighboring frontier populations are differentiated with ethnic terms, such as *Han* and *Fan*. In a few cases, especially in Sichuan and the southwest, the distinction is between subjects of the emperor (*min*) and barbarians (*yi*).

[111] E.g., QSW 132:24.

[112] *Su Che ji*, 2:450.

[113] On legal pluralism on the southwestern and Sichuanese frontiers in the eleventh century, see XCB 313.7593, 453.10872; An Guolou, *Songchao zhoubian minzu*, 159–76. For the southwest in Qing times, see Sutton, "Violence and Ethnicity." For a comparative study of legal pluralism (with a focus on Georgia and New South Wales), see Ford, *Settler Sovereignty*.

[114] XCB 61.1360. See also *Su Che ji*, 2:456.

Table 3.1 *References in Song sources to mixed ethnic populations on the frontier*

Date	Admin. Circuit	Frontier zone	Text	Reference
997	Qinfeng	Northwest	河湟之地, 夷夏雜居.	XCB 42.893; SS 266.9177
1005	Hedong	Northwest	府州蕃漢雜處, 號爲難治.	XCB 61.1360; SHY *fangyu* 21.5
c.1006	Qinfeng	Northwest	景德中...天水近邊, 蕃漢雜處.	SS 250.8818
c.1010	Qinfeng	Northwest	華亭極塞, 蕃、漢雜居.	QSW 77:143
c.1030	Chengdu	Sichuan	聚眾山谷間, 與夷獠雜處, 非遠方所宜.	SS 301.10001
1041	Yongxingjun	Northwest	諸寨側近蕃部... 在近裏與漢户雜居.	QSW 18:218–19
1052	Guangnandong	Southwest	況蕃漢烏合, 其心不一, 力盡勢窮, 寧無疑貳?	QSW 42:9
1066	Zizhou	Sichuan	瀘爲兩蜀之藩,...夷漢錯居.	QSW 75:98
c.1068	Guangnanxi / Guangnandong	Southwest	交廣之地, 距京師幾萬里, 其民俗與山獠雜居.	QSW 67:283
1070	Yongxingjun	Northwest	塞下華戎錯居.	QSW 72:2
1078	Chengdu	Sichuan	蜀之郡邑類夷漢錯居.	QSW 84:203
1079	Chengdu	Sichuan	威、茂、黎三州夷夏雜居	XCB 296.7205; SHY *shihuo* 53.20; SS 176.4287
1080	Chengdu	Sichuan	[蠻人]與華人雜處.	QSW 120:242
1082	Zizhou	Sichuan	瀘州地方千里, 夷夏雜居.	XCB 331.7984; SHY *fanyi* 5.30
c.1086	Chengdu	Sichuan	邊徼之地, 夷漢雜處.	QSW 68:315
c.1087	Jinghubei	Southwest	民夷雜居.	QSW 93:365
c.1087	Guangnanxi	Southwest	欽、誠爲郡, 雖有新舊之異; 而民夷雜處, 不可一以華法治也.	QSW 93:365
c.1087	Zizhou	Sichuan	東蜀地嶮而民貧...而戎瀘被邊, 民夷雜居, 安之尤難.	QSW 93:373
c.1088	Qinfeng	Northwest	夷漢雜處.	QSW 85:218
1091	Jinghubei	Southwest	本州蠻漢雜居.	XCB 462.11031; SHY *fanyi* 5.92
1098	Guangnandong	Southwest	廣州蕃漢錯居.	QSW 132:24
c.1119	Zizhou	Sichuan	先朝念此地夷漢雜居.	SS 353.11154

As we will see in a subsequent chapter, these were people seen by many court elites as brethren of the Song Chinese, who would naturally support a Song *reconquista* out of a feeling of ethnic solidarity. In 1075, for example, Lü Dazhong described the "people beyond the mountains" (in Hedong) as individuals who "all have a heart that pines for the Middle Kingdom," and would fight alongside Song forces if war broke out.[115] Precisely such an attitude may have prompted one border prefect to disregard Song export restrictions on grain in order to alleviate a famine in Liao-controlled Hebei. When explaining his action, he stated quite simply that "they are also my people."[116]

Through the course of the border negotiations of the late eleventh century, however, there developed a deep ambivalence regarding the identity of these Liao Chinese, an ambivalence that fueled an alternative understanding of what it meant to be Chinese. The same population seen by some as the brethren of the Song population and that the border prefect considered to be "my people" became the "enemy" in other accounts. Such was the case of Liao borderlanders who crossed the border to fish or collect firewood. Some accounts described them as "enemy people."[117] Such was also the case with the Liao agriculturalists who encroached on Song farmland near Daizhou. The three farmers in question were undoubtedly ethnic Chinese.[118] Yet, in their accounts of the encroachments, Ouyang Xiu and others refer to the three as "foreigners," "caitiffs," or even "enemies."[119]

One particularly interesting example of the way in which a political border may produce a sense of national division involves Yan Fu, a Song man from the frontier region who at one point served as prefect of Shizhou and vice commissioner of the Crafts Institute.[120] Yan Fu worked closely with Han Zhen during the border negotiations with Liao in the mid-1070s. He became a chief target of criticism in Su Che's series of letters to court attacking Han Zhen, Cai Que

---

[115] XCB 260.6335.

[116] SS 324.10497; XCB 201.4883.

[117] E.g., XCB 205.4969–70.

[118] It is clear that the farmers are ethnoculturally Han by their names, by the fact that they are agriculturalists, and by the fact that there is no evidence of steppe material culture this far south (as demonstrated in Chapter 5).

[119] XCB 154.3749; SHY *bing* 27.36; *Ouyang Xiu quan ji*, 5:1762. In the SHY and *wenji* versions of Ouyang's memorial, the encroaching farmers are described in most cases as "caitiffs"; in the version in XCB (which frequently eliminates derogatory language), they are described as the "enemy." Bao Zheng refers to the encroachers as "foreign households." See QSW 26:45.

[120] For Yan's titles, see XCB 349.8367.

(1037–93), and other supporters of Wang Anshi's policies. According to Su:

> Recently, I have thrice submitted letters [to court] asking for the demotion of chief minister Han Zhen, but this has not yet been implemented. I observe that Zhen is crafty and treacherous beyond bounds . . . As for the demarcation of the border in Hedong, he arrogated all responsibility. I have heard that when Zhen was demarcating the border, he often discussed matters with that borderlander named Yan Fu. Fu advised him to accomplish the matter [quickly]. Taking 700 *li* of our ancestral land and handing it over to our foes was largely through the efforts of Fu. Fu was originally a local leader of the region straddling the Hedong border; many of his kinsmen are in the northern territory [under Liao control]. His mind cannot be fathomed.[121]

Yan Fu was a subject of the Song state and undoubtedly a Han Chinese. It was probably not uncommon to have kinsmen on the other side of the border, especially given that the Liao subjects of northern Hedong were also ethnic Han Chinese. For Su Che, however, Yan was unfathomable and so of uncertain loyalties precisely because of his cross-border ties. Su assumed that ethnic Chinese who lived under Liao control might have agendas that were at odds with the goals of the Song state; they were not the friends of Song China. Whereas ethnicity determined national loyalty on the Song–Xia frontier, for Su, it was not ethnicity that defined who was loyal to Song, but rather where one lived in relation to the demarcated border line.

The impact of political borders on senses of nationhood has been explored by historians of other places and times. Peter Sahlins, in a study of the French-Spanish border in the seventeenth through nineteenth centuries, has proposed a process by which a demarcated border line can itself lead to strong feelings of allegiance. Sahlins's focus was the border that traversed the Cerdagne, a valley in the Pyrenees whose population had once been homogeneous – practicing the same religion, speaking the same dialect of Catalan, and participating in a common social network. Yet when negotiators from Madrid and Paris decided to divide the valley in half, residents on either side of the border came gradually to identify strongly with the states to which they belonged. This transformation was not the result of a deliberate central-government-initiated campaign to promote national pride among its citizens, as other historians of France have argued. Instead, it was the result of a series of local disputes over

[121] XCB 369.8901–02.

property or other issues, disputes that locals deliberately turned into international incidents in order to take advantage of the state's desire to protect its sovereignty. The short-term goal for the locals was to gain the support of a powerful ally (the respective central government) to assist them in their own agendas; the long-term result after two centuries was the emergence of a strong sense of national identity among border populations. In other words, national identity was acquired through a process that did not depend on modern nationalism; it was a process that depended only on the existence of a strong central government willing to play an active role in defending its territorial sovereignty.[122]

It is tempting to imagine that just such a process can explain frontier dynamics in eleventh-century China. Perhaps encroachments by the three Liao farmers near Daizhou had originated as a series of local land disputes involving a few Liao and a few Song farmers; they became a topic at court precisely because Song farmers had found ways to manipulate the state into coming to their defense. One telling account (narrated by Su Che) involves a local strongman named Gao Zheng. After China gave up the sliver of territory in Hedong in 1076, several thousand Chinese households were forced to abandon their homes, their fields, their temples, and their ancestral tombs in order to relocate further south. Gao Zheng was particularly infuriated by this. In his later years, "whenever he encountered somebody discussing with him the perfidy of [Han] Zhen and Yan Fu, he would want to eat [the man's] flesh."[123] So passionate was Gao's fury that he was prepared not only to kill the proverbial messenger, but to eat him as well.

Unfortunately, all of these and other accounts of borders and borderlanders come to the historian today through the accounts of central government officials. The voices of the women and men who lived on the frontier have rarely survived. Thus, what we know about both Yan Fu and Gao Zheng comes from documents included in Su Che's collected works.[124] If one accepts that Gao and Yan Fu were both local strongmen inhabiting the frontier north of Daizhou, as Su's account would have us believe, then one can surmise that they may well have been rivals locally and that their rivalry ultimately had an impact on central government decision-making – as Sahlins's model might predict. What is more

[122] Sahlins, *Boundaries*.
[123] XCB 371.8988–89.
[124] A few additional references to these two men in XCB may have been inserted into the text by its author Li Tao to foreshadow (and therefore give support to) Su Che, whom Li clearly favored.

certain, however, is that Su Che's own attitudes were heavily influenced by the political border. A boundary line that cut across the North China Plain and severed both Hebei and Hedong in half, a boundary line that was deemed unnatural by many, was itself sufficient to transform the way in which some men at court imagined the people living to the north. Ordinary Chinese-speaking farmers who probably had very little stake or interest in the agendas of either the Song or Liao regimes, farmers who remained brethren of Song Chinese in the minds of court officials like Lü Dazhong, became men of uncertain loyalties – or even "enemies" – in the minds of others for no other reason than that they happened to reside or to have family members who resided on the wrong side of the border.

Conclusion

This chapter has sought to demonstrate that the international border established by the Treaty of Chanyuan in 1005 was part of a broader phenomenon. Especially under the activist regimes of the late Northern Song, the Chinese state became directly involved in a number of border demarcation projects along its northern and western frontiers and – to some extent – along its southern frontier as well. Moreover, beginning with the reign of Shenzong in the 1070s, border negotiations went well beyond mere delimitation – that is, simply the identification of rivers or mountain ranges that might serve as a natural boundary. Delimitation was a process that would have required much less effort on the part of the government. Instead, the Song court devoted great resources sending people out into the field to survey and map the border regions, then to mark the landscape with continuous ditches and lines of earthen mounds. It was this same tendency to micromanage the frontier that prompted the Song central government to take sides on property disputes involving individuals, such as the three Liao farmers Nie Zaiyou, Su Zhi, and Du Sirong.

To be sure, central government direct involvement in the frontier under the late Northern Song, and the border demarcation project in particular, shared features that we now associate with the modern international state system. It would be possible, then, for the account in this chapter to provide fodder for a vision of Song China as "early modern," a vision developed a century ago by the Japanese journalist and scholar Naitō Torajirō. But fitting China into such a narrative is not the point here. More interesting is to examine why the state took such an interest in clarifying the frontier at a particular moment in time, and then to explore the implications of border demarcation for Chinese political culture.

The demarcated borders themselves were tied to an alternative notion of sovereignty. An older understanding of China's place in the world, which remained very influential in the Song, derived from the concentric squares model described in Chapter 4. This was a model well suited to linear frontier defenses – most notably the Great Wall. The Great Wall was single-sided. It may have marked the limits of direct and effective military control, but nowhere was it implied that the territory of a neighboring state began immediately on the other side. By contrast, the demarcated borders of the late Northern Song were two-sided. Both neighboring states had rights to farm and herd on their own side of the border; and both states had responsibilities to prevent their people from crossing illegally into the other's territory. In speaking of the emergence in Song times of an East Asian world order, I previously focused on rhetoric and ritual protocol. As it turns out, these constituted only one component of an evolving pan-East Asian culture of international relations in which multiple states (probably largely though not exclusively under Chinese influence) came to share a common understanding of the rights and responsibilities of territorial sovereignty, of the hierarchical nature of inter-state relations, and even of the symbolic meaning of mounds and ditches – what I have called the "language of demarcation."

Demarcated borders also spurred an alternative sense of Chinese identity, in which inter-state boundaries – rather than ethnicity or culture – constituted the determining factor. The model of Chineseness described in the next chapter, a model based on history, ethnicity and culture, as well as the topography of the landscape, seems at times to have underpinned decisions about boundary demarcation with the Xia Kingdom in the far west. But although this model made sense in certain circumstances, it was not particularly useful when dealing with the sorts of tensions that arose among borderland populations along the Song–Liao border. As a result of specific instances of cross-border disputes, some policymakers at court came to imagine the Chinese speakers under Liao control as "enemies," fundamentally no different than their Khitan rulers. Imagining Liao Chinese as being both brethren and enemies was an obvious contradiction, a contradiction that reminds us that a society's understanding of the world and its place within it is rarely consistent and coherent.

What explains these eleventh-century developments? Two factors, it seems to me, were at the heart of the sudden interest in demarcation. First was the geopolitical situation. The Song–Liao border, as defined in 1005, cut across an agricultural zone with a sizable population of farmers. For this reason, it was inevitable that borderlanders would occasionally encroach on the territory of the neighboring state. In fact, agricultural encroachment was reported not only in Hedong, but also along some parts of the Song–Xia border, notably in a region straddling the Quye River in what is now northern Shaanxi Province.[125] Along China's southern frontier, Chinese-speaking agriculturalists also regularly encountered native farming communities.[126] In eras of Chinese history when China's northern frontier lay well beyond the agricultural zone – such as during much of the Tang Dynasty – there probably would have been little need to demarcate a border with such precision. In the eleventh century, demarcation seemed much more necessary.

But geopolitics is only part of the explanation. The Song central government had the option to ignore property disputes along the frontier. Families who chose to live in these regions might have been left to their own resources to deal with the hardships and conflicts they encountered. Or, alternatively, local officials could have handled minor property issues of these sorts without the intervention of bureaucrats in Kaifeng. It was not a coincidence that the state undertook an unprecedented demarcation project precisely when it was under the influence of ideologues committed to state activism to an unprecedented degree. The late Northern Song state was involved in the management of local society on a number of fronts. Whereas in later periods it was local elites who established and managed community granaries and local academies, institutions of this sort were organized by the state under the New Policies. Simultaneously, as Paul Smith has shown, the late Northern Song sought to make the state the "dominant actor in the commercial economy."[127] The central government at this time even sought to expand its influence over popular religion. Valerie Hansen has identified a surge in the granting of state enfeoffment edicts to local deities in the late eleventh century.[128] In such a political environment, state involvement in the nitty-gritty details of border demarcation made perfect sense. Although state activism was associated with expansionism, it also necessitated a clearer understanding of the state's boundaries, both to maximize state revenue and to maximize the ability of the state to control border populations.

---

[125] XCB 185.4469–71, 185.4476–78, 193.4679–80; SHY *bing* 27.41–45.

[126] On the distinction between the northern and southern frontiers, see Lattimore, "Frontier in History," 475–77; on native (non-Chinese) agriculture in the southwest, see Von Glahn, *Country of Streams and Grottoes*, esp. 26–33.

[127] P. J. Smith, "State Power and Economic Activism," 100. See also P. J. Smith, *Taxing Heaven's Storehouse*.

[128] Hansen, *Changing Gods*, 80–81.

PART II

Cultural Space

4

The Chinese Nation

In 1190, six decades after the Jurchen conquest of North China, the Southern Song official Huang Shang (1146–94), who had been appointed Mentor to a prince in line to the throne, presented to his charge a detailed map, carved onto wood, of the territories of past dynasties.[1] Besides labeling the prefectural seats, the mapmaker had carefully drawn dozens of the most important rivers, mountains, and mountain ranges, as well as a remarkably accurate coastline, from Hainan Island in the south to the Liaodong peninsula in the north. Appended to this map was a lengthy colophon explaining in explicit terms the map's purpose. By gazing upon it, the viewer "might be moved, might be filled with indignation, but might also be spurred into action." More specifically, Huang went on to explain, the map would lead the viewer to contemplate the disastrous loss of North China:

> It has long been the case that the territory of the Central Plains included Yan in the north, with the Great Wall marking the boundary. It was only during the Five Dynasties that Shi Jingtang [founding emperor of the Later Jin] abandoned the Sixteen Prefectures and offered them to the Khitans. It has been over three hundred years [since then], and [this territory] has yet to be returned to our possession . . . And now, east of the passes [in Western Shaanxi] and south of the Yellow River, a myriad miles of contiguous territory are in rebel [i.e., Jurchen] hands . . . How can one not shed tears and sigh deeply because of this? This surely fills one with indignation!

Huang's map was striking for several reasons, first and foremost its chief objective – to inspire irredentist passions. Historians typically associate irredentism of this sort more with the world of the nineteenth and twentieth centuries than with twelfth-century China. To be sure, Huang himself may have imagined a future emperor as the chief viewer of his map.

---

[1] For images of Huang's map, see Cao Wanru et al. (eds.), *Zhongguo gudai ditu ji*, pls. 70–72; for a study and transcription of the colophon, see Qian and Yao, "*Dili tu* bei."

A few decades later, however, in 1247, an official serving in Suzhou had the map and colophon carved onto a stele – a stele that stands to this day – "in order to maintain its transmission." Once on a stele, the map and its message would have circulated via rubbings to a broader audience. Another noteworthy feature of the map was the colophon's particular emphasis on the territorial claim to the Sixteen Prefectures. Unlike the lands south of the Yellow River seized by the Jurchens, the Sixteen Prefectures – a region straddling the northern extremity of the North China Plain – was lost to the Khitans before the founding of the Song. Asking to have it "returned to our possession" made sense only insofar as the pronoun "our" referred not merely to the Song state, but rather to a political entity that transcended dynasties.

Huang's map was, of course, the product of a particular cultural context. The irredentist cause garnered wide support among twelfth- and thirteenth-century scholar officials. The most important classical scholars and moral philosophers, from the Neo-Confucian Zhu Xi (1130–1200) to the "utilitarian" Confucians Chen Liang (1143–94) and Ye Shi (1150–1223), pushed for a military reconquest of Jurchen-occupied North China.[2] Numerous poets of the Southern Song – notably Lu You (1125–1210), Yang Wanli (1127–1206), and Xin Qiji (1140–1207) – zealously promoted the irredenta in their verse.[3] Indeed, these poets are remembered to this day as great patriots of the nation. It is common for historians to portray Southern Song irredentism as an inevitable response to the Jurchen invasion. Yet such a conclusion fails to explain why other invasions in earlier times – the steppe nomadic conquests of the fourth century and the Shatuo Turk invasion of North China in the tenth century – did not have a similar impact on Chinese political culture. In fact, it is the contention of this chapter that the Jurchen invasion could elicit such passionate irredentism only because of important conceptual developments during the Northern Song. It was during the eleventh century, well before the Jurchens appeared on the scene, that one first encounters among Chinese elites a national consciousness, as well as a sense that the national territory possessed fixed boundaries.

The previous three chapters dealt with what one might refer to as "political space." Specific political and geopolitical circumstances – the particular configuration of the Song–Liao border, for example, as well as the commitment to state activism in the Wang Anshi and post-Wang

---

[2] Tillman, *Utilitarian Confucianism*, 169–80; De Weerdt, *Competition over Content*, 97–102.
[3] Davis, "Wind against the Mountain," 152–57.

Anshi eras – transformed China's interactions with its neighbors, by driving developments in the East Asian state system, in Chinese military strategy, and in the administration of borders and border lines. This and the following two chapters turn to what one might call "cultural space," focusing on the ways in which Song elites came to conceive in new ways the political entity to which they belonged. Peter Bol, in discussing how Song intellectuals conceptualized the spatial limits of the imperium, emphasized the importance of two factors: geography and culture.[4] From this perspective, the authority of the emperor in theory (if perhaps not in reality) extended to the boundary between the lands under civil administration – where the moral principles inculcated by classical scholarship held sway – and those under tribal control. Alongside geography and culture was a third factor: ethnicity. As they struggled to make sense of the new multi-state system of the eleventh century, Song policymakers also began to exploit ethnic categories originating on the Eurasian steppe. It was the three factors operating in unison that together defined a Song form of the Chinese nation.

Pre-Song Conceptualizations

Table 4.1 proposes a model for understanding the development over time of how educated elites imagined the politico-cultural entity in which they lived. To facilitate the comparative study of nationalisms, the table focuses on elements identifiable in the way the nation-state has been conceived in modern times. As such, the table excludes certain ways in which China was imagined that are irrelevant to twentieth-century conceptualizations, for example, those based on theories of cosmic boundaries described later in the chapter. The goal is not to suggest inevitable teleological progression toward the modern nation-state, but rather to suggest that component traits of modern nationalism could and did develop in premodern times under certain conditions. It should be stressed that the elements listed in Table 4.1 belong to the world of ideas. Taking element 5 as an example, the implication is that educated elites of the Song Dynasty believed that individuals they identified as ethnic "Han people" felt loyalty to the transdynastic entity in question. We do not know if the masses of the population really felt such loyalty, or even identified themselves by the ethnonym *Han*. In addition, the table lists a set of ideas

---

[4] Bol, "Geography and Culture."

Table 4.1 *Development of a Chinese form of nationalism (showing date of first prevalence among Chinese elites of nine component elements)*

Date	Component element	Conceptualization of polity
Pre-Song	1. Set apart from the rest of the world by a distinctive culture.	
Pre-Song	2. Destined to be unified under a single political regime.	Civilized World
Pre-Song	3. Transdynastic, outliving the regimes that temporarily control it.	
Northern Song	4. Populated by a defined ethnic group sharing a common descent, as well as a common language and culture.	
Northern Song	5. Members of this defined ethnic group expected to feel loyalty to the transdynastic entity (and not just to the monarch or to the dynasty).	
Northern Song	6. Can be clearly defined geographically on the basis of the territorial extent of historical dynasties, as well as the geographic range of the majority ethnic group.	Nation-State
Northern Song	7. "Former" territory (even if lost under a previous dynasty) should be recovered, by military force if necessary.	
Northern Song	8. Homogeneous as a space ("sinic space").	
Southern Song	9. Lends itself to symbolic evocation that can arouse passionate responses.	

that was never systematized into a coherent vision; these were ideas that began to circulate at certain periods of time, and subsequently popped up in political discourse only on occasion and somewhat haphazardly. Here, I will outline the key pre-Song developments, before devoting the remainder of the chapter to the Song period.

One can point to three critical developments affecting how educated elites in pre-Song times imagined the place in the world of their polity and their culture. The first involved a heightened sense of cultural distinctiveness (element 1 in Table 4.1), reflected in the development of a discourse contrasting the civilized world with the world of the barbarians.[5] Immediately after the founding of the Zhou state in the middle of the eleventh century BCE, the Zhou kings – based in the Wei and Yellow river valleys of what is now North China – were able to establish relatives and allies as hereditary lords in a broad swathe of territory extending from the northern reaches of the North China Plain to the Yangzi river valley in the south. In subsequent generations, the Zhou kings gradually lost political influence over the hereditary lords, a process culminating in the emergence of the numerous independent states of the Spring and Autumn (770–481 BCE) and Warring States (480–221 BCE) periods. Nevertheless, they retained a symbolic significance as the head of a Zhou ritual order. The hegemony of Zhou rituals may have originated in the propaganda value of inscribed ritual bronze vessels.[6] It was reinforced by the educated men who circulated among the various courts to advise the hereditary lords. Over time, some neighboring peoples once deemed to be "barbarians" were incorporated – either voluntarily or by force – into the Zhou ecumene.[7] Excavated tombs suggest that the homogenization of elite culture was followed by a homogenization of the culture of the lower classes as well. Meanwhile, pastoral nomads, with their radically distinct way of life, began occupying a northern zone on China's immediate periphery, leading to an ever sharper cultural boundary at the margins of the Zhou world. It was precisely at this time – in the middle of the first millennium BCE – that there emerged in Chinese political culture a new discourse contrasting the "barbarians" of the four directions with the Zhou ecumene, in essence between the lands where the Zhou rituals were performed properly and the lands where they were not performed at all. The distinction, however, was not between "China" and foreign lands, but rather between the "civilized" center and the "uncivilized" lands on the periphery. Unresolved was the question

---

[5] The discussion that follows is based on Li Feng, *Landscape and Power*; Falkenhausen, *Chinese Society*, 163–288; Di Cosmo, *Ancient China and its Enemies*, 44–126.

[6] Many bronze inscriptions reproduce appointment letters and other political documents, thereby commemorating ties between the families owning the vessels and the Zhou regime. A few inscriptions (e.g., Shi Qiang *pan* and Yu Qiu *pan*) go a step further by drawing an explicit parallel between the status and power of the family over several generations and the illustrious rule of several generations of Zhou kings. As the texts of these inscriptions were probably intoned during the periodic performance of ancestral rituals, family members would have been recurrently reminded both of their dependence on the Zhou kings for their status and of the emerging myth (which survived into the twentieth century) that the early Zhou kings had ruled over a golden age. For translations of the Shi Qiang *pan* and Yu Qiu *pan*, see Shaughnessy, *Sources of Western Zhou History*, 104; Shaughnessy, "Writing of a Late Western Zhou Bronze Inscription," 852–54.

[7] Di Cosmo, *Ancient China and its Enemies*, 126; Pines, "Beasts or Humans," 85–87.

of whether the distinction was primarily cultural – in which case those classified as "barbarians" could be transformed into civilized people – or whether it was primarily biological. Indeed, the issue of whether it was possible to civilize the "barbarians" repeatedly plagued policymakers in the mid and late imperial periods.[8]

A second important conceptual innovation, also dating to the pre-imperial period, was the idea of "grand unity" (*dayitong* or *yitong*) – that is, the notion that civilization ought to be ruled by a single lord (element 2 in Table 4.1).[9] Throughout the imperial period, this widely shared political ideal legitimated dynastic founders seeking to reunify the Chinese ecumene.[10] When translated into the language of the nation-state in the twentieth century, it provided the basis for the claim by nationalist historians that a unified China was the norm, whereas a disunited China was an aberration. The ideal of unity emerged no later than the early third century BCE. At the time, the Zhou world was divided into independent states that fought each other nearly continuously. Unity represented a solution to the devastating warfare of the period. Political philosophers described "grand unity" in near utopic terms, both in terms of the peace and stability that the "true king" would bring to the world, and in terms of a symbolic ordering of the world through the standardization of weights and measures, of axle gauges, and of the writing system. The influence of this particular utopic vision was such that, when the king of Qin succeeded in 221 BCE in unifying the former Zhou world for the first time under a strongly centralized regime, he consciously performed the role of the "true king" by unifying the weights, measures, and written script.[11] Though "grand unity" remained a foundation of Chinese political philosophy in later times, a counter discourse emerged shortly after the founding of the Qin, once it was realized that a unified empire gave rise

[8] For an eighteenth-century debate between partisans of "ethnic quarantine" on the Qing empire's southwestern frontier (on the grounds that civilizing non-Chinese was impossible) and partisans of "assimilation," see Sutton, "Ethnicity and the Miao Frontier."

[9] The discussion that follows is based primarily on Nylan, "Rhetoric of 'Empire'"; Pines, *Everlasting Empire*, 16–25.

[10] Pines, *Everlasting Empire*, 11–12.

[11] Evidence of a Qin standardization campaign is evident in the archaeological record. Standardized bronze weights and measures dating to the Qin have been found at sites all over China; standardization of the script is evident in excavated documents making use of a new Qin imperial calligraphic style. That the standardization campaign constituted a conscious effort by the Qin First Emperor to emulate the "true king" is implied by how both a contemporaneous imperial inscription and an account dating to just over a century after unification describe the campaign, using language that is nearly verbatim to the call for standardization in the writings of late Warring States political theorists. See Chen Zhaorong, "Qin 'shu tong wenzi'"; Tackett, "Qin Script Reform."

to a new set of problems. The alternative to "grand unity" was *fengjian* – often translated somewhat loosely as "feudalism" – in which the Chinese world was to be apportioned out to regional lords loyal to the emperor. Nostalgia for the pre-unification Zhou order in the form of *fengjian* discourse was resurrected repeatedly throughout history, most recently by Chinese federalists of the early twentieth century.[12]

A third important pre-Song development involved the notion held by educated Chinese that they belonged to something that transcended dynasties (element 3 in Table 4.1).[13] Although there was always an expectation that subjects of a dynasty ought to maintain allegiance to the house they served, political loyalty of this sort did not preclude a sense of belonging simultaneously to something greater than the dynasty. The founder of the Qin Dynasty apparently did not imagine that his political regime would ever come to an end. After unifying what he took to be the entire civilized world, he boldly proclaimed that he had ushered in a new era that would last ten thousand generations.[14] Later emperors did not exhibit such hubris. By the Sui and Tang, it was understood that all states rose and fell, as Heaven's Mandate was transferred from one dynasty to the next. Both the Sui and Tang were seen as successors of the Han; the Song, in turn, was seen as the successor to the Han and Tang.[15] Numerous ambitious scholarly projects of the Tang and Song were transdynastic in conception, surveying the institutions or the history of all of recorded time.[16] Educated elites, in their own genealogical writings, traced their lineages back to ancestors who had served under numerous earlier dynasties.[17] The continuity of elite families, of state institutions, and of the imperial system were not bound by the temporal limits of individual political regimes.

Models of the Cosmos

The discussion so far has focused on elements of Chinese identity that are still recognizable in how the Chinese nation-state is imagined to this day. Here, I describe a set of important conceptual models describing China's place within the cosmos, in this case models that would not

[12] Duara, *Rescuing History*, 147–204.
[13] On the emergent idea of China as a "transdynastic spatiocultural entity," see Bol, "Geography and Culture."
[14] Bodde, "State and Empire of Ch'in," 53–54.
[15] On the Sui seeing itself as successor to the Han, see A. F. Wright, *Sui Dynasty*, 8; on the Song as successor to the Han and Tang, see Chapter 1 above.
[16] Bol, "Geography and Culture," 5.
[17] Tackett, *Destruction*, 27–44.

survive into the twentieth century, but that are nevertheless important for understanding the context in which a sense of nation developed. These cosmographic models developed for the most part in the Han through Tang periods, and they remained influential in Song times. Many of them were rooted in canonical literature. According to the "Canon of Yao" chapter of the *Book of Documents*, the civilized world was defined initially by the mythological Emperor Shun when he "delimited the Twelve Provinces." The subsequent "Tribute of Yu" chapter alludes to an alternative division into Nine Provinces.[18] By their association with Shun and Yu, two of the greatest sage rulers of antiquity, the Nine and the Twelve Provinces became in later times standard means of referring to the proper geographic extent of a unified empire.[19]

In the hands of Warring States and Han thinkers, these fundamental spatiocultural notions were integrated into geometrical models of the cosmos. One model reflected an emerging interest in the quasi-magical properties of the nonary square. The special significance of this three-by-three grid is reflected elsewhere in the mythical well-field system of antiquity, in the layout of capital cities, in the floor plan of the Bright Hall (*mingtang*) at the imperial capital, and in the pattern appearing on certain bronze mirrors of the Han period. Indeed, the entire cosmos was seen by some as composed of a nested hierarchy of grids, whereby the Nine Provinces occupied one of nine subparts of one of nine continents.[20] The Twelve Provinces were integrated into a different cosmological model, the "field allocation" (*fenye*) system, which mapped constellations and Heavenly bodies onto corresponding points on earth, by means of a set of correlations between the Twelve Provinces, the twenty-eight lunar mansions, the twelve earthly branches, and the twelve Jupiter stations.[21] These correlations are frequently alluded to in Tang and Song sources, as when a court official made use of them in 986 to predict the proper planetary alignment for a successful Song invasion of Yan.[22]

---

[18] Karlgren, "Book of Documents," 5, 12–17.

[19] In Tang times and later, nearly all geographical treatises allude to the Nine and Twelve Provinces. For graphical depictions, see *Songben lidai dili zhizhang tu*, 12–15; Tang Zhongyou, *Diwang jingshi tupu*, 5.1a–2b. For the use of these models to justify an irredentist agenda, see QSW 123:87–89. It should be remembered that the "Canon of Yao" and "Tribute of Yu" are late additions to the corpus, dating to no earlier than the third century BCE. See Nylan, *Five "Confucian" Classics*, 134.

[20] Major, "Five Phases"; Henderson, "Chinese Cosmographical Thought"; Lewis, *Construction of Space*, esp. 245–84.

[21] Fang Xuanling, et al., *Jin shu*, 11.307–09.

[22] According to the official, "Between late spring of this year and next year, Jupiter will be in the Song sector [of the sky]; between early fall of this year and the year 989, Saturn will be in

While the Nine and Twelve Provinces provided a way to understand the civilized world, they revealed nothing about the nature of the frontier, nor of the lands beyond. An alternative model, also rooted in the *Book of Documents*, envisioned the earth as composed of five (or, in some later versions, nine) concentric squares radiating outward from the imperial center – the "royal domain," the "vassals' domain," the "pacified zone," the "zone of allied tribes," and the "wilderness zone."[23] By no later than the Han Dynasty, this concentric square framework was further imbued with a moral significance, reflecting the diminishing influence of the Son of Heaven's ethical and cultural sway as one distanced oneself from the capital. The principle of declining levels of civilization implied by these "Five Zones of Submission" was subsequently combined with a *qi*-based metaphysics to explain the link between geography and culture. Thus, several treatises dating to the Tang Dynasty – including by the prominent scholars Cen Wenben (595–645) and Du You (735–812) – posited that pure or correct *qi* at the imperial center produced humane and moral individuals, whereas impure or "blocked" *qi* in the peripheral zones led to barbarism.[24]

Another model of the frontier – which seems to have originated in Han times and to have become prevalent by Tang and Song times – imagined that Heaven had bounded the empire on all four sides with natural frontiers.[25] Such frontiers fit in nicely with earlier geometric models that envisioned both the empire and the world at large as square in shape. Thus, when the minister Di Renjie (629–700) sought to discourage Empress Wu from pursuing her project of military expansion, he invoked the idea of natural physiographic boundaries:

> I have heard that when Heaven created the four barbarian tribes, they were all situated outside of the realm of the ancient kings. Thus, they were blocked by the Deep Blue Sea to the east; divided by the Flowing Sands to the west; bordered by the Great Desert to the north; and impeded by the

---

the Yan sector." See SS 432.12828. For other Tang-Song references to these correlations, see Schafer, *Pacing the Void*, 75–84; Shi Jie, *Culai Shi xiansheng wenji*, 10.116; Tang Zhongyou, *Diwang jingshi tupu*, 6.8a–8b, 6.11a–15b; *Songben lidai dili zhizhang tu*, 80–83.

[23] Karlgren, "Book of Documents," 18; Yü Ying-Shih, "Han Foreign Relations," 379–81; Needham and Wang, *Mathematics*, 501–02; Bol, "Creating a GIS," 33.

[24] Shao-yun Yang, "Reinventing the Barbarian," 20–23, 103. One finds renewed discussion of *qi*-based theories of environmental determinism in the Southern Song, in response to Jurchen rule over the Chinese heartland in the north. See Tillman, "Proto-Nationalism"; Shao-yun Yang, "Reinventing the Barbarian," 330–32.

[25] For examples from the Han Dynasty, see Shao-yun Yang, "Reinventing the Barbarian," 15–16.

Five Peaks to the south. This is the means by which Heaven has separated [us from] the barbarians and divided inside from outside.[26]

A century and a half later, the prominent statesman Li Deyu (787–849) made a similar assertion: "Heaven and Earth have separated north from south by means of deserts, mountains, and rivers . . . How could we dare violate the boundaries of Heaven and Earth?"[27] Northern Song officials invoked these natural frontiers as well, albeit probably more out of concern for Northern Song geopolitical vulnerability than out of a desire to stymie advocates of military expansionism. Li Ruchi (fl. 1120s), for example, spoke of deserts and rivers as "that by which Heaven has delineated inner from outer and separated north from south."[28] Earlier in the dynasty, the scholar and statesman Shi Jie (1005–45), troubled by Khitan control of the passes north of Yan, elaborated on this same idea in a poem entitled "Stirred by Circumstances":

> I have once examined the Central Plains,
> The terrain of which is flat as a whetstone.
> Myriads of miles in circumference,
> It is criss-crossed by the ruts of horse carts.
> The imperial palace is situated at its center,
> Much like the [Palace of] Purple Tenuity, which serves
>   as the pinnacle of the celestial bodies.
> The Yangzi River blocks off the south;
> The frontier passes lie across the north;
> To the east is the sea and to the west the Flowing Sands:
> Heaven has used these to separate out the barbarians.[29]

A previous chapter explored the impact of the loss of the "frontier passes" on Northern Song military decision-making. Here we discover the fundamental cosmic significance of this natural topographic boundary.

Whereas all of these models of the world remained popular in later times, there emerged by the Tang-Song period a new interest in reconciling speculations about the cosmos with observed physiographic features of the landscape.[30] Perhaps the most systematically developed theory of this sort was the Two Boundaries model propounded by the Buddhist monk Yixing (682–727). Yixing focused on two rivers – the Yellow and

---

[26] JTS 89.2889.
[27] QTW 699:7182; Drompp, *Tang China*, 230.
[28] Li Ruchi, *Dongyuan congshuo*, 62.
[29] Shi Jie, *Culai Shi xiansheng wenji*, 3.24.
[30] Needham and Wang, *Mathematics*, 544–45; Henderson, *Development and Decline*, 70.

the Yangzi – and on two east–west mountain ranges, which he termed the Northern Boundary and the Southern Boundary. The Northern Boundary began in the west in the form of the Qilian Mountains lining the southern side of the Gansu Corridor. It then joined the Qinling Mountains separating North China from Hubei and the Sichuan Basin, crossed the Yellow River near Mount Hua at the mouth of the Wei River, and continued along the hills of southern Shanxi. Finally, it took a northward course along the Taihang Mountains, before turning eastward to run along the Yan Mountains. According to Yixing, this chain of mountain ranges was "that by which we are separated from the barbarians of the west and north." The Southern Boundary – "that by which we are separated from the barbarians of the south and east" – circled around the Sichuan Basin before following a course through South China and terminating on the Fujian coast.[31]

Though Yixing himself died two and a half centuries before the founding of the Song, it was, in fact, only in the Song that one begins to find references to the physiographic model attributed to him. Biographical and other anecdotal references to Yixing that date to the tenth century and earlier mention only his expertise in astronomy and calendrical studies.[32] The earliest discussion of his Two Boundaries theory appears in the eleventh-century *New Tang History*.[33] Subsequently, the theory was alluded to in a variety of scholarly genres, including maps of the empire, encyclopedias, and works of classical exegesis.[34] Interest in the Two Boundaries – especially the Northern Boundary – may have been linked to concerns about the Song empire's geopolitical vulnerabilities. But it is also worth noting that the popularization of Yixing's theory coincided with an era when large numbers of prominent men, through their diplomatic service, had opportunities to view firsthand the striking topography of East and Northeast Asia. The new empirical knowledge of geography that they acquired helps explain the remarkable degree to

[31] XTS 31.817.
[32] E.g., JTS 191.5111–13; Li Fang, et al., *Taiping guangji*, 92.608–10, 136.974–75, 140.1009, 149.1072, 215.1647–48, 228.1749, 396.3164. Dunhuang documents also emphasize Yixing's astrological expertise; see Mollier, *Buddhism and Taoism*, 141–43, 214. I was unable to find pre-Song references to the Two Boundaries model.
[33] XTS 31.817.
[34] Tang Zhongyou, *Diwang jingshi tupu*, 6.4a–7a; *Songben lidai dili zhizhang tu*, 84–85; Wang Yinglin, *Yuhai*, 20.26a–28b; Zhang Ruyu, *Qunshu kaosuo*, 59.6b–7a; Lin Zhiqi, *Shangshu quanjie*, 10.4a–4b. In addition, Fang Yue (1199–1262) thrice mentions his strong emotional response to viewing a map of Yixing's Two Boundaries (which depicted land then under Mongol control). See QSW 341:399, 342:64; Fang Yue, *Qiuya shici jiaozhu*, 35:601.

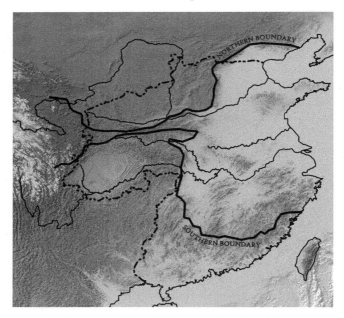

Figure 4.1 Yixing's "Two Boundaries" model
This map approximates the course of the Northern and Southern Boundaries as they
appear on a map of Yixing's Two Boundaries model dating to 1201. See Tang Zhongyou,
Diwang jingshi tupu, 80.

which Song-era maps of Yixing's Two Boundaries adhered to the contours of modern topographic maps (Figure 4.1).

What does one make of these various models of the cosmos? First, it is important to note that, though they were invoked by educated elites in a variety of circumstances – in poetry, in essays, in political debates – there were no attempts to systematize them into a single coherent theory. Models derived from an empirical study of physiography coexisted uneasily with speculative models based on squares or other geometric forms. The Nine Provinces, composed of nine distinct geographic regions arranged in a three-by-three grid, were difficult to reconcile with cosmic theories based on concentric zones of ever diminishing cultural influence.[35] In fact, the various cosmic models in circulation by Song times constituted a good example of how discourses operate. In particular social

[35] On the contradictions between these two models, see Bol, "Creating a GIS," 32.

and political circumstances, members of a society can turn to a repertoire of different ideas and notions, like tools in a tool chest, all deemed legitimate even if they do not fit together into a coherent whole. In much the same way, the component ideas in Table 4.1 were never brought together into a single theory of the nation, though they circulated broadly in elite society, rearing their heads on occasion when needed to construct a convincing argument at court, or to tie together in a compelling manner several lines of literary verse.

Second, the Chinese were, of course, not the only people to devise models to explain their place in the cosmos. Whereas the more speculative theories – *qi* metaphysics, for example – were particular to Chinese or East Asian culture, theories derived from empirical observation or from direct engagement with the human or physical world might coincide with ideas articulated in far-removed societies. Consider this description of the Pyrenees on the Franco-Spanish border, written in 1785 by a French royal geographer:

> Nature, itself, has placed the boundary markers that are to separate forever more France from Spain . . . Following the natural division of the world established from the very beginning by the Creator, all lands in which the rivers enter France must constitute part of this kingdom; and those in which the rivers flow into Spain must constitute part of the states of that power.[36]

Like Yixing's understanding of mountain ranges as separating the Chinese from the people beyond the pale, and Li Ruchi and Shi Jie's assertion that it was "Heaven" that had positioned physiographic elements in order to partition the earth, here, too, we find in this French articulation of the notion of natural frontiers the claim that an impersonal but moral divinity – in this case, the "unmoved mover" of the deists of the Enlightenment rather than the Heaven of Chinese classical scholars – had laid out a plan for the division of the world that humans were in no place to dispute. It is easy to see why Chinese and French ideas were so similar; both were derived from a similar human response to the awe-inspiring sight of mountains rising dramatically on the horizon. The Chinese and European natural boundaries theories shared one more common feature – in both cases, the idea of natural frontiers was rejected in the twentieth century, rendered irrelevant after the globalization of modern nationalist ideology.[37]

---

[36] Nordman, *Frontières de France*, 65.
[37] Sahlins, "Natural Frontiers Revisited," 1450–51.

Han Ethnicity

What we have seen so far is a variety of ideas circulating among Chinese literati that first emerged in the pre-Song period but remained important in later times. Educated elites came to imagine the existence of some sort of transdynastic entity ideally governed by a single emperor and imperial court; and they developed a variety of cosmic models to explain how it fit into the world at large. However, this entity prior to the Song Dynasty is better understood as "civilization" rather than as "China." The idea of the emperor as ruler of the civilized world would persist in political discourse until the early twentieth century. Beginning in the Song Dynasty, however, this understanding of imperial sovereignty came to exist alongside a new sense that transdynastic China was properly defined by a single ethnoculture and by a fixed geographic extent. To the degree that this new political discourse conflated the state both with the nation (i.e., the ethnoculture) and with the national territory, one can speak of the birth of the Chinese nation-state as an idea. In what follows, I will treat, in sequence, how Chinese political elites during the Northern Song came to imagine Han ethnicity, Han ethnic solidarity, and Han territory (elements 4 through 8 in Table 4.1).

Though historians have sometimes questioned the appropriateness of deploying ethnicity as a category of analysis for the premodern period, there is nothing about the classic anthropological studies of ethnicity that suggests it is a phenomenon limited to the modern condition. Ethnic categories are socially constructed on the basis of plausible ethnic markers. They are transactional – meaning that they emerge and are reinforced in the course of social transactions between groups, when they serve a useful social or political purpose. They change over time, such that groups identified by a particular ethnonym today are not necessarily the biological descendants of a historical group with the same name.[38] Simultaneously, they involve "primordial attachments," to use Geertz's term, not in the sense that they derive directly from objective cultural (or genetic) boundaries, but in the sense that they are imagined by participants to be deeply rooted, determined by claims of descent (fictive or not) from a common ancestor.[39] In most of the subsequent discussion, I focus on ethnic

---

[38] E.g., Harrell, "History of the History of the Yi."
[39] Barth, "Introduction"; Geertz, "Integrative Revolution"; Keyes, "Dialectics of Ethnic Change." Geertz's use of the expression "primordial attachments" has sometimes been misconstrued to imply he believed ethnic categories were objectively determined, rather than socially constructed.

categories imagined by Chinese elites, especially policymakers at court.[40] Even before the Song, it is clear there was a sense among educated elites that there existed cultural boundaries between Chinese and non-Chinese, boundaries that one might term ethnic in nature.[41] Nevertheless, there were two important developments in the Song. First was the politicization of ethnicity, whereby the Chinese state came to see itself as closely tied to a single ethnicity, the Han people. Second was a shift in how cultural difference was conceptualized, a shift toward greater emphasis on ancestry rather than geography or environment as determinative of an individual's cultural characteristics.

It is commonly observed that the Tang incorporated foreigners into the imperial system to a far greater degree than the Song. It is for this reason that the Tang – and not the Song – has been labeled a "cosmopolitan empire." Most striking of all were the military men of non-Chinese origin serving in the Tang imperial army. But besides military men, many civilian officials also had non-Chinese ancestries. Numerous families producing chief ministers in the Tang period, for example, had origins on the Eurasian steppe. A number of Korean and Japanese are also known to have traveled to Tang China to serve in the bureaucracy.[42] And there are well-documented examples of the Tang court resettling foreigners within Tang territory. Early in the dynasty, 100,000 Turkish tribesmen were relocated to the Ordos region, on what was then the northern frontier, while close to 10,000 Turkish families were moved to the Tang capital.[43] In addition, as attested by excavated documents from the

---

[40] One might also expect non-elite frontier Chinese populations to have developed a strong awareness of ethnic boundaries as a result of personal encounters with pastoral nomads, though it is difficult to ascertain whether or not their ethnic categories were the same (e.g., based on the same ethnic markers) as those imagined by the sociopolitical elite at the capital.

[41] Abramson, *Ethnic Identity*. As suggested below, in Tang times, cultural difference was more frequently attributed to environment than to descent. Whether or not "ethnicity" existed in Tang elite discourse depends to some degree on whether one's definition of the term requires a claim of common descent.

[42] Holcombe, "Immigrants and Strangers." For chief ministers with steppe ancestries, see XTS 71a.2273, 71b.2289, 71b.2403, 72a.2409, 72b.2818, 75b.3379, 75b.3401, 75b.3437. For ninth-century epitaphs identifying individuals with non-Chinese ancestries, including Persians, Sogdians, Särbi, Turks, Uighurs, Xi, Tibetans, and Koreans, see QTW 505.5140–42, 543.5510–12, 566.5725; Chen Shangjun (ed.), *Quan Tang wen bubian*, 890–92; Guo Maoyu and Zhao Zhenhua, "Tang Shi Xiaozhang muzhi yanjiu"; Mao Yangguang, "Xinjian si fang"; Rong Xinjiang, *Zhonggu Zhongguo*, 238–57; Tackett, "Transformation of Medieval Chinese Elites," 60–61; Wu Gang (ed.), *Quan Tang wen buyi*, 1:282–86, 2:583, 3:143, 3:254–55, 5:36–38, 6:493, 7:414–15; Wu Qingjun and Liu Debiao, "Tangdai Yuan Yun muzhi qianshuo"; Zhou Shaoliang and Zhao Chao (eds.), *Tangdai muzhi huibian*, 2:2110.

[43] Shao-yun Yang, "Reinventing the Barbarian," 57–64; Skaff, *Sui-Tang China*, 55–58.

Turfan region in the far northwest, Sogdian households during the Tang were integrated into the state-regulated land tenure system, as well as the recruitment system for labor and military service.[44]

The Song, by contrast, was very different on all of these points. Song sources make few references to foreign generals or troops in the service of the dynasty, with the singular exception of the Tibetan militias in the northwest (discussed in Chapter 2). In addition, Song sources rarely advertise the non-Chinese backgrounds of civilian officials. In fact, contemporaneous historians looked back on foreign elements in the Tang regime with little approbation. The Neo-Confucian Huang Zhen (1213–80) saw a direct link between foreigners in the military and the decline of the Tang regime: "The Tang, throughout the dynasty, made use of foreign generals (*fanjiang*); then there was the disaster of the An Lushan Rebellion."[45] Indeed, by the Southern Song, many saw civilian officials with foreign backgrounds as an unfortunate long-term conse-quence of the lengthy occupation of North China by the Northern Wei (386–534) and its successor dynasties – founded by the Tabgach, a Särbi (Xianbei) clan from Manchuria. In the view of the thirteenth-century historian Hu Sanxing (1230–1302), a substantial proportion of the great aristocratic families of the Sui and Tang were suspect due to their mixed Särbi-Chinese ancestries:

> After Tabgach Gui rose to power, the characteristic differences between the north and the south became fixed. As soon as the characteristics of the north and the south had become fixed, the south was annexed by the north [i.e., by the Sui]. Alas! After the Sui Dynasty, six to seven tenths of those attaining [political] prominence were descendants of Daibei [tribesmen]; what then was the point of ranking the great families?[46]

In fact, Song-era commentators drew a far sharper distinction between the Tang and the Song than was warranted. As noted in Chapter 2, the founding Song emperors, as well as many of the generals fighting alongside them, were probably themselves of mixed ancestry. This fact is rarely mentioned in Song period sources only because these sources were produced by historians convinced that the territory of their empire was properly inhabited by ethnic Chinese.[47] Whereas the Tang recog-nized itself as a universal or multinational empire, the Song saw itself as

---

[44] Skaff, "Sogdian Trade Diaspora."
[45] Huang Zhen, *Gujin jiyao*, 9.5a.
[46] ZZTJ 108.3429.
[47] Deng Xiaonan, "Lun Wudai Song chu 'huhan.'"

a monoethnic state, even if it took some manipulation of the historical record to live up to this image of itself. This particular self-conception helps explain a number of phenomena, from how the Song determined the precise course of inter-state boundaries (see Chapter 3), to the decision in one instance to cleanse recently conquered territory of its non-Chinese population (see below), to concerns about the integration of Tibetan tribesmen and tribal militia troops on the northwestern frontier, to the conviction that ethnically Han regimes like the Song were fundamentally incapable of fielding effective cavalry armies (see Chapter 2).[48]

Besides the politicization of ethnicity, there was a second important development in the Song: the expanded use of the ethnonym *Han* – the term used to this day to designate the majority ethnic group in China – a development tied to a change in emphasis in the root factors believed to determine differences between peoples.[49] Originally used to refer to the Han Dynasty, *Han* began to serve as an ethnic designator during the Northern Wei, as a means of distinguishing the Särbi ruling class from the indigenous population. It was used less frequently as an ethnonym in the subsequent Tang Dynasty, but re-emerged once again as an ethnic marker under the Song. One can complicate this picture to some extent through a systematic word frequency analysis of a set of related terms (Tables 4.2 and 4.3). In this sort of analysis, it is important to distinguish between different possible meanings of the same word. For example, besides serving as an ethnonym, *Han* could also refer to the Han Dynasty or, as Shao-yun Yang has shown, it could serve as a geopolitical term referring to any state based in the North China Plain.[50]

In brief, what one notes in Table 4.2 is the rise to significance in the Song of a vocabulary still used in the present day to refer to China (*Zhongguo*) and to ethnic Chinese (*Han*). The increased use of *Zhongguo* to talk about China's geographic space – reflecting Ge Zhaoguang's proposal that there emerged in the Song a "China consciousness"[51] – seems to have come at the expense of a set of compound words based on the character *Hua* (Table 4.2a). *Hua* in this particular context referred to the Central Plains of North China, and not to the entire territory

---

[48] Finally, it is tempting to link this new politicization of ethnicity to the Song court's refusal to follow the Han and Tang precedent of establishing imperial marriage alliances with steppe confederation leaders.

[49] On the long and complex history of the *Han* ethnonym, see Shao-yun Yang, "Becoming *Zhongguo*"; Elliott, "Hushuo"; Shao-yun Yang, "*Fan* and *Han*."

[50] Shao-yun Yang, "*Fan* and *Han*," 18–21.

[51] Ge Zhaoguang, "Zhongguo yishi."

Table 4.2 *Word usage patterns in reference to China's geographic space, populations, and culture in Tang through Song prose*[a]

a. Use of *Hua* vs. *Zhongguo* to refer to China's geographic space

	Tang / Five Dynasties		Northern Song	
Hua[b]	407	(53%)	325	(14%)
Zhongguo	363	(47%)	2042	(86%)
Total:	770	(100%)	2367	(100%)

b. Word usage to refer to Chinese populations[c]

	Tang / Five Dynasties		Northern Song	
Hua people	20	(38%)	34	(19%)
Dynastic[d] people	10	(19%)	0	
Zhongguo people	19	(37%)	51	(28%)
Han[e] people	3	(6%)	94	(53%)
Total:	52	(100%)	179	(100%)

c. Word usage to refer to Chinese language and culture[f]

	Tang / Five Dynasties		Northern Song	
Hua language / culture	58	(71%)	30	(38%)
Dynastic[d] language / culture	17	(21%)	0	
Zhongguo language / culture	3	(4%)	27	(35%)
Han[e] language / culture	4	(5%)	21	(27%)
Total:	82	(100%)	78	(100%)

[a] These three tables are based on a count of the number of occurrences of particular words and phrases in two large collections of prose: QTW jj. 1–998 ("Tang / Five Dynasties") and QSW vols. 1–140 ("Northern Song"). Tables "b" and "c" take context into consideration to eliminate false hits; Table "a" does not consider context due to the very large number of hits.

[b] *Hua* = 華夷, 華夏, 諸華, or 中華.

[c] "People" = 人, 民, or 戶; e.g., "*Hua* people" refers to 華人, 華民, or 華戶.

[d] "Dynastic" refers to the Tang in the case of texts written during the Tang, to the Song in the case of Song texts, etc.

[e] *Han* only counted when used as an ethnonym, not when in reference to the Han Dynasty.

[f] "Language / culture" = 語, 言, 文, 音, 字, 風, 俗, 衣, 服, 裳, 裝, 禮, or 教; for example, "*Hua* language / culture" refers to 華語, 華言, 華文, 華音, 華字, 華風, 華俗, 華衣, 華服, 華裳, 華裝, 華禮, or 華教.

Table 4.3 *Usage of the term Fan-Han in Tang through Song prose*[a]

	Tang / Five Dynasties		Northern Song	
Geopolitical (non-ethnic)	14	(26%)	6	(2%)
Frontier military units	35	(65%)	147	(49%)
Frontier civilian populations (merchants, farmers, etc.)	2	(4%)	128	(43%)
Titles of administrators in charge of frontier populations	0		13	(4%)
Other	3	(6%)	6	(2%)
Total:	54	(100%)	300	(100%)

[a] This table is based on a count of the number of occurrences of *Fan-Han* (or *Han-Fan*) in two large collections of prose: QTW jj. 1–998 ("Tang / Five Dynasties") and QSW vols. 1–140 ("Northern Song"). Each occurrence was examined to eliminate false hits. For more on categories of usage ("geopolitical," etc.), see main text.

of the empire. Because it was frequently paired with the character *yi* ("barbarian", or "barbarian lands"), it also carried a very specific connotation of the civilized center. Thus, as alluded to in the Introduction, it can be translated as "illustrious" or "illustriousness." This idea of *Hua* fit in nicely with a model of the cosmos that featured a civilized core surrounded by zones of decreasing degrees of civilization, all of which nevertheless fell (in theory) under the political control of a universal monarch, the Son of Heaven, who ruled over "all under Heaven." The term *Zhongguo*, as Peter Bol has shown, fit much less well with ideas of universal empire.[52] It referred to the cultural zone that properly fell under the emperor's rule. In lieu of multiple concentric zones of diminishing imperial control, it was bounded by a single frontier, reflecting a new world of bilateral boundaries like those described in the previous chapter.

Even more striking is the increased use in the Northern Song of the term *Han* to refer to Chinese populations when, as was common on the frontier, it was necessary to contrast them with other people or peoples (Table 4.2b). In the Tang, the dominant term to refer to ethnic Chinese

[52] On Song uses of the term *Zhongguo*, see Bol, "Geography and Culture." For reasons of clarity, I leave the term untranslated in the discussion that follows; elsewhere, I translate it as "Middle Kingdom."

populations was either "*Hua* people" or "*Zhongguo* people." Though *Hua* and *Zhongguo* both referred to transdynastic notions, it was also common in Tang prose to refer to Chinese by the dynasty-specific term "Tang people." The expression "*Han* people" was rarely used when contrasting Chinese with non-Chinese, though it was used to distinguish contemporaries of the Tang Dynasty from people of the earlier Han Dynasty. In the corpus of Northern Song prose, by contrast, "*Han* people" was the most common term for Chinese – corroborating Mark Elliott's observation based on a different data set[53] – followed by "*Zhongguo* people" and "*Hua* people." The compound "Song people" was never used by Northern Song writers to contrast ethnic Chinese with non-Chinese (though it was used to contrast contemporaries with people of earlier times). Interestingly, a separate survey of eleventh-century political discourse suggests that the use of the term *Han* as an ethnonym increased substantially in frequency over the course of the dynasty.[54]

One finds similar trends when comparing Tang and Song vocabularies dealing with language and culture (Table 4.2c). Educated elites of the Tang and Song typically distinguished different peoples by their language, clothing, diet, ritual practices, and other customs. Thus, for example, when the ethnic Chinese Zhang Li was caught trying to escape Khitan territory in 937, he purportedly explained to his captors, "I am a Hua person. My clothing, language and diet are different from those here. I would rather die than live like this!"[55] A century later, in the preface to a monograph on the Khitans, the author explained that "Liao and *Zhongguo* have mutually unintelligible languages and different foods and diets."[56] As it turns out, in the Tang, *Hua* was the dominant label in compound words referring to Chinese language or culture, followed by "Tang," a reference to the dynasty itself. In Song prose, by contrast, *Zhongguo* and *Han* became much more common in similar contexts,

---

[53] Elliott, "Hushuo," 185. Elliott bases his conclusion on the dynastic histories.

[54] For this separate survey, I calculated the frequency of appearance in XCB (instances per 100 pages of text) of the character *Han* used in an ethnic sense. The data by reign is as follows: Taizu (r. 960–76): 0.51; Taizong (976–97): 1.94; Zhenzong (997–1022): 1.92; Renzong (1022–63): 3.79; Yingzong (1063–67): 0.40; Shenzong (1067–85): 4.02; Zhezong (1085–1100): 4.31. Aside from Yingzong's reign (anomalous in being a brief reign), there was a substantial increase in the use of *Han* in an ethnic sense beginning in the mid-eleventh century.

[55] ZZTJ 281.9170; XWDS 72.898. For details of Zhang Li's career, as well as an alternative interpretation of this incident, see Standen, *Unbounded Loyalty*, 116–20, 124–48.

[56] Su Song, *Su Weigong wenji*, 2:1005. Similarly, a 1074 Buddhist temple inscription observes, in describing the place of origin of Buddhism, that "their language, clothing, utensils, and food and drink do not, for the most part, resemble those of the Central Plains." See QSW 82:107.

while there was a complete disappearance of language identifying Chinese culture with the dynasty.

Though the character *Han* was rarely used in the Tang and Five Dynasties as an ethnonym in the terms included in Table 4.2, it was used in an ethnic sense in one particular compound: *Fan-Han*. *Fan* is often translated as "foreign" or "foreigner" in English (as in the case of the "foreign generals" mentioned above), though it usually referred specifically to Tibetans or Tanguts in the case of Song-era documents. If one examines systematically the uses of *Fan-Han* in Tang and Song prose (Table 4.3), one finds that, in a substantial majority of cases during the Tang and Five Dynasties, the compound referred to mixed ethnic military units, presumably units of the imperial army containing both Han Chinese infantry soldiers, and cavalrymen with pastoralist roots. The compound could also be used in a geopolitical sense, for example, when talking about the Sino-Tibetan frontier. The only two uses of the term to refer to mixed ethnic civilian populations appear in a late Five Dynasties-era imperial edict, composed on the eve of the founding of the Song state.[57] In Northern Song prose, by contrast, *Fan-Han* was used in an ethnic sense in a broader range of contexts. It continued to be used to refer to mixed ethnic military units, but it was also now used more generally to refer to mixed ethnic populations in Song-controlled frontier territories, including, for example, Han and Fan merchants at frontier markets, or Han and Fan villages in close proximity to each other. Finally, the compound *Fan-Han* also appears in Song prose in the titles of bureaucrats administering these mixed populations.

What is the significance of the shift from *Hua* to *Han*? In classic anthropological accounts of ethnicity, sentiments of group cohesion are reinforced by claims of common descent. Some premodern manifestations of ethnicity – in the ancient Eastern Mediterranean, for example – seem to have been rooted almost entirely in such descent claims.[58] In pre-Song China, however, culture was believed to be determined less by ancestry than by geography and environment – more precisely, by the quality of the *qi* at the place where individuals (or their immediate forebears) grew up.[59] Because *Hua* was a toponym that referred to the civilized center, a "Hua person" was somebody whose culture had been determined by high-quality *qi*. The term "Han person," by contrast, had very different

---

[57] QTW 122.1231.
[58] On Greece in antiquity, see Hall, *Ethnic Identity*.
[59] Abramson, *Ethnic Identity*, 95–99.

implications. By definition, it referred to a descendant of the people of the Han Dynasty. The culture of "Han people," thus, was determined not by geography, but rather by ancestry, making the term "Han people" closer in meaning to the classic anthropological understanding of an ethnic group.

There is an interesting explanation for this shift from culture as determined by environment to culture as determined by descent. Shao-yun Yang and Mark Elliott have both provided evidence suggesting that the ethnonym *Han* had steppe origins. It first appeared in the historical record to refer to Chinese during the Särbi-ruled Northern Wei Dynasty; it was then widely used by the Khitans.[60] Undoubtedly, it was for this reason that Zhu Yu, cited in the Introduction, claimed that "northwestern states" referred to *Zhongguo* as *Han*, and that the thirteenth-century historical commentator Hu Sanxing believed it was "barbarians" who had first "referred to *Zhongguo* people as Han people."[61] In fact, the steppe origins of politicized ethnicity of this sort makes perfect sense given the organization of steppe society. Among the pastoral nomads, the fundamental political unit was the descent-based tribe (whereas it was the geographically defined prefecture in the case of Chinese regimes). Moreover, steppe empires and confederations generally preserved tribal substructures, promulgating ethnic policies – such as those described in the next chapter – to help manage intertribal relations.[62]

How would educated Chinese have come to adopt in certain contexts steppe ethnic categories? The intense sociability during Song–Liao diplomatic banquets and other diplomatic exchanges constituted a natural mechanism of transmission. As we saw in Chapter 1, ethnicity was performed at Liao banquets in the process of consuming food. Diplomats of the neighboring states also shared ideas and conceptual categories with each other during their conversations. The Liao Chinese official Liu Liufu, for example, who came on embassies to Kaifeng on at least two occasions in the early 1040s, purportedly once told his escort, the Song official Fu Bi, "I am a man of Yan; along with the officials of the Southern [i.e., Song] Court, we are all of one family. Nowadays, those whom I serve are not of my kind."[63] To claim "family" ties was, of course, to claim a common ancestry. Indeed, according to official Liao ethnic categories, Liu was a "Han person" in contrast to the "Khitan" lords whom he served.

---

[60] Shao-yun Yang, "Becoming *Zhongguo*," 79–99; Elliott, "Hushuo," 180–87.
[61] Zhu Yu, *Pingzhou ketan*, 35; ZZTJ 202.6391.
[62] Barfield, *Perilous Frontier*, 5–8.
[63] QSW 71:315.

What does one then make of the data on the use of the expression *Fan-Han* (Table 4.3)? The fact that much of the early usage of this expression appeared in diplomatic documents might support the thesis of the foreign origins of the term *Han*. But what about the greater use of the expression in the Song, especially in light of Deng Xiaonan's observation that the *Fan–Han* dichotomy was far less frequently deployed in referring to top civilian and military officials? Its expanded usage into new contexts – particularly in reference to non-state actors on the frontier – is the key to understanding this apparent paradox. To transform Song China into an ethnic Han state, it was necessary to homogenize the population by concealing the non-Chinese backgrounds of top officials, while simultaneously clarifying ethnic boundaries in frontier regions. It was for this reason that some Northern Song officials called for the segregation of Fan and Han populations, and others sought to forbid intermarriage.[64]

To conclude this discussion of Han ethnicity, it is worth pointing out that all of these uses of the term *Han* in Song times to refer to a population believed to be culturally and linguistically distinct and homogeneous neglected to recognize the vast differences in regional cultures. Mandarin, Cantonese, Fukienese, and Shanghainese today are all mutually unintelligible languages, as different from each other as are the Romance languages of Europe. There is little doubt that similar language barriers existed among speakers of sinic languages in Song times (though educated elites shared a facility in the court vernacular and the classical written language). There are also great variations in regional Chinese cuisines today – also as different from each other as are the different European cuisines. Undoubtedly, there were similar disparities in diet a thousand years ago. In addition, archaeologists have identified striking contrasts in mortuary cultures between northern and southern Chinese of the Song period, suggesting regional variations in ritual traditions as well.[65] If Han and Tibetan peoples needed to be segregated because their languages were mutually unintelligible, because their meals were incompatible, or because their ritual traditions were different, why were Chinese from different regions not segregated in a similar way? The answer, of course, is that *Han* – like all ethnic categories – was a social construction. The idea of a common culture and language among Han populations was a fiction that made sense from the perspective of eleventh-century central government

[64] E.g., XCB 338.8141–42, 375.9090–91, 476.11343; SS 191.4761; QSW 74:67–68, 108:326, 108:339–40.
[65] Dieter Kuhn, *Place for the Dead*, 65–84.

officials who experienced ethnicity through their diplomatic contacts with Khitans and Tanguts. The naturalization of the category *Han* had far-reaching repercussions. Though *Han* acquired somewhat different connotations in the Yuan, it was revived by Ming sociopolitical elites in its earlier Song meaning.[66] It would survive into the late Qing, at which point it was adopted by anti-Manchu nationalists to describe the people of the new Chinese nation they hoped to establish. To this day, it survives as the ethnonym for the Chinese majority ethnicity, a category of people so capacious in terms of linguistic and cultural difference that its use is analogous to conflating English, Swedes, and Germans today into a single national people.

Han Ethnic Solidarity

Accompanying this new ethnic language were new assumptions about the political loyalties of Han people, notably of those living beyond the boundaries of the Song state (element 5 in Table 4.1). Naomi Standen has shown that, in the tenth century and earlier, there was little expectation of Han ethnic solidarity or loyalty – that is, there was little sense that ethnically Han people should preferentially ally themselves with or proffer allegiance to a regime ruled by an ethnically Han elite.[67] Though the Later Jin would in subsequent centuries be criticized for its alliance with the Khitans, in fact, numerous other regimes of the tenth century – both Chinese (Later Liang and Southern Tang) and non-Chinese (Later Tang and Later Han) – made alliances with the Khitans indiscriminately in their struggles to survive within a complex multi-state system.[68] Meanwhile, frontier warlords of the Tang-Song interregnum seeking to maintain their autonomy commonly switched sides between the Khitan regime to the north and the sequence of regimes to the south based along the Yellow River, with little regard for the ethnic identities of the ruling emperors. Moreover, contemporaneous or near-contemporaneous historians writing in the tenth century did not condemn these men for their shifting allegiances. It was only in the subsequent eleventh century that revisionist historians began to denounce individuals for what were now seen as acts of disloyalty. A primary component of this change in attitude (and the focus of Standen's attention) was an increasingly rigid insistence

---

[66] Elliott, "Hushuo," 188–89.
[67] Standen, *Unbounded Loyalty*.
[68] Wang Jilin, "Qidan yu Nan Tang waijiao guanxi."

on absolute loyalty to the dynasty rather than personal loyalty to an individual ruler. But one can also discern in the eleventh century the increasingly frequent articulation in political discourse of the idea that Han people ought to be loyal to Chinese regimes.[69]

In assessing the nature of political loyalties – including both actual feelings of loyalty and those insisted upon by a hegemonic ideology – one can imagine a variety of different forms, including both loyalty directed toward people and loyalty directed toward ideals, be they ethical principles or systems of government. Thus, one can imagine loyalty to an individual, such as a military commander, a warlord, or a sovereign; to a dynast, in which case the loyalty derives from a commitment to the dynastic principle; to the land and people of a geographically bounded region, as in the cases of modern nationalism or subnational regional attachments; to a transnational community, defined by education, religious affiliation, gender, or socioeconomic class; to an imperial system; to the civilized world, such as what one finds in certain post-Enlightenment moral cosmopolitanisms or among late imperial Confucians as described by Joseph Levenson;[70] or one might imagine loyalty to an ethnicity and culture. In actual practice, we find all of these at different moments in Chinese history. Given strong expectations of allegiance to the reigning emperor, it is not easy to distinguish ethnic loyalty from loyalty to dynasty. The exception involves Han people living beyond the border, in territories that had never been under the control of the Song Dynasty.

As it turns out, in Northern Song political discourse, one finds numerous references to Han people stranded beyond the borders of the Song state. Moreover, it was common to imagine that these Han people wished to be under Han rule. The most frequent such references involve the people of Yan, who, it was well understood, were culturally akin to the Song Chinese.[71] Writing in the mid-eleventh century, the statesman Fan Zhongyan (989–1052) asserted that "in the prefectures of Yan, the population originally was Han in customs; their descendants continue

---

[69] On notions of loyalty during the tenth and eleventh centuries, see Standen, *Unbounded Loyalty*; Wang Gung-wu, "Feng Tao." For the argument that ethnic loyalty did not emerge as an ideal until the eleventh century, see Standen, "Alien Regimes and Mental States," 79–80; Skaff, "Survival in the Frontier Zone," 140–43; Schottenhammer, "Buried Past," 36–39.

[70] For Levenson's succinct discussion of the relationship between "culturalism" and nationalism, see *Confucian China*, 1:95–108.

[71] E.g., according to Chen Shidao, *Houshan tancong*, 6:81, "as for the people of Yan, their clothing and their diets adhere to Chinese standards."

to long for Han."[72] One finds similar accounts regarding a region under Tangut control in the northwest: "Around Xingzhou and Lingzhou, there are many former Han people, all of whom were seized by the [Tangut chief] Yuanhao; they often have feelings of longing for Han."[73] In both cases, the expression "longing for Han" presumably entailed yearning to fall under the political (and therefore moral and cultural) sway of the Song emperor. A 1075 memorial regarding the Hedong frontier is more explicit that the object of longing is Song China: "the people beyond the mountains [in Liao territory], who have long suffered under tyrannical rule, all have feelings of longing for the Middle Kingdom."[74] Finally, one finds additional accounts of this sort in reference to Han populations on the southwestern frontier.[75] To be sure, Xingzhou and Lingzhou had been under Song rule up until 1001. As such, one might imagine that the Song commentators simply believed their populations to have maintained their allegiance to the dynasty that their ancestors had once served. But in other cases – notably the people of Yan and of Liao-controlled Hedong, as well as the Han people living in Tibetan lands – the populations in question had never been under Song control. The feelings they purportedly felt for Song China were the feelings of loyalty that ethnically Han people were imagined naturally to feel for a Han-ruled regime.

Faith in the political allegiance of Han people had important policy-making implications insofar as it spurred a conviction that those living across the borders constituted a potential military resource. Very early in the dynasty, in a 986 edict seeking to justify the seizure of Yan from Liao, Emperor Taizong asserted:

> I cherish this region of Yan, which once was within our frontiers, but has fallen into the hands of the stinking caitiffs for fifty years now. Families there harbor great indignation, having lost their means of livelihood; they look with anticipation to Han [-controlled] territories, but their path there is obstructed . . . These northerners were once known as great warriors. Some will be able to welcome our armies and join forces with us. By means of our imperial campaign, they will cleanse themselves of a generation of shame.[76]

---

[72] QSW 18:159. For similar examples dating to the mid to late eleventh century, see QSW 17:55, 78:266, 129:407; Ding Chuanjing, *Songren yishi huibian*, 20.1103.

[73] XCB 316.7637.

[74] XCB 260.6335.

[75] E.g., after a fortress was abandoned on the southern frontier, one official feared that "there still might be people left behind in the land of streams and grottoes [i.e., tribal territory], who have not managed to come home to Han." See XCB 458.10960.

[76] SHY *bing* 8.4.

In other words, according to Taizong, the people of Yan resented the Khitan occupation of their land to the point that they were ready and willing to join forces with the Song armies to chase out their foreign oppressors. This argument would have resonated with many men at court, an unusually large percentage of whom had family origins in Hebei (either in Liao-controlled Yan or in Song-controlled regions to the south). Indeed, Taizong's own grandfather, great grandfather, and great great grandfather were all buried in Yan, having all three served in the late Tang autonomous provincial government based there.[77] It is plausible that Taizong had some of his own cousins in mind when imagining their "great indignation." Unfortunately for the Song, however, the people of Yan seem not to have been as receptive as expected: ultimately, they decided to assist the Khitans in repelling Taizong's troops. In a frank assessment of the failure of Taizong's 979 and 986 campaigns, the court official Wang Yucheng (954–1001) explained that "the borderlanders [i.e., people of Yan] are ignorant, and were unaware of your wise plan; they all thought you coveted their land, and so they invited the northern barbarians [i.e., Khitan troops] to come south [in their defense]."[78]

Despite Taizong's failures, subsequent generations of political elites – who, in this case, would not have shared Taizong's and some of his courtiers' sentimental attachments to their homeland – persisted in their conviction that the Song regime could count on the solidarity of Han populations across the border. As Fu Bi explained in 1044, after one of his diplomatic missions to Liao:

> Although it has been over one hundred years since the land of Yan was ceded to the Khitans, yet the customs are all those of the Hua people, irrespective of the fact they are controlled by barbarians. In the end, they are of the mind to submit [to Song], and frequently resent the fact that the Middle Kingdom is not able to rule them; they are always filled with frustration, and appear to weep bitterly.

According to Fu, some of the people of Yan had assured him they could raise a militia of several thousand loyalists prepared for martyrdom in defense of the Song cause. "We are after all Hua people; dying would be all the more fortunate!" Fu's informants zealously exclaimed.[79] Fu Bi went

---

[77] Wang Gung-wu, *Structure of Power*, 208–15; Tackett, "Wan Tang Hebei ren," 256–58, 261.

[78] XCB 30.672. Wang went on to propose that, prior to another invasion of Yan, the court should first embark on a propaganda campaign to announce the Song emperor's intentions and promise financial rewards to those taking up arms on behalf of the Song.

[79] QSW 28:317–18; XCB 150.3650.

on to suggest that – though he himself did not advocate war with Liao – the population of Yan would prove a valuable ally if war ever were to break out. In the early 1060s, in a civil service examination essay, Su Shi made a similar argument, first proposing as potential Song allies the "Middle Kingdom [i.e., Han] *shidafu*" at the Liao court, before focusing in greater detail on the population of Yan:

> The land of Yan has, since antiquity, been known for its abundance of vigorous men, who grace the pages of the historical chronicles; it has always been thus. When the Song was established, worthy men everywhere congregated together regardless of distance, all wishing to be deemed deserving of imperial grace [i.e., all wishing to join the Song cause]; only this one territory [of Yan] fell into the clutches of men of another kind. Formerly, Emperor Taizong personally led a campaign to retake Youzhou [i.e., Yan], but failed and withdrew his troops. According to the reports of our spies, the population of Youzhou had plotted to seize [the Khitan] commanders and to surrender the city; when they heard the imperial carriage had returned [back to the south], there was no one who did not shed tears.[80]

Whereas Taizong's own contemporaries, men like Wang Yucheng, had grounds to doubt the ethnic solidarity of the population of Yan, Su Shi's full faith in it colored his account of Taizong's campaigns. Su went on to predict that ethnic tensions in Liao territory would ultimately provide Song with an opportunity for a new campaign.[81] Later in the century, Li Qingchen (1032–1102) made a similar argument, predicting that the day would come when "there will be a man of great valor who will seize [Yan] and join forces with us, asking to become our vassal."[82] In the mid to late eleventh century, one finds numerous other examples of this sort of argument, in the writings of hawks and doves alike.[83]

By the 1110s, hawks at court pushing for an alliance with the Jurchens against Liao exploited much the same claim to further their agenda. One Liao defector brought to court by Song hawks declared that Song armies would be welcomed into Yan with tea- and wine-laden banquets.[84]

---

[80] *Su Shi wenji*, 1:288.
[81] It was only later in the eleventh century that commentators began to insist that the population of Yan had supported Taizong's campaigns (and, even many generations later, continued to bemoan the failures of these campaigns). See, e.g., Wang Pizhi, *Shengshui yantan lu*, 9.111.
[82] QSW 78:396.
[83] E.g., in the 1070s, both doves like Qiang Zhi (1023–76) and hawks like Chao Buzhi (1053–1110) asserted that loyalists in Yan were ready to take up arms for the Song cause. See QSW 66:29, 125:333.
[84] SCBM Zhengxuan, 1.3.

The claim of Yan support for the Song invasion was repeated frequently by the hawks. In a report submitted to the court probably around the year 1115, the official Zhao Dingchen (b. 1070) hypothesized that "those people longing for Han will together take control of the land of Yan and submit it to our administration."[85] Then, just prior to the final invasion of Yan, in early summer 1122, hawks circulated rumors that "the Han people [of Yan] all day long lift their heads and crane their necks, awaiting day after day the imperial troops, yearning to submit to the [Song] emperor's civilizing influence."[86] It is certainly telling that, when the Song troops managed to break into the walled city of Yan (before being chased out the next day), they embarked on a campaign of ethnic cleansing, systematically killing all non-Han people among the city's population. According to one account, "the slayings numbered in the tens of thousands; the main thoroughfares were drenched in blood."[87] Evidently, due to their expected loyalty to the Song, Han Chinese among the population of the city were not assumed to be the same threat. Finally, in 1123, in a congratulatory memorial presented to court after the Jurchens transferred control of Yan to the Song, Cai Jing asserted that, among the "population left behind" of Han residents of Yan, "young and old alike cheered with joy."[88]

In fact, as in the case of Taizong's failure in 986, there is little evidence of a groundswell of support in Yan for the Song cause. According to one account, the local population was "stupefied" when they read a placard brought in by Song troops that sought to rally their support.[89] Later, when Song troops arrived at the city walls of Yan, during one of the two failed campaigns of 1122, the Liao Chinese in charge refused to open the city gates. By contrast, these same Liao Chinese would a few months later surrender the city to the Jurchens without a fight.[90] Indeed, the more level-headed official Hong Zhongfu (1049–1131), in a letter to the court submitted just before the invasion, mocked the "groundless talk" that the "Han people" of the Sixteen Prefectures "will greet us at the border with pavilions of incense and flowers." The Liao government had welcomed educated Chinese into their administration with open arms, offering them high salaries. Why, Hong asked, would these Chinese give up

---

[85] QSW 138:156.

[86] SCBM Zhengxuan, 9.83.

[87] Ibid., 11.98. Subsequently, as part of the 1123 Sino-Jurchen agreement, the Song court agreed to relocate all remaining non-Han residents of the Yan region into Jurchen territory (ibid., 14.125).

[88] Ibid., 17.158.

[89] Ibid., 6.54.

[90] Tao, *Two Sons of Heaven*, 92.

everything to defect to the Song? Moreover, in recognition of the critical role of the Sixteen Prefectures as a breadbasket of their empire, the Liao had reduced taxes and labor requirements, a policy well appreciated by the local Han population. "How can we rely on this talk of pavilions of incense and flowers?" Hong asked in conclusion.[91] Looking in hindsight on the invasion of Yan a few years later, another commentator concluded that "from the beginning, the people of Yan did not have feelings of longing for Han."[92]

In the first decade or two after the Jurchen invasion of North China, the idea of a loyalist population behind enemy lines began to circulate once more, a population that purportedly "day after day awaited the return of the imperial armies."[93] In the words of one poem from this period imagining life at the former Northern Song capital of Kaifeng, "The people left behind look at each other and cry out to Heaven."[94] In most cases, the population in question consisted of former subjects of the Song in the North China Plain, who, in the immediate aftermath of the invasion, may very well have hoped for a Song restoration.[95] But not all were former Song subjects. Even after the Jurchen invasion, one still finds accounts of a purportedly loyalist population in Yan, a population that, according to one source, so hated the Jurchens that they "wished to devour their flesh."[96] Moreover, claims of ethnic solidarity continued into the 1180s and 1190s, at which point – now a good two generations after the loss of North China – it is unlikely that a loyalist population still persisted. In the early 1190s, the "patriot poet" Lu You wrote several poems imagining the sentiments of the Han population in Jurchen-occupied lands – "The tears of the people left behind seep into the Tartar dust [i.e., the dust stirred up by the nomads' horses]; / Looking southward, for yet another year, they await the imperial armies!"[97] The Southern Song political elite's mistaken faith in Han ethnic solidarity led to at least one more disastrous

---

[91] QSW 119:127–28; SCBM Zhengxuan, 19.179–81.

[92] SCBM Zhengxuan, 24.231.

[93] For various claims of this sort dating roughly to the 1130s or 1140s, see QSW 253:9; SS 475.13801; Li Xinchuan, *Jianyan yilai xinian yaolu*, 20.400; SHY *zhiguan* 41.9; Levine, "Welcome to the Occupation," 401–02.

[94] QSS 35:22395; De Weerdt, "Maps and Memory," 161.

[95] Indeed, there are numerous accounts of "righteous and patriotic armies" in parts of North China organized locally to fight for the Song cause immediately after the Jurchen invasion. See Trauzettel, "Sung Patriotism," 204–06.

[96] QSW 144:313.

[97] Lu You, *Jiannan shigao jiaozhu*, 4:1774. For two similar poems from the same period, see ibid., 2:552, 2:623.

military debacle. In 1206, the Southern Song chief minister Han Tuozhou (1152–1207) initiated a reconquest of Jurchen-controlled North China, basing his overall strategy on the assumption that the population of the region would, eighty years after the Jurchen invasion, still feel loyalty to the Song and join forces with its army. He was wrong; the population of North China did no such thing. As a result, the Song armies were annihilated, and Han lost his head (which was sent to the Jurchens in a box as part of the ensuing peace agreement).[98]

In all of these accounts of Han ethnic loyalty, one cannot know for sure what the "populations left behind" really thought. As we shall see in the next chapter, the Liao empire had in place an ethnic policy that could have served to reinforce in the minds of the people of Yan their ethnocultural distinctiveness from their Khitan overlords. But the repeated failure of Song armies to find the allies they hoped for in enemy territory at best suggests Song political elites overestimated the strength of Han ethnic solidarity.[99] In the case of Benedict Anderson's "imagined community," it is the masses of the populations of modern nation-states who, under the influence of mass media, universal education, and organized propaganda campaigns, come to see themselves as belonging to a community of fellow citizens. The community is "imagined" in the sense that individuals will never meet the vast majority of its members, even though, in the fervor of patriotic passions, they would gladly die on the battlefield on behalf of this community of strangers. What is fascinating about the Song is not that ethnic Han Chinese everywhere really were willing to sacrifice their lives for their fellow Chinese, but that Song political elites believed that they were. It was an imagined "imagined community." As in the case of the Han ethnic category, the expectation of Han solidarity outlived the Song Dynasty. Both nationalists and revolutionaries in the early twentieth century and Communists in later decades called on ethnic Chinese abroad to contribute to the Chinese nation, through investments, financial contributions, or even by coming back to the motherland to work on Overseas Chinese Farms.[100]

---

[98] Franke, "Chin Dynasty," 247–49.

[99] Even in much more recent times, many of the armed uprisings against foreign occupiers – against the British in the mid-nineteenth century and the Japanese in the mid-twentieth century – failed to provoke the sort of nationalist responses among the populace that contemporary nationalist historians might assume. See Wakeman, *Strangers at the Gate*, esp. 56–58; Wakeman, "Hanjian."

[100] Duara, "Nationalists among Transnationals"; Ford, "Guiqiao." As in the case of the Song, twentieth-century nationalists and Communists only managed to convince a small percentage of ethnically Han people abroad to contribute to their causes.

Han Territory

Accompanying developments in ideas of ethnicity and ethnic loyalty was the emerging notion under the Northern Song that it was possible to define the proper geographic extent of the imperial realm on the basis of historical, ethnocultural, and – in some cases – ecological principles (element 6 in Table 4.1). We already saw evidence of this notion in the previous chapter, in the decision to demarcate the Xia–Song border according to cultural ecology and the geographic distribution of ethnic populations. It was not uncommon to refer to the transdynastic political entity occupying this zone by the term "Middle Kingdom" (*Zhongguo*). Thus, one Song scholar observed in a temple inscription dating to the year 1035: "The barbarian tribes to the south, east, west, and north all belong to all under Heaven (*tianxia*); it is only our Han territory that we refer to as the Middle Kingdom (*Zhongguo*)."[101] From this perspective, the occupation of any part of this territory by a non-Han regime was an inherent violation of the proper ordering of the world, a conclusion that fueled in the Song a new interest in so-called "conquest" dynasties, discussed in more detail below. More fatefully, it fueled a series of wars of expansion driven explicitly by irredentist territorial claims (element 7 in Table 4.1). Military expansionism was, of course, not new to the Song; what was new was its ideological justification.

This irredentist ideology was not yet in place in the first two decades of the dynasty, a period when the military conquest of core Chinese regions was necessary to establish Song dynastic legitimacy; "lost" territories on the frontier were of little concern. As a successor to five short-lived dynasties that had coexisted with numerous independent southern kingdoms, one of the important Song claims to legitimacy rested on its ability to accomplish what had not been achieved by any other post-Tang regime – the reunification of the civilized world. Thus, even after the Song consolidation of most of South China with the defeat in late 975 of the Southern Tang, the founding emperor Taizu refused a new imperial title offered to him by his courtiers that referred to him as a "unifier." "As of now, Fen and Jin [in southern Hedong] have not been pacified, and Yan has not been recovered," he observed. "How is it not an exaggeration to refer to [what I have done] as 'unification'?"[102]

---

[101] QSW 20:98.

[102] *Song da zhaoling ji*, 3.11. This anecdote was often repeated. See, e.g., SHY *dixi* 1.3; SHY *li* 49.5; Sima Guang, *Sushui jiwen*, 1.6. In Sima Guang's version, which may have reflected late Northern Song concerns, Taizu only mentions Yan and not southern Hedong.

By the 980s, under Emperor Taizong, the Song position was far more secure. By then, the Song had forced the Wuyue Kingdom (907–78) in the southeast to capitulate, and had annexed southern Hedong, thereby eliminating the Northern Han regime (951–79). At this point, the Song could plausibly claim to have unified the world insofar as it coexisted with no other autonomous Chinese regime. A 974 stele celebrated this accomplishment by asserting that the dynasty had "recovered the distant limits of the Tracks of Yu" – that is, the lands traversed by one of the great sage kings of remote antiquity – "and recuperated the former territories of the Central Plains."[103] In subsequent decades, no one doubted (or dared suggest) that the Song had failed to complete its unification project. From the perspective of Liu Chang (1019–68), there was no mistaking the stark contrast between the Song and the preceding period:

> From the Tang through the sequence of Five Dynasties, the world was divided up for over a hundred years. Among Wu, Shu, Jiao, Yi, Jing, Jin, Min, and Yue, the largest [of these states] proclaimed themselves empires, while the smallest proclaimed themselves kingdoms. They collected tax revenue for themselves, without joining together under a [single] emperor and imperial bureaucracy. After Taizu finally secured the throne, within ten years, Wu, Shu, Jiao, Yi, [and Jing] were gradually forced to surrender. Soon after Taizong ascended the throne, Min and Yue [i.e., Wuyue] asked to submit to the court, and Binzhou [i.e., the Northern Han] was pacified, such that the world was for the first time [since the Tang] unified.[104]

With no longer a need to seize Yan for the sake of dynastic legitimacy, Taizong began to articulate a different set of justifications to pursue his wars of conquest. Such justifications became all the more important after the failure of the 979 invasion of Yan, when some imperial advisors started questioning whether continued warfare was wise. In response to their concerns, Taizong initially argued that the 979 attack had been punitive, in retaliation for Khitan aggression.[105] Later, beginning in the 980s, he turned more than once to a far more interesting justification, revolving around the premise that the people of Yan were culturally Chinese. In an edict issued on the eve of the 986 invasion, he declared:

> I cherish this region of Yan. It was originally [inhabited by] people of the Middle Kingdom, but, since the [Later] Jin and Han, it has been

---

[103] QSW 3:238. Others used very similar language to describe Song unification. E.g., Sima Guang asserted in 1085 that, after Taizong's seizure of Hedong, "the tracks of the Great Yu were all possessed by the Song." See XCB 363.8689.

[104] QSW 59:379.

[105] SHY *xingfa* 2.2–3.

expropriated by barbarians. To this day, fifty years later, it has not yet been recovered. Our dynasty has already transformed the world [with its civilizing influence]; imperial grace has extended to all animals and plants. How can we allow the territory of Yan to persist as a land of [uncivilized people with] disheveled hair, and allow the survivors among the well-born to remain in a society where one consumes [an uncivilized diet of] raw meat?[106]

In an edict dating to the same year, Taizong expressed a desire to "sweep away the accumulated humiliation of the borderlanders [of Hebei]."[107]

The argument that the people of Yan were brethren of the Song people, one recalls, would have made sense to the many courtiers (and imperial clansmen) with family origins in Yan or neighboring regions. Indeed, many of the hawks goading Taizong to take Yan in 986 and even in later years – including Song Qi (917–96), Hu Dan (j.s. 978), Han Guohua (957–1011), and the rumored cannibal Liu Kai (948–1001) – were men from Hebei.[108] But, according to extant sources, it was the emperor himself who took the lead in promulgating an ethnocultural argument for taking Yan. Even after the failure of the 986 attack, after which Taizong gave up trying to conquer the region, the emperor continued to express concern for a people he viewed as culturally akin to the Song Chinese.[109]

The situation in the early Song differed in a number of ways from the situation later in the dynasty. The expansionist movement at this point was focused almost entirely on Yan – the eastern eight of the Sixteen Prefectures. There was no particular interest in regions further west.[110] Moreover, even with regard to Yan, there was vigorous debate at court on whether or not this territory was an essential part of a Chinese empire. Court doves were particularly skeptical. Many of them saw Yan

---

[106] SHY *bing* 7.10. Of the numerous sources citing this edict, one attributes it to Taizu, but most attribute it to Taizong. For another articulation of this same idea by Taizong in 986, see XCB 27.617. Taizu has also been credited with first proposing that the people of Yan were brethren of the Song people, purportedly establishing a special treasury to finance the purchase or reconquest of Yan. See, e.g., XCB 19.436. Elements of this story may be apocryphal.

[107] SHY *bing* 8.4. Three years earlier, Taizong had also spoken of "brushing away the humiliation" of his immediate imperial predecessors, Taizu and the Later Zhou emperor Shizong (r. 954–59). See XCB 24.556.

[108] For their memorials encouraging a reconquest of Yan, see SS 264.9123–28, 432.12828–29; QSW 6:273–76, 29:48.

[109] For a 989 edict reiterating this concern, see SHY *dixi* 9.2.

[110] For a rare early Song policy proposal (dating to 997) promoting the conquest of both Yan and Hehuang in the northwest, see QSW 9:177. By contrast, when a few years later Yang Yi (974–1020) identified both Yan and Hehuang as "lost territories," he did so to argue against the idea that the Song needed to maintain control of Lingzhou simply because it had once been under Chinese control. See QSW 14:257.

as a semi-barbaric frontier zone, an idea inspired both by the concentric squares model – whereby Yan would have been less civilized due to its distance from the imperial center – and by the fact that Yan had been an autonomous province in the second half of the Tang. One early Song court official went so far as to describe the people of Yan with language generally reserved for "greedy" steppe nomads: "what they most love is the hunt, and what they covet is material profit; aside from this, they have no other abilities."[111]

Other opponents of war with Liao insisted that legitimate dynasties simply had no need to expand. After all, the sage kings of antiquity had ruled over relatively modest territories.[112] Imperial unification was achieved by eliminating all rival claimants to the throne, not by seizing a defined set of territories. According to the influential official Zhao Pu (922–92), writing in 986:

> With the pacification of [Wuyue] and the forcible seizure of Hedong, [the emperor] has bequeathed his extraordinary valor to posterity, while cleansing the indignation of the previous dynasties. The lands between the Four Seas [i.e., the civilized world] have all returned to our grasp; for ten years up through the Yongxi era [i.e., the present day] there have just been those barbarians [i.e., the Khitans], but how are they our rivals? Nomads, who can fly off like birds, have since antiquity been difficult to control.[113]

From Zhao's perspective, controlling Yan was immaterial once the last remaining rival was a steppe-based empire. Pastoral nomads were part of the natural order of things, with whom even the sage kings of antiquity had agreed to coexist. Zhao's colleague at court, Zhang Qixian (943–1014), made much the same point in blunter terms, in a memorial dated 980: "The Khitans are not worth annexing; Yan is not worth seizing."[114] It was precisely this sort of thinking that became outdated over the course of the Northern Song. By the mid-twelfth century, historians like Li Tao (1115–84) criticized Zhang's 980 memorial on the grounds that its author "only understood that the Khitans could not be attacked, but did not understand that the region of Yan had to be taken."[115] Li Tao went on to list Zhao Pu, as well, among a list of other men who had failed to understand the vital need to conquer Yan.

---

[111] XCB 44.943.
[112] XCB 50.1096.
[113] Shao Bowen, *Shao shi wenjian lu*, 6:48.
[114] XCB 21.484.
[115] XCB 21.485.

Sima Guang provides an interesting historicization of Northern Song irredentism in a brief narrative overview of three hundred years of frontier history:

> From the mid-Tang, when the provinces came to dominate [at the expense of the central government], down to the Five Dynasties, when numerous warlords contended for supremacy, the Nine Provinces between the Four Seas rotted like a carved up melon; armies swallowed each other up, while the common people wallowed in misery. This lasted over two hundred years. When Taizu received Heaven's brilliant mandate, he sent out his armies against all those who would not submit, gloriously initiating the imperial way. Taizong succeeded him, bringing to fruition [Taizu's] achievements, whereupon the Tracks of the Great Yu were all possessed by the Song. Subsequently, the weapons of war were put away, and the populace was granted a respite. People now can live to a very advanced age without witnessing warfare at any point in their lives. Administrators keep watch over the laws and standards, while the people are undisturbed in their occupations. Cocks crow, dogs bark, and smoke and flames [from the hearths] are in dense profusion. One might call this the ultimate in eras of peace; it is something that has rarely been matched since antiquity. When Shenzong inherited the throne [in 1068], the spirit [of his ministers] was heroic and martial. Because You, Ji, Yun, and Shuo [the Sixteen Prefectures] are in the hands of the Khitans; Lingwu and Hexi [in the northwest] are under the sole command of the [Tanguts]; and Cochin and Annam [in the far south] are controlled by the Ly family, it is no longer possible to establish bureaucrats there, nor to exact taxes or corvée labor. Compared to the territorial extent of the Han and the Tang, we are not yet whole. Fueled by the shame of this, there is now the fervent will to send out armies to open up [the frontier]. The result has been that military men on the frontier – who lie in wait for small gains, wantonly talking big and taking credit for the achievements of others without regard for the harm done to the state – vie to show off their bravado . . . And pasty-faced bookworms – steeped in texts and diagrams, who delight in ancient precedents without a sense of how to adapt them to contemporary circumstances – compete with each other to present bizarre policy proposals at court.[116]

Sima Guang was typical of the doves at court in the second half of the eleventh century. He celebrated the peace of the post-Chanyuan period as something "rarely matched since antiquity," while mocking the amateurish military adventurism of those among his contemporaries pushing for war. In fact, as we saw in Chapter 1, hawks at court focused their attention on the Tanguts and Tibetans in the northwest (and, to a lesser extent, on the southern frontier), not on the Khitans in the northeast. But Sima

[116] XCB 363.8689.

simplified the situation, conveniently treating expansionism on all three frontiers as a single phenomenon. Finally, and of particular relevance here, Sima described what he saw as a new conviction held by many of his colleagues: that the territories of the Han and Tang empires defined what it meant for China to be "whole." Although Sima specifically dates the first emergence of this new mentality to Shenzong's reign – presumably a veiled barb aimed at Wang Anshi and other rivals at court – as we shall see, one already finds in the 1040s evidence of new sorts of territorial claims, based at least in part on a claim to the "former lands of the Han and Tang."[117] In tracing the development of this discourse, it is worth, however, distinguishing Tangut and Tibetan lands in the northwest from the Liao-occupied Sixteen Prefectures in the northeast.

In justifying northwestward expansionism in the decades after the first Sino-Tangut war, Song hawks turned to arguments based on a combination of historical and ethnocultural principles. Historical arguments identified territories beyond the frontier that had once been under Chinese rule. Thus, Suizhou – seized by a Song army acting without court approval in 1067 – was called "our former land."[118] So, too, was the portion of the Qinghai plateau wrestled from the Tibetans at the turn of the twelfth century.[119] None of these lands had ever been under Song control. They were "former lands" only insofar as they had been under the control of earlier Chinese dynasties. Other examples abound. In the early 1040s, Yang Xie (980–1049) referred to Lingzhou and Xiazhou as "ancient commanderies of the Tang and Han"; Fan Zhongyan described the broader Shaanxi frontier region as "former territories of the Han and Tang"; and, some decades later, after the Song conquest of Hehuang, a congratulatory memorial referred to this region, as well, in nearly identical language.[120] In all of these cases, Song officials in essence claimed land on behalf of a political entity that transcended dynasty.

This claim to historical territory in the northwest was closely linked to another sort of argument – one based on ethnicity and culture. Warmongers pushing for expansion into the northwest were particularly fascinated by the so-called "people left behind" – Han people living

---

[117] This interest in Han and Tang territories coincided with a broader obsession with trying to demonstrate that the Song had "surpassed the Tang and exceeded the Han."

[118] QSW 110:103.

[119] QSW 38:330, 48:337, 83:284.

[120] XCB 134.3189; QSW 18:157; XCB 506.12265. For a similar remark by Wang Anshi, see P. J. Smith, "Shen-tsung's Reign," 465. In a somewhat different version of this historical claim, Chinese control of these territories was said to extend back to the time of Yu the Great. See QSW 123:88–89.

in Tangut- or Tibetan-controlled lands, who had been "abandoned" when the region fell out of Tang control in the second half of the eighth century. After the reconquest of some of the Tibetan-controlled lands, for example, one memorial noted that, with the seizure of "the former land of Hehuang," the Song court was able to reregister "the people left behind since Tang and Han times."[121] Hawkish policymakers used similar language in describing Tangut territories further north. In 1041, in his "Ten Proposals for Pacifying the Barbarians," Zhang Fangping (1007–91) observed:

> The village elders of those [Tangut] prefectures are our people who have been left behind; though they drink milk and drape themselves in felt [in steppe nomadic fashion], they still think longingly of the land of Hua. When our imperial armies surround them, we can win them over by means of kindness and good faith, thereby bringing Shuofang [i.e., the original core of the Tangut state] back to the fold.[122]

In this last example, the ethnic Chinese population – descendants of the people of past dynasties – constituted not only a justification for conquest, but also an imagined ally that would welcome in Song armies.

If hawks pushing for war in the northwest justified themselves by means of historical and ethnocultural-based territorial claims, their opponents at court turned to more pragmatic concerns. One argument focused on another sort of transdynastic principle – natural ecological constraints. In 1039, just after the outbreak of war with the Tanguts, one of the military commanders in charge of the northwestern defenses, Liu Ping, offered a general strategy for dealing with the frontier adjacent to the original four core prefectures of the Tangut state. "Ling, Xia, Sui, and Yin [prefectures] do not produce the five grains," he wrote. "[In consisting of] hundreds of miles of desert, they were not originally among the lands of Hua."[123] Due to the difficulties of supplying Chinese garrisons and administrative outposts in this region, Liu advocated dislodging the Tanguts by means of alliances with locally based tribesmen. In later decades, critics of northwestward expansionism frequently condemned the conquest of land that would not produce tax revenue. When Su Che (1039–1112) advocated returning Lanzhou, which had been seized from the Tanguts in 1081, he described it as "useless land originally beyond our borders."[124] When Chao

[121] QSW 144:351. For similar examples, see QSW 77:239, 82:359, 138:123–24.
[122] QSW 37:34.
[123] XCB 125.2957.
[124] XCB 381.9281.

Yuezhi (1059–1129) sought in 1100 to dissuade the court from further expeditions into the northwest, he asked rhetorically, "Why must we throw away vast quantities of gold, silk, and grain to fight over a small amount of barren land?"[125] Qin Guan (1049–1100) provided an interesting assessment of the difference between two fundamentally different strategies for dealing with the northwest, in a discussion of four sites in the vicinity of Lanzhou in the Gansu Corridor. According to Qin, whereas one group of policymakers regarded all of these sites as "the Middle Kingdom's former territory," the other side noted that it had long been a "nest of Tibetans and other barbarians," and that by sponsoring local chieftains to govern the region, it would be possible to save millions in supply costs.[126] On the basis of this ecological argument, it was a moot point whether or not a Chinese regime had once directly administered these lands if the costs of maintaining control were too great. As Bi Zhongyou (1047–1121) put it, "territories beyond the pale, even those that were once counties and prefectures of the Middle Kingdom, are equally of no use to us."[127]

A second criticism of northwestward expansion focused on territory defined in dynastic terms, rather than relying on a transdynastic logic. For example, when arguing in 1092 against establishing two new fortified cities near Lanzhou, Fan Bailu (1030–94) observed that such a provocation might trigger new warfare with the Tanguts. After all, he reminded the court, the region in question "was not originally our land."[128] In fact, Lanzhou was incorporated into both the Han and Tang empires; it was not "our land" because it had never been under Song control. Around the same time, a debate erupted at court on whether to return land seized earlier from the Tanguts. Both Wang Cun (1023–1101) and Han Wei (1016–1098) referred to this land as "their former land" – that is, land once belonging to the Tangut Xia dynasty.[129] Su Che offered an interesting justification to explain why he supported the return of this land, even though he had previously excoriated the officials who had given up a sliver of land in Hedong to the Khitans:

> Places around Lanzhou cannot be discussed in the same context as the Hedong border. The Hedong border is a strategic point for the state, and was handed down to us by the founding emperors. Who would dare give

---

[125] QSW 129:406.

[126] QSW 120:64–65. According to Feng Shan, expansionism in the northwest and south had as its goal to seize a mere one hundredth of the territories of the Han and Tang, yet at very high cost. See QSW 78:265.

[127] QSW 111:78.

[128] XCB 479.11412.

[129] QSW 93:208, 110:129. The land in question had been seized purportedly to punish the Tangut queen mother for deposing her son.

it up? . . . As for the places around Lanzhou, these were originally former lands of the Western barbarians [i.e., the Tanguts]; obtaining these lands brings us costs but no profits.[130]

Given the contractual basis of the peace agreements – discussed in the previous chapter – there was an ethical component to this focus on dynastic territory, especially in the case of territory defined through past diplomatic negotiations. When recommending the return of the Tangut lands, Han Wei reminded the court that "that which makes the Middle Kingdom worthy of acclamation is its trustworthiness and adherence to propriety; what makes the distant lands worthy of contempt is their rapaciousness and brutality." Su Che was particularly adamant on this point. He insisted that it would be "crooked" to annex Tangut territory even in the wake of a successful Chinese military campaign.[131] Elsewhere, Su was unambiguous on who was to blame for the civilian casualties that resulted from Tangut incursions: "This is not the fault of the Westerners; it is entirely the result of the [Song] court's lack of righteousness."[132] Annexation had caused the Song to lose the moral high ground.

The issue of military expansionism into the Khitan-controlled northeast adhered, in certain regards, to a similar conceptual framework. Indeed, Yan and northern Hedong were at times explicitly treated on par with the northwest. According to one mid-century memorial:

> Nowadays, the northern barbarians [i.e., the Khitans] occupy the garrisons of Yan and northern Hedong, while [the Tangut leader] Yuanhao plunders Lingwu, Yin, and Xia. All are our [former] prefectures and commanderies. Their ceremonial carts and costumes, their children, their precious goods are all identical to those of the Han.[133]

And, according to Qin Guan's own account of his hawkish fantasies as a young man:

> I wished to take after the greatest of strategies [used in the past] in order to exact Heaven's punishment; I would recover the former lands of Yan and Xia, thereby offering comfort to the people left behind since the Tang and [Later] Jin. I would [thereby] spread my reputation beyond all bounds, by implementing plans that would stand the test of time. How grand would that have been![134]

[130] XCB 381.9283.
[131] XCB 381.9280; SS 339.10832–33.
[132] XCB 460.11001. Besides Su Che, Sima Guang and Su Shi made similar observations. See P. J. Smith, "Shen-tsung's Reign," 478.
[133] QSW 20:25.
[134] QSW 123:333.

In both of these two cases, arguments were based on a combination of historical and ethnocultural principles.

As with the northwest, some court officials argued that, for pragmatic and ethical reasons alike, it was better to limit territorial ambitions to dynastic lands. One frequently cited example concerned Fu Bi's 1042 embassy to Liao. To combat the Liao claim to Guannan – two prefectures seized from the Khitans by the Later Zhou a few years before the founding of the Song – Fu observed to the Khitan emperor:

> Emperor Gaozu of Jin relinquished the province of [Yan] to the Khitans; emperor Shizong of Zhou recaptured Guannan. All these are matters of other dynasties. It has been ninety years since the founding of the Song; if both of us start claiming the former territories of other dynasties, how would this be to the advantage of the Northern Court [i.e., Liao]?

While hunting with the emperor the next day, Fu Bi brought up the Guannan issue once more: "How could the Southern Court . . . agree to give up the former lands of the [Song] imperial ancestors?"[135] The dynastic principle was brought up again on the eve of the Jurchen invasion, for example, by the official Wang Shu (d. 1143):

> Our state has been at peace with the people of Liao for a hundred years. Now we sit by and watch as their state disintegrates [before the Jurchen onslaught] without providing assistance, and then exploit their land. How is this not laying the foundation for the Jurchens to bring disaster on us?[136]

"Their land" referred, of course, to Liao dynastic territory. It is worth noting that, in these examples, the dynastic principle was invoked under two specific circumstances: first, in the context of diplomatic negotiations, when pragmatism was essential; and second, in the desperate final pleas by doves hoping to ward off an imminent invasion of Yan.

But if the Song claim to Khitan-controlled territories in the northeast shared conceptual similarities with the claim to Tibetan and Tangut lands, the two claims differed in two important ways. First, whereas doves invoked ecological constraints in arguing against military expansionism in the northwest, nobody at court argued that Yan – an agricultural breadbasket – was ill-suited for supporting a Chinese administrative infrastructure. In his unsolicited letter to the emperor, Chao Buzhi

---

[135] XCB 137.3284–85. Fu Bi was later remembered for such quips, which are cited in his spirit path inscription. See *Su Shi wenji*, 2:526–27.

[136] SS 372.11545.

(1053–1110) contrasted the northwest and the northeast in especially stark terms:

> How can the wealth of the six cities of Hehuang compare to the wealth of Yan? Hehuang is remote; only by emptying the cities' coffers can the Middle Kingdom defend it with some degree of confidence. By contrast, with the wealth of Yan, we can be sure it will be easy to defend. As for its urban layout, its agricultural work, the literary conventions of its administrative documents, and its military formations and ranks, none do not derive from the Middle Kingdom's old customs. If we were today to rule it in accordance with the Middle Kingdom's laws, its people would be easily pacified. Once we rule Yan, we would quickly control all former territories of the Later Jin.[137]

Second, during the century after the peace of Chanyuan of 1005, there was a new consensus among Song political elites that the people of Yan were ethnically Han and the territory of Yan belonged to the "Middle Kingdom" – even as these same men overwhelmingly opposed war with Liao. It was not uncommon to portray peace with Liao as a tragic necessity. Yu Jing (1000–64), for example, who was resolutely opposed to the conquest of Yan, admitted that he was "pained that the land of Yan is in the clutches of the barbarians."[138] Zhang Lei (1054–1114) described his sorrow at the loss of Gansu and Yan – both of which he noted were former territories of the Han and Tang – even while urging the court to "proceed with caution," a common euphemism for avoiding an all-out war:

> As for the fact that our prestige exceeds that of all others on earth, yet two corners of the land cannot be [under our control] as before. How does this make any sense? It is for this reason that I feel deep resentment and profound regret, and call on our great generals to render on behalf of the emperor meritorious services unsurpassed in their excellence. I only ask that we plan carefully and proceed with caution.[139]

And, in 1078, the official Huang Tingjian (1045–1105), in a poem, praised the peace agreements negotiated under Zhenzong and Renzong, yet not without a hint of ambivalence:

> Emperor Zhenzong's many policies were superb;
> Emperor Renzong's achievements were superior.
> After re-establishing the imperial capital upon founding our dynasty,

---

[137] QSW 125:329.
[138] SS 162.4428.
[139] QSW 128:35.

We defeated the Tartars, though we still relinquish vast sums of gold
    [i.e., as an annual payment].
For a century, we have rested our soldiers,
After appeasing our foe on that day.
Rather than striving to break the back of the Xiongnu [i.e., Khitans],
It is better to stay the course [of paying for peace].[140]

Needless to say, the fact that the eleventh-century commitment to peace coexisted with an increasingly passionate conviction that Yan was rightfully Chinese did not bode well for the long-term stability of the post-Chanyuan order.

The culmination of the new irredentist logic was evident in a particularly striking way in the final decade of the Northern Song, as the court began plotting with the Jurchens on how to carve up Liao territory. In the second month of 1120, during the first substantive negotiations, the Song envoy asked his Jurchen counterpart for all "former Han prefectures" to be granted to the Song.[141] Given that reference here was only to "Han" and not to "the Han and the Tang," the expression "Han prefectures" designates almost certainly the former lands of the ethnic Han people (or lands formerly under the rule of Han people), rather than the lands once under the control of the Han Dynasty. The invocation of ethnic lands here is not surprising, of course, in the context of a transcultural discourse designed to make sense to the Jurchen negotiators. This language was used repeatedly in subsequent negotiations. In a letter to the Song emperor following important Jurchen military victories over the Khitans later that year, the Jin ruler Aguda proclaimed his right to all Khitan territory, but agreed to "hand over Yan and Yun [the Sixteen Prefectures] to the Southern Court as a special concession, both in appreciation of the good intentions of the emperor of the Southern Court, and because Yanjing [the principle city of Yan] was originally Han land."[142] In the seventh month of the year, a Jin envoy arrived in Kaifeng with a state letter confirming once more that "Yanjing and its attached prefectures were originally Han lands."[143] The response from the Song emperor, dated two months later, then reasserted that "the land of Yan, under occupation since the Five Dynasties, including the former Han lands, the

[140] *Huang Tingjian shi jizhu*, 3:868.
[141] SCBM Zhengxuan, 4.32.
[142] Ibid.
[143] Ibid., 4.35.

Han people [residing there], and the [strategic] passes of Juyong, Gubei, Songting, and Yu, should be returned [to us] as already discussed."[144]

To recap, what we have seen, in brief, is a tendency in the second half of the Northern Song to lay claim to territories not under the Song's de facto control on the basis of historical and ethnocultural principles. But how did this aspect of Northern Song political culture differ from pre-Song times? One approach to answering this question is to examine pre-Song uses of irredentist vocabulary. In texts dating to the Tang and earlier, the expression "former lands" referred almost exclusively to the homeland of individuals, or, in some cases, to the homelands of individual tribes or peoples.[145] Even when it referred to lost territories once under the state's control, the issue at hand was former lands of the dynasty, not lands that had belonged to a past dynasty. Moreover, such references seem not to have been invoked to justify expansionist policies.[146] In a similar way, the expression "Han lands" was not used to refer to territories occupied by Han people. In diplomatic documents – notably in the Sino-Tibetan treaties – it was used in a geopolitical sense to refer to territories under de facto Tang rule; alternatively, it referred in historical texts concerning the Han Dynasty to lands under that dynasty's control. The exceptional pre-Song references to land occupied by ethnically Han people – references attributed to the Liao founder Abaoji and to a Chinese envoy to the Khitans – are suggestive.[147] As we shall see, it was indeed the experiences of the Song ambassadors to Liao that, more than anything else, account for a new sense of what constituted the proper limits of the territory of the "Middle Kingdom."

[144] Ibid., 4.36. Finally, after the Jurchens transferred control of Yan to the Song in early 1123, numerous Song officials submitted congratulatory memorials to their emperor. A typical one of these memorials praised the emperor for having "seized the former land of Yan, and consoled the people left behind in the clutches of the enemy." See ibid., 17.158, collated against the *Siku quanshu* edn. of this same text. For other contemporaneous documents using such language, see SHY *fanyi* 2.35–36; QSW 134:60, 142:241, 144:285–86, 149:140–41, 155:137, 157:107.

[145] By "former lands," I generally refer to one of the following terms: 舊土, 舊地, 故地, 故土.

[146] E.g., after the reconquest of the Four Garrisons in the Tarim Basin, Empress Wu praised a general for reconquering "former lands" once under Tang control: "In the Zhenguan era, the western frontier stood at the Four Garrisons. Subsequently, they were not well defended, and were abandoned to the Tibetans. Now, this former land has been entirely recovered." Later in the dynasty, Emperor Xianzong (r. 805–20) "wished to recover the former land of Longyou [i.e., Gansu]." See JTS 133.3681; XTS 111.4148. In both cases, the monarchs referred to "former lands" of the dynasty (or, in the case of Empress Wu, of her deceased husband's dynasty), not of a transdynastic "Middle Kingdom," and they did so only in passing, not as a basis to justify military action.

[147] For Abaoji's reference to ethnic "Han lands," see JWDS 88.1148, 137.1830–31; CFYG 14:7901–02, 20:11519. For reference to the Sixteen Prefectures as "former Han lands" in Hu Qiao's embassy account, see XWDS 73.907.

For another useful point of comparison between the Song and earlier times, one can turn to arguments at the courts of the Sui and early Tang to justify military expansion into Korea, the Eurasian steppe, and Central Asia.[148] Opponents of expansionism foreshadowed some of the arguments made much later at the Song court, noting both topographic and ecological barriers constraining the reach of Chinese armies and of the Chinese state apparatus.[149] What one does not find in Sui and Tang political discourse is allusion to an irredentist agenda to recover "former" territories of historical dynasties.[150] The campaigns against Koguryo and the Korean peninsula during the reigns of Sui Yangdi, Tang Taizong, and Tang Gaozong, for example, were driven by inter-state politics. By getting involved in the management of the relations between the Korean kingdoms, the Tang hoped to cultivate loyal allies and enhance its prestige on the world stage.[151] In addition, the megalomaniac Tang Taizong seems to have been inspired to take Korea in part to fulfill his personal ambition to match or even surpass the accomplishments of great kings and emperors of the past.[152] Though some of Taizong's advisors – notably Pei Ju (547–627) and Wen Dalin (575–637) – recognized that parts of the Koguryo Kingdom occupied territories once under the administrative control of the Han Dynasty, their primary concerns lay not with establishing direct rule over this land, but rather with preventing Koguryo from rejecting its vassal status, thereby setting a precedent for other neighboring states to follow. "We cannot allow them to disavow their subordination to us," Wen insisted.[153]

Tang expansion toward the Eurasian steppe and into the Tarim Basin (in modern-day Xinjiang) under Tang Taizong, Tang Gaozong, and Empress Wu can be accounted for in a similar way. Although historians

---

[148] I thank Victoria Ma for compiling some of the material that follows while working on her undergraduate thesis, "Defining Imperial Territory during the Tang and Song Dynasties" (May 2015).

[149] E.g., Shao-yun Yang, "Reinventing the Barbarian," 5.

[150] Cf. Twitchett, "Introduction," 32, which mentions in passing that Sui-Tang expansionism sought the "recovery of territories formerly under Han rule"; later chapters of the *Cambridge History*, however, rarely bring up this motive. E.g., A. F. Wright, "Sui Dynasty," 138, 146, suggests that Sui Yangdi was driven by a desire for "geo-political dominance" and by a vision of himself as destined for glorious victories. Similarly, though Wang Zhenping, *Tang China in Multi-Polar Asia*, 55 suggests that Korea was perceived as "*terra irredenta*," he later observes that *Realpolitik* was the Tang's primary driving force.

[151] Wechsler, "T'ai-tsung the Consolidator," 231–35; Wang Zhenping, *Tang China in Multi-Polar Asia*, 266–72.

[152] Wechsler, "T'ai-tsung the Consolidator," 232; Shao-yun Yang, "Reinventing the Barbarian," 5–10.

[153] JTS 199a.5321; Shao-yun Yang, "Reinventing the Barbarian," 30–32.

have proposed a gamut of explanations, including the desire to secure Silk Road trade routes or to exert sovereignty over an ever larger territory, military-strategic reasons seem to have been particularly critical.[154] In the early years of the dynasty, the Mongolia-based cavalry armies of the Turkish confederation posed a grave threat to the Tang regime. It was in order to neutralize the Turks that Taizong first sent armies into the steppe. To further weaken them, he subsequently turned to a strategy first used in the Han Dynasty, annexing the oases of the Tarim Basin in order to limit the flow of vital agricultural supplies to the nomads.[155] A century later, after the decline of the Turks, the Tarim Basin played a key role in the "grand strategy" against the powerful Kingdom of Tibet. By controlling this region together with the Gansu Corridor, the Tang was able to block Tibetan access to the Wei river valley (site of the Tang's primary capital), while also preventing Tibet from joining forces with steppe nomads further north.[156]

In sum, unlike during the Song, irredentist territorial claims based on historical or ethnocultural principles played at best a minor role in spurring the territorial expansion of the Sui-Tang period. Throughout this period, the court was far more interested in preserving the authority and prestige of the regime than in seizing "former" territory. One can hardly imagine an official in the Tang proposing what Chao Buzhi proposed in the late eleventh century, in his unsolicited letter to the Song emperor:

> Once our soldiers have pacified [Yan], the former territories of the [Later Jin] will have been recovered. I ask that we then respect the frontiers, scrupulously run patrols, and admonish border officials not to seek to profit on behalf of the throne from any lands not [belonging to] the Middle Kingdom . . . Though the caitiffs [i.e., Khitans] will have lost Yan, they will recognize that it was originally former territory of the Middle Kingdom and will not be stingy on the matter. The Middle Kingdom will once again make peace with them and re-establish diplomatic exchanges.[157]

---

[154] Skaff, "Straddling Steppe and Sown," 62–89.

[155] Wang Zhenping, *Tang China in Multi-Polar Asia*, 39–45. Although Taizong would later invoke the presence of ethnic Chinese in Gaochang, apparently in an ex post facto justification for the annexation of the region, he did not initially embark on his military campaigns with these populations in mind. See Shao-yun Yang, "Reinventing the Barbarian," 35–36. A century and a half later, an imperial rescript ordered the repatriation of Han soldiers and settlers to the Tang interior after the loss of the Western Regions; it did not lay claim to the territory they occupied. See QTW 464:4738–39.

[156] Twitchett, "Tibet in Tang's Grand Strategy"; Wang Zhenping, *Tang China in Multi-Polar Asia*, 150, 277–79.

[157] QSW 125:335.

So convinced was Chao that the Song had a fundamental right to take Yan that he could not imagine that the Khitans would harbor resentment after an invasion. It was no small irony that, as we shall see, the Khitans in fact conceived of their state in entirely different terms – as multinational rather than monoethnic.

A final way to get at the novelty of the Song sense of Chinese territory is to examine the evolution in discourse regarding non-Chinese regimes that controlled the Chinese heartland. The first lengthy period of non-Chinese control of North China followed the Xiongnu invasions that forced the Western Jin court to flee south in the year 316. Among the dynasties subsequently established in the north, variously by steppe or Manchurian tribesmen, the most successful was the Särbi Northern Wei. Textbooks of Chinese history today treat the Northern Wei as the first effective "conquest dynasty," which established the precedent followed later by the Khitan Liao, Jurchen Jin, Mongol Yuan, and Manchu Qing dynasties. But, in contrast to the Southern Song, which obsessed over the alien occupation of the north, the native Chinese regimes based in the south during the Northern Wei period showed very little interest in reconquering North China, preferring to safeguard their own positions, while promulgating the idea that their own cultural refinement distinguished them from the coarse but virile northerners – northerners that included both ethnic Särbi and the sorts of ethnic Chinese that later Song commentators might have identified as "people left behind." Military forays into the north were spurred by military men seeking to expand their power and influence at the southern courts, not with a mind toward the reconquest of lost Han Chinese territory.[158] The southern regimes had so little notion of conquering the north that they simply re-established administrative units in the south named after northern counties and prefectures, providing northern émigrés with new places to call home.[159]

A second period of non-Chinese control began after the fall of the Tang, when, in 921, a Shatuo Turkish regime based in the northeast overthrew the Later Liang Dynasty (907–21), ushering in a thirty-year period when North China was ruled in succession by three short-lived

---

[158] Tian Xiaofei, *Beacon Fire and Shooting Star*, 310–66; Tian Xiaofei, "From the Eastern Jin through the Early Tang," 266–68, 277; Graff, *Medieval Chinese Warfare*, 127–28.

[159] Chittick, *Patronage and Community*, 20–21. From the perspective of an evolving southern identity, the Yangzi River sometimes represented the northern limits of the civilized world; see the discussion of Guo Pu's "Rhapsody on the Yangzi River" in Tian Xiaofei, "From the Eastern Jin through the Early Tang," 204.

Shatuo dynasties – the Later Tang (923–36), the Later Jin (936–47), and the Later Han (947–50). Once again, there is little evidence that the native Chinese dynasties in the south were particularly concerned by the non-Chinese origins of the Shatuo regimes. Even the more powerful of the southern dynasties – including Wu (902–37), the Southern Tang (937–75), Wuyue (902–78), and the two Sichuan-based Shu kingdoms – paid greater attention to rivalries with each other than to the situation in the north, establishing alliances when it was useful either with one of the Shatuo states or even with the Khitans.[160] The Shatuo regimes were never singled out as less legitimate than other rival states due to their non-Chinese origins.[161]

Attitudes toward both the Shatuo and the earlier Särbi dynasties changed markedly in the Song. Because the Song imperial clan had itself emerged to prominence from within the Shatuo power structure, the Later Tang, Later Jin, and Later Han dynasties were enshrined early on by the Song court as the legitimate successors to the Tang, at the expense of the southern regimes. By the mid-eleventh century, however, many prominent intellectuals were evidently uncomfortable with these three non-Han-ruled dynasties. For good evidence of this shift in perspective, one can compare the late tenth-century *Old History of the Five Dynasties* with the mid-eleventh-century *New History of the Five Dynasties*. The former does not bring up ethnicity as an issue when discussing the Shatuo. The latter – a work composed by the scholar, statesman, and pre-eminent historian Ouyang Xiu with the explicit goal of correcting errors of historical interpretation in the earlier work – exhibits far more skepticism.[162] Particularly apparent is Ouyang's distaste for the second Shatuo dynasty, the Later Jin, a regime that was ultimately overthrown in the 947 Khitan

---

[160] Wang Jilin, "Qidan yu Nan Tang"; Worthy, "Diplomacy for Survival"; Kurz, "The Yangzi"; Wang, *Power and Politics*, 228–41.

[161] Moreover, the legitimacy of the southern regimes was derived often as much from appeals to regionalist sentiments as from a claim to have inherited the Tang mandate. Even while portraying itself as the legitimate successor of the Tang, the Sichuan-based Former Shu Kingdom (907–25) established monuments commemorating local Sichuanese heroes, and claimed to have inherited the mantle of Sichuan-based regimes of the past, notably Shu Han of the Three Kingdoms period. See Wang, *Power and Politics*, 185–93. After the founding of the Song, some southerners maintained strong regionalist attachments to their defunct states even after receiving appointments in the new Song bureaucracy. E.g., after relocating from Jiangnan to Kaifeng to serve the Song, the former Southern Tang official Xu Xuan (917–92) continued to write inscriptions primarily for Jiangnan religious institutions, to maintain social ties primarily with people from Jiangnan, and to provide charity to impoverished natives of Jiangnan. See Tackett, "Story of Xu Xuan"; Woolley, "From Restoration to Unification."

[162] Davis, *Historical Records of the Five Dynasties*, lxi; So, "Negotiating Chinese Identity," 223–32.

invasion of North China. "The Jin Dynasty arose from among the barbarians [i.e., the Shatuo]," he asserted. "In the end, it was destroyed by barbarians [i.e., by Khitans]."[163] Though Ouyang never went so far as to propose that the Southern Tang or other southern regimes possessed greater legitimacy than the northern dynasties as successors to the Tang, he was explicit about his unease at treating the southern states as mere tributary vassals of the Shatuo regimes. "When looking at the barbarians from the perspective of the Middle Kingdom, it is acceptable to treat them as barbarians," he wrote in a question-and-answer dialogue that follows the Table of the Ten Kingdoms in the *New History of the Five Dynasties*. "[But] looking at the Ten Kingdoms from the perspective of the rulers of the Five Dynasties, it is not acceptable to treat them as barbarians."[164]

Song condemnation of the earlier Särbi regimes was more unambiguous. Previously, under the Sui and Tang dynasties, there had been widespread agreement among scholars that the Mandate of Heaven (possessed by the one and only legitimate emperor) had been held by the Särbi dynasties in the north, not the Han-ruled regimes in the south.[165] It was only under the Song that the Tabgach Northern Wei came to be viewed as illegitimate insofar as it was a non-Han regime. An essay on court ritual and music included in the *New Tang History* bluntly noted the "barbarian" origins of the Northern Dynasties: "After the chaos at the end of the Han Dynasty, and after the [Western] Jin fled south of the Yangzi, the Central Plains fell to the barbarians."[166] When warning the court of the Tanguts' imperial pretensions, the powerful mid-Song statesman Fan Zhongyan compared them to a series of non-Chinese regimes of the past, in a 1043 memorial composed on behalf of himself and other like-minded court officials:

> Advisors [favoring the peace terms] all assert that Yuanhao [the Tangut leader] is a Tartar, who [consequently] has no desire to occupy the Middle Kingdom, seeking only to establish his prestige among the frontier tribes. [But] we assert that the followers of Tabgach Gui, Shi Le, Liu Cong,

---

[163] XWDS 17.181. For a similar observation, see XWDS 17.188. Ouyang's ambivalence toward the Later Tang emperor Mingzong (926–33) is interesting. Though Mingzong "arose from among the northern barbarians," he was both incorruptible and an effective ruler, according to Ouyang. But Ouyang also notes that "the character of the barbarian is stubborn . . . such that [Mingzong] often executed innocent ministers." See XWDS 6.66.

[164] XWDS 71.881; So, "Negotiating Chinese Identity," 232.

[165] Tian Xiaofei, *Beacon Fire and Shooting Star*, 318; Holmgren, "Northern Wei as a Conquest Dynasty," 2–4.

[166] XTS 21.460.

Fu Jian, and Helian Bobo [founding emperors of fourth-century "conquest" dynasties] were all Tartars, yet every one of them took residence in [i.e., invaded] the Central Plains. More recently, Li Keyong and his son [founder of the Later Tang], who were Shatuo, established a base in Taiyuan and later a capital at Luoyang . . . Indeed, rebels against the Han house [i.e., Chinese regimes] do not enjoy living amid the barbarian lands; they scheme in their hearts to conquer Han territory. They then force Han people to administer the cities that they seize, much like when the Khitans, after obtaining the [Sixteen] Prefectures south of the mountains, ordered Han people to administer them on their behalf.[167]

Fan's contemporary Zhang Fangping described the situation after the Western Jin court fled south in similar terms:

The world was torn asunder. In the chaos of the Yongjia era [307–13], all moral principles were shattered; Qiang and Tartar [tribesmen] lived scattered about the various Xia lands [i.e., the Central Plains], while [Han Chinese] officials spread out in Jing and Wu [in the South].[168]

In earlier times, the fact that the Northern Dynasties had – in principle at least – performed the imperial rituals in accordance with tradition and had made use of the Chinese administrative infrastructure was sufficient to establish the legitimacy of their rulers. By the mid-eleventh century, in the eyes of Ouyang, Fan, and Zhang, they were suspect because they were not Han Chinese. Finally, in the Southern Song and early Yuan, condemnation of the Tabgach clan reached a sort of apogee, notably in the writings of the Song loyalist Zheng Sixiao (1241–1318):[169]

A minister performing the functions of the lord, barbarians performing the functions of the Middle Kingdom – throughout history, among the sinister things of the world, none are greater than these. For barbarians to perform the functions of the Central State, this is not a blessing from the barbarians, but is actually a calamity brought on by them. It is as if an ox or a horse were one morning suddenly to understand the language of men while still wearing a hairy tail and standing atop four hoofs. Even a young child no more than three feet in height would, on seeing such a sight, do no more than exclaim "ox-horse demon!" He would dare not call such a thing a "human"; truly, it would be too bizarre a thing! . . . As for Tabgach Gui [founder of the Northern Wei] and the sixteen barbarian states [i.e., the Northern Dynasties], none of them properly performed the functions of

---

[167] QSW 18:225.
[168] QSW 38:117.
[169] It should be remembered that Zheng Sixiao was not typical of the Song loyalists who survived the Mongol invasion. See Jay, *Change in Dynasties*, 186–90, 195. On whether Zheng's text cited here is a Ming forgery, see ibid., 74–76.

the barbarians. Even if Tabgach Gui made use of the musical and ritual implements [of the Chinese imperial tradition], and usurped the functions of the Middle Kingdom, thus bringing chaos to the natural order of things, this was no different from clothing an ox or a horse and calling it a human . . . Lord and minister, the civilized center and the barbarian – these have constituted the great divisions of the world throughout history. How can one muddle [these distinctions]? . . . Some will say, "The Tabgach clan, including tribesmen of the extreme north, are all descendants of the Yellow Emperor. . ." I say, if the scions of great ministers of state abandon the *Songs* and the *Rites*, some delighting in serving as yamen runners, some drifting off to be bandits, how is it acceptable to bring up the achievements of their ancestors and place them among the ranks of grandees? This is to say nothing of the lands beyond the remote frontiers, which, possessing a monstrous *qi*, produce barbarians – lands such as the country of hairy men, the country of apes, the country of dogs, and the country of women. Their kinds are very strange; they are not at all of the [same] seed and kind as people of the Middle Kingdom. Since [the world] was created, these have existed. To say they are descendants of the Yellow Emperor or descendants of the Xiahou clan [of the Xia Dynasty of antiquity] is, thus, false.[170]

Amid his flamboyantly vitriolic chauvinism, for which Zheng is well known, one can discern the classic articulation of ethnic difference in his refusal to accept that the Tabgach might have shared a common ancestor with the Chinese. In addition, Zheng clearly rejected the idea that the descendants of a man of a "strange kind" – who was not ethnically Han – could legitimately rule over China.

To sum up so far, the discussion above has traced the emergence over the course of the eleventh century of the idea that it was possible to define the proper geographic limits of the imperial realm on the basis of the territorial extent of historical dynasties, as well as the geographic range of ethnically Han populations (element 6 in Table 4.1). Moreover, this notion spurred irredentist claims to "former" lands beyond the limits of Song political control. We saw signs of this perspective early in the dynasty in the edicts of Song Taizong, though Taizong focused exclusively on Yan, and was probably driven by a sentimental attachment to his own homeland. By the middle of the Northern Song, policymakers across the political spectrum – including, notably, the doves at court – came to accept the logic underlying such irredentist claims, both in talking about Yan and in talking about other frontiers. Though I have focused on the northeast and northwest, one late eleventh-century imperial geography included dozens

[170] QSW 360:56–57. On the Tabgach claim of descent from the Yellow Emperor, see ZZTJ 140.4393.

of southern and southwestern prefectures alongside the Sixteen Prefectures in a list of "prefectures beyond the pale" that had once been under Tang control.[171] Though the territorial claims coexisted for decades alongside a continued commitment to peace with Liao, they, nevertheless, provided ideological fuel for irredentist military campaigns (element 7 in Table 4.1), first in the northwest and the south, and then – late in the Northern Song – in the northeast. Finally, as will be clear in a subsequent chapter, the idea of a common historical and ethnocultural zone implied a homogeneity in the ethnic and cultural landscape (element 8 in Table 4.1) that was, in fact, at odds with the wide cultural and linguistic variability across the Song empire. This imagined homogeneous space – what I call "sinic space" – defined the territory of a transdynastic "Middle Kingdom," rather than of the Song Dynasty alone, as it included areas that the Song had never controlled.

Implicit in this entire discussion, of course, is the suggestion that the Song elite imagined Chinese territory in ways that resembled how national territory was later conceived by Europeans. To be sure, one must draw such a comparison with care. Even among Europeans, the fundamental logic at the heart of territorial claims could vary significantly at different times and under different circumstances. Particularly dramatic were differences in the ways that Europeans justified their ambitions over "empty," or, in some cases, genuinely uninhabited lands in the Americas and elsewhere. In 1612, the French sought to secure rights to São Luís do Maranhão (now in Brazil) by rounding up natives to participate in a "ceremony of possession" performed before God and modeled on the coronation of a European monarch. At roughly the same time, English colonists in North America instead laid claim to land by erecting houses, planting gardens, and in other ways developing the land.[172] Later, in the nineteenth and early twentieth centuries, in the great era of geographers and naturalists, Europeans turned to the right of first discovery, establishing their claims to territory by naming the natural features of a place, or by publishing a description of its geography, fauna, and flora.[173] An alternative way of establishing first discovery – still used to this day – involved unfurling the national flag, a practice that at times has reached comic proportions, such as when the Nazis sought to secure rights to a portion of Antarctica

---

[171] Wang Cun, *Yuanfeng jiuyu zhi*, 10.478–85. This geographic treatise became notorious among doves for implicitly promoting expansionism in the northwest and south.

[172] Seed, *Ceremonies of Possession*, 16–68. In 1765, England countered a Spanish claim to the Falkland Islands by insisting that a vegetable garden had been planted there by a member of a previous English expedition. See Day, *Conquest*, 160.

[173] Day, *Conquest*, 11–12, 49–68.

by dropping flags from airplanes, or when, much more recently, a Russian submarine planted a flag underwater at the North Pole.[174]

But if cultural differences in the logic of territory are to be expected when comparing Song China to early modern and modern Europe, one must not disregard the striking similarities. We previously saw resemblances in how natural frontiers were invoked, and, in the last chapter, we encountered a similar relationship between the language of national territory and the legal language surrounding property ownership. As it turns out, one can also distinguish comparable uses of historical and ethnocultural principles. Already in the early modern period, Western European diplomats turned to historical charters and precedents when negotiating territorial disputes.[175] And, in the nineteenth and twentieth centuries, one encounters numerous claims to territory based on ethnocultural principles – for example, German claims to the *große Deutschland* or Italian claims to the *terra irredenta*. These overarching similarities between Europe and China may have differed in ideological rationales. In Europe, claims to territory based on ethnocultural principles ultimately stemmed from Romantic ideals of self-determination for all people; in Song China, by contrast, they derived from the concept of grand unity. Nevertheless, the similarities in how Chinese and Europeans used history and notions of imagined descent suggest the appeal that both may come to have in human societies under appropriate contingent conditions. Simultaneously, the dangers of nationalist politics have always been apparent. In recent decades, Euro-American foreign policy has generally insisted upon preserving the status quo – for example, Ukrainian control over the Crimea, or Japanese control over the "Senkaku" Islands – precisely because it is viewed as the most reliable way to prevent reckless irredentists from igniting another world war. It was for very similar reasons that doves like Su Che preferred to disregard transdynastic claims and limit territorial ambitions to the lands currently under Song control.

National Symbols, Irredentist Passions

Thus far, this chapter has focused on key developments in conceptualizations of China through the end of the Northern Song. By examining how Han ethnicity and Chinese territory were imagined and then politicized at court, one can, in essence, watch the idea of the Middle Kingdom

---

[174] Prescott, *Political Frontiers*, 300–01; Chivers, "Russians Plant Flag."
[175] Sahlins, *Boundaries*, 32–39.

as nation unfold for the first time among political elites. A critical element of modern national consciousness absent from the discussion so far (and, indeed, absent from many discussions of nationalism) involves emotions.[176] It is emotions in the form of passionate feelings of loyalty that drive people to act and sacrifice on behalf of the nation, thereby making nationalism such a potent political force. We have seen hints of irredentist passions in the speeches and writings of Northern Song policymakers. It was during the Southern Song, however, that these passions blossomed among educated elites. They were fueled by new ways of symbolically evoking the transdynastic nation, corroborating Norbert Elias' observation that, in nationalism, the "focus of emotional attachments" revolves around "impersonal symbols of a hallowed collectivity."[177]

One of the best examples of this phenomenon involves maps, such as the one described at the beginning of the chapter. Whereas Huang Shang's map was eventually disseminated via stele rubbings, a large number of others were published during the Southern Song, and circulated more widely. The historical atlas *Handy Geographical Maps of Successive Dynasties*, for example, first printed in the early twelfth century, went through multiple editions over the course of the Southern Song, eventually becoming a household name among educated elites preparing for the civil service exams.[178] Cartographic representations of the empire on maps and in atlases played a particularly critical role in fostering a sense of China's proper geographic extent. In part, these maps communicated with viewers through textual annotations, such as Huang Shang's colophon. But one must also not discount their power to communicate through visual means alone. Some maps were so similar to each other in appearance that one can readily imagine that the shape of the empire – outlined by seas to the east and south, rivers to the west, and the Great Wall to the north – became iconic, imprinted in the collective psyche of educated Chinese elites in ways similar to the "geo-body" of modern nation-states.[179]

[176] Although emotions constitute both a critical constitutive element of historical phenomena and a factor essential for understanding and explaining historical change, they have often been neglected by historians. See Rosenwein, "Worrying about Emotions in History," esp. 821. Thus, Benedict Anderson's *Imagined Communities*, which explicitly addresses why people sacrifice their lives for their nation, focuses on the cognitive side of national consciousness, not its emotional side. Even a topic like the French Revolution – which has over two centuries accrued a vast scholarship – has only recently been explored from the perspective of the emotions of its participants. See T. Tackett, *Coming of the Terror*, esp. 5–7.

[177] Elias, *Germans*, 148.

[178] De Weerdt, "Cultural Logics of Map Reading," esp. 242–45, 263–67.

[179] For maps with very similar outlines, see Cao Wanru et al. (eds.), *Zhongguo gudai ditu ji*, pls. 61–62, 92, 94–101, 152, 174, 196. On the iconic shape of the "geo-body of a nation," see Thongchai, *Siam Mapped*, esp. 137–39.

To assess more directly the emotional impact of these maps on contemporaries, one can turn to the poems and other literary pieces written in direct response to the viewing of a map.[180] Hilde De Weerdt has identified dozens of such texts, and has demonstrated that, by displaying in such a prominent way the lost territory in the north, maps indeed inspired passionate responses.[181] Upon gazing at one map of the consecutive dynasties of the past, the monk Wenxiang (b. 1211) wrote, "I beat my breast in distress." His contemporary Liu Kezhuang (1187–1269) was "overcome by solitary anger" after looking at a map of the empire.[182] The "patriot poet" Lu You wrote several such poems,[183] including one penned in 1173 after viewing a map of Dasan Pass near the old Qin-era capital at Xianyang, a region then under Jurchen control:

> I would mount my horse to attack the crazed Tartars [i.e., the Jurchens];
> I would dismount to compose military dispatches.
> These were the ambitions I harbored at the age of twenty, [yet]
> At the age of fifty, I remain but an emaciated scholar.
> Between Dasan [Pass] and Chen Depot,
> There are mountains, rivers, thick forests, and sinuous terrain.
> The vigorous *qi* [of the region] produces people of great integrity;
> Together with them, one might make great plans [of reconquest].
> The mountainous city of Xianyang
> Is site of the old capital of the Qin and Han dynasties. [But now]
> The imperial *qi* dissipates in the evening mist;
> The palace halls are overgrown with spring weeds.
> How might I, in the tow of the imperial army,
> Sweep clean [this region] and welcome back the emperor's carriage?[184]

One recognizes the *qi*-based theories of environmental determinism discussed previously, as well as a faith in the ethnic loyalty of some of the remaining Chinese in the north – "people of great integrity" – whom one could still expect to side with the Song nearly two generations after the Jurchen conquest. Of greater relevance here is the ambition of this

---

[180] Though I contend that the passions expressed by Southern Song irredentists reflected new ways of conceptualizing the polities to which they belonged, one should also consider the possibility that new genres of poetry provided educated elites with vehicles for expressing their emotions in new ways. According to Chang, *Late-Ming Poet Ch'en Tzu-lung*, 83–101, a new interest in celebrating romantic love in poetry during the late Ming explains the sudden appearance of a new language for expressing patriotic love.

[181] De Weerdt, "Maps and Memory." For an additional poem of this genre, written upon seeing a map of the Western Regions, see QSS 65:41083.

[182] De Weerdt, "Maps and Memory," 159–60.

[183] Lu You, *Jiannan shigao jiaozhu*, 1:449, 3:1124, 3:1440–41, 5:2282, 5:2331, 8:4464.

[184] Ibid., 1:357–58.

"emaciated scholar" to lead the charge to reconquer the north, an ambition apparently inspired by the map itself.

Besides visual representations of the empire or of lost territories in the north, other sorts of symbols could conjure similarly passionate responses. In the call to arms in Huang Shang's colophon, the mapmaker explicitly invokes two specific symbols of territorial loss, the historical Great Wall – remnants of which survived in Song times in the mountains north of Yan and at sites further west – and the Sixteen Prefectures: "It has long been the case that the territory of the Central Plains included Yan in the north, with the Great Wall marking the boundary. It was only during the Five Dynasties that Shi Jingtang abandoned the Sixteen Prefectures and offered them to the Khitans." These two symbols represented, by their very natures, transdynastic territorial claims. Via these claims, both fueled irredentist sentiments in Song times, showing up on other maps of the period, as well as in a variety of literary texts. Because both would remain potent cultural symbols for centuries, notably for twentieth-century nationalists, it is worth saying a bit more about their cultural histories.[185]

Today, the Great Wall stands as one of the most recognizable symbols of the Chinese nation, appearing, for example, on paper currency and tourist visas. In fact, the Great Wall as a symbol has a long history, having maintained its cultural significance even in periods like the Song when no lengthy frontier walls had been constructed for hundreds of years. We saw in Chapter 2 its use as a reference to the tyrannical excesses of the First Emperor of Qin. In the Song, it was more common than in earlier times to paint the Great Wall in a positive light. To begin with, one encounters renewed discussion of the efficacy of the Wall as a military tool, an idea undoubtedly driven by grave concerns over the loss of the strategic passes through the Yan Mountains – what Song Qi (998–1061) had, in fact, referred to as the "Great Wall line of defense."[186] As Qin Guan (1049–1100) observed:

> In former times, as soon as the Qin had proclaimed its empire, because the six [warring] states were already defunct, there was nothing worth worrying about across the land. It was only the Tartars that still brought trouble to the Qin, whereupon Qin dispatched [the general] Meng Tian to the north to build the Great Wall, and to expel the Xiongnu to over 700 *li* further out.[187]

---

[185] Another symbol of significance in defining Chinese historical territory consisted of the "Surrender-Here Cities" on the Tang frontier.
[186] QSW 23:268.
[187] QSW 120:58.

The author does mention the subsequent rebellions – previously treated as a direct consequence of Qin tyranny – but concludes only that techniques for handling steppe nomads apparently differed from those needed for dealing with an internal uprising.[188] By the Southern Song, revisionist views of the Great Wall were more unabashed. According to Ye Shi, one of the key participants in the Confucian statecraft movement of the Southern Song, the Qin Great Wall was an effective Chinese response to what Ye saw as the earliest instance of state formation among the pastoral nomads. Like Qin Guan, Ye dissociated the collapse of the Qin Dynasty from the construction of the Wall itself.[189] An early thirteenth-century memorial penned by one of Ye's contemporaries, Lou Yue (1137–1213), developed much the same line of argument:

> I once traveled to Yan on a minor assignment [accompanying the Song ambassador] and saw firsthand the old frontier. The so-called Baigou River [marking the Northern Song–Liao border] was really no more than a trickle. The remains of the pools of water, elm and willow trees, and embankments at Ansu and elsewhere [i.e., the hydraulic defenses and tree palisade] were all man-made creations, and not a natural barrier. The Qin Great Wall has, since ancient times, been deemed [the product of] worthless policymaking, but at least it imposed restrictions . . . Ever since Zhou Dewei lost the strategic stronghold of Yu Pass, and the Later Jin gave up the territory of the Sixteen Prefectures, it has not been possible to restore the Middle Kingdom [in full]. It is as if a properly registered household adjoins that of a thief, and depends entirely on a wall for protection. One day, the thief breaks through the wall, whereupon the household draws a line on the flat ground for defense.[190]

The fact that the author points to his own voyage to Yan as a source of inspiration is worth noting; as we shall see later, the embassy travel experience was critical in forming Song Chinese worldviews. More to the point, in rehabilitating the Qin Great Wall – essentially on the grounds that "good walls make good neighbors" – he implies that it was an effective military tool.

It also became more common in the Song to invoke the Great Wall as a timeless, cosmic frontier between Chinese and the lands beyond.[191]

---

[188] Cf. Xia Song, who believed the Great Wall of the Qin (and Han) constituted "the hard labor of past dynasties that has been to the benefit of later kings." See QSW 17:55.

[189] QSW 285:263.

[190] QSW 263:237.

[191] To be sure, the Great Wall was also invoked on rare occasions in earlier times to denote a timeless division between civilization and barbarism. But it is noteworthy that it was Song scholars who popularized these earlier references. E.g., Liu Kuang's (8th c.) argument in a memorial that the

In a poem written in response to viewing a map of Shaanxi, on what was then the frontier with the Tanguts, Liu Chang (1019–68) described the Great Wall as part of the natural frontier that separated China from the outermost "zone of submission":

> The azure sea [of Qinghai] traverses the Western Regions,
> The Great Wall rises up in the north.
> One can clearly make out the physiography –
> I long for when these separated us from the "wilderness zone."[192]

Though the map that Liu Chang examined does not survive, numerous extant Song maps of the empire confirm that the Great Wall often featured prominently, in each case making a dramatic upside-down "v", stretching first westward from the Bohai Sea, then southwestward across the great bend of the Yellow River toward the Gansu Corridor.[193] The course of the Wall was sufficiently similar on a number of different Song-era maps to suggest that its v-shaped curve – like the shape of China, itself – had become iconic. Captions on two of the maps provide a simplified history of the "ancient Great Wall," indicating the multiple Chinese regimes that contributed to its construction – the states of Zhao and Yan during the Warring States period, the Qin and Han dynasties, as well as the Later Wei and the Sui.[194] The implication, of course, was that the Great Wall ran a timeless course across the northern landscape. Indeed, in the *Handy Geographical Maps of Successive Dynasties*, one finds the Great Wall running its v-shaped course across every single map, even those representing periods of time before the first frontier wall was ever constructed. In fact, besides failing to properly historicize the construction of the Wall, the suggestion that Great Walls from different eras ran an identical path was erroneous. Northern border walls were built along multiple different courses in different periods of time. The v-shaped course on the maps – which roughly corresponds to the path of the much later Ming Great Wall – was far removed from the Qin and Han

---

Great Wall served to "separate inside from outside" is quoted in XTS 215a.6023 and Wang Yinglin, *Yuhai*, 25.22a-23b. The assertion in Ban Gu (32–92 CE), *Han shu*, 96a:3872 that the Wall "marks the border of China" is repeated in WJZY, part 1, 19.16b and Wang Yinglin, *Yuhai*, 152.9b.

[192] QSS 9:5822.

[193] For Song maps depicting the Great Wall, see Cao Wanru et al. (eds.), *Zhongguo gudai ditu ji*, pls. 60–62, 70, 72, 94–101, 103, 152. It is not known whether the Great Wall appeared on pre-Song maps, as no pre-Song maps of the empire survive.

[194] Cao Wanru, "Youguan *Huayi tu* wenti de tantao," 42.

fortifications, which were built much further to the north.[195] This wall appearing on Song maps seems rather to have been a conglomerate of the Warring States Qin Wall, built across Shaanxi in the third century BCE, and, further east, the Northern Qi Wall of the sixth century CE. It was probably not a coincidence that it was remnants of these walls that Song officials encountered while in the field, on diplomatic or other missions.[196]

For interesting examples of the spectrum of Southern Song allusions to the Great Wall, one can turn to the work of Lu You, a man known for zealously promoting the irredentist movement to reconquer the north from the Jurchens. In some poems, Lu adhered to the earlier pre-Song view that talented commanders were more valuable than border walls for ensuring a peaceful frontier. As he explained in a poem about one famous frontier fort of the Tang, "The men of Qin who built the Great Wall over the span of thousands of miles, / Were not worth those [Tang-era] braves who defended Beiping [in Hebei]."[197] In another poem, he stated explicitly that military generals might, themselves, "serve as a Great Wall."[198] In a play on this metaphor, the poet elsewhere implied that poetic verse, itself, could play the role of a Great Wall, forming part of the arsenal with which a poet could fend off his literary rivals. "There is a Great Wall in his five-syllable verse," Lu wrote of a certain exam candidate named Cheng, whose "fresh poetry strives to fly and stir, / bringing light to old and tired eyes."[199]

But Lu You also at times followed his Song peers in portraying the Great Wall in a more favorable light. In a poem describing laborers hard at work diking a river in southwestern Sichuan, the new embankment appears "like a single shield that can block a hundred arrow shots, / tortuous its whole length, and great in height, / obstructing [the waters] like the Great Wall holding back the northern barbarians."[200] Whereas an earlier poet would have implied by invoking the Wall in this situation that the state was oppressing the local populace with the dike project, this was not Lu's intention here. The Great Wall was simply an effective barrier. In several poems, Lu You goes a step further, portraying the Great Wall as a

[195] Xu Pingfang, "Archaeology of the Great Wall."
[196] Tackett, "Great Wall," 107, 109–20.
[197] Lu You, *Jiannan shigao jiaozhu*, 3:1158.
[198] Ibid., 6:3001.
[199] Ibid., 2:956. For other uses by Lu You of a similar metaphor, see ibid., 1:433, 5:2717, 6:3119. For an example from the poetry of Fan Chengda, see *Fan Shihu ji*, 1:114.
[200] Lu You, *Jiannan shigao jiaozhu*, 1:387.

remarkable military achievement of the Qin and Han. In "Thoughts on the Past," he expressed the dream of reliving the heydays of the Qin and Han. The Great Wall served as an evocative symbol of this glorious past:

> Recruiting warriors with a thousand coins,
> Building the Great Wall across ten thousand *li*:
> When will the moon over the Green Grave [in Mongolia]
> Also shine upon the Han barracks?[201]

The Wall played a similar role in another poem, in which Lu lamented the Song court's unwillingness to take on the Jurchens in battle, while simultaneously mocking his own failure to put his words into action:

> The fortifications are interminably calm; there have been
>   no calls to arm,
> Although we frequently raise our wine glasses and recite
>   poems [about war].
> The Great Wall spanning thousands of miles was the
>   concern of heroes;
> We [by contrast] banter lightheartedly about the Classics,
>   then nap through the afternoon.[202]

It was as a symbol of the grandeur of past dynasties that the Wall could serve to inspire irredentist passions. Even if Lu You himself could merely fantasize about war over a glass of wine, a true hero – aroused like Lu by the memory of the Great Wall – might one day lead the charge to recover the north.

Besides the Great Wall, the Sixteen Prefectures ("of Yan and Yun") served as a second powerful symbol of the irredentist cause, invoked on Huang Shang's map, as well as on other Song-era maps. In later centuries, the symbolic significance of the Sixteen Prefectures as a *terra irredenta* was unambiguous. Under the Ming, their importance derived in part from the fact that the Ming was the first native Chinese regime to control the territory following nearly half a millennium of foreign occupation. In the words of the Ming scholar and encyclopedist Zhang Huang (1527–1608):

> After the [Later] Jin paid off the Khitans [with the Sixteen Prefectures] in 936, this land fell under caitiff control for over 450 years in total. Only after [Emperor] Taizu of our dynasty chased out the Yuan and restored the Middle Kingdom was [this land] pulled out from the mire [of barbarian control].[203]

---

[201] Ibid., 8:4306.
[202] Ibid., 3:1582.
[203] Zhang Huang, *Tushu bian*, 44.26a–26b. For a very similar observation, see *Ming shilu*, 103: 7601–02 (Shizong 446.2a–2b).

It is for similar reasons that the Ming essayist Gui Youguang (1507–71) "never once failed to sigh" during his travels to Beijing, as he traversed land that had been inaccessible during the Song era, "after the Later Jin bestowed the Sixteen Prefectures to the Khitans."[204] So engrained were the prefectures in collective consciousness that they even made their way into vernacular literature. In a tale by Ling Mengchu (1580–1644), they appear as the destination of a fictional eleventh-century chess prodigy who leaves Song territory after failing to find a soul-mate of equal talent.[205] In the early Qing, the Khitan occupation of the Sixteen Prefectures became a subject of renewed fascination for Ming loyalist writers, serving as a convenient metaphor for the Manchu invasion of China.[206] They were then invoked once more by early twentieth-century nationalists. In the 1905 preface to the very first issue of the *Journal of National Essence*, the chief editor Huang Jie (1873–1935) uses the Sixteen Prefectures to denote one of several eras when "the governance of our China involved despotic governance by a foreign race, and not governance by our own people."[207]

In contrast to these later times, however, Song representations of the territory were more nuanced. The commitment in the Northern Song to maintaining the Chanyuan Peace tended to moderate irredentist language aimed at the northeast.[208] By the Southern Song, by contrast, many felt that Yan – the eastern half of the Sixteen Prefectures – had served as a poisoned apple, luring the Song to violate their oath with the Khitans, while laying the foundation for the loss of all of North China. The Confucian statecraft scholar Ye Shi (1150–1223) bluntly declared that "what brought about the disaster of the Jingkang era [the final two years of the Northern Song] was the seizure of Yan." He repeated himself for emphasis: "Those seeking to explain the failure of the Jingkang era must conclude that it was [due to] the seizure of Yan."[209] Indeed, a sense of the loss resulting from the foolhardy occupation of Yan provoked

---

[204] Gui Youguang, *Zhenchuan xiansheng ji*, 853. Gui makes this observation in a travel diary recounting his 1562 trip to Beijing.

[205] Ling Mengchu, *Erke pai'an jingqi*, 25–26.

[206] See, e.g., the reference to "Yan and Yun" in the preface to *Hou shuihu zhuan*. On the relationship between this anonymously authored work and Ming loyalist literature, see Li, "Full-Length Vernacular Fiction," 628.

[207] Huang Jie, "Guocui xuebao xu," 1b. For a contextualization of this preface, see Hon, *Revolution as Restoration*, 71.

[208] For an exceptional eleventh-century poem calling in passionate terms for the liberation of Yan, see QSS 6:3874–75.

[209] QSW 285:214.

condemnations sometimes as passionate as the cries of the irredentists. Thus, in the final lines of his fourteen-chapter *Explications of the
Geography of the Comprehensive Mirror*, in a section entitled "A Study
of the Sixteen Prefectures of the Later Jin," Wang Yinglin (1223–96)
described his own impressions as he read Sima Guang's monumental
chronicle *Comprehensive Mirror to Aid in Governance*:

> When the founder of our dynasty brought out the map of Yan and showed
> it to [his close advisor] Zhao Pu, Pu believed what would be difficult was
> defending this territory [after its conquest]. [Yet] evil ministers during the
> Xuanhe era got together with the Jurchens for a joint attack to take the
> desolate cities of Yan and Yun, [the result of which is that] our former capi-
> tals are in ruins, and the Central Plains suffer from utter misery. According
> to the top line statement of the *shi* hexagram of the *Book of Changes*, "Petty
> men must not be used lest chaos be brought to the state." My feelings swell
> with indignation over this, and so I end my *Explications* on this note.[210]

But simultaneously, even after the loss of all of North China, many members of the Southern Song political elite remained confident that Yan was
properly Chinese territory. Much of their argument rested on a theory of
natural frontiers. The strategic mountain passes north of Yan served as a
"protective screen" for the North China Plain; the occupation of these
passes by the Khitans provided the steppe nomads with an unnatural
military advantage.[211] These topographic barriers revealed unambiguously
the underlying structure of the cosmos, as Lu You explained:

> I have heard that, both today and in antiquity, topographic features have
> not changed. [Thus,] both Hua and the barbarian lands have well-defined
> territorial extents. As a result, while they [i.e., the nomads] must not cross
> southward into Yan, we must not establish garrisons in Liaodong. Even Yao
> and Shun did not try to impose civilized practices on the barbarians. [At
> the same time,] how can Heaven and Earth tolerate having North China
> stink of goats and sheep [of the nomads]?[212]

In a poem composed on "First Mountain" – on the south bank of the
river marking the Sino-Jurchen border – the official Wang Xin (d. 1194)
made a similar point, once again using Yan to denote what ought to be
China's northernmost territory:

> The Traces of Yu are vast, the sky immense,
> Everything in sight consists of our former mountains and rivers.

---

[210] Wang Yinglin, *Tongjian dili tongshi*, 14:225.
[211] Luo Bi, *Shiyi*, 3.15a–b.
[212] QSW 222:284.

Who thought to use the Huai River to demarcate north and south?
Only when one has gotten as far as Yan does one first reach the
    frontier.[213]

Under these circumstances, Yan – and the Sixteen Prefectures more broadly speaking – became the subject of passionate irredentist verse. Lu You concluded one poem by asking, "When will we hear of an imperial edict dispatching generals to move into Yan?"[214] In another poem – in which, much as we have seen before, he poked fun at himself for his failure to put his words into action – he declared:

In my breast reside a hundred thousand mighty soldiers,
With military flags and imperial banners, but unrealized ambitions.
Do not laugh at this old man by the thatched window;
In a bit, I will joke around about seizing Youzhou [i.e., Yan].[215]

And, in another poem, inspired by the thought of Emperor Gaozong (r. 1127–62) buried in an unassuming tomb while awaiting reburial back in the north, he wrote:

I remember encountering Emperor Gaozong and recognizing
    the physiognomy of a great man;
Who would have thought I would [outlive him and] be left
    to grow old alone!
To this day, his bones lie in a tomb but five meters in height;
Yet although his bones may turn to dust, his heart will not decay.
Why do we not send an army as mighty as a comet to sweep
    Youzhou [i.e., Yan] clean [of our enemy]?
Why do we not, like the men of old, set about to satisfy our
    undying need for vengeance?
Whereas Great men are honored in temples with [posthumous]
    titles,
To my great shame, I do not take action for fear of losing my life![216]

The poet's reference to the dead emperor reminds us that, despite their nationalist rhetoric, educated men continued to see themselves as loyal subjects of their dynasty. But it is not insignificant that the poet then alludes to Yan – land lost before the dynasty's founding.

Lu You was, of course, not alone in invoking the Sixteen Prefectures in stirring irredentist verse. His older contemporary, Cao Xun (1098–1174),

---

[213] QSS 47:29562.
[214] Lu You, *Jiannan shigao jiaozhu*, 4:1894.
[215] Ibid., 4:1969. For poems invoking a similar theme, see ibid., 2:615–16, 7:3952.
[216] Ibid., 4:2197.

did much the same thing. In "Spring Breeze Ode," which begins with an account of the Song court's flight to Hangzhou after the Jurchen invasion, the land of Yan represented once again China's northernmost territory:

> A rainbow in the Heavens disappeared in the daylight,
> As the Central Plains became a territory of sheep and dogs.
> A stream of imperial banners crossed [south to] Jiang-Han,
> And the court officials hid out in one [remote] corner of the world.
> South as far as Wu, north as far as Yan,
> West to Qin and East to Lu, all destroyed by the Tartars.
> It has been three to four dozen years now;
> The people who fled [long for home like] birds pining for their nests.
> Whenever I think of home, the Huai River stands in my way;
> But my heart drifts far away alongside the soaring clouds.[217]

Though certainly less exuberant than Lu You, Cao nonetheless bares his feelings with the image of clouds drifting toward Yan, across a border he himself cannot cross. Nostalgia for the Sixteen Prefectures re-emerged in another poem by Cao Xun, about a solitary swan goose who migrated south, like many Song officials in the wake of the Jurchen invasion:

> To this day, Yan and Dai [i.e., the Sixteen Prefectures] are teeming
>   with Tartars;
> Whenever [the goose] dreams of flying home, he fears their archers.
> He fears their archers: Who is able to expel the Tartar caitiffs for us?
> Once the Tartar caitiffs are expelled, the way of the Han will flourish,
> Whereupon, despite a lifetime of misery [in exile], we will forget our
>   suffering.[218]

Given that neither Cao nor his ancestors were natives of the Sixteen Prefectures, the swan goose was not a metaphor for the poet himself. The passionate call to expel the Jurchens from Yan and Dai was made on behalf of the people of the "Middle Kingdom" as a whole.

All of this passionate irredentist verse was, of course, the work of educated elites. Is there any reason to believe that the masses of the Chinese population shared in these emotions? Although maps of the empire and symbols like the Great Wall may not have meant much to illiterate peasants, one might imagine that idealistic administrators would have considered ways to inspire the masses to fight the state's cause. In 1120, the prefect of Kuizhou, in eastern Sichuan, erected a pavilion in honor of Zhuge Liang, the famous Sichuanese military strategist of the

---

[217] QSS 33:21049.
[218] QSS 33:21078.

third century. In the preface to a rhapsody he wrote to commemorate the event, he explained that Zhuge Liang would inspire the local population to remember the "people left behind" in the "former lands of the Han and the Tang." If the people of Kuizhou were made to chant the rhapsody each year, he explained, "not a few will be filled with indignation."[219] It is unclear, however, whether such concerted efforts of indoctrination would have elicited a national consciousness among the peasantry. In a poem composed, it seems, upon the visit of an acquaintance to the rural outpost where he was then serving in office, the twelfth-century Southern Song official Liao Xingzhi (1137–89) sharply contrasted the patriotic ambitions of the men of his class – who traveled across the empire in service of the throne – with the simple needs and desires of the local populace:

> In a past year, with the crops about to sprout after the spring planting,
> I was pleased to see you arrive, your shoes tattered [from the long voyage].
> This year, with peasants hard at work amid the poldered fields,
> You arrive with your brother aboard a clacking boat.
> Throughout our lives, across the realm, we exert great effort,
> Everywhere intoning poetry, without a day of rest.
> With lofty aspirations and a laugh, [we soar like] drifting clouds,
> In the evening, foddering [our horses] in Yan; in the morning
>   breakfasting in Wu.
> Now ambling along a waterway with rustic knowledge of the nearby
>   fields;
> Now trapped in the net [of officialdom], with the countenance of
>   a roving dragon.
> When great heroes meet, their exploits will be fruitful,
> But would we not be better off just aspiring for warmth, rest,
>   and nourishment?[220]

In speaking of the men of his own class, one recognizes the same self-deprecatory tone we saw in Lu You's poems, poking fun at the fantastic dreams of educated elites – articulated in effete poetry penned after an evening of drinking – to lead a cavalry charge to retake the north. And one recognizes as well the metaphor of the drifting clouds that we saw in Cao Xun's poem. In this case, however, it is clear the author knew full well that the great masses of the Chinese peasantry were concerned not with alien control of the north, but with the more pressing mundane needs of day-to-day life.

---

[219] QSW 135:278.
[220] QSS 47:29167–68.

Conclusion

This chapter has described the development in the Northern Song of a set of ideas that I have equated with the emergence of a form of Chinese nationalism. Critical to this development was a novel way of thinking about territory, articulated by the Song court in the process of formulating policies for dealing with its neighbors. In exploring ways of defining the proper spatial limits of the empire – an empire now seen as bounded rather than universal – policymakers invoked both the geographic extent of historical dynasties and the de facto range of the Han ethnoculture. This new logic of territory helped fuel the irredentist politics of the late Northern Song, and set the stage for the passionate patriotic calls to arm in the Southern Song. Implicit in this way of thinking about territory was the idea that there existed a transdynastic entity – often referred to in Chinese as *Zhongguo* or, in translation, as the "Middle Kingdom" – that was distinct from the Song regime, but that the Song could claim to defend or possess. The notion of a political entity that transcended dynasty and regime and whose territorial extent had deep roots in the past is, in fact, not unlike the manner in which modern nation-states are conceived.

The question remains as to whether culture or ethnicity was more important in defining the "Middle Kingdom." Peter Bol has provided a great deal of evidence to suggest that the ideological basis of political legitimacy in Song China primarily involved culture.[221] The *Zhongguo* was conceived to be spatiocultural in nature, embodying both a fixed territory and a defined culture. Discourse on the *Zhongguo* often revolved around a dichotomy between the interior, where people lived according to the moral principles of the Classics, and an exterior that lay beyond the sway of civilization. And theories of government, including the widely cited eleventh-century treatise on the legitimacy of past dynasties by Ouyang Xiu, focused on two standards: territorial unity and moral rule.[222] The fact that, in works of political theory of this sort, the ideological basis for government depended on culture (which could be learned) and not on ethnicity (which was inherited) was crucial in later times for providing "conquest" dynasties – notably the Jurchen Jin, Mongol Yuan, and Manchu Qing dynasties – with a basis of legitimacy in the eyes of educated Chinese.

---

[221] Bol, "Geography and Culture."
[222] Chan, *Legitimation in Imperial China*, 38–39.

If culture trumped ethnicity in Chinese political theory, what does one make then of the use of the ethnic category *Han* in Song frontier policy? The geographic range of "Han people" was used both to determine the course of a demarcated border and to lay claim to territory beyond the frontier. Here, it is important to recognize the distinction between a political ideology and the unspoken sentiments that underlie a consciousness or sense of identity. The world of today provides ample evidence that ethnicity can operate under the surface, even when in contradiction to sanctified ideologies.[223] In Northern Song China, when working out the details of frontier policy at a practical level, policymakers revealed underlying assumptions about who properly belonged to their political community, irrespective of the ideals of their political theories. Though the category *Han* originated on the Eurasian steppe, I have argued in this chapter that it was naturalized at some point in the Song. Thus, a temple inscription dating to the 1030s equated the "Middle Kingdom" (i.e., *Zhongguo*) with "Han territory." Later in the century, it became common to assume "Han people" inhabiting the territory of a neighboring state naturally felt loyalty to the "Middle Kingdom," while prominent Northern Song literati like Su Shi came to think of their counterparts among the people of Yan as "Middle Kingdom *shidafu*." And Song sources could imagine a Liao Chinese official proclaiming Song Chinese as his "family" and Khitans as not of his "kind." In sum, by the later decades of the eleventh century, political discourse concerning the frontier was governed as much by the strong sentiment that there existed a community of people sharing a common ancestry as by an ideology defining the imperium on the basis of a particular cultural zone.

The nation in Song times was, of course, very different from modern nations in a number of critical ways. It was a social construct in the Song, just as in modern times, but one circulating only among educated elites and not transmitted to the masses of the population. There is no evidence that the Song worldview resembled the modern nationview, in which a multitude of nations have together divided up all territory and all people on earth. There was also nothing in the Song resembling the ideal of popular sovereignty, wherein the nation-state was thought to belong to the people and to be the product of their will. But if the nation in Song times was not rationalized on the same ideological grounds, what

---

[223] E.g., ethnic-based nativisms are prevalent in the United States and Western Europe today, despite state promotion of inclusive ideologies defining the people of the nation in cultural rather than ethnic terms.

it did share with the modern nation was something more fundamental, a mode of consciousness, in which educated elites strongly identified with their "imagined community." One is tempted to see this something that is more fundamental than ideology as constituting a characteristic common to humankind, with the potential to inspire nationalist thinking in multiple places and times under particular conditions.

Why was the eleventh century so critical to the appearance of a form of Chinese national consciousness? As discussed in the Introduction, one recognizes in the Northern Song several close parallels to Benedict Anderson's description of the development of "imagined communities" in the nineteenth-century West. The breakdown of aristocratic hierarchies in Europe finds an analogy in the destruction of the medieval Chinese aristocracy at the turn of the tenth century. The popularization of woodblock printing in the eleventh century, the dramatic expansion in size of the educated population, and the geographic spread of this sociopolitical elite – which had once been confined to the capital – meant that there existed by the late Northern Song a self-conscious empire-wide community of educated elites – the so-called *shidafu*. The meritocratic ideal built into the civil service examination system of the Song period in turn made it possible, in theory, for even humble members of society to study hard and join this community. The closed social hierarchy of the earlier Tang period had disappeared.

Such an account of the emergence of a sense of community that was both homogeneous and empire-wide does not, however, explain how Song political elites came to define the boundaries of their community in ethnic terms, nor does it explain why they came to conflate the state both with the Han ethnoculture and with a clearly defined national territory. What I will propose in the next two chapters is that the origins of the Chinese nation were powerfully influenced by the travel experiences of the ambassadors, who constituted a significant component of the high political elite. During their embassies, the ambassadors not only had opportunities to internalize steppe ethnic categories in the course of diplomatic banqueting (as discussed in Chapter 1), they also had the opportunity to see for themselves the stark ecological and cultural divide that existed between the Chinese world south of the Yan Mountains and the world of the steppe in the lands beyond. Given the importance of the cultural ecology of Northeast Asia to my argument, before exploring the travel experiences of the ambassadors (in Chapter 6), it is necessary first to reconstruct the ethnocultural landscape as it existed in the eleventh century.

5

Mortuary Cultures across the Chinese–Steppe Divide

In 1993, when archaeologists first unsealed the tomb of Zhang Wenzao (1029–74) and his wife at a site near the city of Xuanhua just northwest of Beijing, they were treated to a feast.[1] Set upon two wooden tables placed before a coffin entirely enveloped in Sanskrit characters was an array of porcelain dishes containing offerings of now desiccated pears, chestnuts, jujubes, and other victuals, left untouched for over 900 years. On the floor of the tomb off to one side were additional vessels believed once to have held wine. The pictorial program of the wall murals complemented this display of food. In the antechamber, an orchestra played music as servants – sometimes in Chinese and sometimes in Khitan clothing and hairstyles – prepared hot beverages that were then served by attendants in the main hall. In accordance with Buddhist customs, Zhang and his wife were cremated. However, as was not uncommon in tombs of the region, their ashes had been placed in compartments contained within near life-sized straw manikins, perhaps providing them with the physical bodies they needed to enjoy the banquet.

About ten years prior to this remarkable find, archaeologists unearthed another well-preserved tomb a few hundred miles to the northeast, near the border between Liaoning Province and Inner Mongolia. Although it dated to just a few decades earlier, this second tomb – that of the Liao princess of Chen (1001–18) – was strikingly different in a number of its features.[2] It had clearly not been conceived as the site of grand festivities; the small offering table held few ceramic dishes. Other types of grave goods, however, were in great abundance. One side chamber was filled with horse accoutrements, including iron stirrups inlaid with gold, and

---

[1] In the nomenclature of Chinese archaeologists, the tomb in question is Xuanhua Xiabali Liao tomb number M7; it appears as tomb #918 in the database described in Appendix B. For a full archaeological report, see *Xuanhua Liao mu*, 69–125.

[2] This is tomb #746 in the database. For a full archaeological report, see *Liao Chenguo gongzhu mu*.

a wooden saddle. Unlike Zhang and his wife, the princess and her husband were not cremated, nor were their remains even placed in a coffin. Instead, the couple lay on a funerary couch, their heads resting on silver pillows, their faces concealed behind stunning gold masks, and their bodies shrouded in silver mesh suits.

The two tombs described here both date to the eleventh century. Both were discovered at sites well within the territory of the Liao empire. How then does one account for their great differences? From an epitaph stone contained in Zhang's tomb, we learn that he came from an important local family that had lived in the region for generations. Whereas his brother and nephew held minor positions in the local government, he himself had made a small fortune, perhaps in trade, and had become a great patron of the local Buddhist monastery.[3] The princess of Chen, by contrast, as her title might suggest, was a blue-blooded aristocrat. She was a member of the Liao imperial clan, the granddaughter of Emperor Jingzong (r. 969–82).[4] And she had married the brother-in-law of the reigning emperor, shortly before succumbing to an illness at the age of eighteen. To be sure, a vast gulf in social status existed between the two individuals, perhaps explaining the abundance of precious metals found in one tomb and not the other. But other distinctions – the cremation burial of Zhang as opposed to the interment of the princess without a coffin – surely reflected very different beliefs about death and the commemoration of the dead.

In fact, as we shall see below, the two tombs were typical of two strikingly different mortuary cultures, one Chinese and one originating on the Eurasian steppe, two cultures that coexisted during the Liao Dynasty. By exploiting a large number of published excavation reports of eleventh-century Northeast Asian tombs, this chapter identifies the geographic limits of the Chinese and Khitan cultural zones on an empirical basis. It then explores the role of politics – notably of Liao ethnic policies – in reinforcing the cultural and geographic segregation of peoples. Unlike the previous chapter, focus here is not on the worldview of Song Chinese political elites. Nevertheless, as Chapter 6 will make clear, the geographic distribution of two radically different cultures had a direct impact on how Song travelers to Liao came to understand the limits of the Chinese ecumene.

---

[3] For transcripts of Zhang's epitaph, as well as of those of three close family members, see Xiang Nan, et al. (eds.), *Liaodai shike wen xubian*, 214–17, 294–96.
[4] For a transcript of her epitaph, see Liu Fengzhu et al. (eds.), *Liao Shangjing*, 79.

Tombs of Eleventh-Century Northeast Asia

At the heart of the present study is a database of Northeast Asian tombs compiled from a more or less systematic survey of archaeological monographs and journals dating back to the 1940s. The database – described in more detail in Appendix B – contains information on over one thousand individual tombs discovered in a broad zone straddling the Song–Liao border, a zone composed of the North China Plain, the Shanxi uplands east of the Yellow River, the eastern extremity of the Eurasian steppe, and central and southern Manchuria. The tombs in the survey all date roughly to the "long" eleventh century, equivalent to the period of the Liao and Northern Song dynasties.[5] Each entry in the database includes information on tomb architecture, grave goods, and the major themes of the wall murals. In addition, the location of each tomb is identified using latitude and longitude coordinates.

To be sure, there are numerous methodological problems in the reconstruction of a culture on the basis of excavated remains. Many of these methodological problems are described in Appendix A. In general, one can think of tombs as constituting the material embodiment of a society's mortuary culture, which itself represents only one component – albeit an important component – of the totality of beliefs and practices that defines that society. Often, it is very difficult to provide an interpretive framework for understanding the "meaning" of particular grave goods or tomb features, although I have attempted in some cases to do just this when extant literary sources provide sufficient clues. But even when the meaning of objects is unclear, these objects can be thought of as cultural markers. Fortunately, the vast differences between the two material cultures that are the focus of this chapter leave little room for doubt that they can be used to define quite precisely the Chinese and steppe cultural zones.

Besides problems of interpretation, one must deal with the fact that tombs are never in their original states at the time they are discovered by archaeologists. Most tombs of the eleventh century were robbed of much of their contents centuries ago; and all tombs of this period have suffered from the ravages of time. Thus, even in the case of a tomb for which there exists a particularly thorough archaeological report, its entry in the database will be incomplete, insofar as the entry will list only grave goods and

---

[5] Because stone epitaphs are rarely encountered in eleventh-century tombs, very few excavated tombs of this period can be dated precisely. In general, I followed the intuition of the excavators when assessing whether specific tombs dated to the Liao–Northern Song period, except in cases where I found their dating to be particularly problematic.

tomb features that have not disintegrated over the ages. But it should also be noted that, even in their original states at the time of burial, different tombs of the same culture did not contain exactly the same assortment of objects. People always have a range of possibilities at their disposal; a culture, then, should be defined on the basis of the repertoire of available choices, rather than on the particular choices made in a single case. For this reason, one can rarely draw conclusions based on the *absence* of a particular grave object or mural motif in any one individual tomb.

Fortunately, all of these problems are partially resolved because of the large sample size of the database. To begin with, using statistical techniques, one can identify the probability that any two tomb features are found in the same tomb. One can then determine which sets of features tend to cluster together, allowing one to reconstruct a particular cultural repertoire – that is, the repertoire of choices that defines a culture – despite the fact that most individual tombs do not survive in their original states. In addition, when determining the geographic extent of particular cultures, rather than mapping all tombs included in the database, one can situate only the sample of tombs containing particular features. With a database that is sufficiently large, this sample allows us to draw useful conclusions. The next two sections describe two distinct cultural repertoires apparent in Northeast Asian tombs dating to the Liao and Northern Song periods. I refer to these two repertoires as "Khitan" and "North Chinese," taking the North Chinese repertoire to represent the culture of Chinese living under either Song or Liao political control.[6]

Khitan Mortuary Culture

Table 5.1 lists the objects and tomb features that define the "Khitan" cultural repertoire. These goods include the epitaphs and other inscriptions written in the Khitan script that archaeologists occasionally encounter in Liao-era tombs. Several of the other elements of the repertoire can be linked to Khitan culture on the basis of contemporary or near contemporary literary sources. Song ethnographic literature describing Khitan funerary practices makes note of the unusual coverings placed on the

---

[6] The elements of the two repertoires were initially determined impressionistically after a broad reading of excavation reports and previous scholarship on Khitan mortuary culture – notably Wang Qiuhua, "Liaodai muzang fenqu yu fenqi" and Dong Xinlin, "Liaodai muzang xingzhi yu fenqi." Subsequently, the definitions of the two repertoires were refined on the basis of cluster analysis, as described below.

Table 5.1 *Grave goods and tomb features of the "Khitan" cultural repertoire*

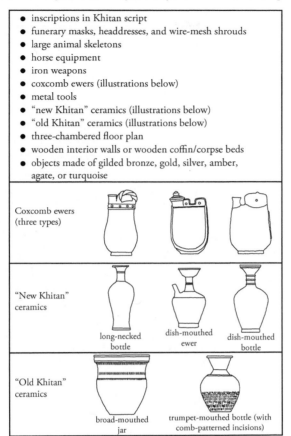

- inscriptions in Khitan script
- funerary masks, headdresses, and wire-mesh shrouds
- large animal skeletons
- horse equipment
- iron weapons
- coxcomb ewers (illustrations below)
- metal tools
- "new Khitan" ceramics (illustrations below)
- "old Khitan" ceramics (illustrations below)
- three-chambered floor plan
- wooden interior walls or wooden coffin/corpse beds
- objects made of gilded bronze, gold, silver, amber, agate, or turquoise

Coxcomb ewers
(three types)

"New Khitan"
ceramics

long-necked
bottle

dish-mouthed
ewer

dish-mouthed
bottle

"Old Khitan"
ceramics

broad-mouthed
jar

trumpet-mouthed bottle (with
comb-patterned incisions)

deceased in some tombs – including that of the Liao princess of Chen – coverings composed of a full-body wire-mesh shroud or wire-mesh gloves and a gold, silver, or gilded bronze mask with headdress.[7] In the words of the twelfth-century writer Wen Weijian, corpse preparation among

---

[7] For descriptions and photographs of Khitan funerary masks, headdresses, and shrouds, see Ji Chengzhang, "Haoqianying di liu hao Liao mu"; Du Chengwu and Lu Sixian, "Qidan nüshi"; Chollet, "Treasures from the Liao Period." It has been variously proposed that these articles are tied to shamanistic, Buddhist, or pan-steppe practices. For a recent study, see Louis, "Iconic Ancestors."

wealthy Khitan families involved "using gold and silver to make masks and copper wire to envelop the hands and feet in a net."[8]

Other literary sources seem to confirm that skeletons of large animals, especially of horses, were also characteristic of Khitan mortuary culture. As early as 992, the Liao state banned horse sacrifices, as well as the interment of armor and of gold and silver objects.[9] A half century later, in 1042, the government broadened the ban to include the sacrifice of cattle as well. This proscription was then reiterated the following year.[10] The only sacrifices apparently deemed permissible were those of sheep, a practice incorporated into the account of Khitan burial customs preserved in the dynastic history of the Liao.[11] The reiteration of the ban suggests that the practice may have been widespread and difficult to stop.

Although not attested in contemporaneous sources, scholars today agree that a series of other burial goods was typical of Khitan burial culture. Many of these goods consist of objects one would associate with a society of pastoral warriors – iron stirrups, horse bits, spherical bells, and other pieces of horse equipment. In addition, although saddles were made of highly perishable wood and leather, Liao-era tombs frequently contain the decorative gilded silver and bronze elements once affixed to the saddle or to the straps attaching the saddle to the horse.[12] Khitan tombs also commonly contain iron weaponry, notably swords, spears, and arrowheads of various types.[13] In very rare cases, wooden arrows and birch bark or leather quivers have survived.[14] One of the more interesting and frequently encountered articles associated with Khitan pastoral culture are the "coxcomb ewers" (*jiguan hu*), ceramic vessels roughly in the shape of a rooster's crown apparently intended to emulate leather saddlebags. These ceramic saddlebags have flattened bodies; often they have small holes, instead of a handle, through which a rope might once have passed.[15]

---

[8] Tao Zongyi, *Shuofu*, 8.49a.
[9] LS 13.142.
[10] LS 19.228, 229.
[11] LS 50.840.
[12] For examples of saddles that have survived almost intact, see "Aluke'erqinqi Dao'erqige faxian yi zuo Liao mu," 150–51; *Liao Chenguo gongzhu mu*, 108–09.
[13] For a survey of commonly excavated Liao weaponry, see Liu Jingwen and Wang Xiulan, "Liao Jin bingqi yanjiu."
[14] Su Ritai, "Keyou zhongqi Bazhalaga Liao mu," 68; "Neimeng Huolinguoleshi Liao mu," 39–40; "Aluke'erqinqi Dao'erqige faxian yi zuo Liao mu," 149; *Zhongguo wenwu ditu ji* (Neimenggu) 2:431, 467.
[15] Yang Jing, "Luelun jiguan hu"; Zhang Songbo, "Guanyu jiguan hu." Coxcomb ewers are also referred to as "stirrup ewers" (*madeng hu*) or "imitation leather bag ewers" (*fang pi'nang hu*).

Other articles frequently found in Khitan-type tombs include tools and ceramic vessels plausibly used by the deceased in life. Archaeologists have on numerous occasions discovered sets of iron carpentry tools – including axes, chisels, files, awls, and adzes – as well as other metal devices, such as shovels, tongs, and scissors. In addition, there are a number of specific ceramic vessel types that seem to have been unique to the Khitan cultural repertoire. These vessels include long-necked bottles (*changjing ping*), dish-mouthed ewers (*pankou hu*) and bottles (*pankou ping*), and Liao three-color (*sancai*) ware, including notably a certain type of three-color oblong dish referred to by archaeologists as a "crabapple blossom platter" (*haitang pan*). Although this particular type of platter was popular in the late Tang capital, by the eleventh century, it seems to have remained in use only in Liao (and not in Song) territory.[16] An older set of earthenware vessels dating to the pre-Liao or very early Liao period included broad-mouthed jars (*changkou guan*), trumpet-mouthed bottles (*labakou guan*), and a variety of vessels with comb-patterned (*biwen*) incisions.[17]

The more elaborate brick tombs containing Khitan-type grave goods were built according to a three-chambered floor plan that seems to have been unique to the region surrounding the Supreme and Central Capitals of the Liao empire. The sloping entry passageways resemble those of Tang imperial tombs, with dirt walls sometimes coated in plaster. However, brick-walled "gate halls" – structures unknown in the Tang world – are typically found just outside the underground door leading into the tomb proper. This door opened into an antechamber, which itself led to a main chamber to the north. Unlike Tang imperial tombs which were laid out along a single axis, these large-sized Liao tombs typically had three chambers, two of which extended out to the east and the west of the north–south axis. In the more elaborate Khitan tombs, one also commonly encounters metal implements made of gilded silver or bronze, as well as ornamental jewelry made of amber, agate, crystal, or turquoise. All such objects – death masks and wire-mesh shrouds, horse equipment, weapons, tools, precious stones, and "Khitan"-type ceramics – are rarely found in Chinese-type tombs.

---

[16] Cf. Dong Xinlin, "Liaodai muzang xingzhi yu fenqi," 65–69, which includes a less comprehensive list of Khitan-type ceramics, and which also includes pumpkin-lobed jars and "chicken-thigh" bottles, which I do not treat as part of the Khitan cultural repertoire.

[17] These last vessels are often found together in the same tomb with other Khitan-type objects (weapons, horse equipment, etc.), but rarely in conjunction with the later types of ceramic vessels.

Table 5.2 *Grave goods and tomb features of the "North Chinese" cultural repertoire*

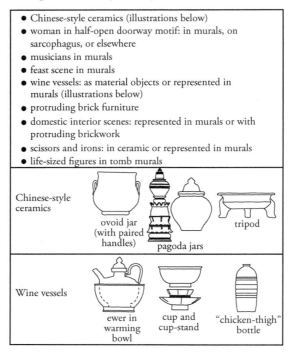

- Chinese-style ceramics (illustrations below)
- woman in half-open doorway motif: in murals, on sarcophagus, or elsewhere
- musicians in murals
- feast scene in murals
- wine vessels: as material objects or represented in murals (illustrations below)
- protruding brick furniture
- domestic interior scenes: represented in murals or with protruding brickwork
- scissors and irons: in ceramic or represented in murals
- life-sized figures in tomb murals

Chinese-style ceramics

ovoid jar (with paired handles)

pagoda jars

tripod

Wine vessels

ewer in warming bowl

cup and cup-stand

"chicken-thigh" bottle

North Chinese Mortuary Culture

Table 5.2 lists the elements typical of "North Chinese" mortuary culture. As will be evident below, this cultural repertoire spanned the Song–Liao border. It included grave goods and tomb features characteristic of Song tombs in Henan, as well as of both Song and Liao tombs in the portions of Hedong and Hebei south of the Great Wall. Due to the migration of Chinese into Manchuria, some Chinese-type tombs of this period have been discovered north of the Yan Mountains as well. Although this repertoire represents a culture shared by populations inhabiting the North China Plain on both sides of the Song–Liao divide, as we shall see, the political border did spur some degree of cultural divergence between Liao and Song Chinese.

One problem encountered when trying to reconstruct this trans-border Chinese mortuary culture stems from the fact that tombs discovered in

Song-controlled regions of Hedong and the North China Plain tend to contain few grave goods, a pattern discussed below. Nevertheless, there are certain ceramic vessel types commonly found in eleventh-century tombs on either side of the border, including ovoid jars – often with small paired handles or with knobbed "pagoda"-style lids – as well as a variety of tripod vessels.[18] There are also characteristic motifs that frequently appear on the walls of Chinese-style tombs, as well as on other tomb surfaces. One such motif – depicted both in painted murals and in carved relief on brick walls or on the surfaces of sarcophagi – consists of a woman standing in a half-open doorway. This motif has variously been interpreted to represent a servant entering the tomb chamber to serve the deceased, a spirit beckoning the deceased to cross the threshold into the afterlife, or an alluring beauty in a sexually suggestive pose.[19]

A particularly useful approach to handling the paucity of grave goods in Song tombs is to pay attention to how tombs functioned as a whole rather than to try to identify isolated elements. One can focus, in particular, on two specific characteristics of the North Chinese understanding of the afterlife. The first involves the idea – quite apparent in the tomb of Zhang Wenzao – that the burial chamber functioned as the venue for a grand post-mortem feast in which the deceased enjoyed music, food, and wine. The second presumes a particular North Chinese understanding of the afterlife, according to which the tomb murals and walls functioned as extensions of the interior of the tomb chamber, creating a "virtual reality" for the enjoyment of the deceased.[20]

Ubiquitous in Chinese tombs on both sides of the Song–Liao border are allusions to a great banquet, allusions apparent in both the grave goods and the wall murals and reliefs. Many tombs contain painted scenes of near life-sized musicians, dancers, and acrobats. Even more common are murals depicting food and beverage preparation or consumption. In some tombs, such as the famous tomb number one excavated at Baisha, Henan in 1951, the deceased couple appears on one wall of the tomb chamber, facing each other at a table while enjoying delicacies set

---

[18] For a good introduction to the ceramic vessels contained in "Han" tombs of the Liao Dynasty, see Yang Jing, "Liaodai Han ren muzang"; Dong Xinlin, "Liaodai muzang xingzhi yu fenqi," 68–69. Many of these vessel types have been encountered by archaeologists excavating the Ding kilns in Song-controlled Hebei. See, e.g., the ewer and jar depicted in "Hebei Quyang xian Jiancicun Ding yao yizhi," 401; and Mu Qing, "Zaoqi Dingci chutan," 31–36.

[19] Goldin, "Motif of the Woman in the Doorway."

[20] Cf. Wu Hung, *Art of the Yellow Springs*, 38–47, 88–89.

before them.[21] As is typical in such murals, a ewer of wine is kept warm in a bowl of hot water placed on the table. In front of each individual is a cup for the wine, posed on a cup stand. Beneath the table is a large wine storage bottle held upright in a bottle rack. And off to the side, a servant holds in both hands a spittoon, an object that had become a necessary component of elegant and refined living since Tang times.[22] The neighboring tomb number two at Baisha has a similar mural, but with dishes of fruits or vegetables accompanying the wine cups on the table.[23]

In the tomb of Zhang Wenzao, one finds a common variation of this banquet scene. Although the murals depict a musical ensemble and the preparation of beverages, the deceased couple does not appear anywhere on the richly painted walls. That is not to say, however, that the dead did not partake of the feast. As we have seen, dishes full of food were set on a table in front of the coffin.[24] Archaeologists also found a cup with cup-stand and a spittoon on the offering table, and a yellow ceramic ewer on the floor – which had apparently been knocked off the table when the wooden tomb door collapsed at some point in the past.[25] Finally, in one corner of the tomb were several wine storage containers, of the type usually referred to as "chicken-thigh bottles" (*jitui ping*) in archaeological reports. One of these storage bottles, hermetically sealed with lime, still contained nearly a liter of a red liquid believed to have once been grape wine.[26] In other words, the same objects that appear in the mural of Baisha tomb 1 were found in material form in Zhang's tomb. In either case, it is clear that the consumption by the deceased of wine and delicacies was integral to the function of the tomb.

Su Bai has theorized that the scenes of a feasting couple in the Baisha tombs is a depiction of the "fragrant banquet" described in one Song Dynasty tale.[27] In this tale, a married couple face each other at a table while listening to music – an activity that, the storyteller informs us, "represents the mutual love between husband and wife."[28] Although the term "fragrant banquet" appears nowhere else in Song literary sources, it has become common currency in archaeological reports. But regardless of

---

[21] Su Bai, *Baisha Song mu*, col. pl. 5.

[22] Ye Wa, "Mortuary Practice in Medieval China," 172–73.

[23] Su Bai, *Baisha Song mu*, col. pl. 9.

[24] *Xuanhua Liao mu*, 347–51.

[25] Ibid., col. pls. 21, 34.

[26] Ibid., 341–46. Archaeologists have also discovered a red liquid in a sealed vessel found in a Liao tomb in Liaoning Province. See "Faku Yemaotai Liao mu ji lue," 27.

[27] Su Bai, *Baisha Song mu*, 48–49 (n.53).

[28] Luo Ye, *Zuiweng tanlu*, 102.

the name one gives to this feast motif, it is clear that it accords well with contemporary literary and artistic representations of good times. One need go no further than the famous painting of Han Xizai's (902–70) notorious night entertainments, attributed to the tenth-century painter Gu Hongzhong (937–75), to encounter a table containing delicacies as well as a ewer, warming bowl, and cups with cup-stands.[29] In his nostalgic account of Northern Song Kaifeng, Meng Yuanlao (fl. 1126–47) imagines a similar scene in his description of an evening in an eleventh-century tavern: "In any wine house, regardless of who they were, whenever two or more people sat down face-to-face to drink wine, they were invariably served a ewer with a warming bowl, two cups with cup stands, fruits and vegetables (five slices per dish), and a bowl of three to five pickles."[30] Thus, the "fragrant banquet" of North Chinese tombs seems to have provided the dead with the delights they might have enjoyed in life, whether in urban taverns or at private soirées.

The "sacrifice of repose," designed to "calm" the soul of the recently deceased, provides clues for understanding more precisely how rituals performed aboveground were linked to the underground feast. This ritual was considered particularly important because, in the days immediately after death, the deceased's two souls were believed to have not yet settled in their proper places – the *hun* soul in the deceased's spirit tablet, and the *po* soul in the tomb. According to descriptions in three different Song-era ritual manuals, by Sima Guang (1019–86), Lü Zuqian (1137–81), and Zhu Xi (1130–1200), the sacrifice in question, which took place in a hall aboveground after the burial, involved laying a table of offerings in front of (i.e., to the south of) the soul seat, on which had been placed the spirit tablet of the deceased.[31] The offering table, thus, had the same spatial relationship to the deceased as in Zhang Wenzao's tomb. On this offering table were placed vegetables, fruits, wine cups with cup-stands, and spoons and chopsticks. A wine bottle was placed in its rack to one side and a brazier for hot water to the other side. The wine was later transferred to a ewer, from where it was poured into the wine cups. Here once again, the arrangement of objects in the sacrifice accorded remarkably well with how these objects were positioned in Zhang's tomb. Zhu Xi also mentions

---

[29] For a detailed image of these vessels, see Sullivan, *Night Entertainments*, dust jacket and 27.

[30] Meng Yuanlao, *Dongjing menghua lu*, 1:420–21. For the identification of *zhuwan* (注碗) as a ewer-warming bowl set, see ibid., 1:424–25; Su Bai, *Baisha Song mu*, 37–38, 50 (n.56).

[31] Sima Guang, *Shuyi*, 8.8a–11a; *Lü Zuqian quanji*, 1:336–39; Zhu Xi, *Jiali*, 41a–42a. For a translation of Zhu's account, see Ebrey, *Chu Hsi's Family Rituals*, 126–30. Note that Ebrey translates *zhu* (注) as "decanter," rather than "ewer."

a table of dishes, including meat dishes, set up outside of the hall; at a designated moment, these dishes were brought into the hall for the offering. Although meats were not found in Zhang's tomb – as a fervent patron of Buddhism, he may have been a vegetarian – murals in the antechamber depict cooks preparing delicacies that then reappear in the hands of servants in murals in the main hall. The descriptions of post-burial rites in Song-era ritual manuals seem, thus, to explain one of the key functions of North Chinese tombs. The "Sacrifice of Repose" served to appease the *hun* soul, helping it settle properly in the ancestral tablet; meanwhile, a feast occurring in the tomb perhaps simultaneously appeased the *po* soul, encouraging it to remain in the tomb, and not to wander off.

So critical was this banquet to Chinese understandings of death that any references to it amid the grave goods or other tomb features constitute good evidence of Chinese cultural influence. Such references might include vessels used for wine consumption – the ewers, warming bowls, cups with cup-stands, and "chicken-thigh bottles" – objects generally placed in front of (i.e. south of) the coffin of the deceased. Included also are tomb murals depicting musicians, cooks preparing food and wine, or the couple seated in chairs at a table. Finally, because it was common for the table and chairs to be constructed from bricks protruding out of the wall, signs of this masonry technique are often sufficient to identify a banquet scene, especially in cases where the murals have long since disintegrated.

The masonry technique in question is fundamental to a second important characteristic of North Chinese mortuary culture. Large numbers of Chinese chambered tombs appear to integrate the space of the tomb chamber with a coherent pictorial and architectural program. Besides tables and chairs, other furniture frequently juts out of the wall as well, including lamp stands, wash basins, clothing racks, and mirror stands. Painted figures often interact directly with this furniture. In the case of two tombs discovered near Datong, Shanxi Province, for example, women in the murals add oil to chandeliers that protrude from the wall.[32] In some cases, there is an analogous interplay between grave goods and elements of the chamber walls. In the tomb of Zhang Kuangzheng – Zhang Wenzao's father – one little yellow cup-stand supporting a white porcelain bowl appears both in represented form on the mural of the east wall of the antechamber and in physical form set amid the ceramic vessels

[32] Wang Yintian, "Shanxi Datong shi Liaodai Xu Congyun mu," pl.1; Wang Yintian, "Shanxi Datong shi Liao mu," pl.5.

arrayed upon the wooden offering table in the main hall.[33] In numerous Northern Song tombs, archaeologists have found ceramic oil lamp bowls balanced atop protruding brick chandeliers.[34] All of this interplay has the effect of pulling elements of the wall into the space of the tomb.

Also common among Chinese chambered tombs of the North China Plain is the use of masonry to mimic wooden architectural elements.[35] Brick pillars are often connected to the roof of the tomb chamber by complex brick bracketing systems that very much resemble structures found in the few remaining wooden buildings in China that date to the eleventh century. Song tombs, in particular, frequently contain false doors and window frames, also built of brick, that suggest the existence of additional adjacent rooms. Scenes from these adjacent rooms sometimes appear in the murals, where one might find women applying make-up before a mirror, servant girls washing clothing in a basin, household managers receiving strings of cash and rolls of silk, or a desk equipped with the "four treasures of the scholar's study." Adding color to some of these scenes are paintings of gaudy interiors decorated with drapery, screens, and even hanging scrolls.[36] In this way, the tomb chamber became the central courtyard of a lively "virtual" mansion.

Eleventh-century Chinese tombs thus reveal an understanding of the afterlife adhering to a logic very different from that of the real world, a logic involving the seamless interplay between representation and reality. Painted servants might carry cups and cup-stands that then appeared elsewhere as physical objects; virtual chandeliers appearing in relief on the walls might be set ablaze with real flames from an oil lamp balanced on top; and the spirits of a deceased couple might leave the coffin to enjoy wine from vessels depicted in murals. The popularization of cremation burial during this period apparently posed an interesting problem: how could tomb occupants enjoy the feast without a physical body? As it turns out, often they were given virtual bodies with which to enjoy the virtual feasts. In some cases of cremation, stone figurines of the wife and husband were placed on the coffin bed. In other cases, as we have seen in

---

[33] Shen, "Body Matters," 135.

[34] Li Mingde and Guo Yitian, "Anyang Xiaonanhai Songdai bihua mu," 76; Zhang Zengwu, "Henan Linxian chengguan Song mu," 41; Jiang Sheng and Yu Jinfang, "Hubei Xiangfan Liujia geng Tang Song muzang," 35; "Jinan shi Song Jin zhuandiao bihua mu," 48.

[35] The use of protruding brickwork to mimic wooden architectural elements originated in late Tang Hebei. It spread to Henan in the tenth century, in conjunction with large-scale elite migrations. See Tackett, "Wan Tang Hebei ren."

[36] E.g., see "Luoyang Mangshan Songdai bihua mu" and color plates in *Xuanhua Liao Mu*.

the case of Zhang Wenzao's tomb, manikins might be used. The more elaborate of these manikins were life-sized, with articulated wooden joints.[37]

By comparison, Khitan mortuary culture seems to have had no use for such virtual reality. Grave goods in Khitan tombs – especially the horse equipment, weapons, and metal tools – were typically functional objects that may well have been used by the deceased during life. As discussed below, whereas working metal scissors have been discovered in Khitan tombs, ceramic scissors or scissors carved in relief are common to Chinese-type tombs. Moreover, rather than incorporating extensive brickwork to mimic wood architecture, Khitan tombs often contain real timber structures, especially wooden interior walls (*huqiang*), wooden burial chambers (*xiaozhang* or *guo*), and wooden "beds" for the coffin or corpse (*guanchuang* or *shichuang*). Khitan tombs reflect a mortuary culture that posited a general continuity between life and the afterlife. The logic of space and of materiality applicable in the real world of the living remained the same after death.

The Cultural Geography of the Song–Liao Frontier

By taking advantage of the latitude and longitude coordinates assigned to each tomb in the database, it is possible to ascertain the geographic range of Khitan and North Chinese mortuary cultures, as they have been defined above. The two maps in Figure 5.1 mark the locations of excavated tombs containing one or more elements of the Khitan cultural repertoire. On the basis of these maps, one can reconstruct a cultural boundary spanning the Liao empire that skirted the northern limits of the North China Plain at the Yan Mountains, and in fact generally followed the course of the Northern Qi (and Ming) "Outer" Great Wall further west. Tombs with Khitan features are largely limited to the region north of this line, with a particularly large number found in a region between the Central, Eastern, and Supreme capitals of the Liao empire, a region nowadays straddling the Liaoning–Inner Mongolia border. However, in the zone south of this line – marked as the "Liao Southern Zone" on the maps, and roughly equivalent to the territory of the Liao-occupied Sixteen Prefectures – archaeologists have rarely encountered tombs containing Khitan features. The few exceptions turn out to be tombs that are overwhelmingly Chinese in basic features despite containing one or

---

[37] Jie Xigong, "Taiyuan Xiaojingyu Song Ming mu," esp. 255–56; Shen, "Body Matters."

a. Metal and ceramics

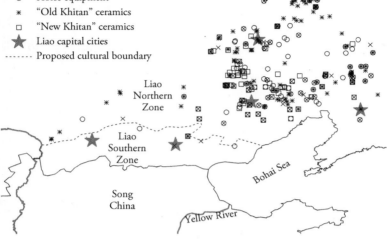

- ✕   Weapons / tools
- ○   Horse equipment
- ✳   "Old Khitan" ceramics
- ▢   "New Khitan" ceramics
- ★   Liao capital cities
- ------ Proposed cultural boundary

Liao Northern Zone

Liao Southern Zone

Bohai Sea

Song China

Yellow River

b. Miscellaneous features

- ✳   Khitan inscriptions
- ○   Khitan-style three-chambered tombs
- ✕   Gold and precious stones
- ▢   Funerary masks and mesh garments
- ★   Liao capital cities
- ------ Proposed cultural boundary

Liao Northern Zone

Liao Southern Zone

Song China

Bohai Sea

Yellow River

Figure 5.1 Geographic distribution of tombs with "Khitan" features

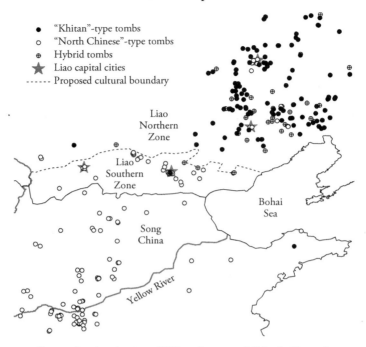

Figure 5.2 Geographic distribution of "Khitan"-type and "North Chinese"-type tombs "Khitan"-type tombs are defined as tombs with two or more features of "Khitan" mortuary culture and no features of "North Chinese" mortuary culture; "North Chinese"-type tombs have two or more features of "North Chinese" mortuary culture and no features of "Khitan" mortuary culture; "hybrid" tombs have two or more features of both "Khitan" and "North Chinese" mortuary cultures.

two Khitan-type grave goods. As a general rule, Khitan culture seems not to have infiltrated the Sixteen Prefectures in the southern portion of the Liao empire.

Figure 5.2 summarizes the geographic extent of the Chinese and Khitan cultural repertoires using a somewhat different approach. Rather than examining the distribution of individual tomb features, it maps the locations of three different types of tombs – those exhibiting exclusively "North Chinese" characteristics, those exhibiting exclusively "Khitan" characteristics, and "hybrid" tombs, which exhibit both Chinese and Khitan features. In this last type of tomb, one typically finds primarily Khitan tomb elements, with the addition of the grave goods typically associated with the "fragrant banquet" (wine vessels, spittoons, etc.)

placed on an offering table. In brief, Figure 5.2 reveals that the portions of North China under both Song and Liao control shared a common mortuary culture. In the Liao Southern Zone, there is only one "Khitan"-type tomb that appears on the map, in the vicinity of the Liao Southern Capital (modern-day Beijing). By contrast, there are sixty-five "North Chinese"-type tombs (several of which are undiscernible on the map due to overlapping symbols). There are also six hybrid tombs, all situated immediately south of the cultural boundary line. Finally, in Song-controlled China, there is a single unusual tomb in eastern Shandong containing several Khitan-type objects. Very few Chinese-type tombs have, in fact, been found in this region, which may imply the existence of a distinct cultural zone encircling the Bohai Sea. Indeed, archaeologists specializing in other historical eras have noted cross-Bohai cultural ties.[38]

In the Liao Northern Zone, on the other hand, the situation is more complex. Overall, the majority of excavated tombs exhibit predominantly Khitan features. However, the cultural boundary did not have the same impact on the northward spread of Chinese mortuary culture as it did on the southward spread of Khitan culture. Chinese-type tombs, though perhaps in the minority, are especially common in the vicinities of the Central and Supreme Capitals of the Liao, where hybrid tombs are also encountered fairly frequently. There has been a tendency in scholarship on the Liao to assume that the Sixteen Prefectures were the site of the most active cultural intermixing during the eleventh century. Intuitively, this may make sense; in fact, however, there was almost no such mixing of populations south of the Yan Mountains. The zone north of the mountains was far more culturally diverse.

Interestingly, in this same region north of the Yan Mountains, there is no evidence in the archaeological record of distinct Khitan, Xi, and Parhae peoples, although all three groups are documented in contemporaneous Chinese descriptions of the Liao empire. This discrepancy between archaeological and literary data may suggest that the Xi and Parhae shared much in common with the Khitans, and that distinguishing between their largely overlapping cultural repertoires will require the identification of a different set of cultural markers. Alternatively, the Xi and Parhae may have built much simpler burial sites – either for cultural or for socioeconomic reasons – so that their tombs are rarely reported in the archaeological literature.

---

[38] A search for "circum-Bohai archaeology" (*huan Bohai kaogu*) in article databases yields abundant discussions of the common material culture around the Bohai Sea.

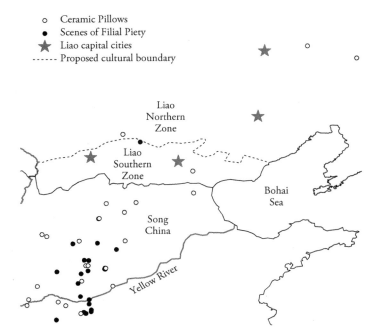

Figure 5.3 Geographic distribution of tombs with ceramic pillows or murals depicting
the paragons of filial piety

But although the Yan Mountains constituted a significant cultural
divide separating Chinese and Liao culture, the political border further south between the two states seems to have led over time to a
certain degree of cultural divergence. Certain tomb features are much
more common in Song-controlled regions of North China than within
the Liao-controlled Southern Zone, such as ceramic pillows (placed
under the head of the deceased) and murals depicting the paragons of
filial piety (Figure 5.3).[39] There is also the tendency for tombs in Liao-
occupied Hedong and Hebei to contain a much larger total number of

---

[39] Mural scenes of the paragons of filial piety have tentatively been identified in several Liao-era
tombs excavated in the vicinity of Anshan, Liaoning, site of the former Liao Eastern Capital. See
Xu Yulin, "Liaoning Anshan shi Wangjia yu Liao huaxiang shimu"; Torii, *Sculptured Stone Tombs of
the Liao Dynasty*, esp. 23–26, 42–46, 57–58. These scenes probably reflect a distinct tradition.
They appear in a central location on the tomb walls and are carved in relief, whereas in Song
tombs they appear as small, painted images in the upper registers of the tomb murals.

Table 5.3 *Prevalence of tombs with large numbers of grave goods (by region)*[a]

	Song China		Liao Southern Zone		Liao Northern Zone	
Zero or one grave good	115	(41%)	18	(15%)	105	(21%)
More than one grave good	166	(59%)	105	(85%)	405	(79%)
Of which: Very large number of grave goods[b]	5	(2%)	23	(19%)	85	(17%)
Total:	281	(100%)	123	(100%)	510	(100%)

[a] See Appendix B for description of database used for this table.
[b] Grave goods deemed "very large" in number if "grave goods" field of database entry for tomb in question contains more than eighty characters.

grave goods (Table 5.3). Whether or not this discrepancy is the result of cultural or socioeconomic factors is unclear. One curious pattern involves the domestic animals that appear on occasion in tomb murals – Song Chinese seem to have preferred cats, while Liao Chinese preferred dogs (Pekingese to be specific).[40] The broader implications of this last difference for our understanding of fundamental cultural differences between Song and Liao Chinese are left to the reader's interpretation.

The relative paucity of grave goods in Song tombs may be linked to yet another interesting pattern, depicted in Figure 5.4. It has long been noted that scissors seem to have played an important role in Chinese tombs, perhaps symbolizing the cutting of the bond between the living and the deceased.[41] Frequently, these objects appear in tombs in conjunction with a clothes iron, the symbolic significance of which is less clear. In Song tombs, these two objects usually appear together in brick relief or painted on tomb walls. In Chinese tombs in the Liao region, by contrast, one frequently encounters physical scissors made of ceramic or porcelain, sometimes in conjunction with ceramic irons. Finally, Khitan tombs of the Northern Zone often contain actual functional metal scissors, reflecting perhaps a Khitan cultural preference for the real over

[40] See Tomb Database for relevant data.
[41] Ye Wa, "Mortuary Practice in Medieval China," 346–47.

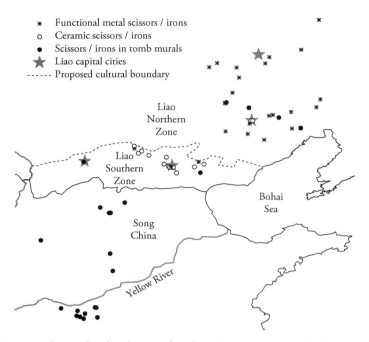

Figure 5.4 Geographic distribution of tombs with scissors or irons (real or virtual)

the virtual. But although Chinese-type tombs on both sides of the political border contain scissors in the form of non-functional representations, the Song–Liao political border does, nevertheless, appear to demarcate additional, more subtle distinctions in mortuary culture. Aside from scissors and irons, a few other ceramic objects common to Liao Chinese tombs tend to appear almost exclusively on murals in tombs south of the border. Ewers and warming bowls decorated with carved lotus petals, apparently produced at the Ding kilns in Song-controlled Hebei, are common in tombs north of the border.[42] South of the border, these same

---

[42] For examples of lotus-flower-carved porcelain vessels produced at the Ding kiln, see *Chūgoku tōji zenshū*, vol. 9, pls. 24, 28, 31, 37, 40, 53, 60; Su Tianjun, "Shunyi xian Liao Jingguang sheli taji," 52–53. For a porcelain *kundika* with lotus-flower carvings discovered in a Liao-era pagoda crypt in Ding County, see "Hebei Ding xian faxian liang zuo Song dai taji," pl. 6; Yang Xiaoneng, *New Perspectives on China's Past*, 2: 485.

objects are rare, though they often appear represented on tomb walls, with the very same carved lotus-petal motif.[43]

While the significance of such distinctions is not always easy to disentangle, another striking difference between Liao and Song Chinese tombs involves the role of Buddhism in mortuary culture. A number of elements associated with Buddhist ritual practices – including *dharani* pillars, *kundikas*, inscriptions written in Sanskrit, and manikins containing cremated remains – are found almost exclusively in Chinese tombs north of the Song–Liao border.[44] The tendency in Liao tombs to incorporate scenes of tea preparation (rather than the heating of wine) on murals depicting the "fragrant banquet" may also reflect a Buddhist influence. Most striking of all are the sharp differences in the prevalence of cremation burials – generally considered one of the most accurate indicators of Buddhist burial practice. Figure 5.5 compares the geographic extent of cremation burials to that of tombs containing complete skeletons. In fact, in contrast to Song Chinese tombs, Chinese tombs in the Liao Southern Zone were far more likely to involve cremation. The role of Buddhism in mortuary culture, then, constitutes one of the most striking distinctions between Chinese living on either side of the Song–Liao political border.

The influence of Buddhism on Liao mortuary practices is not entirely unexpected given the Liao state's well-known patronage of Buddhism, and the importance of Buddhism in Khitan funerary ritual.[45] Nevertheless, we are left with a puzzling paradox. The Buddhist grave goods commonly found in Chinese-type tombs in Liao territory are almost entirely absent from Khitan-type tombs. Moreover, in contrast to the Liao Chinese preference for cremation burials (evident in both the Northern and Southern

---

[43] E.g., "Henan Xin'an xian Song cun Bei Song diaozhuan bihua mu," 22, 26; Wu Dongfeng, "Hebei Wuyi Longdian Song mu fajue baogao," 325, 326; Yang Yubin, "Shangcai Song mu"; Zhang Jian and Wang Kai, "Luoyang Jianxi san zuo Song dai fangmugou zhuanshimu," pl. 2; Su Bai, *Baisha Song mu*, 74; Zhao Hong and Gao Ming, "Jiyuan shi Dongshi lutou cun Song dai bihua mu," inside rear cover.

[44] By my count, there are eleven tombs with such Buddhist elements in the Liao Southern Zone, another eleven tombs in the Liao Northern Zone, and only one tomb of this sort in Song China. The one exception involves an unusual multi-chambered tomb dating to 1087 excavated in southern Shanxi Province, which contains a *dharani* pillar in the central chamber, albeit one with an inscription in Chinese rather than Sanskrit. See Wang Jinxian and Wang Yonggen, "Shanxi Huguan Nancun Song dai zhuandiao mu."

[45] E.g., an inscription discovered in 1995 records that, upon the death of a high-ranking member of the Liao imperial consort clan, 4,400 monks chanted for 62 days, intoning the name of the Buddha a total of 2,454,400 times. See Liu Fengzhu et al. (eds.), *Liao Shangjing*, 161. For more on Liao Buddhism, see Wittfogel and Feng, *History of Chinese Society: Liao*, 291–309.

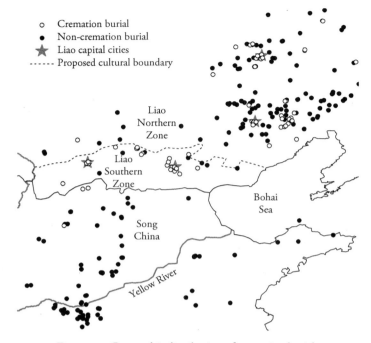

Figure 5.5 Geographic distribution of cremation burials

Zones), Khitan tombs tend overwhelmingly to contain full skeletons. The only notable examples of cremation burials in non-"North Chinese"-type tombs of the Northern Zone involve a certain number of simple tombs excavated in the suburbs of the Liao Supreme Capital at the sites of Liao-era Buddhist monasteries. Some scholars have argued that these tombs – especially those containing ceramic urns in the shape of model yurts – may reflect traditional Khitan cremation practices, though it is equally possible that they were the tombs of Buddhist monks.[46]

Nancy Steinhardt has suggested one possible solution to the paradox. She has observed that some of the timber structures found in Khitan-type tombs – such as the wooden sarcophagus from the tomb at Tu'erji Hill (Figure 5.6a) – resemble Buddhist temples in their basic architectural

[46] Jin Yongtian, "Liao Shangjing chengzhi fujin fosi yizhi"; Jin Yongtian, "Shangjing fujin faxian de xiaoxing muzang"; Wen Yu, "Qionglu shi guhui guan."

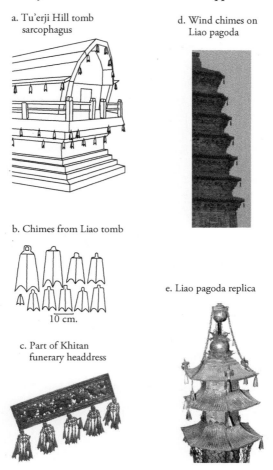

a. Tu'erji Hill tomb sarcophagus

d. Wind chimes on Liao pagoda

b. Chimes from Liao tomb

10 cm.

e. Liao pagoda replica

c. Part of Khitan funerary headdress

Figure 5.6 Wind chimes as Buddhist symbols in Khitan culture

features.[47] One can make a similar argument regarding wind chimes. Chimes appear prominently on the sides of the Tu'erji Hill sarcophagus. In many other Khitan tombs, in which the original wooden structures have not survived, one encounters sets of chimes very similar in basic appearance (Figure 5.6b). Miniature chimes have also been found attached to Khitan-style funerary headdresses (Figure 5.6c). There is reason to believe that

[47] Steinhardt, "Architectural Landscape," 47–49; Steinhardt, "Liao Pagodas."

such chimes, when found in Liao tombs, constitute meaningful Buddhist symbols. They are found almost ubiquitously on Liao-era pagodas (Figure 5.6d). The fact that chimes constitute one of the most prominent decorative elements on one miniature pagoda replica (Figure 5.6e) – from the crypt of the North Pagoda in Chaoyang, Liaoning Province – suggests that they were viewed as symbolically significant elements of Buddhist architecture. A plausible explanation for their potency as Buddhist symbols might lie in the fact that their clanging in the wind can often be heard at some distance away, helping to guide pilgrims to sites of worship. Although Liao state patronage of Buddhism facilitated the propagation of Buddhist practice throughout Liao territory, there were, nevertheless, striking differences with regard to how Khitans and Chinese living in those territories integrated that religion into their mortuary cultures.

Hybrid Tombs

Thus far, in discussing cultural boundaries on the basis of the material culture of tombs, focus has been on the geographic range of particular sets of artifacts. On the basis of this analysis, we saw that the Song–Liao border did have an impact on mortuary culture, albeit a relatively subtle impact. The far more significant cultural boundary lay along the Yan Mountains separating the Sixteen Prefectures from the Liao empire's Northern Zone. If one assumes that this particular cultural distribution reflected the relative distribution of ethnic Chinese and ethnic Khitan populations, it becomes apparent that the Liao occupation of the Sixteen Prefectures did not prompt a detectable influx of Khitans into the region. By contrast, ethnic Chinese apparently did relocate in substantial numbers into the steppe, especially into the regions in the vicinity of the Liao Central and Supreme Capitals. The link between migration and Liao ethnic policies will be discussed in more detail below.

On the basis of the same data, what can one conclude about boundaries in the sociological rather than the geographic sense? To what extent did individual families residing within the Liao multiethnic empire incorporate elements of other cultures into their own practices? One way of measuring the extent of this sort of cultural border-crossing on the basis of archaeological data is via cluster analysis. Figure 5.7 cross-tabulates the chances that one tomb feature appears in a tomb given the presence of another tomb feature. The resulting table demonstrates that Khitan features (on the upper left of the matrix) strongly correlated with other Khitan features; Chinese features (lower right) strongly correlated with

A B C D E F G H I J K L M N O P Q R S T U V W X Y Z 1 2 3 4 5 6 7 8

A. Khitan inscriptions
B. Masks & mesh garments
C. Large animal bones
D. Horse equipment
E. Weapons
F. Coxcomb ewers
G. Metal tools
H. "New Khitan" ceramics
I. "Old Khitan" ceramics
J. Floor plan with 3 chambers
K. Wooden interior
L. Wooden bed
M. Gilded bronze objects
N. Precious stones
O. Multiple gold items
P. Wine vessels
Q. Chicken-thigh bottles
R. Spittoons
S. Vessels with lotus pattern
T. Utensils
U. Protruding masonry
V. Mural with wine vessels
W. Mural with spittoon
X. Scenes of feasting
Y. Mural with screen/drapery
Z. Mural with musicians
1. Chinese-style ceramics
2. Woman-door motif
3. Ceramic pillows
4. Scenes of filial piety
5. Scissors/irons in murals
6. Ceramic scissors/irons
7. Cremation burial
8. Buddhist objects

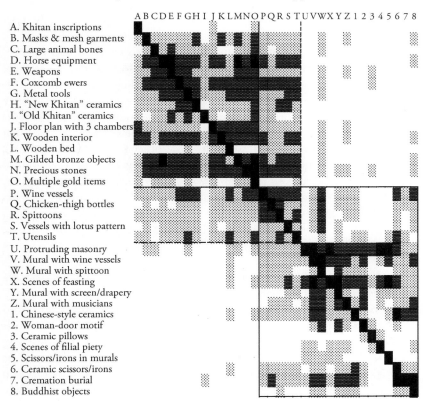

Figure 5.7 Cross-tabulation of tomb features in eleventh-century Northeast Asian tombs
This figure identifies patterns in the clustering of tomb features tabulated on the basis
of data culled from 979 eleventh-century tombs from the North China Plain, Shanxi,
and regions further north. Letters/numbers in the top row refer to the corresponding
features identified by letters/numbers in the left-most column. Clustering is calculated
on the basis of what percentage of tombs with the feature identified in the top row also
contains the feature identified in the left-most column. A blank space indicates less than
8.3%; a light-colored block (▨) indicates 8.3–25%; a darker-colored block (▦) indicates
25%–58.3%; a black block (■) indicates 58.3–100%. Solid lines distinguish the two main
cultural repertoires: "Khitan" features (A through O) and "North Chinese" features (P
through 8). The dashed lines demarcate a number of "North Chinese" features that commonly appear in Khitan tombs.

other Chinese features. In addition, Figure 5.7 identifies certain specific
Chinese grave goods often found in Khitan tombs, including wine vessels and chicken-thigh bottles. As a general rule, disregarding this last set
of objects, a tomb was either unambiguously Chinese or unambiguously

Khitan in its features. Cultural border-crossing seems to have been relatively limited, at least as pertaining to mortuary practice.

Nevertheless, as we saw in Figure 5.2, hybrid tombs were not uncommon in the Liao empire's Northern Zone. What does one make of these tombs? For what reasons and by what processes did some families come to incorporate both Chinese and Khitan elements into their mortuary practices? Here it is worth considering to what extent Chinese elements in Khitan tombs (or vice versa) were deemed to be conceptually distinct sets of artifacts. In order to ascertain how objects were categorized in people's minds, one can pay attention to where objects were placed within the tombs and which objects were typically grouped together into sets. Unfortunately, most excavated tombs were disturbed by looters (or by natural events like flooding) well before archaeologists could document their contents. In many other cases, excavation reports are too cursory, and provide no details about the placement of grave goods. But in a few cases, the careful arrangement of objects within a tomb suggests that when both Khitan and Chinese goods were present, they were conceived to be distinct sets of objects.

The best example involves Khitan tombs containing ewers, chicken-thigh bottles, and other wine vessels that one also commonly finds in "North Chinese"-type tombs. In Khitan-type tombs lacking these Chinese elements (Figure 5.8), there is a tendency to find Khitan-type ceramics placed together in a set either near the head of the deceased, generally on the east side of the tomb, or – in the case of three-chambered tombs – in the eastern side chamber. Horse equipment and weapons are usually found together on the opposite (west) side of the tomb, or in the western side chamber in the case of three-chambered tombs. In the case of Khitan tombs containing Chinese-style wine vessels (Figure 5.9), these Chinese ceramics are generally found physically set apart from the Khitan ceramics. Moreover, they are typically situated in front of the bodies of the deceased, as prescribed for the "sacrifice of repose" and in accordance with their positions in the Chinese-type Xuanhua tombs. In other words, "sinicized" Khitans (and "khitanized" Chinese) – who supplemented their own customary practices with elements of Chinese (or Khitan) rituals – did so without eliminating their own traditions. Such Khitans continued to incorporate weapons, horse equipment, and Khitan-type ceramics in their tombs, presumably performing associated Khitan rituals in accordance with their own traditions, yet while simultaneously placing objects on an offering table in front of the deceased in the Chinese fashion.

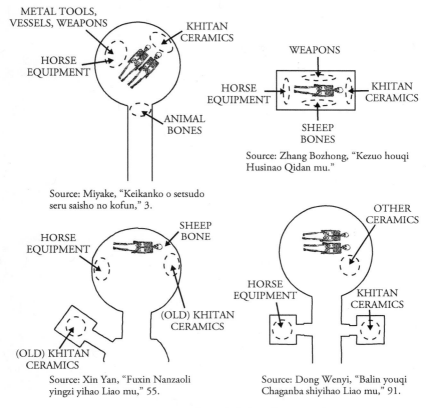

METAL TOOLS,
VESSELS, WEAPONS

KHITAN
CERAMICS

HORSE
EQUIPMENT

ANIMAL
BONES

Source: Miyake, "Keikanko o setsudo
seru saisho no kofun," 3.

WEAPONS

HORSE
EQUIPMENT

KHITAN
CERAMICS

SHEEP
BONES

Source: Zhang Bozhong, "Kezuo houqi
Husinao Qidan mu."

HORSE
EQUIPMENT

SHEEP
BONE

(OLD) KHITAN
CERAMICS

(OLD) KHITAN
CERAMICS

Source: Xin Yan, "Fuxin Nanzaoli
yingzi yihao Liao mu," 55.

OTHER
CERAMICS

HORSE
EQUIPMENT

KHITAN
CERAMICS

Source: Dong Wenyi, "Balin youqi
Chaganba shiyihao Liao mu," 91.

Figure 5.8 Layouts of sample "Khitan"-type tombs

Why some Khitans decided to adopt Chinese practices (or vice versa) is difficult to surmise. In some cases, mixed marriages may have been the cause. Whereas the Xuanhua tombs are almost entirely Chinese in their features, a single tomb does contain a few Khitan elements.[48] In this tomb, the male deceased was buried in a wire-mesh shroud in accordance with Khitan practices; his wife, by contrast, was cremated and her ashes placed in a life-sized articulated manikin in accordance with the Buddhist practices of Liao Chinese. It is very plausible that the husband was an ethnic Khitan and the wife Chinese. Besides intermarriage, some cultural

[48] "Hebei Xuanhua xin faxian liang chu Liao Jin bihua mu"; *Xuanhua Xiabali er qu*, 22.

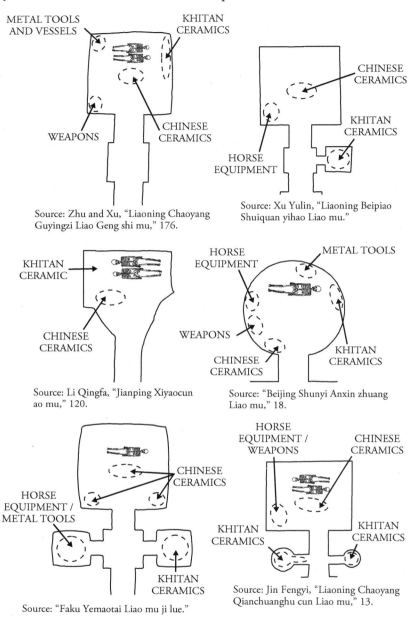

METAL TOOLS
AND VESSELS

KHITAN
CERAMICS

WEAPONS

CHINESE
CERAMICS

Source: Zhu and Xu, "Liaoning Chaoyang
Guyingzi Liao Geng shi mu," 176.

CHINESE
CERAMICS

KHITAN
CERAMICS

HORSE
EQUIPMENT

Source: Xu Yulin, "Liaoning Beipiao
Shuiquan yihao Liao mu."

KHITAN
CERAMIC

CHINESE
CERAMICS

Source: Li Qingfa, "Jianping Xiyaocun
ao mu," 120.

HORSE
EQUIPMENT

METAL TOOLS

WEAPONS

CHINESE
CERAMICS

KHITAN
CERAMICS

Source: "Beijing Shunyi Anxin zhuang
Liao mu," 18.

CHINESE
CERAMICS

HORSE
EQUIPMENT /
METAL TOOLS

KHITAN
CERAMICS

Source: "Faku Yemaotai Liao mu ji lue."

HORSE
EQUIPMENT /
WEAPONS

CHINESE
CERAMICS

KHITAN
CERAMICS

KHITAN
CERAMICS

Source: Jin Fengyi, "Liaoning Chaoyang
Qianchuanghu cun Liao mu," 13.

Figure 5.9 Layouts of sample "Khitan"-type tombs containing Chinese-type ceramics

hybridization may have been the result of Khitans living in close proximity to Chinese, probably a relatively common phenomenon in the immediate vicinities of the Central and Supreme Capitals. As a result, Chinese and Khitans may have attended each other's funerals, thereby in the long run mutually influencing each other's traditions. In both cases, however, non-native cultural elements were maintained as a discrete component of the mortuary ritual. The hybridization mechanism did not involve a process of syncretism, whereby foreign elements were fused with native elements to create entirely new traditions, within which one could no longer conceptually disaggregate the two original sources of influence. Instead, what we find is that non-native elements (for example, Chinese ceramics) were incorporated into native mortuary practice through a process of accretion. Even the builders of hybrid tombs remained consciously aware of the distinctiveness of Chinese and Khitan cultural elements.

Liao Ethnic Policy

How does one account for the sharp geographic division between a Chinese cultural zone in the southern portion of the Liao empire and the mixed Chinese-Khitan zone to its north? Within the mixed Northern Zone, how does one account for the maintenance of a conceptual distinction between Chinese and Khitan cultural elements? Part of the explanation for the geographic boundary at the Yan Mountains lies, to be sure, in the formidable ecological difference between the Chinese agricultural heartland and the much drier and colder pastoral grasslands of the steppe to the north. The impact of this difference in ecology on culture remains glaring to this day. Even in contemporary times, many Mongols retain elements of a pastoral nomadic lifestyle. In Mongolian supermarkets, meat and other animal products are cheap, while vegetables – the mainstay of the Chinese peasant diet – are expensive when available at all. In addition, unlike Chinese, Mongols continue to this day to ride horses from a very young age. And, though they now winter in towns where their children can attend school, most still migrate to higher elevations in the summer months, moving camp with SUVs and pickup trucks in lieu of animal trains. Given the starkness of the pastoral–agricultural cultural divide even in contemporary times, one should not be surprised to find a similar divide a thousand years ago.

But ecological conditions aside, it is also important to recognize the crucial role played by the Liao state in creating and reinforcing ethnic categories, as well as in maintaining the geographic segregation of different populations. The ethnic policies of the Khitan empire were, in fact, typical of the regimes originating in the forests and steppe of Northeast Asia. In steppe societies, tribes constituted the fundamental social, political, and military unit. Tribes were natural building blocks for ethnic categories, because their members were perceived to share a common ancestry – a belief critical for bolstering feelings of solidarity and community among a population of migrating nomads.[49] Thus, for example, funerary epitaphs in the Khitan language (as opposed to those written in classical Chinese) pay particular attention to the deceased's position within a tribal hierarchy.[50] Much like ethnic categories, tribes were also dynamic entities, sometimes breaking apart or merging with other tribes. They also on occasion joined together – either voluntarily or by force – to form supratribal political structures, sometimes in the form of a loose confederation, and sometimes in the form of an organized steppe empire.[51] Subordinate tribes might maintain their internal structures after joining a loose confederation, making it relatively easy for them to break away later. However, in the case of the better organized empires – including the Khitan as well as the Mongol and the Manchu empires – tribes were entirely reorganized to diminish the possibility of rebellions.[52]

In light of tribal reorganizations of this sort, it became critical during the consolidation of steppe empires to manage ethnic politics. The top-down process of ethnogenesis, by means of which basic ethnic divisions were reimagined, has been well studied by historians of the Qing Dynasty. The ethnonym "Manchu" was itself a political creation of the 1630s. A concocted foundation myth provided a genealogical basis for determining who was a Manchu, and also for justifying the pre-eminent position of the imperial Aisin Gioro clan. The early Qing emperors also

---

[49] Lindner, "What Was a Nomadic Tribe," esp. 696–97; Fletcher, "Mongols," 16–17; Barfield, *Perilous Frontier*, 24–28. For a similar account of Southeast Asian tribal politics and ethnogenesis, see Scott, *Art of Not Being Governed*, 256–70. The importance of ancestry did not preclude the development of class hierarchies within tribes. In addition, as Lindner observes, tribal genealogies were commonly rearranged to produce an "ex post facto justification" for particular political imperatives. What was important was the "idiom" of kinship, not shared DNA.

[50] E.g., the title of the Chinese funerary epitaph for Yelü Xinie identifies him as the Deputy Governor of the Xingfu Army; the title of his Khitan epitaph, by contrast, only identifies the branch of the imperial clan to which he belonged, without mentioning his bureaucratic title. See Liu Fengzhu et al. (eds.), *Liao Shangjing*, 123, 125. For other similar Khitan epitaphs, see ibid., 102, 111. On the tribal structure of Khitan society, see Aisin-Gioro, *Kittanbun boshi*, 56–102.

[51] Fletcher, "Mongols," 19–21; Barfield, *Perilous Frontier*, 5–8. Barfield surveys several anthropological theories accounting for the formation of supratribal structures.

[52] Fletcher, "Mongols," 29–30. For examples of the Khitan court reorganizing subordinate tribes, see Wittfogel and Feng, *History of Chinese Society: Liao*, 47–49.

played an active role in defining the common cultural characteristics of the Manchu people.[53] Though we know far less about Khitan ethnogenesis, it is clear that a Khitan foundation myth was also created, providing the important tribes of the regime with common genealogical origins.[54] Like the Manchus, the Khitans also sought to define – or invent – a set of distinct cultural traditions. Early in the tenth century, the Khitan ruler ordered the creation of a written script.[55] The Khitans also made use of a distinctive hairstyle to serve as an ethnic marker, though they did not impose their hairstyle on the conquered Chinese population, as would both the Jurchens and the Manchus.[56] Later in the dynasty, the Liao court commissioned the production of ritual texts that coordinated Chinese ritual practice with Khitan traditions.[57] Attempts to reform Khitan funerary mores, described above, may have reflected additional efforts to establish a set of ritual practices analogous to, yet distinct from, Chinese practices.

But it was not always possible (or politically desirable) to construct a single ethnicity out of all tribes in a steppe empire, especially when there existed particularly stark cultural or linguistic divides. For this reason, large steppe empires were conceived to be multinational. From its inception, the Qing Dynasty institutionalized a distinction between Manchus, Mongols, and Han Chinese.[58] The Liao empire also distinguished between several peoples: Khitans, Parhae, Xi, and Han. The institutionalization of these

[53] Crossley, "Introduction to the Qing Foundation Myth"; Crossley, "*Manzhou Yuanliu Kao*"; Elliott, *Manchu Way*, 42–47, 63–72. Elliott, 69–70 points out that included among the Manchus were both speakers of related dialects of the Jurchen language, and also speakers of mutually unintelligible languages.

[54] Twitchett and Tietze, "The Liao," 51–52. In addition, for Turkish foundation myths, see Golden, *Introduction*, 117–20; for the Mongol foundation myth, see de Rachewiltz, *Secret History*, esp. 1–16.

[55] More precisely, the Khitans invented distinct "large" and "small" scripts, neither of which has been fully decoded. For a relatively up-to-date study of the Khitan written language, see Kane, *Kitan Language*.

[56] Khitan men shaved the tops of their heads, letting the hair around their temples grow out and hang down over their shoulders. See Twitchett and Tietze, "The Liao," 46; for depictions in tomb murals, see *Xuanhua Liao mu*, col. pls. 5, 7, 10, 30, 31. Male hairstyles appear to have been widely used on the steppe to identify ethnicity. Whereas Xiongnu men had braids, Turks let their hair hang loose, Mongols wore plaits of twisted hair behind their ears, and Jurchen and Manchu men wore a queue. For photographs of excavated Xiongnu braids, see Eregzen (ed.), *Treasures of the Xiongnu*, 110–11; for depictions of Turkish hairstyles, see de la Vaissière, *Histoire des marchands sogdiens*, pl. 2; on Mongol hair, see de Rachewiltz, *Secret History*, 310–11; on Jurchen and Manchu hair, see Franke, "Forest Peoples of Manchuria," 417; Franke, "Chin Dynasty," 281; Wakeman, *Great Enterprise*, 60, 646–50.

[57] Wittfogel and Feng, *History of Chinese Society: Liao*, 263.

[58] The institutionalization of ethnicity in the early Qing is most evident in the distinction between Manchu, Mongol, and Chinese Eight Banners. See Elliott, *Manchu Way*, 72–78.

four ethnic groups was apparent in the names of certain bureaus – for example, the "Chief Administration Office of the Han and Parhae People of the Chongde Ordo."[59] It was also apparent in the fact that, as we saw in Chapter 1, the Liao ambassador to Song was always an ethnic Khitan, while his deputy was always ethnically Han. Ethnic difference was also encoded into court ritual. Thus, Liao bureaucrats representing the steppe and those representing the Chinese zones were distinguishable from each other by their styles of dress.[60]

The multinational nature of large steppe empires created obvious logistical problems, especially with regard to Chinese populations, who vastly outnumbered their conquerors while also not sharing in steppe political culture.[61] One solution was to promulgate a theory of "ethnic sovereignty," in which the conquerors were deemed most fit to rule on the basis of their ethnicity. Mark Elliott has elaborated in some detail on Qing efforts to construct a "Manchu Way," which celebrated the Manchus' warrior ethos as a marker of distinction justifying Manchu control over China and other lands.[62] So, too, under the Liao, it was critical for the Khitans to maintain their own distinctiveness as warriors in order to legitimate their rule over their own multinational empire.[63] Thus, whereas Song sociopolitical elites celebrated their classical educations and literary talent, Khitans exalted their martial and physical prowess. This alternative identity explains the presence in Khitan tombs but not in Chinese-style tombs of weapons and horse equipment. In addition, the unique characteristics of Liao timber frame and brick architecture, as well as the unique layout of Khitan imperial mausoleums, may have reflected a conscious attempt to establish a Khitan imperial tradition analogous to but yet also distinct from the Chinese tradition.[64]

---

[59] Xiang Nan (ed.), *Liaodai shike wenbian*, 185, 250.

[60] Twitchett and Tietze, "The Liao," 77.

[61] According to Wittfogel and Feng, *History of Chinese Society: Liao*, 58, Han Chinese constituted at least 63 percent of the population of the Liao empire, whereas Khitans constituted only 20 percent. The Chinese population of the Qing Dynasty exceeded the Manchu population by an even wider margin.

[62] Elliott, *Manchu Way*, esp. 4–10.

[63] Cf. Bol, "Seeking Common Ground," 485, regarding Jurchens: "it was clearly in their political interest to remain distinct."

[64] Steinhardt, "Liao: An Architectural Tradition in the Making"; Steinhardt, *Liao Architecture*, esp. 401–05. The tomb of Abaoji, the founder of the Khitan state, offers a good example of how Khitan imperial tradition differed from Chinese imperial tradition, insofar as its configuration is in many ways the inverse of the configuration of Chinese imperial tombs. Whereas Tang and Song emperors were buried beneath tumuli sometimes the size of small mountains, Abaoji was buried in a valley surrounded on all sides by mountain ridges. See Dong Xinlin et al., "Neimenggu Balin zuoqi Liaodai Zuling"; the valley is visible on satellite maps at coordinates 43.888N, 119.109E.

A second solution was to set up a "dual organization," by means of which Chinese and other non-steppe peoples were governed according to their own bureaucratic and legal traditions.[65] Thus, immediately after the Khitan annexation of the Sixteen Prefectures, it became state policy to "use national institutions to govern the Khitans, and Han institutions in treating the Han people."[66] The Liao state went on to establish government organs modeled on the Tang bureaucracy and instituted a civil service examination to recruit men to staff these bureaus.[67] To make "dual organization" feasible, however, it was necessary to keep Han populations segregated geographically from the rest of the empire. To be sure, the ethnic geography of Northeast Asia was complex after centuries of migration by Chinese and steppe peoples alike. But the Liao state proved able and willing to manage this intricate ethnic landscape. To avoid competitions over grazing lands, for example, it forcibly moved numerous nomadic tribes to new pastures. The state also relocated entire villages of Han and Parhae subjects on numerous occasions – to diminish the chance of rebellion, to establish colonies of craftsmen and agriculturalists, or for other strategic reasons.[68] Given the Liao state's widespread use of forced migration to manage its empire's ethnic geography, one better understands how it was able to maintain the Sixteen Prefectures as a relatively homogeneous Chinese cultural zone. The result was that, despite the Liao annexation of this region, its inhabitants continued well into the eleventh century to resemble their Song brethren to the south in terms of cultural practices.

Conclusion

This chapter has sought to reconstruct the ethnic and cultural landscape of eleventh-century Northeast Asia, and to evaluate its relationship to geopolitical circumstances, on the basis of the excavated remains of tombs. The geopolitics of eleventh-century Northeast Asia was unusual. The political border between Song China and the Khitan Liao empire to the north

---

[65] Franke, "Role of the State," 102–04; Barfield, *Perilous Frontier*, 97–98. The tendency for conquerors from the steppe – from the Särbi to the Mongols to the Manchus – to rule Chinese-populated territories in Chinese fashion as part of a pragmatic imperial strategy has fueled the erroneous theory that "conquest dynasties" inevitably "sinicized" over time. For a critique of the "Sinicization School" as pertains to the Manchus, see Elliott, *Manchu Way*, 26–32.

[66] LS 45.685.

[67] Twitchett and Tietze, "The Liao," 77–79; Wittfogel and Feng, *History of Chinese Society: Liao*, 454–56.

[68] For tables indicating where Han Chinese, Parhae, and other populations were resettled at various sites around the Liao empire, see Wittfogel and Feng, *History of Chinese Society: Liao*, 62–83.

was set along a river that cut directly across the vast North China Plain. Although there is little doubt that the populations on both sides of the frontier shared a common culture, archaeological evidence suggests that, in the long run, the political border may have spurred some degree of cultural divergence. Most notably, whereas cremation burial was prevalent among Liao Chinese, it was rare in the Song-controlled portion of the North China Plain. Liao state patronage of Buddhism helps to account for this difference in mortuary cultures. The relatively rigid restrictions on cross-border travel incorporated into the Chanyuan Oath also played a role, by isolating the populations on either side of the border.

Much more dramatic than the emerging differences between Liao and Song Chinese, however, was the cultural gulf that separated the North China Plain from the steppe. An analysis of the material culture of tombs from across Northeast Asia suggests that Chinese and steppe cultures were radically different in their fundamental practices and beliefs. Khitan tombs contained the weapons and horse accoutrements one might associate with pastoral nomadic warriors. Such objects were almost never found in Chinese tombs. By contrast, Chinese tombs – in both Liao and Song territory – were conceptualized as the sites of great feasts of the afterlife. The popularity of this "fragrant banquet" derived in part from an apparent conviction that representations of musicians and of victuals in tomb murals were sufficient to satisfy the needs of the deceased. Belief in the efficacy of such a "virtual reality" is also evident in other Chinese funerary customs, such as the popularity – described in accounts dating to as early as the eighth century – of burning money, miniature houses, and other goods made of paper.[69]

How does one explain the persistence of radically different world-views north and south of the Yan Mountains two hundred years after the Khitans took control of the Sixteen Prefectures? Why are there virtually no traces of objects and features associated with Khitan mortuary culture in tombs excavated south of the Yan Mountains? Key to understanding the endurance of the Chinese–steppe cultural divide is to recognize the impact of Liao ethnic policies. Unlike Song China, the Liao did not see itself as a monoethnic nation-state. It was a multinational empire that expended great effort managing the populations under its rule. In accordance with principles underlying tribal structures, it classified people according to ancestry and culture. It also recognized the legitimacy of culturally distinct

---

[69] Feng Yan, *Fengshi wenjian ji*, 6.60–61.

legal and administrative systems, establishing the Sixteen Prefectures as a zone where Chinese could be ruled according to their own customs. It was these ethnic policies that helped both to preserve the cultural distinctiveness of Chinese and Khitan cultures and to maintain the geographic segregation of the two cultures.

In the next chapter, we return to the primary focus of the book – the ways in which Chinese at the Northern Song court conceptualized China and its place in the world. Court officials traveled in great numbers across Northeast Asia. As they made their way from the Song capital in Henan to the Liao court, they had opportunities to witness firsthand the ethnic geography and politics of Northeast Asia. Not only were they influenced by the particular ways in which the Liao categorized people on ethnic grounds, they also observed the radical cultural gulf distinguishing populations north and south of the Yan Mountains.

6

Sinic Space and Han Chinese

In a previous chapter, we encountered the Sixteen Prefectures of Yan and Yun serving as a symbol of the Chinese nation, arousing the passions of patriots in Song times and later. One of the underlying premises was that these prefectures, although occupied by the Khitans since before the founding of the Song, constituted "former lands of the Han and Tang," still inhabited by a population of ethnic Han people who yearned to return to Chinese rule. Insofar as this region consisted of landscapes deemed by Song times to be characteristically Chinese in nature – agricultural lands populated by Chinese-speaking peasants – one might refer to it as a "sinic space." The idea of "sinic space" accords well, of course, with the modern way of conceptualizing the territory of a nation-state – as a homogeneous space, possessing everywhere equally the characteristic qualities that distinguish it from the national spaces of neighboring states.

Under the Tang, by contrast, the northeast – and especially the region of Yan – was viewed very differently. In the early eighth century, it was common to depict the people of Hebei as semi-"barbaric," as well as both "fierce" and "proud."[1] After serving as a launch pad for the great An Lushan Rebellion of the mid-eighth century, Hebei acquired in addition a reputation for rebelliousness.[2] The term "Hebei precedent" came to serve as a derogatory reference to the practice of hereditary succession used by Hebei provincial governors, a practice that, by defying the august authority of the emperor, was interpreted as "provincial hubris."[3] It is certainly with this view of the northeast in mind that the ninth-century writer Du Mu (803–52) imagined the Hebei origins of a certain Lu Pei, whose pastimes seemed more to resemble those of steppe nomads

---

[1] Pulleyblank, *Background of the Rebellion of An Lu-shan*, 79.
[2] E.g., JTS 200b.5386.
[3] Peterson, "Court and Province," 548.

than those of educated Chinese elites. By the age of twenty, according to Du, Lu "had never heard of men of antiquity like the Duke of Zhou and Confucius." Instead, "he played polo, drank alcohol, and hunted rabbits on horseback; when he spoke, his words without exception concerned matters of warfare, attack, and defense."[4] The mid-twentieth-century Tang historian Chen Yinke used this very passage from Du Mu to put forward his thesis that Hebei was "barbarized" over the course of the Tang, as large numbers of non-Chinese migrated in from regions further north.[5] Whether or not the mores of this region were actually transformed in the way Chen suggests is less significant than the fact that Hebei was believed in Tang times to be different, populated by people fundamentally less civilized than the Chinese of the heartland.

How does one account for this sharp divergence in views of the northeast, from the Tang, when it epitomized the semi-barbaric frontier, to the mid-Northern Song, when even doves at court recognized it as China's "lost" territory inhabited by ethnic brethren? Indeed, this conceptual transformation of the position of Yan and the northeast in the Chinese imaginary was part and parcel of a new way of conceiving state territory. How one explains the transformation is critical for better understanding the emergence among Chinese educated elites of a national consciousness.

This chapter explores the conversion of Yan into "sinic space" by examining the experiences of Song ambassadors to Liao, men who, as we have seen, represented the pinnacle of the Chinese sociopolitical elite. Previously, in Chapter 1, the accounts of these ambassadors helped document the intense sociability that developed between Song and Liao diplomats. This sociability may well account for the transmission from the Liao to the Song of certain conceptual categories underlying the Liao ethnic policies described in the previous chapter. But an equally important component of the cosmopolitanism of Song ambassadors – as Christian Lamouroux has previously observed – involved the travel experience itself.[6] While journeying to the fringes of the Eurasian steppe, they gained firsthand knowledge of the cultural and ecological landscape of Northeast Asia, recording many of their observations in diaries and poetry. This new firsthand knowledge transformed how they understood China's place in the world.

---

[4] *Du Mu ji xinian jiaozhu*, 3:767.
[5] Chen Yinke, *Tangdai zhengzhi shi*, 26.
[6] Lamouroux, "De l'étrangeté à la différence."

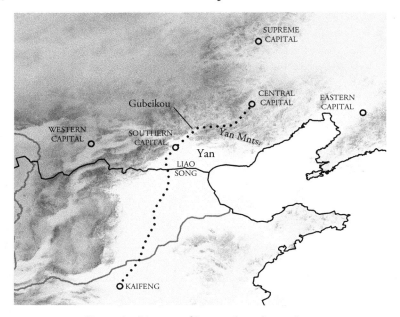

Figure 6.1 Itinerary of Song ambassadors to Liao

Elite Travelers in Song China

Throughout the post-Chanyuan century, Song embassies to Liao began their journeys along a fixed itinerary (Figure 6.1). All entered Liao territory after crossing the Baigou River just north of the Song prefecture of Xiongzhou.[7] It was there that they first met their escorts, who would accompany them to the Khitan court. Four more days of travel brought them to the Liao Southern Capital of Yanjing. After typically two nights in Yanjing, they then headed northeast through Wangjing – roughly anticipating the route of the airport expressway in modern Beijing – and on toward the Yan Mountains, reaching Gubei Pass five days later. After ten more days of traveling, the Song envoys reached the Liao Central Capital, the ruins of which lie today just west of Ningcheng in Chifeng, Inner Mongolia. In some cases, the Liao emperor met them there, and their journeys came to an end. For embassies that traveled further,

---

[7] This itinerary is based on a synthesis of several of the embassy travelogues mentioned below. The route is described briefly in Nie Chongqi, "Song Liao jiaopin kao," 22.

the routes varied somewhat, depending on where the mobile Khitan court was then encamped. Most envoys would travel another half month northward, skirting the Greater Khingan Range that bounded the western edge of the Manchurian Plain, before crossing the broad Xar Moron River. Soon afterwards, they reached their final destination, either the Liao Supreme Capital (situated at the site of modern-day Bairin Left Banner, Inner Mongolia), or else the nearby camp of the Liao emperor. In total, the trip required a month or more of travel in each direction. At least a third of this time – between the Baigou River and Gubei Pass – was spent in the region of Yan.

Travelers to Liao documented their impressions while on the road in embassy diaries and travel poetry. By the second half of the eleventh century, all ambassadors were apparently required by the court to submit a travelogue providing a day-by-day account of the round trip to the Liao capital.[8] Eight of these embassy diaries survive in complete or fragmentary versions (Table 6.1).[9] Some, such as the one written by Wang Zeng (978–1038), are especially terse, indicating only the route and distances travelled, and making a few additional observations that struck the author as particularly noteworthy. Other diaries were longer and more informative. The travelogue by the polymath Shen Gua (1031–95), for example, is particularly rich in details. When submitted to the throne in 1075, it was even accompanied by illustrations depicting the physiography and the customs of the people, though these illustrations no longer survive.[10] Also included in Table 6.1 is a report on Liao administration and society, compiled by Yu Jing (1000–72), that incorporates what appear to be excerpts of records of his three trips to the Khitan court. In addition, there is Xu Kangzong's (d. 1135) account of his 1125 embassy to the Jurchens, then based to the east of Khitan territory.

Besides embassy diaries, ambassadors and other members of their retinues also composed poetry in great abundance while on the road. In Chapter 1, we focused on the banquet poetry of Song and Liao diplomats. But envoys did not limit their compositions to banquets. They also wrote verse describing their impressions of the scenes they encountered during their journeys. This invaluable source material has not received the attention it deserves, partly because it tends to be scattered haphazardly throughout the collected works of its authors. Table 6.2

---

[8] Fu Lehuan, "Song ren shi Liao yulu"; Christian Lamouroux, "De l'étrangeté à la différence," 104.

[9] D. C. Wright, *From War to Diplomatic Parity*, 175–83. See also D. C. Wright, *Ambassadors Records*; Fu Lehuan, "Song ren shi Liao yulu"; Franke, "Sung Embassies."

[10] SS 331.10655; Subrenat, "Shen Kua."

Table 6.1 *Extant embassy diaries and related reports*

Author	Date of embassy	Reference[a]
Hu Qiao (fl. 950s)	947–53	Text: XWDS 73.905–08; Ye Longli, *Qidan guozhi*, 25.237–40. Study: Jia Jingyan, "Hu Qiao xian Liao ji shuzheng."
Lu Zhen (957–1014)	1009	Abbreviated text: Lu Zhen, *Chengyao lu*. Fragments of full text: Jiang Shaoyu, *Songchao shishi leiyuan*, 77.1010–16. Study: Jia Jingyan, "Lu Zhen *Chengyao lu* shuzheng gao."
Wang Zeng (978–1038)	1012	Text: Ye Longli, *Qidan guozhi*, 24.230–32; XCB 79.1794–96; SHY *fanyi* 2.6–9. Study: Fu Lehuan, "Song ren shi Liao yulu," 176–81.
Xue Ying (948–1021); Zhang Shixun (964–1049)	1016	Text: XCB 88.2015; Ye Longli, *Qidan guozhi*, 24.232; LS 37.441–42. Study: Fu Lehuan, "Song ren shi Liao yulu," 172–74. *Qidan guozhi* erroneously attributes this account to Fu Bi, who went on an embassy to Liao in 1042.
Song Shou (991–1040)	1021	Fragmentary text: XCB 97.2253–54; SHY *fanyi* 2.9–11.
Yu Jing (1000–72)	1043	Text: QSW 27:104–07.
Chen Xiang (1017–80)	1068	Text: QSW 50:228–37.
Shen Gua (1031–95)	1078	Text: QSW 77:377–83. Study: Jia Jingyan, "Xining shi Qidan tuchao shuzheng gao."
Zhang Shunmin (c.1034–c.1100)	1093	Fragmentary text: Ye Longli, *Qidan guozhi*, 25.240–42.
Xu Kangzong (d. 1135)	1125	Text: Jue'an and Nai'an, *Jingkang baishi jianzheng*, 1–43; Yuwen Maozhao, *Da Jinguo zhi jiaozheng*, 2:559–81.

[a] Several texts available in English; see Wright, *Ambassadors Records*.

Table 6.2 *Reconstructed sequences of embassy poetry*

Poet	Date of embassy	Reference[a]
Han Qi (1008–75)	1038	Han Qi, *Anyang ji biannian jianzhu*, 1:166–70.
Wang Gui (1019–85)	1051	QSS 9:5957, 5969–71, 5991–92, 6005.
Liu Chang (1019–68)	1055	QSS 9:5658, 5731, 5793, 5801, 5810, 5835, 5844–45, 5852, 5856, 5869, 5871, 5876, 5880, 5903, 5905, 5907–10, 5913, 5916–17, 5926, 5928–29, 5939, 5942–43.
Ouyang Xiu (1007–72)	1055	Ouyang Xiu, *Ouyang Xiu quan ji*, 1:87, 1:91–93, 2:202–04, 3:769, 3:811, 3:818. For reconstruction of this sequence, see Liu Deqing, *Ouyang Xiu jinian lu*, 275–79.
Shen Gou (1025–67)	1059	QSS 11:7519–23.
Zheng Xie (1022–72)	1062	QSS 10:6819, 6821, 6852, 6882–83.
Wang Anshi (1021–86)	1063	Wang Anshi, *Wang Jing Gong shizhu bujian*, 3.59–60, 7.143–45, 12.235–36, 14.269, 16.300–02, 23.408, 23.411–12, 24.430, 24.440, 25.454, 29.538–39, 30.553–54, 33.618–20, 34.625–26, 45.881–82. For reconstruction of this sequence, see Zhang Diyun, "Guanyu Wang Anshi shi Liao"; *Quan Liao shi hua*, 286–90.
Chen Xiang (1017–80)	1067	QSS 8:5082, 5090–92.
Su Song (1020–1101)	1068/1077	Su Song, *Su Weigong wenji*, 1:160–77.
Su Che (1039–1112)	1089	Su Che, *Su Che ji*, 16:317–23.
Peng Ruli (1042–95)	1091	QSS 16:10471, 10491, 10504–05, 10546, 10552–54, 10565–66, 10589, 10602, 10614–15, 10617, 10635–37.
Zhang Shunmin (c.1034–c.1100)	1093	QSW 83:260–61; QSS 14:9678, 9679, 9685, 9692.
Liu Qi (d. 1117)		QSS 8:12196–98, 12213–14.

[a] Many poems also included in *Quan Liao shi hua*, 266–333.

reconstructs sequences of poems by a diverse assortment of eleventh-century writers. Included are two of the most famous Northern Song literati, Ouyang Xiu (1007–72) and Su Che (1039–1112). Also represented are several late eleventh-century chief ministers, including Wang Anshi (1021–86), Wang Gui (1019–85), and Su Song (1020–1101). The two lengthy poetic sequences preserved in Su Song's collected works are particularly interesting. Like Shen Gua, Su Song was a scientist and inventor, having co-edited the illustrated pharmacopoeia *Tujing bencao* (1061) and submitted to the throne a detailed plan for the construction of a mechanical clock.[11] Perhaps because of his interest in science and the natural world, he seems to have been particularly attentive to empirical observations during his travels. He later put together a 200-chapter guide to Liao customs and to Song–Liao diplomatic practice.[12] Although this guide does not survive, his extant embassy poetry sequences recapitulate a wealth of data on ecology, geography, and nomadic customs.[13]

It is important to bear in mind when analyzing this material that official travel and travel literature under the Song had become an integral element of elite life. Elite travel in this period still occurred mostly in the context of official business, unlike in the Ming Dynasty and later, when one begins to encounter large numbers of independent, gentlemen travelers. Song officials were dispatched from Kaifeng to far-flung posts all around the empire, providing them with a panoramic vision of Song territory. While journeying to their appointments, they made use of government roads and spent nights at government inns and post stations not unlike the accommodations provided to ambassadors en route to the Liao court.[14] Moreover, they were entertained along the way by colleagues or friends at gatherings that resembled embassy banquets in many ways, replete with food, wine, and poetry-writing. Song appointees to office were usually given ample time to reach their posts, allowing them to make detours to visit places of interest along the way.[15] Spurred in part by these new opportunities to tour famous sites, and in part by the emergence of a print culture in the eleventh century, travel literature flourished in the Northern Song. Included among this literature were

[11] Miyashita, "Su Sung."
[12] Only the preface of this guide survives. See Su Song, *Su Weigong wenji*, 66:1003–06.
[13] See, e.g., Su Song, *Su Weigong wenji*, 13:170, 171, 173, 175; QSS 9:5845, 9:5917.
[14] Zhang Cong, *Transformative Journeys*, 43–68, 83–110.
[15] Ibid., 76–81.

prose essays and travel diaries – many not unlike embassy travelogues in their basic formats – as well as vast quantities of verse.

The travel literature in turn fueled a new elite practice of "cultural pilgrimages." Over time, certain mountains, temples, and historical sites became ever more renowned as generations of travelers, en route to official appointments, celebrated these places in poems that were engraved in situ on steles or cliff faces, or that circulated in published form among the literati class.[16] By the Southern Song, one could consult local or national gazetteers to identify the famous places to visit in the various prefectures of the empire.[17] Though these sites may have been places of great scenic beauty, what really attracted the visitors was their cultural aura, as well as what they had come to signify in historical memory.[18] Embassy literature came to play a similar role. Previously unknown sites along the standardized route traveled by the ambassadors to Liao became attractions – almost the equivalent of tourist destinations. First described in the poetry or diaries of the earliest travelers to the Khitan court, subsequent travelers paused to admire the same vistas, and to compose verse encapsulating their own impressions. Thus, several successive envoys composed poems, when traversing Gubei Pass, about a temple there dedicated to the Song general Yang Ye (d. 986).[19] Many travelers also stopped to write lines of verse commemorating Huixian Rock[20] – a geological formation that apparently resembled an assemblage of spirits – as well as the aptly named Sixiang ("Thinking-of-Home") Ridge.[21]

Travel and the Transformation of Worldviews

At the heart of the new popularity of travel literature in the Song was the widely held belief among educated Chinese – explored in some detail by Zhang Cong – that the travel experience was invaluable as a source of

---

[16] Ibid., 154–79.

[17] Ibid., 202–06.

[18] A good example involves the Red Cliff, site of a third-century battle. Because the famous literatus Su Shi wrote two prose poems about it, it became the topic of verse by the twelfth-century poets Lu You and Fan Chengda, who were themselves more interested in following in Su Shi's footsteps than in either the surrounding scenery or the third-century battle. For more on "Su Shi sites," see ibid., 180–206.

[19] Su Song, *Su Weigong wenji*, 1:162; *Su Che ji*, 1:319; QSS 9:5916, 16:10504.

[20] Su Song, *Su Weigong wenji*, 1:164; QSS 9:5992, 16:10546, 16:10589; QSW 77:380.

[21] *Su Che ji*, 1:319; QSS 9:5871, 9:5909, 9:5991, 14:9692; Lu Zhen, *Chengyao lu*, 2; XCB 79.1795; QSW 77:379.

edification.[22] As the mid-eleventh-century scholar Hu Yuan (993–1059) put it:

> If a scholar only stays in one place, he will stagnate there, and become narrow-minded and ignorant. One must travel the four corners of the earth, and scrutinize the patterns of human affairs, the social customs of the north and the south, and the layout of the mountains and rivers, in order to broaden one's knowledge.[23]

Su Che – whose embassy poems survive – made much the same point, while describing the transformative influence of travel on his own formation:

> At the age of nineteen, when I lived at home, the people with whom I associated were limited to those around my hometown; what I got to see was limited to what was within a few hundred *li*. There were no tall mountains or vast plains from which I could expand my horizons. I had read all of the works of the masters, but these were all things of the past . . . So I resolved to leave home and seek out the strange phenomena and magnificent sights of the world, in order to become aware of the magnitude of Heaven and Earth. I passed by the old capital cities of the Qin and Han dynasties, then gazed at the heights of Mt. Zhongnan, Mt. Song, and Mt. Hua, then turned to the north to look upon the flowing waters of the Yellow River . . . In the capital, I beheld the majesty of the imperial palace . . . Thus, I became aware of the great beauty of the world.[24]

Travel expanded one's horizons in ways that book-learning simply could not do, by providing one with firsthand empirical knowledge about both the workings and the grandeur of the world. Given this appreciation of the transformative power of travel, the writings of men with firsthand knowledge of the world at large acquired a certain prestige. Song scholars expressed particular admiration for the works of the early historian Sima Qian (*c*.145–*c*.86 BCE), as it was said he had journeyed to the four corners of the empire while gathering information for his celebrated historical study.[25]

The same conviction about the value of travel applied to embassy missions as well. Each evening during his 1029 embassy to Liao, Su Qi (987–1035) religiously recorded in his poetry all of his observations about the terrain and landscape; "everything was included." When he returned to

[22] Zhang Cong, *Transformative Journeys*, esp. 162–67.
[23] Wang Zhi, *Moji*, 3.51. Translation adapted from Zhang Cong, *Transformative Journeys*, 162.
[24] *Su che ji*, 2:381. Translation adapted from Zhang Cong, *Transformative Journeys*, 162.
[25] Zhang Cong, *Transformative Journeys*, 163–66.

Kaifeng, he circulated a compilation of his poems at court that "people competed with each other to recite."[26] It was also common during policy debates to claim to have gained a new expertise in foreign affairs after an embassy. Su Che composed a series of five "Memorials Discussing Northern Border Affairs upon Returning from a Northern Embassy," which included suggestions on how to enforce existing trade restrictions on printed books and Song bronze coins.[27] Earlier in the century, "Jolly" Wang Gongchen (1012–85) had also made policy proposals grounded in knowledge he acquired as an ambassador. In this case, he argued for the establishment of a local militia system along the Song–Liao frontier, claiming to have heard during his travels that Khitan soldiers feared local fighters far more than Song government troops.[28] A number of other such memorials were composed by influential statesmen who had returned from Liao, including Fu Bi (1004–83), Lü Tao (1031–1107), and Zhang Fangping (1007–91).[29] Given the value attributed to knowledge acquired on embassy missions, it is not surprising that ambassadors' travelogues were used as sources of military intelligence as well.[30] Parts of the description of Yanjing in the mid-eleventh-century military treatise *Wujing zongyao*, for example, contain material copied almost verbatim from an embassy journal submitted to the court in 1012.[31]

In reality, of course, the writings of Song travelers and diplomats often reveal as much about pre-existing conceptual categories and frameworks as about objective reality. As a general rule, Chinese views of peripheral lands throughout the Song and later periods can productively be compared to Western "Orientalism." Not only did Song travelers interpret the phenomena they encountered in their own culturally defined manner, they also chose what to include in their diaries and what to commemorate in verse. Thus, in Song travel writings, one can often discern distinct "gazes" – be it an "imperial gaze" or simply the gaze of a curious traveler – reflecting the author's perceived relationship to his surroundings. But all this is not to assert that the travel experience had no impact on worldviews. In a careful study of Renaissance-era accounts of South India, Joan-Pau Rubiés

---

[26] QSW 41:110.
[27] *Su Che ji*, 2:747–48.
[28] XCB 127.3007.
[29] XCB 150.3639, 3650, 3654; QSW 73:180–81; XCB 138.3326–27. See also QSW 50:41–42; XCB 242.5906.
[30] Franke, "Sung Embassies," 137–39; D. C. Wright, *From War to Diplomatic Parity*, 179–80, 183–84.
[31] Compare the passage beginning with "出北門, 過古長城" in WJZY, part 1, 22.2a–2b, with XCB 79.1795–96.

has demonstrated that European travelers did, in fact, possess the ability to decode foreign cultural systems, even if they sometimes resorted to homologous European practices to help them make sense of what they saw. In Rubiés's account, "Orientalism" in the Saidian sense emerged not in the firsthand reports of the travelers to India, themselves, but rather in the summaries and syntheses of these firsthand accounts by later writers.[32]

At the heart of Rubiés's argument is a recognition of the power of firsthand transcultural encounters to expand horizons and transform the understanding of one's position within a larger world. Northern Song China in the post-Chanyuan period was unusual precisely because of the substantial number of individuals who, through diplomatic missions, came to know such transcultural experiences. In contrast to Renaissance travelers to India, moreover, the travelers to Liao included a sizable component of the political elite, as well as some of the most celebrated writers of the period, including the prose and verse masters Ouyang Xiu and Su Shi. Such men possessed an unmatched ability to shape both state policy and elite culture. To the extent that one can reconstruct how these men were transformed by their journeys beyond the frontier, one can better understand why a fundamentally new consciousness emerged in eleventh-century China.

The remainder of this chapter will explore how what ambassadors witnessed and experienced during their missions to Liao – as attested in their travel writings – affected the Song worldview. Three specific features of the Northeast Asian landscape impressed the envoys above all else. First, almost without exception, they were fascinated by the dramatic topography of the mountains north of Yan, which had all the features of a "natural" boundary. Second, they were struck by the alien landscape appearing immediately after traveling into the mountains, which made them all the more aware of the distinctiveness of "sinic space." Third, many travelers described with great interest the ethnically Han population of Yan. These three sets of observations are all the more noteworthy because empirical data confirms the significance of the Yan Mountains as a topographic, ecological, and cultural boundary in the eleventh century. One readily understands why the travelers were so impressed by what they saw, and how these impressions influenced their vision of the world and their sense of a Chinese identity.

---

[32] Rubiés, *Travel and Ethnology*. For a discussion of the birth of Orientalism in later syntheses of firsthand travel accounts, see esp. 291–92.

"Heaven's Barrier"

On one of the increasingly rare clear days in China's capital city, perhaps following a significant rainstorm, the modern-day tourist can still experience what envoys to Liao would have seen as they crossed the region of Yan. From an elevated position in the city center – the top of Jingshan Park, for example – one can make out the range of mountains that dramatically line the northern and western horizons (Figure 6.2). It is these mountains that bring to an abrupt end the vast North China Plain, which extends southward as far as the eye can see. If one then takes a bus tour to see the remains of the Ming-era Great Wall just north of Beijing, one will note how quickly the flat farmlands north of the city come to an end. A tourist with more time, who may have traveled by train from Shanghai or elsewhere in the south, will have experienced the vastness of the North China Plain: the foothills of the Yan Mountains will constitute some of the first hills encountered after hundreds of miles of travel.

One of the themes encountered most consistently in the travel writings of Song envoys to Liao concerns the topography of the Yan region. Immediately upon crossing the Baigou River that demarcated the Song–Liao border, the Song envoy Su Song aptly described this scene in a line of verse, as he gazed northward toward the Yan Mountains: "the cyan mountains are like a wall, the land like a platter."[33] A bit further north, in Shunzhou, Liu Chang was similarly impressed by the contrast between the mountains and the plains. Looking toward the mountains while atop his horse, he wrote, "A boundless plain faces this cluster of peaks – a green wall that winds back and forth in myriad layers."[34] It was easy for these travelers to imagine this topographic "wall" as a natural barrier separating China from their neighbors living to the north. Su Che remarked:

> The Yan Mountains are like a long snake,
> Separating Han from barbarians for a thousand *li*.
> Its mouth grasps the base of the Western Mountains;
> Its tail drapes across the shores of the Eastern Sea.[35]

In a second poem composed at Gubei Pass, the pass through which most Song envoys exited the North China Plain, he reiterated this point: "barbarian and Han territory are separated here."[36] The defensive value

---

[33] Su Song, *Su Weigong wenji*, 1:161.
[34] QSS 9:5913.
[35] *Su Che ji*, 1:319.
[36] Ibid.

Figure 6.2 Yan Mountains viewed from central Beijing

of Juyong Pass near Badaling – where "the cliff walls are like a fortified passageway through which pedestrians pass like fish in a stream" – was succinctly summarized in a poem by Zheng Xie (1022–72): "With a single man blocking its key point, a myriad horses could not rush through."[37] Hu Qiao's embassy diary included a similar portrayal of Shimen Pass: "[Next to] the road at the pass, the cliffs are narrow; one man can block a hundred [men]; this is the strategic spot by which the Middle Kingdom can control the Khitans."[38] Gubei Pass was no less strategic, as Wang Zeng made clear in his travelogue:

> On both sides are high cliffs, with the road in between only suitable for the tracks of a single carriage; north of the pass is a stockade, [manned by] a row of archers, their bows fully drawn; this was originally where Fanyang defended against the Xi and Khitans; it is the most strategic of spots.[39]

Wang concluded by noting that most territorial encroachments in former times had occurred via Yingzhou and Pingzhou – that is, along the one prominent gap in this topographic barrier, the narrow stretch of coastal flatland linking the North China Plain to the fertile lowlands of southern Manchuria.

Given the striking topography of the Yan Mountains and the role they were perceived to play in defending the North China Plain from attack, it is not surprising that travelers often imagined them as a manifestation of Heaven's will. Thus, as he approached Gubei Pass, the early eleventh-century envoy Lu Zhen recorded in his journal that "the cliff walls are high and precipitous; Heaven has set apart the Rong caitiffs by means of this very place."[40] Trekking through several decades later, Su Song noted that the mountains there constituted "Heaven's barrier" and served to "separate north from south."[41] Liu Chang was equally struck, describing mountains that "stretched for a myriad *li* east to west"; on the day he crossed through them, he commented, "This morning, I recognized Heaven's will, which is to separate Hua from the land of barbarians."[42] And Han Qi described the scene at Gubei Pass as follows: "East and west, the layers of peaks stand profuse and tall . . . It was Heaven's will that north and south should be divided here."[43]

---

[37] QSS 10:6821.
[38] XWDS 73.905.
[39] XCB 79.1795.
[40] Lu Zhen, *Chengyao lu*, 2.
[41] Su Song, *Su Weigong wenji*, 1:162.
[42] QSS 9:5835.
[43] Han Qi, *Anyang ji biannian jianzhu*, 1:170.

To be sure, imagining the Yan Mountains as "Heaven's barrier" accorded well with the emerging popularity of topography-based models of the world. Indeed, if one examines Song-era cartographic representations of Yixing's Two Boundaries model (Figure 4.1), one observes that Yixing's "Northern Boundary" at its eastern end incorporated the Yan Mountains. Yixing himself lived long before the Song Dynasty, so his model in principle predated the Chanyuan Oath, and may have played a role in framing how eleventh-century envoys understood what they encountered in their travels. Simultaneously, however, there is little doubt that the dramatic topography north of Yan was as striking to eleventh-century travelers as it is to tourists today. The experiences of Northern Song ambassadors, as attested in their travel poetry and prose, served then to reinforce their conviction that the Yan Mountains constituted China's natural northern border, established by Heaven in part to protect China from steppe invaders. The ambassadors' experiences may explain – as much as be explained by – the growing popularity in the Song Dynasty of Yixing's cosmographic theory.

Yan as Sinic Space

It was not just the topography of the Yan Mountains that attracted the attention of the Song travelers. They were also struck by the very different landscapes they encountered north and south of the mountains. Upon crossing the Song–Liao political border and entering the Khitan-controlled portion of northern Hebei, the surrounding environment remained familiar. Beyond the mountains, however, the envoys witnessed a sudden and dramatic transformation, involving not only the disappearance of historical and other markers of civilization as they knew it, but also the appearance of an alien cultural ecology and of non-Han peoples. At this point, it is worth recalling that the diplomats, as prominent political elites, would have had previous experiences journeying to diverse bureaucratic appointments around the Song empire. They possessed a panoramic understanding of China that provided them with a particular way of envisioning generic Chinese space.

For educated Chinese, all well versed in classical and historical scholarship, historical remains from earlier dynasties constituted clear markers of their own culture and civilization.[44] The fact that embassies

---

[44] Lamouroux, "De l'étrangeté à la différence," 109–10.

encountered Chinese historical remains in the Yan region, but not beyond the mountains, helped to establish Yan as a "sinic space." Not long after entering the Liao-controlled portion of northern Hebei, for example, Shen Gua followed a canal that, according to him, was built by Sui Yangdi (569–618) to supply his armies during one of his failed Korea campaigns.[45] Several decades later and further to the east, Xu Kangzong encountered a supply canal he claimed had been excavated centuries earlier by the famed warlord Cao Cao (155–220). Subsequently, upon reaching the prefectural seat of Yingzhou, Xu noted that the city had been initially established by none other than Shun, the great sage king of remote antiquity.[46] In Yanjing and its vicinity, the travelers also described several historical temples: the Huayan Temple, one wall of which was said to feature calligraphy penned by Song Taizong (939–97) during his 979 invasion of Yan;[47] the Minzhong Temple, built by Tang Taizong to honor fallen soldiers;[48] and the Tang-era Guoye Temple, which housed a "Hall of Stone Scriptures," undoubtedly a reference to the thousands of Tang-era Buddhist inscriptions that are preserved to this day in caves atop Shijing Mountain southwest of Beijing.[49]

As they approached the Yan frontier, the Song envoys recognized indications that they were approaching the limits of historical China. Three different envoys crossing beyond the Yan Mountains using three different routes – Hu Qiao through Juyong Pass, Wang Zeng through Gubei Pass, and Xu Kangzong through Yu Pass – all noted the sudden disappearance of the stone mile markers that lined the roads of the Chinese empire.[50] Indeed, in Song travel literature more generally speaking, mile markers held a particular symbolic significance to officials journeying along government roads.[51] In addition, even the tersest of embassy diaries mentioned the remains of the "Ancient Great Wall." Lu Zhen, Wang Zeng, and Shen Gua all encountered this Wall between Yanjing and the Wangjing (Sunhou) hostel to the northeast.[52] Both Shen

---

[45] QSW 77:378.

[46] Jue'an and Nai'an, *Jingkang baishi jianzheng*, 10 (stage 5), 16 (stage 13).

[47] Jiang Shaoyu, *Songchao shishi leiyuan*, 77.1012.

[48] XCB 79.1795. This temple would have been one of the seven established by Taizong in 629 to honor soldiers who had died in the battles leading to the founding of the Tang. See Weinstein, *Buddhism under the T'ang*, 13.

[49] Lu Zhen, *Chengyao lu*, 1.

[50] XWDS 73.905; XCB 79.1795; Jue'an and Nai'an, *Jingkang baishi jianzheng*, 19 (stage 15). According to the ninth-century Japanese monk Ennin, the Tang erected markers every five *li* on the main roads. See Reischauer (trans.), *Ennin's Diary*, 175–76.

[51] Zhang Cong, *Transformative Journeys*, 59–62.

[52] Lu Zhen, *Chengyao lu*, 1; XCB 79.1795; QSW 77:378.

Gua and Zhang Shunmin observed the Wall a bit further north as well, as they entered the hills north of Shunzhou.[53] Su Song sighted the "ten-thousand *li* wall of the king of Qin" at Gubei Pass.[54] And Xu Kangzong described remains of the "Ancient Great Wall" at Shanhaiguan on the Bohai coast. Beyond the Wall, he wrote, "there are no historical remains to talk about."[55] Historians and archaeologists have now confirmed that this "Ancient Great Wall" was a construction built by the Northern Qi Dynasty in the mid-sixth century.[56] Yet Su Song was not alone in misidentifying it as the more famous Great Wall of Qin. In his "Rhapsody on the Great Wall," Zhang Shunmin even claimed to have seen the withered bones of Qin-era corvée laborers beneath the wall remains at Gubei Pass.[57] The erroneous identification of these remains with a structure built well over a millennium before the founding of the Song is suggestive. To the travelers, these remnants of ancient fortifications represented a timeless boundary between their own land and the lands beyond.

Besides demarcating the limits of a characteristic and familiar historical landscape, the Yan Mountains were also seen as separating two very different cultural ecologies. Just past the Song–Liao border, while still south of the mountains, Su Song observed a scene he might have encountered anywhere in Song territory: "1000 *li* of [farmers] plowing and cultivating mulberry trees."[58] According to Shen Gua, around Shunzhou, in the foothills of the Yan Mountains, "mulberry trees and grain are fertile and flourishing."[59] After traveling beyond the mountain passes further north, however, envoys made note of the immediate transformation of the landscape. In describing the view from Yu Pass, Xu Kangzong observed:

> Ascending to a high spot and looking back toward Jieshi in the east and Wutai in the west, the land of [Yan] consists of 1000 *li* of fertile ground, bordered to the north by great mountains . . . In the lands south of the mountains, nowhere does one not find the five grains, the hundred fruits, and fine vegetation and trees. Not more than a few dozen *li* beyond the passes, however, the mountains are bare of trees, the rivers are murky, and everywhere [the soil] is poor and salty. One sees nothing but yellow thatch and dry grass, extending out who knows how far.[60]

[53] QSW 77:378–79; QSW 83:260.
[54] Su Song, *Su Weigong wenji*, 1:169.
[55] Jue'an and Nai'an, *Jingkang baishi jianzheng*, 19 (stages 16–17).
[56] Tackett, "Great Wall," 109–12.
[57] QSW 83:260.
[58] Su Song, *Su Weigong wenji*, 1:161.
[59] QSW 77:378.
[60] Jue'an and Nai'an, *Jingkang baishi jianzheng*, 17 (stage 14).

And, according to Su Che, who crossed the mountains a few decades earlier at Gubei Pass:

> The frontier of Yan ends at Gubei Pass,
> Beyond which the mountains dissipate into numerous flat fields.
> Here, Xi people build grass huts for themselves,
> And Khitan horse carts rest near the springs.
> Camels, sheep, and horses scatter in the river valley,
> Moving on when the water and grasses dry up.[61]

The strict divide, between sedentary agriculturalists farming their fertile fields and pastoral nomads accompanying their herds in search of water and fresh pasture, could not have been more clear.

So stark was the cultural-ecological divide that many of the travelers attributed it – once again – to the will of Heaven. Xu Kangzong, after describing the ecological boundary at Yu Pass, asserted that "Heaven must have established this to set apart Hua from the barbarian lands."[62] According to Wang Gui, observing the scene from Gubei Pass:

> No riding horses arrive here; no wheels leave from here.
> Heaven's barrier is clearly marked, with only one passage
>   through.[63]

Whereas Xu focused on the limits of the agricultural zone, Wang stressed the divide between a world of wheeled carts and a world of horse-riding nomads. But like Xu, Wang also invoked Heaven. For Peng Ruli (1042–95), then on his way home from regions further north, Gubei Pass was where he finally encountered the familiar sound of a rooster's cry, a cry that to him marked his return to a land of agriculturalists, and to people of his own culture:

> After the snows, the hue of the sky has become clearer;
> At a rustic inn, suddenly I hear a cock's crow.
> Mountains, rivers – topographic features – all accord with
>   Yu's plan;
> Thus, the customs and habits of the people here resemble those
>   of Yanjing.[64]

Although Peng did not mention Heaven, the Yan Mountains surrounding Gubei Pass were of cosmic significance nonetheless: they were the

---

[61] Su Che, *Su Che ji*, 1:320.
[62] Jue'an and Nai'an, *Jingkang baishi jianzheng*, 17 (stage 14).
[63] QSS 9:5992.
[64] QSS 16:10504.

material embodiment of the sage king Yu's partitioning of the world at the dawn of human civilization.

In fact, not all Song travelers described the ecological divide in quite such black-and-white terms. It was well past the Yan Mountains, as they continued northward beyond the Central Capital, that Song envoys finally encountered the more purely pastoral societies of the Eurasian steppe proper. According to the reports of both Song Shou and Shen Gua, only after leaving the Central Capital did ambassadors begin to spend nights regularly in felt yurts rather than traditional Chinese-style hostels.[65] It was also only in this distant region that the envoys began to notice steppe-style urban centers, featuring large empty spaces within the city walls where nomads could set up their camps.[66] Similarly only when traveling in the vicinity of the Central Capital and beyond did Su Song first pay attention to elements of the pastoral-nomadic lifestyle. His sequence of poems describes Khitan yurt carts, vast herds of horses, and the steppe hunting technique of encircling rabbits and other game with an army of horsemen.[67]

Many Song observers described a transitional zone between the Yan Mountains and the Central Capital, with an economy that combined stock farming with crop cultivation. Agriculture was still possible, albeit difficult due to the extremes in temperature. According to Peng Ruli, north of Gubei Pass "the land is sparse in grain crops; / throughout the year frost and snow are in abundance."[68] Although "sparse," cereal farming did exist. Similarly, in an annotation to a poem written at the Liu River, not long after crossing the Yan Mountains, Su Song observed that "Liao soil is very rich, but the land is cold and one cannot plant [much]; plowing begins in late Spring and [farming] ceases in early Fall."[69] Elsewhere, Shen Gua specified that the growing season in this region was not much more than three months long, between the fourth and seventh months of the year.[70]

[65] XCB 97.2253; QSW 77:380–81.

[66] XCB 97.2253; QSW 77:381. Lu Zhen also describes an open space occupied by yurts within the inner city walls of the Central Capital. See Jiang Shaoyu, Songchao shishi leiyuan, 77.1012, 1014. For an excellent description of steppe urbanization, see Rogers, "Urban Centres."

[67] Su Song, Su Weigong wenji, 1:171, 173, 175. What Su describes as "hunting by encircling" is equivalent to the nerge ("Great Hunt") of the Mongols. See Lane, Daily Life in the Mongol Empire, 107–14.

[68] QSS 16:10602.

[69] Su Song, Su Weigong wenji, 1:176.

[70] QSW 77:377.

Given these ecological limitations, stock herding was an important supplement to agriculture in this transitional zone beyond the Yan Mountains. According to Liu Chang, "beginning at Gubei Pass is the land of the Xi people, all of whom live in the mountains, drawing water from the valleys, where they plow and herd."[71] Not long after crossing the same pass, Su Song painted a similar scene:

> Everywhere the inhabitants are occupied plowing and herding,
> While yurt carts carrying entire families move back and forth.[72]

Wang Zeng described a mixture of primitive agriculture and stock herding in somewhat more detail:

> Once one has crossed Gubei Pass, one is in tribal territory. The inhabitants live in grass huts or wooden cabins. They still occupy themselves plowing and cultivating, but there are neither mulberry nor cudrania trees. [The seeds] which they plant are all placed atop the [ridges of the] furrows, probably because they fear [the grooves] would be covered up by wind-blown sand. In the mountains, the pine trees are abundant, so, in the more remote valleys, they make a living burning charcoal. Frequently, one sees them herding cattle, horses, camels, and, especially, black sheep and yellow pigs. There are also some who lead yurt carts in search of water and pasture or in pursuit of game.[73]

Wang's description, to be sure, did not paint an ecological divide as stark as some of the earlier portrayals of a cosmic boundary established by Heaven. But the mixed transitional zone was, nonetheless, an alien land. Not only did one suddenly encounter herders living alongside farming families, one also found agriculturalists planting crops in strange ways.

As in the case of the descriptions of the topography, one recognizes how traveling envoys made sense of what they encountered according to pre-existing conceptual frameworks. In the case of the topography, the travelers invoked natural boundaries theories, as well as the notion of a frontier established by Heaven. In the case of the changing cultural ecology north of the mountains, they brought up once again the will of Heaven. They also identified the historical ruins they encountered on the basis of their own preconceptions, at times mistaking them for much earlier structures. But though there existed culturally specific ways in which Song envoys made sense of their observations while journeying

---

[71] QSS 9:5917.
[72] Su Song, *Su Weigong wenji*, 1:163.
[73] XCB 79.1796.

to the north, it is also clear that certain specific sights were sufficiently remarkable to attract the attention of numerous among them, and to merit a reference in even the most summary accounts. Not only did the Yan Mountains constitute a dramatic physical barrier, it was also – as is clear from Chapter 5 – a striking cultural divide. Though travel accounts describing the diverse territories of the Song empire frequently emphasized regional cultural disparities, the distinctive lifestyle of pastoral and agropastoral populations was far more strikingly different. The Song envoys' travels through Yan and the regions beyond made them more certain than ever both of the fundamental characteristics of Chinese space, and of the precise location of the timeless boundary separating China from the lands beyond.

The People of Yan

Besides serving as a divide between two different cultural ecologies, the Yan Mountains were also conceived as an ethnocultural frontier. Travelers' accounts largely reflected what we know of Liao ethnic categories and policies. According to these accounts, four distinct ethnic groups occupied the region between Yan and the Liao Supreme Capital: Khitan, Parhae, Xi, and Han people. Each was identifiable on the basis of gastronomic, sartorial, and linguistic characteristics. As Yu Jing observed regarding these four groups, "as for their clothing, food and drinks, and language, each followed their own customs."[74] Thus, embassy diaries and travel poetry frequently distinguished people wearing "Han clothing" from those wearing "Tartar clothing," the latter typically made of leather or fur.[75] Song embassy accounts also paid great attention to "caitiff food," which – as we saw in Chapter 1 – consisted of unappetizing meats cut into pieces too large to be eaten with chopsticks.[76]

According to the travelers' reports, the homelands of these ethnicities could be mapped into a neat spatial framework. As Shen Gua explained, "East of Enzhou is Parhae; south of the Central Capital is Eastern Xi . . .; in the mountains to the southwest is Western Xi, which includes the ancient district of the Hsi."[77] An earlier travel account by Xue Ying and Zhang Shixun provided a similar account: "Beginning just past the

---

[74] QSW 27:106.
[75] E.g., Jiang Shaoyu, *Songchao shishi leiyuan*, 77.1011, 1013.
[76] Ibid., 77.1011; Jue'an and Nai'an, *Jingkang baishi jianzheng*, 13 (stage 10).
[77] QSW 77:377.

Chongxin Hostel [near the Central Capital] is the ancient territory of the Khitans; further south must all be the land of the Xi."[78] Roughly speaking, then, the original Khitan homeland was situated in the region between the Supreme Capital and the Central Capital; and Xi territory extended from the Central Capital south to the Yan Mountains and Gubei Pass. It was on the basis of this framework that Liu Chang observed, "beginning at Gubei Pass is the land of the Xi people."[79] The reality of the situation, as suggested in the previous chapter, was not quite as neat as this ethnic geography would imply. Indeed, Lu Zhen and Shen Gua both encountered a mixed population that included Han people in the broad zone between the Central Capital and the Yan Mountains.[80] Although Song Shou observed that "from Gubei Pass to north of the Central Capital is the territory of the Xi," he went on to explain that, ever since the Khitan invasion of the region, Khitan, Han, and Parhae people all began to reside there as well.[81]

But whereas the ethnic composition of the region north of the Yan Mountains may have been quite complex – a complexity indeed reflected in the material culture of tombs – such was not the case for the region of Yan itself. Many Song envoys noted that the population was overwhelmingly Han. Shen Gua remarked, "South of the mountains is none other than the eight prefectures of Yan and Ji; the clothing and language are all according to old customs."[82] Shen went on to identify only a small discrepancy between clothing styles in Yan and those in the "Middle Kingdom." Similarly, according to Lu Zhen, "The residents [of Yan] . . . customarily all wear Han clothing. Among them are some who wear Tartar clothing, probably just miscellaneous Khitan and Parhae women."[83] Anyone wearing non-Han clothing in Liao-controlled Yan, thus, was "miscellaneous" and out of place.

Also suggested in such ethnographies of Yan was the idea that its inhabitants, as Han people, identified strongly with the Song. As we have seen, several poets, including Su Song, Liu Chang, Su Che, and Peng Ruli, commemorated in their verse a temple at Gubei Pass purportedly dedicated to the martyred Song general Yang Ye (d. 986).[84] Yang – also

---

[78] XCB 88.2015.
[79] QSS 9:5917.
[80] Jiang Shaoyu, *Songchao shishi leiyuan*, 77.1012; QSW 77:380.
[81] XCB 97.2253.
[82] QSW 77:378.
[83] Jiang Shaoyu, *Songchao shishi leiyuan*, 77.1011.
[84] Su Song, *Su Weigong wenji*, 1:162; QSS 9:5916; *Su Che ji*, 1:319; QSS 16:10504. According to Liang Zhangju, *Langji congtan*, 6.98–99, this temple was still standing in the eighteenth century.

known as "Peerless Yang" – had, in an act of supreme loyalty, starved himself to death after his capture by Liao in the year 986.[85] Implied in the poetry was that only feelings of solidarity with the Song could have led the locals to construct and maintain a temple in his honor.

So attached were the people of Yan to the "Middle Kingdom" that, according to numerous Song travel accounts, the sight of the traveling Song envoy and his retinue could move them to tears. Su Che painted just such a scene:

> When they see the [ethnic] Han envoy, they are sad in their hearts:
> "It's been over a century since Shi Jingtang
> Usurped the throne, bringing calamity to Yan and Ji.
> I raise my head and ask heaven what were my crimes,
> And harbor resentment against my forebears who had followed
>   [An] Lushan."[86]

In this case, Su linked the loss of Yan to the population's support of the mid-eighth-century rebellion of An Lushan. But despite noting a historical instance of disloyalty – resurrecting perhaps the older Tang stereotypes of Hebei – Su did not doubt that the people of Yan in his own day identified with the Song. For them, the transfer of Yan to the Khitans under the Later Jin emperor Shi Jingtang was an unmitigated disaster.

In a poem by Zheng Xie, composed while on his way back to the North China Plain through Juyong Pass, one finds a similar scene of older ethnic Han men – identifiable by their headdresses – lamenting the Liao takeover of a century earlier:

> By the roadside are two or three old fellows,
> Wearing headscarfs, white beards hanging down.
> Delighted they are to see a Han official;
> They kowtow, while one of them sighs:
> There is no way now to resolve their troubles,
> For it has been a hundred years since this remote territory was lost.
> The Heavenly numbers [of fate] ultimately have their
>   pre-determined correspondences,
> Thus, the map of Dukang was given up.
> I pour a libation of wine to commemorate the people left behind,
> Whose tears moisten this corner of the blue mountains.[87]

---

[85] Jiang Shaoyu, *Songchao shishi leiyuan*, 55.721–22.
[86] *Su Che ji*, 1:320.
[87] QSS 10:6821.

The "map of Dukang" was the map that the would-be Yan assassin Jing Ke had offered to the king of Qin as a feigned gesture of surrender on the eve of China's first unification in 221 BCE. Thus, in this case, Zheng Xie was comparing the Liao annexation of Yan to the much earlier Qin seizure of the Warring States Kingdom of Yan. The powerful eleventh-century statesman Wang Anshi (1021–86), who once escorted a Liao envoy at least as far as the border at the Baigou River, offered a similar description in a poem commemorating the pomp surrounding the return of the envoy to Khitan territory:

> Dreary clouds and cold rain, water in abundance;
> Saddled horses to the east and west, the musicians pause.
> Still now there are people of Yan who shed streams of tears,
> As they turn to look back, at the flowing waters south of the border.[88]

Whereas Zheng imagined men of Yan moistening the land with their tears, Wang painted the picture of tears in far greater abundance. By deliberately juxtaposing streams of rain water south of the border with the tears of the inhabitants, Wang leaves the reader with the impression that the tears themselves might flow back "home" across the border into Song territory.

Given their perceived allegiance to Song China, there was little doubt among the Song travelers that the people of Yan yearned for the *reconquista* that would make them once more subjects of the "Middle Kingdom." According to Lu Zhen, during Taizong's siege of Yanjing in 979, the residents of the city were so ecstatic that they plotted to expel the defending Liao generals and surrender the city. When Taizong was forced to withdraw, the city's elders could not conceal their dismay: they "caressed their children, telling them with a sigh, 'You will not get to be subjects of Han. This is your fate.'"[89] At Gubei Pass over a century later, Peng Ruli imagined locals still dreaming of the reconquest:

> Elders of Yuyang still shed tears:
> Where is there a fierce general to campaign against the enemy?
> But the emperor's lenience and tolerance do not distinguish south
>   from north,
> And so I realize his imperial virtue is on par with Heaven.[90]

---

[88] Wang Anshi, *Wang Jing Gong shizhu bujian*, 45.881–82.
[89] Jiang Shaoyu, *Songchao shishi leiyuan*, 77.1012.
[90] QSS 16:10504.

Although Peng sympathized with the elders of Yuyang, he also recognized the benefits of decades of peace on the northern frontier – the product of "imperial virtue."[91]

While the Song travelers did not doubt that Han people were the natural inhabitants of Yan, they were far more ambivalent about those living north of the mountains. Probably since very early times, there had been a steady trickle of Chinese immigration into Manchuria and other territories to the north. By the eleventh century, their presence is readily apparent in the archaeological record, as we have seen. In later times, these migrants would constitute the "transfrontiersmen" who played such an important role in Frederick Wakeman's account of the Manchu "Great Enterprise."[92] From the perspective of the Song envoys, there were few legitimate reasons for Han people to voluntarily leave Yan for regions further north. Su Che noted in a preface to a poem about a Han community he encountered in Huizhou that it consisted of the descendants of many an "absconded traitor" fleeing Song territory.[93] Other Han populations were identified as victims of forced relocation, as in the case of one village populated by families hailing from Weizhou in southern Hebei.[94]

One reason individual Chinese might have left by choice was to eke out an existence away from rapacious tax collectors. Such was the case with a Han population Su Che encountered just north of Gubei Pass:

> When Han people immigrated is not clear;
> Their clothing has gradually changed, but their language
>   remains the same.
> For generations, they have been guests here, toiling at
>   the plow and dividing up the harvests.
> The taxes and corvée duties were light, providing them
>   with temporary comfort.[95]

This last example is particularly revealing. According to Su, these Han people north of the Yan Mountains went through a process of de-sinification: they continued to speak their ancestral language, even as they gradually abandoned Han-style garments.

---

[91] Peng's dovish position is more apparent in some of his other poems, such as one that praises the "noble king who understands how to still the halberds." See QSS 16:10602.
[92] Wakeman, *Great Enterprise*, esp. 1:37–49.
[93] *Su Che ji*, 1:321.
[94] XWDS 73.906.
[95] *Su Che ji*, 1:320.

In a preface to one of his poems, Su Song described a similar de-sinification process, in this case involving hairstyle rather than clothing:

> Among the enemy, there are many individuals from Yan and Ji who were kidnapped and [now] live scattered through foreign territory. All of them shave the tops of their heads and let loose their hair in accordance with [local Khitan] customs. Only their headscarves and shirts are a little different, permitting one to distinguish Han people from foreigners.[96]

It is notable that neither Su Che nor Su Song treated the migration of Han people north of the Yan Mountains as the expansion of Chinese civilization. Instead, what they saw corroborated in their minds the notion of a rigid ethnic boundary that they imagined separated Han people from those further north. The Yan Mountains constituted the limit of the Chinese ecumene, and therefore the limit of the natural geographic extent of Han populations. Those crossing beyond the mountains were an aberration of sorts, regardless of whether they were escaped criminals or the victims of forced relocation.

In descriptions of the customs of the population north and south of the Yan Mountains, one finds, once again, that the envoys brought with them a certain interpretive baggage that impacted how they made sense of what they saw. Particularly suspect is the implication that large numbers of people in eleventh-century Yan felt allegiance to the Song emperor. The region had never been under Song rule, and had been under Khitan control for a century or more by the time the Song envoys traveled through. Nevertheless, numerous elements of the ethnic landscape of Northeast Asia, as portrayed in embassy literature, are consistent with empirical data. Specific ethnographic observations regarding nomadic practices – steppe urbanism and the great hunts, for example – resemble later descriptions of the customs of Mongols and other steppe peoples. Moreover, the four ethnicities (Han, Khitan, Xi, and Parhae) noted by the envoys match Liao ethnic categories, and their distribution on either side of the Yan Mountains parallels the cultural geography reconstructed in the previous chapter on the basis of archaeological remains. The fact that the ethnic geography was the product of Liao ethnic policies is no small irony. The result was that Song diplomats to Liao came to see the Yan Mountains as a physical, ecological, cultural, and ethnic boundary, and returned home all the more convinced of the natural geographic limits of sinic space and, therefore, of Chinese national territory.

---

[96] Su Song, *Su Weigong wenji*, 1:163.

Conclusion

As a result of a century of peace between Song China and its steppe neighbor to the north, an unprecedented number of influential statesmen and prominent cultural elites traveled across the Song state's northeastern frontier en route to the court of the Liao empire. The result was a cosmopolitan outlook that differed in fundamental ways from the more famous "cosmopolitanism" of the High Tang. During the Tang, the capital city of Chang'an became a magnet for foreign merchants, monks, and students arriving from all over Asia. The resulting environment – in which political and cultural elites for the most part encountered foreigners only at the imperial center (viewing them through a particular sort of imperial gaze) – probably did no more than reinforce an understanding of the world that put the imperial capital at the center of civilization. By contrast, political elites of the Northern Song also witnessed an entire alien world during their travels as diplomats to the Eurasian steppe and the court of the Song's northern neighbor.[97] With so many prominent statesmen and intellectuals experiencing these distant lands firsthand, it is little wonder that there emerged among educated elites of the eleventh century a new worldview that redefined age-old categories such as *Zhongguo*, *Han*, and *Hua*, such that these elites for the first time conceived of both China and Chinese identity.

When analyzing extant writings of envoys to Liao, it is not always easy to disaggregate the underlying interpretive framework from the empirical observations themselves. Many elements of eleventh-century embassy literature reflect older conceptualizations, as well as older literary conventions. One must be skeptical, for example, of the claim that the people of Yan strongly identified with Song China, weeping with emotion at the sight of a Song envoy. But two features of the northeastern landscape were so striking that they could not fail to impress the Song travelers: the dramatic topography of the Yan Mountains, and the sharp Han–Khitan cultural divide described in Chapter 5. Ambassadors were in a particularly good position to appreciate the significance of these features, having spent several days crossing the flat, culturally homogeneous North China Plain as they traveled from Kaifeng to the Song–Liao border. Indeed, as one would expect, the travelers consistently made note in their embassy reports and in

---

[97] These literati elite cosmopolitans should also be distinguished from yet another type of cosmopolitan encountered increasingly frequently across the Tang–Song Transition: Chinese merchants engaged in international trade.

their travel poetry of "Heaven's barrier" north of Yan and of the dramatic ecological and cultural divide between Yan and the regions beyond.

The firsthand experiences of the envoys and the members of their retinue had the effect of fostering several notions typically associated with the ideological foundation of the modern nation-state, as explored in Chapter 4. First, the impressions of the travelers to Liao reinforced a sense that China possessed natural frontiers evident both in the lay of the land and in the distribution of peoples. The rising popularity over the course of the Song of Yixing's "Two Boundaries" model may well have been inspired by the sight of the Yan Mountains draped across the northern horizon as the travelers reached the end of the North China Plain. Indeed, the Yan Mountains were the embodiment of the "Northern Boundary" on cartographic representations of Yixing's model. The sense that these mountains marked the limits of the Chinese ecumene was further reinforced by seeing the remains of an ancient Great Wall at Gubei Pass, the pass through which so many ambassadors to Liao in the post-Chanyuan era left the North China Plain.

Second, ambassadors acquired a much clearer sense of what it was that distinguished a "Chinese" landscape from the lands beyond. Rather than focusing on the ways in which northern Hebei differed from Sichuan, the Yellow river valley, or, perhaps, parts of South China – all places an official might have visited in the service of the court – the travelers were struck by the far more dramatic distinction between North China and the mixed agro-pastoral zone beyond the mountains. Yan was a sinic space in which Song travelers could feel at home. A past emperor's calligraphy on a temple wall, stone mile markers along a road, and well-tended fields of cereal crops and mulberry trees were the familiar characteristics of a recognizably Chinese environment. Simultaneously, the clothing, food, and language of the people of Yan identified them as Han, distinct from Khitans and other non-Han peoples. Immediately north of the mountains, however, the countryside rapidly transitioned into something starkly different, with alien people practicing alien ways of life. The clarity with which these travelers distinguished a sinic Yan from the lands beyond implies that, at least in the minds of the Song envoys, China possessed an ecological and cultural homogeneity that was as apparent in Yan as it was in central Henan at Song China's political core. From this perspective, the conceptualization of Chinese space was very different from the older concentric square model of the world – in which civilization declined by degree as one distanced oneself from the center – and it was not unlike that envisioned by Chinese nationalists today.

Third, it was perhaps as a result of their travels to Liao that Song political elites came fervently to imagine that the population of Yan was part of their own community. In observing that the residents of Yan spoke and looked like Chinese, it was logical to think of this population as a "people left behind," a phrase appearing in eleventh-century embassy literature that later became a refrain for early twelfth-century revanchists. Repeated descriptions of individuals weeping at the sight of the Song envoy, vocally lamenting the Khitan takeover of their province, may well have reflected the growing conviction that both Yan Chinese and their brethren to the south were part of a single "imagined community," bound together by a common sense of identity and purpose. From the envoys' perspective, it was this sense of political community that motivated the people of Yan to shed "streams of tears" at the sight of the Han envoy and that drove some of them to proclaim a willingness to die for the Song cause.

The sense that sinic space and the geographic range of Han populations ended abruptly at Gubei Pass north of Yan rather than at the political border along the Baigou River meant that one could envision an entity – which one might call the "Chinese nation" – that was defined not by the de facto limits of the Song state, but rather by unambiguous and timeless physiographic and ethnic boundaries. This distinction between nation and state was fundamental to the modern European idea of the nation-state. Only with this distinction did the ideological cry to unite the nation under one state banner make sense. Although the basis on which Yan was portrayed as Chinese may have differed in critical ways from the thinking of nineteenth-century European nationalists – whether it be Germans calling for the annexation of the Sudetenland in order to reconstitute an imagined *Groß Deutschland*, Italians seeking to recapture Trentino and the *terra irredenta*, or French vying for control of Alsace and other territories within its *frontières naturelles* – they all shared in common the notion of a state–nation distinction.

The comparability with elements of nineteenth-century European subjectivities does not mean, however, that the idea of China in the eleventh century was the product of the same circumstances. Nineteenth-century European irredentism was the outcome of a complex set of contingent developments, including post-Enlightenment notions of popular sovereignty that would have had little meaning to Song Chinese. The origin of the Chinese nation lay in an alternative set of developments. First was the unusual geopolitical situation, whereby the Song–Liao political frontier in Hebei, as determined by diplomatic negotiations, did not coincide with a more "natural" boundary: the Yan Mountains further north. Second was the fact that the standard itinerary of Song envoys to Liao led them to behold firsthand a particularly dramatic topographic barrier. Had the Song court been based at the site of the Tang capital in the Wei river valley, envoys might have traveled through Hedong, where the Song–Liao border was already set along a relatively imposing mountain range. A third contingency concerned Liao ethnic policies, by which the Liao state enforced a clear geographic line of separation between a homogeneous ethnic Chinese population in Yan and a more mixed population further north. Finally, it was critically significant that the envoys to Liao consisted of powerful members of the political class. As officials who had served both in the capital and at a variety of provincial posts, who possessed therefore a panoramic vision of the empire, they were particularly sensitive to how the landscape and customs of Yan fit into the broader ethnic and political world. As agents of the state, they had a particular interest in defining the physical limits of Chinese territory and equating this territory with lands that "rightfully" belonged to the Song regime. Though their new worldview was the product of travel experiences across only one of China's many political borders, it was not difficult for them to conceptualize other frontiers in similar ways, frontiers similarly populated with Han "people left behind" yearning for a Chinese *reconquista*.

Conclusion

The previous chapters have sought to explore China's shifting position in the world at a critical moment in its history. At the heart of the study is the contention that both the East Asian inter-state system and Chinese notions of identity had extensive and complex histories that extended back well before the arrival of Europeans in significant numbers in the nineteenth century. The Northern Song was a particularly important period of change, especially in the decades following the momentous 1005 Chanyuan agreement between the Song and Liao empires. Whereas scholars have previously recognized the novelty of the multi-state system that emerged in the eleventh century, in which Song China stood "among equals," I have sought to identify a broader set of repercussions of the peace agreement. Diplomatic practice in the post-Chanyuan period fostered an unprecedented cosmopolitan sociability between Song and Liao political elites. In addition, the unusual configuration of the Song–Liao border, which ran directly across the North China Plain, prompted the Song to establish linear military defenses (in contrast to the earlier Tang approach to frontier defense). Subsequently, after the Song gained a greater sense of security following decades of peace with Liao – a peace bolstered by an exceptional degree of diplomatic sociability – it embarked on a project to demarcate bilateral boundaries on multiple frontiers.

But perhaps the most striking and far-reaching of post-Chanyuan developments was the emergence of what essentially amounted to a Chinese national consciousness. As we have seen, this development entailed the reconceptualization of China's population as a monocultural and monoethnic people – the "Han people." Simultaneously, Chinese educated elites acquired an increasingly clear sense of the nature and characteristics of what I have termed "sinic space," defined on historical, ecological, and ethnic grounds. The fact that "sinic space" so conceived went well beyond the de facto political boundaries of the Song state implied a discrepancy between the geographic extent of the Chinese nation and that of the Chinese state. This perceived discrepancy – fueled by a conviction that Han populations beyond the border would naturally side with a Chinese regime – constituted the driving force for the irredentist ambitions of the late Northern Song and, following the Jurchen invasion, of the Southern Song as well. It also meant that Chinese sovereignty was now seen as bounded, a conceptual development that helps to explain the extensive late eleventh-century boundary demarcation project.

In some respects, the picture I have painted of the Northern Song accords neatly with the early twentieth-century "Naitō thesis," which proposed that China entered the "early modern" era at this time. Proponents of this thesis have typically focused on a commercial revolution, on the demise of the medieval aristocracy, and on certain aspects of the Neo-Confucian "Renaissance" – phenomena they saw as analogous to characteristic features of the early modern period in Europe. Needless to say, one might also incorporate into this story a "modern" approach to boundary demarcation, as well as a nationalist irredentism analogous to similar European movements in the eighteenth and nineteenth centuries. But it is not necessary to fit the story of China in the eleventh century into a narrative of modernity. Many of the phenomena explored in the book – border demarcation, for example, or the notion that political and ethnic boundaries ought to align – are not so unusual as concepts that one cannot imagine them to have emerged under premodern conditions. More interesting, then, is to explore the historical factors responsible for the developments in question at a particular moment in time.

How did the new idea of the Chinese nation come about in Song times? In this book, I have proposed a complex combination of contingent circumstances. The notion of a cohesive Chinese nation depended in part on the ability of educated elites to see individuals from all social strata, living in all corners of Song territory, as their brethren rather than as social others. Critical to their ability to view other Chinese in this way were two significant post-Tang transformations. First, whereas the Tang was dominated by families whose prestige derived from a centuries-long tradition of bureaucratic service, there emerged in the Song a meritocratic ideal that made it now imaginable for any male to educate himself and serve in government. Second, while Tang aristocrats and much of the political elite had been concentrated in the immediate vicinity of the capital cities, by the mid-Song, educated men from all over the empire came to see themselves as belonging to a broad community of *shidafu*, bound together by their common pursuits and by the common course of studies necessary to prepare for the civil service examination. Insofar as education was in principle (if not in reality) available to all – including women, who were expected to educate their sons – it was possible now to envision a national community that incorporated all inhabitants of a vast swathe of Song territory.

But the Chinese nation was ultimately defined as much by its boundaries as by the internal cohesion of its community of members. The Chanyuan Oath and the particular geopolitics of the post-Chanyuan period played key roles. Chanyuan created a pattern of diplomatic exchanges unprecedented in terms of their frequency and in terms of the number of prominent policymakers who participated. The result was that a significant percentage of the most powerful statesmen and the most influential cultural elites enjoyed cosmopolitan experiences unusual in China's premodern period. One aspect of this cosmopolitanism involved intensive social interactions between Song and Liao political elites, most notably during embassy banquets. As a result, some Song participants – the pre-eminent literatus Su Shi, for example – found it plausible to treat ethnic Chinese officials of the Liao state as fellow *shidafu*. The implication was that Chinese living beyond the political borders of the Song state might also belong to the Chinese nation. Sociability between Song and Liao diplomats can also explain how ethnic categories rooted in steppe tribal politics made their way into Song elite discourse. Indeed, the term "Han" itself seems to have had steppe origins. The earliest use of this word as an ethnonym was by the non-Chinese Särbi regimes during the pre-Tang period. It was later widely employed by Liao administrators in conjunction with a Liao ethnic policy that sought to maintain both ethnic distinctions and boundaries, as well as the geographic segregation of different peoples. The extensive Song use of "Han" as an ethnonym – as well as the common Song and Liao visual representations of Khitans and their daily life – can be explained in part by the intense diplomatic and social interactions between Song and Liao bureaucrats.

The cosmopolitan experience of the Song envoys involved more than a new sociability. As part of the Chanyuan system, political elites embarked multiple times a year on lengthy journeys from the Song capital of Kaifeng to the sites of the mobile Khitan court on the Eastern Mongolian steppe. The experience of following a standard itinerary, first across the vast North China Plain, then through Liao-controlled Yan, and on beyond Gubei Pass in the Yan Mountains – an itinerary described in official reports and private poetry – reinforced the sentiment that the northern mountains marked China's natural boundary. Not only were they physically imposing, they also constituted an important cultural barrier that, as a result of Liao ethnic policies, separated a relatively homogeneous ethnic Chinese population based in Yan from a mixed steppe–Chinese culture in the lands further north. Although Song literati frequently wrote about the great variety of regional customs in the Chinese interior – regional customs they also encountered firsthand as traveling bureaucrats – none of these internal boundaries compared in significance to the stark divide between Chinese agriculturalists and the non-Chinese pastoralists and agro-pastoralists of the zone to the north. This experience, I argue, was the major factor prompting the Song political elite to envision the territory of Yan as being rightfully Chinese. It also became possible more generally to treat a Chinese population that was culturally and linguistically heterogeneous as a single "Han" people. Although the cross-border travels of Song bureaucrats were usually limited to Liao territory, it was no great conceptual jump – especially given the bureaucrats' panoramic perspectives on the entire empire – to imagine *terre irredente* on other frontiers, also inhabited by ethnic Han "people left behind."

Historians of nationalism tend to be skeptical of the idea of premodern nationhood. Indeed, one of their primary goals in the past decades has been to denaturalize modern nations and claims about their purported antique pasts. But the contention in this book is not that the Song represented the moment in which the modern Chinese nation first came into being, but rather that one can recognize in the Song a number of elements that lie at the heart of modern nationalism. The notion that there existed in the Song an alternative nationalism – resembling modern nationalism in some ways but not in others – makes sense if one thinks of nationalism as the product of a combination of culturally specific factors and factors common to the human condition. The latter might include the propensity to treat awe-inspiring mountains as "natural frontiers," or the proclivity to see cultural differences as deeply rooted, or the tendency to feel a sense of solidarity with members of one's community (whether "imagined" or not). One might also expect certain commonalities in how a society's sense of identity is affected by a geopolitical environment in which the state coexists with others on roughly equal terms, and in which elites envision the state's entire population as constituting a roughly homogeneous community.

How did Song nationalism differ from its modern alternative? One can answer this question in a systematic way by treating in sequence four closely related phenomena: national consciousness, nationalist ideology, nationalist movements, and the nationview. It is in terms of national consciousness (the feeling of belonging to a homogeneous nationwide community) that Song nationalism most resembled its modern incarnation. By the late eleventh century, men at the Song court conceived of a bounded "imagined community" of brethren, and of a national territory partially "lost" under a past dynasty. Although in Song times one encountered such sentiments primarily among educated elites, it is worth remembering that, in Benedict Anderson's classic account, national consciousness also emerged initially among elites, first among "creole elites" in the Americas, then among Eastern European intellectual elites, then among native elites of colonial Africa and Asia. Moreover, as in Song China, it arose in the Americas (according to Anderson) as a self-contained phenomenon. One could imagine one's own national community without necessarily having on one's mind other such communities in neighboring states.

In contrast to national consciousness, Song nationalist ideology (the principle that the boundaries of the state ought to coincide with the geographic extent of the national community) diverged in more significant ways from the ideology of modern times. Although Song Chinese clearly associated *Zhongguo* (the transdynastic entity to which they belonged) with a single people – the Han people – when defining *Zhongguo*, they more commonly focused on its culture and its geography, not its ethnic composition. It was only when forced to make certain pragmatic decisions concerning frontier policy – where to demarcate the Song–Xia border, for example, or whether to exterminate ethnic Khitans in territories captured by Song armies – that Song decision-makers revealed their intuitive sense that ethnicity (i.e. ancestry) was a determinant of culture. Whereas modern nationalists usually define their state in terms of a particular people, whose culture they then strive to characterize, Song elites defined their state in terms of a particular culture which they then equated with a particular people.[1]

As for nationalist movements (which seek to implement the nationalist agenda), these in Song times resembled those of the nineteenth and twentieth centuries insofar as some policymakers sought to implement

---

[1] One should not take this distinction too far. Even in today's world, certain nations – the United States and France, for example – define themselves according to the culture of the national people rather than its ethnic composition. Thus, the United States during certain periods of its history welcomed in immigrants who accepted American civic principles and agreed to learn the national language. Though one might argue Song Chinese also differed from modern nationalists insofar as they believed their culture defined what it meant to be civilized, the American impulse to civilize the world with "democracy" and "freedom" suggests that modern populations can hold a similar faith in the superiority of their culture.

their irredentist ambitions through military action. However, unlike in later times, the Song state did not seek to indoctrinate the masses of the population in order to harness the power of mass action for the national-ist cause. In fact, technologies of propaganda were available to Northern Song bureaucrats. Woodblock printing was widespread by the eleventh century, and policymakers understood its value for purposes of indoctri-nation. In order to propagate orthodox interpretations of the Confucian classics, for example, the Song state sought for a time to monopolize the printing of these texts.[2] A more creative use of print for propaganda purposes was outlined in a memorial by Fan Chuncui (1046–1117), in response to a court call for proposals on how to deal with the Tangut Xia regime. According to Fan, the Tangut ruler had succeeded in rally-ing his people only by spreading lies about the Song. The solution was straightforward:

> Order the various circuits to produce printed pamphlets, with everything written in both Chinese and Tangut. Dispatch lone horsemen to gallop at least a hundred miles into [Tangut] territory. With one [pamphlet], [our message] can be conveyed to ten people; with ten, it can be conveyed to a hundred people. Thus, [the Tangut ruler's] perfidy will be known to all.[3]

If the eleventh-century Song court had the technology and the imagina-tion to disseminate political messages, why did it not do so to rally its own people to the irredentist cause? Why did it only think to spread propaganda to the subjects of the Tangut monarch? One possibility is that the military value of the mobilization of mass sentiments is not self-evident. Mass indoctrination for military purposes was a technology of governance that was recognized in the nineteenth and twentieth centuries only after the power of armies of indoctrinated soldiers had been demon-strated empirically on the battlefield.

Finally, we turn to the fourth component of nationalism: the nation-view. It is in terms of this component that modern times are most at odds with how educated elites of the Northern Song envisioned their world. By the second half of the twentieth century, after the demise of Western colonial empires, it became the norm to see all territory and all people as belonging to one and only one nation-state.[4] Each nation-state was in

---

[2] Cherniack, "Book Culture," 28.

[3] XCB 466.11136–37.

[4] Prior to World War Two, as a result of social Darwinism and other related ideologies, Western colonial powers deemed some peoples insufficiently advanced to have their own state. See, e.g., Duara, *Sovereignty and Authenticity*, 16–17.

turn conceptualized according to a common modular framework, with each having its own flag, its own national anthem, its own cuisine, and its own national pastimes. There is no evidence that educated elites of the Song imagined the world in modular terms. The "Chinese nation" was not perceived to exist in a sea of other nation-states. Nevertheless, there are a few intriguing hints that suggest how the eleventh-century East Asian world order might have spurred over time the development of an alternative modular nationview based on the concentric square model, in which multiple centers of civilization coexisted, each with its own distinct cultural practices and its own uncivilized peripheries. The Liao court seems to have self-consciously developed a Khitan imperial culture, with its own set of costumes, court rituals, and written script. Further to the west the Tanguts followed suit in conscious imitation of the Liao. By the 1030s, they insisted upon the right to "establish a state" (thereby freeing themselves of Song suzerainty) partly on the grounds that they had fashioned their own Tangut script, clothing, court rituals, and music.[5] Some eleventh-century Song statesmen embraced this logic. Following his diplomatic mission to Liao, Su Song wrote a treatise describing Liao court rituals and costumes, in which he implied that the Liao empire, like China, was composed of a civilized center – defined by distinct Liao cultural practices – surrounded by an uncivilized "wilderness zone."[6] Indeed, in describing their respective civilizations, other East Asian states – the Korean Koryŏ regime, for example – also turned on occasion to a discourse based on peripheral "zones of submission" encircling a unified center ruled by a single monarch.[7] The Vietnamese Chu Nom script, modeled on and yet distinct from the Chinese script, constitutes another intriguing example. Developed no later than the twelfth century, it apparently served partly as a tool to "tame" the uncivilized people of the south.[8]

Most of this book has dealt with the "long" eleventh century. What happened in subsequent centuries? After the Jurchen invasion of the 1120s, the East Asian world order remained much the same for another century. Although the Khitans disappeared from the scene, the Jurchen

---

[5] McGrath, "Reigns of Jen-tsung and Ying-tsung," 302; XCB 123.2893–94.
[6] Su Song, *Su Weigong wenji*, 2:1005.
[7] Breuker, "Koryŏ as an Independent Realm." For a more extensive discussion of Koryŏ's perception of itself as an "ontological equal to the Chinese [i.e., Song] and Manchurian [i.e., Khitan and Jurchen] Sons of Heaven," see Breuker, *Establishing a Pluralist Society*.
[8] Phan, "Chu Nom and the Taming of the South." For the argument that the Chu Nom script developed around the twelfth century, see Nguyen, "Graphemic Borrowings," 384–97.

Jin regime replaced them as the most powerful rival of the newly reconstituted Southern Song. Both empires continued to coexist with the Tangut Xia state, which persisted into the twelfth century, as well as the Koryō Kingdom and the Vietnamese Ly Dynasty. The Song leadership established a peace agreement with the Jin modeled on the Chanyuan agreement, and they exchanged frequent embassies with their new neighbor to the north, much as they had done with the Liao in the previous century. Simultaneously, Southern Song elites maintained the idea of the Song as an ethnic Han nation. Indeed, the Southern Song is remembered for its passionate irredentism, an irredentism driven to some extent by widely circulating cartographic representations of what was considered to be the true geographic extent of the empire.

The Mongol tsunami of the thirteenth century brought an end to the multi-state system of the post-Chanyuan period, ensuring that, in subsequent centuries, the idea of the Chinese nation and the structure of the East Asian world order would follow complex evolutionary paths. In the post-Song period, China was ruled by two types of dynasties.[9] The Mongol Yuan (1271–1368) and Manchu Qing (1636–1911) dynasties, representing the first type, were both multinational in conception, not unlike the Liao and Jin. These regimes, founded by non-sinic peoples from the north, conceived of ethnic Han populations and the territories they inhabited as merely one part of a much larger empire. The ruling minorities sought to preserve their political dominance through the careful implementation of a policy of "ethnic sovereignty," which emphasized the special abilities of their ethnic group to rule the empire, and maintained a clear distinction between conqueror and conquered.[10] Meanwhile, ethnic Han intellectuals at the Yuan and Qing courts, partly in order to preserve their own relevance, sought to highlight the universal appeal of Confucian values, and rejected earlier Song efforts to equate Confucian culture with sinic space alone. The Ming Dynasty (1368–1644), by contrast, which was founded by an ethnic Chinese military man in the middle of the fourteenth century, was much more like the Song Dynasty in terms of conceptualizing itself as a Chinese nation.[11] In the Ming, one found literati once again arguing for the maintenance

[9] Cf. Seo, "Toshi no seikatsu to bunka," 411–16.
[10] Elliott, *Manchu Way*, 2–8.
[11] As observed by one prominent historian of China, "Ming China was arguably a nation-state emerging in the wake of the Mongol empire, with borders roughly following the Han Chinese ethnic frontier, a shared culture, and a 'national' education system institutionalized through the examinations." See Esherick, "Introduction," 9.

of a clear cultural, ethnic, and geographic divide between China and the lands and people beyond.[12]

As for the People's Republic of China today, though founded by Han Chinese, it is a multinational state modeled more closely on the Manchu empire than on the Song or the Ming. Like the Manchu empire, its territory includes Manchuria, part of Mongolia, Eastern Turkestan, Tibet, Yunnan, as well as China Proper. Nevertheless, elements of the earlier Song vision of the Chinese nation persist to the present day. First and foremost is the belief in the objective reality of a homogeneous Han people. The sense that Chinese civilization is fundamentally Han at its core has fueled the awkward relationship that continues to exist between the Chinese state and its fifty-five non-Han minority nationalities.[13] One also recognizes in the twentieth century an enduring expectation of Han ethnic solidarity, whereby both early twentieth-century nationalists and the People's Republic of China have expected Han Chinese abroad (but not necessarily Uighurs or other minority nationalities) to exhibit loyalty to their motherland.[14] Finally, whereas European and American nation-states are portrayed as sharing together in the heritage of "Western civilization," Chinese nationalists today lay claim to an entire "civilization" as its past heritage, demonstrating the persistence of the old ideal of a grand unity of the civilized world.

[12] Bol, "Geography and Culture," 98.
[13] In the early twentieth century, many Chinese nationalists preferred a monoethnic Han state that excluded non-Han territories in the northeast, west, and southwest. See Esherick, "How the Qing Became China."
[14] Duara, "Nationalists among Transnationals"; Ford, "Guiqiao."

Tomb Analysis and Cultural Difference

Here, I clarify methodological issues relevant to the use of the material culture of tombs to differentiate between Northeast Asian cultural zones. In the context of the present study, culture is considered to include both beliefs and practices. It is distinct from ethnic identity, which is an emic phenomenon pertaining to how a society itself uses cultural or other markers to discriminate between peoples. The relationship between culture and material culture is complex. The material culture of tombs can be seen as the material embodiment of a society's mortuary culture. As such, it provides a snapshot of one small part of the totality of beliefs and practices that defines a culture. In some cases, new developments in tomb characteristics mirrored more general society-wide trends. The well-known fascination with foreign exotica that permeates literature of the High Tang, for example, is reflected in Tang tomb figurines of foreigners and ceramic grave goods mimicking Central and West Asian objects. But even when it is not possible to reconstruct the precise beliefs and practices that account for particular tomb features – as is the case more often than not – these tomb features can serve as cultural markers, allowing one to discriminate between two or more cultures on the basis of the material record.

The discrete cultures at the heart of this discussion, however, do not exist wholly independently of each other. One can think of them as existing within a multilevel hierarchy or heterarchy of cultures and subcultures. One might think of the top of the hierarchy as consisting of features common to tombs all over Northeast Asia. For example, the entryways of Northeast Asian tombs tend to be situated on the south side; the deceased is typically laid to rest on the opposite (north) side with feet to the west and head to the east; and bronze mirrors and coins are commonly found within. These features might help distinguish East Asian from European tombs, but would be of little value in distinguishing Chinese from Khitan tombs.

At the bottom of the hierarchy, one might place the funerary traditions of a single clan. For example, Ye Wa has identified a number of family funerary traditions in a Tang cemetery just east of Luoyang. One family tended to bury its dead with unusual soapstone boxes, another with particular apotropaic iron objects, and yet another with objects referencing the twelve animals of the zodiac.[1] In addition, some families demonstrated a propensity to include in their tombs greater (or lesser) quantities of metal utensils or of tomb figurines.[2] There is similar evidence of family burial traditions among the Liao-era tombs excavated in the Longquanwu cemetery just west of modern-day Beijing. Tombs laid out in clusters – apparently belonging to the same family – had a tendency to share certain features. Cluster I tombs were the only tombs to include exclusively vessels made of porcelain. All other tombs included both porcelain and earthenware vessels. Cluster I tombs also had a greater tendency to include coins. On the other hand, Cluster III tombs were the only ones to include chicken-thigh bottles as well as ceramic winnowing baskets; these were also the only tombs to have semi-circular coffin platforms occupying the entire northern half of the tomb chamber.[3]

Family traditions are, of course, not the focus of this study, the goal of which is rather to explore "higher" levels of the East Asian cultural hierarchy. There is ample room to disagree on which level of this hierarchy reflects a distinction in "culture" and which reflects a distinction in "subculture." A survey of the material culture, however, makes clear that the distinction between "Khitan" and "Chinese" mortuary practices is starker than between Song Chinese and Liao Chinese mortuary practices. One could, thus, think of the first as representing a cultural difference and the second as a subcultural one. Indeed, distinguishing between these two levels of the culture hierarchy is at the heart of the descriptions of Khitan and Chinese mortuary cultures in Chapter 5.

When using material objects to characterize a culture, one should take care to avoid a number of possible interpretive errors. To begin with, as Arjun Appadurai has shown, identical objects can possess very different

---

[1] Ye Wa, "Mortuary Practice in Medieval China," 99 (for soapstone boxes), 236 (for animals of the zodiac), 316 (for iron objects).

[2] Ibid., 211–16 (for metal utensils), 237–45 (for figurines).

[3] For the full excavation report of the Longquanwu cemetery, see *Beijing Longquanwu Liao Jin muzang*. Cluster I tombs include tombs M1, M2, M3, M4, M5, and M9; cluster III tombs include tombs M17, M19, M20, M23, and M24. See map of cemetery at 11. For a discussion of cluster I as a family cemetery, see esp. 240.

meanings in different cultural contexts.[4] This phenomenon is well exemplified by two objects commonly encountered in tombs throughout Northeast Asia, bronze coins and bronze mirrors, both of which seem to have served multiple functions. Coins could be placed inside the mouth of the deceased,[5] under the head of the deceased,[6] or elsewhere within the coffin;[7] in other cases, coins are found in urns intermixed with cremated remains;[8] and in yet other cases, they are found on an offering table placed in front of the corpse[9] or between an epitaph stone and its limestone cover.[10] These different locations within the tomb more than likely reflected differences in ritual practice and in associated beliefs. Coins placed within the coffin, for example, played a role in the encoffinment ceremony, a ritual that might precede the burial itself by several months.[11] Similarly, one can assume that placing coins on an offering table rather than in the deceased's mouth reflected different sets of beliefs regarding how money was transmitted to the afterlife, or perhaps regarding notions of the afterlife itself.

Bronze mirrors constitute a similar example. In Xuanhua tomb number seven, mirrors were discovered in three different contexts: within the well-preserved wood coffin amid the clothing of the deceased; beneath a collapsed mirror stand on which it had certainly once been placed; and embedded into the very center of the brick dome dominating the tomb chamber.[12] These three very different contexts imply that mirrors played several different functional and symbolic roles within a tomb. With regard to mirrors, then, tomb number seven reflects an amalgam of three different cultural or subcultural traditions. Unfortunately, if excavation reports do not identify the placement of mirrors and coins within a pair

---

[4] Appadurai, "Introduction."

[5] Li Qingfa, "Jianping Xiyaocun Liao mu," 121; "Jilin Shuangliao xian Gaolige Liao mu qun," 140; Hansen, "Introduction," 4.

[6] "Neimeng Tuquan xian faxian Liaodai wenwu," 211.

[7] "Shanxi Datong jiaoqu wu zuo Liao bihua mu," 39; Li Zhongyi, "Handan shiqu faxian Songdai muzang," 20; Ye Wa, "Mortuary Practice in Medieval China," 159–66.

[8] "Shanxi Datong jiaoqu wu zuo Liao bihua mu," 37.

[9] *Xuanhua Liao mu*, 41, 100.

[10] Zhang Xiande, "Beijing shi Daxing xian Liaodai Ma Zhiwen mu," 31; Wang Ce and Zhu Zhigang, "Fengtai lukou nan chutu Liao mu," 319; Kervyn, "Tombeau de l'empereur Tao-tsong," 300. It is not uncommon to find rusty traces of bronze coins on the surfaces of excavated tomb epitaphs.

[11] Ye Wa, "Mortuary Practice in Medieval China," 153–54.

[12] *Xuanhua Liao mu*, 89, 99–101. For mirrors embedded in the ceiling of the tomb or hanging from a hook in the ceiling, see "Chifeng xian Dayingzi Liao mu," 18; "Keyou zhong qi Daiqintala Liao mu," 654. Mirrors were also hung from the ceilings of pagoda crypts; see "Hebei Ding xian faxian liang zuo Song dai taji," 4.

of tombs, one should be wary of concluding that the two tombs necessarily belonged to the same cultural or subcultural tradition.

Whereas similarities in tomb content might belie differences in underlying cultural traditions, the opposite is also true: not all variations in tomb features constitute evidence of a significant cultural divide. Consider minor stylistic variations in the flourishes appearing in the corners of a tomb mural or in the forms of ceramic vessels. Although perhaps noted with care in excavation reports written by specialists who have pored over every detail of the scant finds from a particular tomb, one should avoid overinterpreting their significance to the participants of the funeral rituals. Minor variations did not necessarily impact the success of the mortuary rites or the proper functioning of the tombs. Such variations – whether the product of happenstance or the expression of an artisan's individual predilections – might well lie within a single culture's accepted range of permitted variability. As such, they do not reflect a cultural divide.

In addition, even among apparently more meaningful variations in tomb features, some are undoubtedly related to socioeconomic strata rather than to cultural groups. For example, in many regions of China, one might classify tombs into two types: single-occupancy pit tombs with crude ceramics and double-occupancy brick-chambered tombs with higher-quality grave goods. To be sure, these two tomb types may represent different cultural preferences. Dieter Kuhn has argued that some of the simplest Song tombs reflected new intellectual trends among Chinese elites – articulated in Song-era ritual texts – that favored "economy, modesty and simplicity in burials."[13] But it is equally likely that these two tomb types simply differentiate wealthier and poorer segments of society.

One should also bear in mind the possible impact of ecological conditions on tomb construction techniques and on the long-term survival of tomb elements. For example, Al Dien has observed that, during the Six Dynasties era, water drainage systems were more common in tombs in South China, where rain falls in far greater abundance.[14] Song-era observers described a related phenomenon. Whereas one prominent eleventh-century ritual manual (whose author was from the north) advocated placing wine and food in a side chamber of the tomb itself, a later manual compiled by a southerner recommended that – because of the consistency of soil in South China – it was dangerous to enlarge

---

[13] Kuhn, "Decoding Tombs," 102. For analogous examples from elsewhere in the world, see Parker Pearson, "Mortuary Practices"; Hodder, "Social Structure and Cemeteries."
[14] Dien, Six Dynasties, 114.

the tomb to accommodate these extra goods; he recommended placing the goods in an entirely separate pit.[15] Thus, neither the existence of drainage systems nor the overall layout of the tombs themselves necessarily reflects a different set of beliefs; they could reflect ways in which people adapted their tombs to particular environmental conditions.

Similarly, whereas stone tombs are prevalent north of the Yan Mountains, they are rare further south. Although this geographic discrepancy may reflect distinctions between Khitan and Chinese cultures, it is equally plausible that stones were simply more readily available further north and that clay for bricks was more readily available further south. Because tomb walls were often coated with plaster or hidden behind wood panels, the material composition of the walls was, in any case, not necessarily significant to ritual practice, and so did not reflect fundamental differences in core cultural beliefs. Variations in rainfall – and in soil composition as well – might also affect the rate of survival of tomb content. The discovery of wooden objects in tombs from one region could be the product of drier climate rather than of a cultural predilection for wood. Similarly, the absence of bone remains in tombs in one area may have resulted from noncalcareous soils (which tend to dissolve bone) rather than from an unusual culturally specific way of disposing of corpses.[16]

Yet another factor affecting the regional clustering of particular tomb features was the geographic range of trade networks distributing manufactured mortuary goods. Perhaps Ding ceramics were more likely found in proximity of the Ding kilns in central Hebei. Even architectural features might have been affected by commercial networks. The boards used to construct the wooden interior chambers common in Khitan tombs, for example, often had numbers and other positional information written in Chinese, apparently providing instructions for the reassembly of structures initially manufactured elsewhere.[17] However, the impact of trade networks should not be exaggerated. One should also bear in mind that concern over the proper performance of mortuary rituals helped to ensure that the demand for particular grave goods had a greater impact on supply than vice versa. The impact of demand on supply could explain the large numbers of *imitation* Ding ceramics found in Liao tombs.

---

[15] Sima Guang, *Shuyi*, 7.5a–6a, 8.5a–5b; *Lü Zuqian quanji*, 1:333.

[16] Parker Pearson, *Archaeology of Death and Burial*, 200.

[17] E.g., "Neimenggu Jiefang yingzi Liao mu," 330; Xiang Chunsong, "Zhaomeng diqu de Liaodai muzang," 76; "Aohan qi Qijia Liao mu," 49. By contrast, bricks were sometimes produced in situ. See "Neimenggu Aohanqi Shazigou, Dahengou Liao mu," 889.

A final problem to consider involves what might be termed the "problem of silence." One should be careful not to draw too many conclusions from the absence of a characteristic feature in a given tomb. Specific grave goods might have been looted from one tomb but not from another; murals might have decayed at different rates depending on soil and moisture conditions; and archaeologists' own interests may have affected the details included in a published excavation report. Moreover, individuals in most cultural contexts enjoyed some flexibility in selecting from a repertoire of permissible choices. When commissioning a muralist, for example, the family of the deceased probably had a range of options regarding the particular motifs that could appear on the tomb wall. One might define a culture by the range of choices available rather than by the actual choices made by an individual. Distinguishing between the actual choices made and the larger repertoire of possibilities essentially involves distinguishing between an individual's predilections and the culture to which the individual belonged. Thinking of culture as consisting of a range of possibilities has the benefit of minimizing the impact of the problem of silence. The presence of an object becomes important as a cultural marker; on the other hand, its absence is not necessarily significant. Practically speaking, what this means in the context of Chapter 5 is that discrete cultures can be identified and characterized by determining (through cluster analysis and other techniques) which sets of objects are more likely found together in the same tomb and which sets of objects are never or only very rarely found together.

Guide to the Databases

Tomb Database

In order to allow readers to examine and utilize for their own purposes the data on which Chapter 5 is based, a simple database in .mdb format entitled "Database of Tang, Song, and Liao Tombs, version 1.0" (TSLT010.mdb) is available for free download on the author's website. Included in the database is a basic form for viewing and searching the data, as well as a query that classifies tombs according to "Khitan" and "North Chinese" features. The database was compiled from a systematic survey of archaeological monographs and journals from the 1940s to approximately 2010. It covers tombs dating to the Tang through Northern Song/Liao periods within a broad region of Northeast Asia that can be defined roughly as the zone north of 32°N latitude and east of 110.5°E longitude. For practical reasons involving the availability of excavation reports, the database only includes tombs excavated within the modern borders of the People's Republic of China. Below is a description of the data fields:

1 Basic Data
    ID: Unique identification number of the tomb.
    Latitude, Longitude: Latitude and longitude coordinates of the
        tomb, determined using Google Maps in conjunction with
        the maps and descriptions contained in relevant archaeological
        reports. In most cases, the coordinates are accurate to within
        about 5 kilometers; in rare cases in which the excavation reports
        refer to unidentifiable place names, the latitude–longitude
        coordinates of the county seat are used.
    Burial date: Date of tomb construction and/or burial (if known).
    Period: Time period of tomb construction; either "Tang,"
        "Five Dynasties," "Northern Song," or "Liao."

Tomb name: Name of the tomb as it is identified in archaeological reports.

Tomb occupant: Name of the tomb occupant (if known).

Excavation date: Date of tomb excavation.

Reference: List of relevant archaeological reports and other published material.

2   Type of tomb

Tomb type: Classification of the tomb, for example, as a "pit tomb" or a "chambered tomb."

Construction material: Composition of the tomb walls, usually "earth," "brick," or "stone."

Number of chambers: Number of tomb chambers, usually "one," "two," or "multiple." In addition, "three (Khitan-style)" identifies Khitan-style three-chambered tombs, which include a main chamber and two smaller chambers on either side connected together by a central corridor.

3   Type of burial

Cremation: Identifies cremation burials. Field is set to "yes," "no," "both" (if one occupant is cremated and a second occupant is not), or "unclear."

Coffin type: Identifies coffin as "wooden," "stone," "unclear," or "none."

Occupants: Number of occupants, usually "one," "two," "multiple," or "unclear."

4   Tomb architecture and contents

Chamber shape: Shape of the floor plan of the principle chamber, usually "square," "rectangular," "circular," "hexagonal," or "octagonal." Though not exploited in Chapter 5 of the book, the data in this field was used in a published study examining the southward and northward spread of Hebei mortuary culture over the course of the tenth century.[1]

Wooden structures: Notes wooden structures contained within the tomb, including wooden interior walls (護牆), wooden burial chambers (小帳), and wooden coffin or corpse beds (棺床 or 屍床).

---

[1] Tackett, "Wan Tang Hebei ren."

<u>Timber mimicry</u>: Identifies protruding brickwork (if any) designed to imitate timber architecture.

<u>Mural content</u>: Lists principle mural motifs (if any).

<u>Grave goods</u>: Lists grave goods (if any).

The database also includes a query entitled "Khitan/Chinese contents." This query identifies tombs containing Khitan-type and Chinese-type tomb features, as defined in Chapter 5. By examining the query, one can reconstruct the methodology used to produce most of the figures in the chapter. In most cases, tomb features were identified by means of a keyword search in <u>Grave goods</u>, <u>Mural content</u>, or one of the other text fields.

Database of Song Policymakers and Diplomats

In addition, a second, smaller database of Song policymakers and diplomats (also in .mdb format) is available for free download on the author's website. This database contains three tables, as well as the queries used to calculate the figures contained in Tables 1.1–1.5. The three tables are as follows:

(a) "Bio_data", which contains three fields: (1) <u>cbdb_personid</u> (equivalent to c_personid, the Chinese Biographical Database's person identification number); (2) <u>name</u>; and (3) <u>birthyear</u>. Most birth years are taken from the Chinese Biographical Database. Estimated birth years were usually calculated by subtracting 59 from the Chinese Biographical Database's c_index_year.

(b) "Policymakers," which is a list of Northern and Southern Song policymaking appointments based on Xu Ziming, *Song zaifu biannian lu jiaobu*. The table identifies appointees (by <u>cbdb_personid</u> and <u>name</u>), <u>office</u>, as well as the start and end dates of each appointment (<u>s_date</u> and <u>e_date</u>, respectively). Following Xu Ziming, five policymaking offices are included: chief minister (宰相), deputy chief minister (副宰相), commissioner of military affairs (樞密使), deputy commissioner of military affairs (樞密副使), and notary of the Bureau of Military Affairs (簽書樞密院事). The latter office is not treated as a "top" policy position in Chapter 1, and so is excluded from the calculations in Tables 1.1–1.5. The table takes into consideration that chief ministers (宰相) and deputy chief ministers (副宰相) were identified by different titles at different times.[2] In addition,

---

[2] For a useful table, see Zhang Xiqing, *Songchao dianzhang zhidu*, 42.

commissioners of military affairs variously held the titles of either 樞密使 or 知樞密院事, and their deputies variously either 樞密副使 or 同知樞密院事.

(c)   "Diplomats", which is a list of Northern Song ambassadors and deputy ambassadors to the Liao court, as well as Northern Song escorts – welcoming commissioners (接伴使), hospitality commissioners (館伴使), and parting commissioners (送伴使) – accompanying Liao diplomats. The list of ambassadors is based primarily on Nie Chongqi, "Song Liao jiaopin kao"; escorts were identified by means of a comprehensive keyword search for the terms 接伴, 館伴, and 送伴 in XCB, SHY, SS, and vols. 1–140 of QSW (i.e., roughly speaking the Northern Song volumes of QSW). The table includes the following fields: cbdb_personid, name, appointment, date, and reference.

Bibliography

Abbreviations Used

CFYG   *Cefu yuangui.* Taipei: Qinghua shuju, 1967.

JTS   Liu Xu et al. *Jiu Tang shu.* Beijing: Zhonghua shuju, 1975.

JWDS   Xue Juzheng et al. *Jiu Wudai shi.* Beijing: Zhonghua shuju, 1976.

LS   Toghtō et al. *Liao shi.* Beijing: Zhonghua shuju, 1974.

QSS   Fu Xuancong et al. (eds.). *Quan Song shi.* Beijing: Beijing daxue chubanshe, 1991–98.

QSW   Zeng Zaozhuang and Liu Lin (eds.). *Quan Song wen.* Shanghai cishu chubanshe, 2006.

QTW   Dong Gao et al. *Quan Tang wen.* Beijing: Zhonghua shuju, 1983.

SCBM   Xu Mengxin. *Sanchao beimeng huibian.* Shanghai: Haitian shudian, 1939.

SHY   Xu Song. *Song huiyao jigao.* Beijing: Zhonghua shuju, 1957.

SS   Toghtō et al. *Song shi.* Beijing: Zhonghua shuju, 1977.

WJZY   Zeng Gongliang and Ding Du. *Wujing zongyao.* Vols. 3–5 of *Zhongguo bingshu jicheng.* Beijing: Jiefangjun chubanshe, 1988.

XCB   Li Tao. *Xu zizhi tongjian changbian.* Beijing: Zhonghua shuju, 2004.

XTS   Ouyang Xiu and Song Qi. *Xin Tang shu.* Beijing: Zhonghua shuju, 1975.

XWDS   Ouyang Xiu. *Xin Wudai shi.* Beijing: Zhonghua shuju, 1974.

ZZTJ   Sima Guang. *Zizhi tongjian.* Beijing: Zhonghua shuju, 1956.

Other Pre-1900

Ban Gu. *Han shu.* Beijing: Zhonghua shuju, 1962.

Chen Pengnian. *Jiangnan bielu.* Vol. 9 of *Wudai shishu huibian,* 5125–43. Hangzhou chubanshe, 2004.

Chen Shangjun (ed.). *Quan Tang wen bubian.* Beijing: Zhonghua shuju, 2005.

Chen Shidao. *Houshan tancong*. Beijing: Zhonghua shuju, 2007.

Ding Chuanjing. *Songren yishi huibian*. Beijing: Zhonghua shuju, 1981.

Du Mu. *Du Mu ji xinian jiaozhu*. Beijing: Zhonghua shuju, 2008.

Du You. *Tongdian*. Beijing: Zhonghua shuju, 1988.

Fan Chengda. *Fan Shihu ji*. Hong Kong: Zhonghua shuju, 1974.

Fan Zhen. *Dongzhai jishi*. Beijing: Zhonghua shuju, 1980.

Fan Zhongyan. *Fan Zhongyan quanji*. Nanjing: Fenghuang chubanshe, 2004.

Fang Xuanling et al. *Jin shu*. Beijing: Zhonghua shuju, 1974.

Fang Yue. *Qiuya shici jiaozhu*. Hefei: Huangshan shushe, 1998.

Feng Yan. *Fengshi wenjian ji jiaozhu*. Beijing: Zhonghua shuju, 2005.

Gui Youguang. *Zhenchuan xiansheng ji*. Shanghai guji, 1981.

Han Qi. *Anyang ji biannian jianzhu*. Chengdu: Ba Shu shushe, 2000.

Hou shuihu zhuan. Shenyang: Chunfeng wenyi chubanshe, 1985.

Huang Jie. "Guocui xuebao xu." *Guocui xuebao* 1 (1905), *xu*.1a–4a.

Huang Tingjian. *Huang Tingjian shi jizhu*. Beijing: Zhonghua shuju, 2003.

Huang Zhen. *Gujin jiyao*. Vol. 384 of *Yingyin wenyuange siku quanshu*. Taipei: Taiwan shangwu yinshuguan, 1983.

Huang Zunxian. *Riben guozhi*. Vol. 745 of *Xuxiu siku quanshu*. Shanghai: Guji chubanshe, 1995.

Jiang Shaoyu. *Songchao shishi leiyuan*. Shanghai guji, 1981.

Jue'an and Nai'an. *Jingkang baishi jianzheng*. Beijing: Zhonghua shuju, 1988.

Li Fang et al. *Taiping guangji*. Beijing: Zhonghua shuju, 1961.

Li Ruchi. *Dongyuan congshuo*. Shanghai: Shangwu yishuguan, 1937.

Li Xinchuan. *Jianyan yilai chaoye zaji*. Beijing: Zhonghua shuju, 2000.

Jianyan yilai xinian yaolu. Shanghai: Shangwu yinshuguan, 1936.

Lin Zhiqi. *Shangshu quanjie*. Vol. 55 of *Yingyin wenyuange siku quanshu*. Taipei: Taiwan shangwu yinshuguan, 1983.

Ling Mengchu. *Erke pai'an jingqi*. Shanghai: Jiangsu guji chubanshe, 1990.

Liu Zhi. *Zhongsu ji*. Beijing: Zhonghua shuju, 2002.

Lu You. *Jiannan shigao jiaozhu*. Shanghai: Shanghai guji chubanshe, 1985.

Jiashi jiuwen. Beijing: Zhonghua shuju, 1993.

Lu Zhen. *Chengyao lu*. Beijing: Zhonghua shuju, 1991.

Lü Zuqian. *Lü Zuqian quanji*. Hangzhou: Zhejiang guji chubanshe, 2008.

Luo Bi. *Shiyi*. Vol. 854 of *Yingyin wenyuange siku quanshu*. Taipei: Taiwan shangwu yinshuguan, 1983.

Luo Ye. *Zuiweng tanlu*. Shanghai: Gudian wenxue chubanshe, 1957.

Meng Yuanlao. *Dongjing menghua lu jianzhu*. Beijing: Zhonghua shuju, 2006.

Ming shilu: fu jiaokan ji. Nan'gang: Zhongyang yanjiuyuan lishi yuyan yanjiu-suo, n.d.

Ouyang Xiu. *Ouyang Xiu quan ji*. Beijing: Zhonghua shuju, 2001.

Quan Liao shi hua, ed. Jiang Zuyi and Zhang Diyun. Changsha: Yuelu shushe, 1992.

Shao Bowen. *Shao shi wenjian lu*. Beijing: Zhonghua shuju, 1983.

Shen Gua. *Mengxi bitan*. Shanghai shudian, 2003.

Shen Yue. *Song shu*. Beijing: Zhonghua shuju, 1995.

Shi Jie. *Culai Shi xiansheng wenji*. Beijing: Zhonghua shuju, 1984.

Sima Guang. *Shuyi*. Vol. 142 of *Yinying wenyuange siku quanshu*. Taipei: Taiwan shangwu yinshuguan, 1983.

    Sushui jiwen. Beijing: Zhonghua shuju, 1989.

Sima Qian. *Shiji*. Beijing: Zhonghua shuju, 1994.

Song da zhaoling ji. Beijing: Zhonghua shuju, 1962.

Songben lidai dili zhizhang tu. Shanghai guji chubanshe, 1989.

Su Che. *Longchuan biezhi*. Beijing: Zhonghua shuju, 1997.

    Su Che ji. Beijing: Zhonghua shuju, 1990.

Su Shi. *Su Shi wenji*. Beijing: Zhonghua shuju, 1986.

Su Song. *Su Weigong wenji*. Beijing: Zhonghua shuju, 1988.

Tang Zhongyou. *Diwang jingshi tupu*. Vol. 76 of *Beijing tushuguan guji zhenben congkan*. Beijing: Shumu wenxian chubanshe, 1987.

Wang Anshi. *Wang Jing Gong shizhu bujian*. Chengdu: Ba-Shu shushe, 2002.

Wang Cun. *Yuanfeng jiuyu zhi*. Beijing: Zhonghua shuju, 1984.

Wang Pizhi. *Shengshui yantan lu*. Beijing: Zhonghua shuju, 1981.

Wang Yinglin. *Tongjian dili tongshi*. Shanghai: Shangwu yinshuguan, 1936.

    Yuhai. Taipei: Huawen shuju, 1964.

Wang Zhi. *Moji*. Beijing: Zhonghua shuju, 1981.

Wei Tai. *Dongxuan bilu*. Beijing: Zhonghua shuju, 1983.

Wu Gang (ed.). *Quan Tang wen buyi*. Xi'an: San Qin chubanshe, 1994–2007.

Xiang Nan (ed.). *Liaodai shike wenbian*. Shijiazhuang: Hebei jiaoyu chubanshe, 1995.

Xiang Nan et al. (eds.). *Liaodai shike wen xubian*. Shenyang: Liaoning renmin chubanshe, 2010.

Xu Ziming. *Song zaifu biannian lu jiaobu*. Beijing: Zhonghua shuju, 2012.

Ye Longli. *Qidan guo zhi*. Shanghai guji, 1985.

Yingyin wenyuan ge siku quanshu. Taipei: Taiwan shangwu yinshuguan, 1983–86.

Yue Ke. *Tingshi*. Beijing: Zhonghua shuju, 1997.

Yuwen Maozhao. *Da Jinguo zhi jiaozheng*. Beijing: Zhonghua shuju, 1986.

Zhang Fangping. *Zhang Fangping ji*. Zhengzhou: Zhongzhou guji chubanshe, 1992.

Zhang Huang. *Tushu bian*. Yangzhou: Yangzhou guji shudian, 1988.

Zhang Ruyu. *Qunshu kaosuo*. Vols. 936–38 of *Yinying wenyuange siku quanshu*. Taipei: Taiwan shangwu yinshuguan, 1983.

Zhao Lingzhi. *Houqing lu*. Beijing: Zhonghua shuju, 2002.

Zhao Yanwei. *Yunlu manchao*. Beijing: Zhonghua shuju, 1996.

Zhou Hui. *Beiyuan lu*. Beijing: Zhonghua shuju, 1991.

    Qingbo zazhi jiaozhu. Beijing: Zhonghua shuju, 1994.

Zhou li zhushu fu jiaokan ji. Vol. 3 of *Shisan jing zhushu fu jiaokan ji*, collated by Ruan Yuan. Taipei: Yiwen yinshuguan, 1976.

Zhou Shaoliang and Zhao Chao (eds.). *Tangdai muzhi huibian*. Shanghai guji, 1991.

Zhu Xi. *Jiali*. In *Zhuzi chengshu*, ed. Huang Ruijie, 1341 edn. Repr. in Patricia Buckley Ebrey. *Chu Hsi's Family Rituals*. Princeton University Press, 1991.

Zhu Yu. *Pingzhou ketan*. Shanghai guji chubanshe, 1989.
Zhuang Chuo. *Ji le bian*. Beijing: Zhonghua shuju, 1983.

Post-1900

Abramson, Marc Samuel. "Deep Eyes and High Noses: Physiognomy and the Depiction of Barbarians in Tang China." In *Political Frontiers, Ethnic Boundaries, and Human Geographies in Chinese History*, ed. Nicola di Cosmo and Don J. Wyatt, 119–59. New York: RoutledgeCurzon, 2003.
Ethnic Identity in Tang China. Philadelphia: University of Pennsylvania Press, 2008.
Adelman, Jeremy and Stephen Aron. "From Borderlands to Borders: Empires, Nation-States, and the Peoples in Between in North American History." *American Historical Review*, 104/3 (1999): 814–41.
Aisin-Gioro Ulhicun. *Kittanbun boshi yori mita Ryō shi*. Kyoto: Shōkadō, 2006.
"Aluke'erqinqi Dao'erqige faxian yi zuo Liao mu." *Neimenggu wenwu kaogu*, 1–2/1992: 149–51.
Alyagon, Elad. "Inked: Song Soldiers, Military Tattoos, and the Remaking of the Chinese Lower Class, 960–1279." PhD Thesis, University of California, Davis, 2016.
An Guolou. *Songchao zhoubian minzu zhengce yanjiu*. Taipei: Wenjin chubanshe, 1997.
Anderson, Benedict. *Imagined Communities: Reflections on the Origin and Spread of Nationalism*. Rev. edn. New York: Verso, 2006.
Anderson, James A. *The Rebel Den of Nùng Trí Cao: Loyalty and Identity along the Sino-Vietnamese Frontier*. Seattle: University of Washington Press, 2007.
"'Treacherous Factions': Shifting Frontier Alliances in the Breakdown of Sino-Vietnamese Relations on the Eve of the 1075 Border War." In *Battlefronts Real and Imagined: War, Border, and Identity in the Chinese Middle Period*, ed. Don J. Wyatt, 191–226. New York: Palgrave Macmillan, 2008.
Ang, Melvin Thlick-Len. "Sung-Liao Diplomacy in Eleventh- and Twelfth-Century China: A Study of the Social and Political Determinants of Foreign Policy." PhD Thesis. University of Pennsylvania, 1983.
"Aohan qi Lama gou Liaodai bihua mu." *Neimenggu wenwu kaogu*, 1/1999: 90–97.
"Aohan qi Qijia Liao mu." *Neimenggu wenwu kaogu*, 1/1999: 46–66, 104.
"Aohan qi Yangshan 1–3 hao Liaomu qingli jianbao." *Neimenggu wenwu kaogu*, 1/1999: 1–38, 43.
Appadurai, Arjun. "Introduction: Commodities and the Politics of Value." In *The Social Life of Things: Commodities in Cultural Perspective*, ed. Arjun Appadurai, 3–63. Cambridge University Press, 1986.
Backus, Charles. *The Nan-chao Kingdom and T'ang China's Southwestern Frontier*. Cambridge University Press, 1981.
Barfield, Thomas J. *The Perilous Frontier: Nomadic Empires and China*. Cambridge, MA: Blackwell, 1989.

Barth, Fredrik. "Introduction" to *Ethnic Groups and Boundaries: The Social Organization of Cultural Difference*, ed. Fredrik Barth, 9–37. London: Allen & Unwin, 1969.

Baud, Michiel and Willem van Schendel. "Towards a Comparative History of Borderlands." *Journal of World History*, 8/2 (1997): 211–42.

Beijing Longquanwu Liao Jin muzang fajue baogao. Beijing: Kexue chubanshe, 2009.

"Beijing Shunyi Anxin zhuang Liao mu fajue jianbao." *Wenwu*, 6/1992: 17–23.

Bodde, Derk. "The State and Empire of Ch'in." In *Cambridge History of China*, vol. 1: *The Ch'in and Han Empires*, ed. Denis Twitchett and Michael Loewe, 20–102. Cambridge University Press, 1986.

Bol, Peter K. "Creating a GIS for the History of China." In *Placing History: How Maps, Spatial Data, and GIS Are Changing Historical Scholarship*, ed. Anne Kelly Knowles, 27–59. Redlands, CA: ESRI Press, 2008.

  "Geography and Culture: Middle-Period Discourse on the Zhong guo." In *Space and Cultural Fields: Spatial Images, Practices and Social Production*, ed. Huang Ying-kuei. Taipei: Center for Chinese Studies, 2009. Accessed 31 October 2014. http://nrs.harvard.edu/urn-3:HUL.InstRepos:3629313.

  Neo-Confucianism in History. Cambridge, MA: Harvard University Asia Center, 2008.

  "Seeking Common Ground: Han Literati under Jurchen Rule." *Harvard Journal of Asiatic Studies*, 47/2 (1987): 461–538.

  "The Sung Examination System and the Shih." *Asia Major*, 3rd ser., 3/2 (1990): 149–71.

  "This Culture of Ours": Intellectual Transitions in T'ang and Sung China. Stanford University Press, 1992.

Bossler, Beverly J. *Powerful Relations: Kinship, Status, and the State in Sung China (960–1279)*. Cambridge, MA: Council on East Asian Studies, 1998.

Breuker, Remco E. *Establishing a Pluralist Society in Medieval Korea, 918–1170: History, Ideology and Identity in the Koryŏ Dynasty*. Leiden: Brill, 2010.

  "Koryŏ as an Independent Realm: The Emperor's Clothes." *Korean Studies*, 27 (2003): 48–84.

Bulliet, Richard W. *Hunters, Herders, and Hamburgers*. New York: Columbia University Press, 2005.

Cao Wanru. "Youguan *Huayi tu* wenti de tantao." In *Zhongguo gudai dituji: Zhanguo-Yuan*, ed. Cao Wanru et al., 41–45.

Cao Wanru. et al. (eds.). *Zhongguo gudai ditu ji: Zhanguo-Yuan*. Beijing: Wenwu chubanshe, 1990.

Chaffee, John. *The Thorny Gates of Learning in Sung China*. New edn. Albany: State University of New York Press, 1995.

Chan, Hok-lam. *Legitimation in Imperial China: Discussions under the Jurchen-Chin Dynasty*. Seattle: University of Washington Press, 1984.

Chang, Kang-i Sun. *The Late-Ming Poet Ch'en Tzu-lung: Crises of Love and Loyalism*. New Haven, CT: Yale University Press, 1991.

Chen Feng. *Bei Song wujiang qunti yu xiangguan wenti yanjiu*. Beijing: Zhonghua shuju, 2004.

Chen Yinke. *Tangdai zhengzhi shi shulun gao*. Shanghai guji chubanshe, 1982.

Chen Zhaorong. "Qin 'shu tong wenzi' xintan." *Zhongyang yanjiuyuan lishi yuyan yanjiusuo jikan*, 68/3 (1997): 589–641.

Cheng Long. *Bei Song Xibei zhanqu liangshi buji dili*. Beijing: Shehui kexue wenxian chubanshe, 2006.

Cherniack, Susan. "Book Culture and Textual Transmission in Sung China." *Harvard Journal of Asiatic Studies*, 54/1 (1994): 5–125.

"Chifeng xian Dayingzi Liao mu fajue baogao." *Kaogu xuebao*, 3/1956: 1–31.

Chittick, Andrew. *Patronage and Community in Medieval China: The Xiangyang Garrison, 400–600 CE*. Albany: State University of New York Press, 2009.

Chivers, C. J. "Russians Plant Flag on the Arctic Seabed." *The New York Times*, August 3, 2007.

Chollet, Hélène. "Treasures from the Liao Period at the Musée Cernuschi." *Orientations*, 36/5 (2005): 40–46.

Chūgoku tōji zenshū, vol. 9: *Tei yō*. Kyoto: Binobi, 1981.

Crossley, Pamela Kyle. "An Introduction to the Qing Foundation Myth." *Late Imperial China*, 6/2 (1985): 13–24.

"*Manzhou yuanliu* kao and the Formalization of the Manchu Heritage." *Journal of Asian Studies*, 46/4 (1987): 761–90.

Csete, Anne. "Ethnicity, Conflict, and the State in the Early to Mid-Qing: The Hainan Highlands, 1644–1800." In *Empire at the Margins: Culture, Ethnicity, and Frontier in Early Modern China*, ed. Pamela Kyle Crossley et al., 229–52. Berkeley: University of California Press, 2006.

Dai Zunde and Lei Yungui. "Shuozhou Liaodai bihua mu fajue jianbao." *Wenwu jikan*, 2/1995: 19–26.

Dardess, John W. "Did the Mongols Matter? Territory, Power, and the Intelligentsia in China from the Northern Song to the Early Ming." In *The Song-Yuan-Ming Transition in Chinese History*, ed Paul Jakov Smith and Richard Von Glahn, 111–34. Cambridge, MA: Harvard University Asia Center, 2003.

Davis, Richard L. *Historical Records of the Five Dynasties*. New York: Columbia University Press, 2004.

Wind against the Mountain: The Crisis of Politics and Culture in Thirteenth-Century China. Cambridge, MA: Council on East Asian Studies, 1996.

Day, David. *Conquest: How Societies Overwhelm Others*. Oxford University Press, 2008.

de la Vaissière, Étienne. *Histoire des marchands sogdiens*. 2nd edn. Paris: Collège de France, 2004.

de Rachewiltz, Igor (trans.). *The Secret History of the Mongols*. Leiden: Brill, 2004.

De Weerdt, Hilde. *Competition over Content: Negotiating Standards for the Civil Service Examinations in Imperial China (1127–1279)*. Cambridge, MA: Harvard University Asia Center, 2007.

"The Cultural Logics of Map Reading: Text, Time, and Space in Printed Maps of the Song Empire." In *Knowledge and Text Production in an Age of Print*, ed. Lucille Chia and Hilde De Weerdt, 239–70. Leiden: Brill, 2011.

"Maps and Memory: Reading of Cartography in Twelfth- and Thirteenth-Century Song China." *Imago Mundi*, 61/2 (2009): 145–67.

"What did Su Che See in the North? Publishing Regulations, State Security, and Political Culture in Song China." *T'oung Pao*, 92/4–5 (2006): 466–94.

Deng Xiaonan. "Lun Wudai Songchu 'hu-han' yujing de xiaojie." *Wenshizhe*, 5/2005: 57–64.

Deng Xiaonan and Christian Lamouroux. "The 'Ancestors Family Instructions': Authority and Sovereignty in Song China." *Journal of Song-Yuan Studies*, 35 (2005): 79–97.

Di Cosmo, Nicola. *Ancient China and its Enemies: The Rise of Nomadic Power in East Asian History*. Cambridge and New York: Cambridge University Press, 2002.

Dien, Albert E. *Six Dynasties Civilization*. New Haven, CT: Yale University Press, 2007.

Dong Wenyi. "Balin youqi Chaganba shiyihao Liao mu." *Neimenggu wenwu kaogu*, 3 (1984): 91–93.

Dong Xinlin. "Liaodai muzang xingzhi yu fenqi luelun." *Kaogu*, 8 (2004): 62–75.

Dong Xinlin. et al. "Neimenggu Balin zuoqi Liaodai Zuling kaogu fajue de xin shouhuo." *Kaogu*, 2/2008: 3–6.

Drompp, Michael R. *Tang China and the Collapse of the Uighur Empire*. Leiden and Boston, MA: Brill, 2005.

Druckman, Daniel. "Nationalism, Patriotism, and Group Loyalty: A Social Psychological Perspective." *Mershon International Studies Review*, 38/1 (1994): 43–68.

Du Chengwu and Lu Sixian. "Qidan nüshi de wangluo yu mianju." In *Qidan nüshi: Haoqianying Liao mu qingli yu yanjiu*, 89–109. Hohhot: Neimenggu renmin chubanshe, 1985.

Duara, Prasenjit. "Nationalists among Transnationals: Overseas Chinese and the Idea of China, 1900–1911." In *Ungrounded Empires: The Cultural Politics of Modern Chinese Transnationalism*, ed. Aihwa Ong, 39–60. New York: Routledge, 1996.

Rescuing History from the Nation: Questioning Narratives of Modern China. University of Chicago Press, 1995.

Sovereignty and Authenticity: Manchukuo and the East Asian Modern. Lanham, MD: Rowman & Littlefield, 2003.

Dunnell, Ruth. "The Hsi Hsia." In *Cambridge History of China*, Vol. 6: *Alien Regimes and Border States, 907–1368*, eds. Herbert Franke and Denis Twitchett, 154–214. Cambridge University Press, 1994.

"Significant Peripheries: Inner Asian Perspectives on Song Studies." *Journal of Song-Yuan Studies*, 24 (1994): 334–39.

Ebrey, Patricia Buckley. *The Aristocratic Families of Early Imperial China: A Case Study of the Po-ling Ts'ui Family*. Cambridge University Press, 1978.

Chu Hsi's Family Rituals. Princeton University Press, 1991.

Emperor Huizong. Cambridge, MA: Harvard University Press, 2014.

"Surnames and Han Chinese Identity." In *Negotiating Ethnicities in China and Taiwan*, ed. Melissa J. Brown, 11–36. Berkeley: Institute of East Asian Studies, 1996.

Egan, Ronald. "To Count Grains of Sand on the Ocean Floor: Changing Perceptions of Books and Learning in the Song Dynasty." In *Knowledge and Text Production in an Age of Print: China, 900–1400*, ed. Lucille Chia and Hilde De Weerdt, 33–62. Leiden and Boston, MA: Brill, 2011.

Elias, Norbert. *The Germans: Power Struggles and the Development of Habitus in the Nineteenth and Twentieth Centuries*, trans. Eric Dunning and Stephen Mennell. New York: Columbia University Press, 1996.

Elliott, Mark. "Hushuo: The Northern Other and the Naming of the Han Chinese." In *Critical Han Studies: The History, Representation, and Identity of China's Majority*, ed. Thomas S. Mullaney et al., 173–90. Berkeley: University of California Press, 2012.

The Manchu Way: The Eight Banners and Ethnic Identity in Late Imperial China. Stanford University Press, 2001.

Elvin, Mark. *The Pattern of the Chinese Past*. Stanford University Press, 1973.

The Retreat of the Elephants. New Haven, CT: Yale University Press, 2004.

Eregzen, Gelegdorj (ed.). *Treasures of the Xiongnu*. Ulaanbaatar: Mongolian Academy of Sciences, 2011.

Esherick, Joseph W. "How the Qing Became China." In *Empire to Nation: Historical Perspectives on the Making of the Modern World*, ed. Joseph W. Esherick et al., 229–59. Lanham, MD: Rowman & Littlefield, 2006.

Esherick, Joseph W. et al. "Introduction" to *Empire to Nation: Historical Perspectives on the Making of the Modern World*, ed. Joseph W. Esherick et al., 1–31. Lanham, MD: Rowman & Littlefield, 2006.

Fairbank, John King (ed.). *The Chinese World Order: Traditional China's Foreign Relations*. Cambridge, MA: Harvard University Press, 1968.

"Faku Yemaotai Liao mu ji lue." *Wenwu*, 12/1975: 26–36.

Falkenhausen, Lothar von. *Chinese Society in the Age of Confucius*. Los Angeles, CA: Cotsen Institute of Archaeology, 2006.

Fletcher, Joseph. "The Mongols: Ecological and Social Perspectives." *Harvard Journal of Asiatic Studies*, 46/1 (1986): 11–50.

Ford, Caleb. "Guiqiao (Returned Overseas Chinese) Identity in the PRC." *Journal of Chinese Overseas*, 10/2 (2014): 239–62.

Ford, Lisa. *Settler Sovereignty: Jurisdiction and Indigenous People in America and Australia, 1788–1836*. Cambridge, MA: Harvard University Press, 2010.

Franke, Herbert. "The Chin Dynasty." In *Cambridge History of China*, vol. 6: *Alien Regimes and Border States, 907–1368*, ed. Herbert Franke and Denis Twitchett, 215–320. Cambridge University Press, 1994.

"Chinese Historiography under Mongol Rule: The Role of History in Acculturation." *Mongolian Studies*, 1 (1974): 15–26.

"The Forest Peoples of Manchuria: Kitans and Jurchens." In *Cambridge History of Early Inner Asia*, ed. Denis Sinor, 400–23. Cambridge University Press, 1990.

"The Role of the State as a Structural Element in Polyethnic Societies." In *Foundations and Limits of State Power in China*, ed. S. R. Schram, 87–112. London: School of Oriental and African Studies, 1987.

"Sung Embassies: Some General Observations." In *China Among Equals: The Middle Kingdom and its Neighbors, 10th–14th Centuries*, ed. Morris Rossabi, 116–48. Berkeley: University of California Press, 1983.

Franke, Herbert and Denis Twitchett. "Introduction" to *Cambridge History of China*, vol. 6: *Alien Regimes and Border States, 907–1368*, ed. Herbert Franke and Denis Twitchett, 1–42. Cambridge University Press, 1994.

Fu Lehuan. "Song ren shi Liao yulu xingcheng kao." *Guoxue jikan*, 5/4 (1935): 165–93.

Gat, Azar. *Nations: The Long History and Deep Roots of Political Ethnicity and Nationalism*. Cambridge University Press, 2013.

Ge Zhaoguang. *Zhongguo sixiang shi*. Shanghai: Fudan daxue chubanshe, 1998–2000.

"'Zhongguo' yishi zai Songdai de tuxian." In *Zhai ci Zhongguo*, 41–65. Beijing: Zhonghua shuju, 2011.

Geary, Patrick J. *The Myth of Nations: The Medieval Origins of Europe*. Princeton University Press, 2002.

Geertz, Clifford. "The Integrative Revolution: Primordial Sentiments and Civil Politics in the New States." In *Old Societies and New States: The Quest for Modernity in Asia and Africa*, ed. Clifford Geertz, 105–57. London: Collier-Macmillan, 1963.

Gellner, Ernest. *Nations and Nationalism*. 2nd edn. Ithaca, NY: Cornell University Press, 2008.

Golden, Peter B. *An Introduction to the History of the Turkic Peoples*. Wiesbaden: Otto Harrassowitz, 1992.

Goldin, Paul R. "The Motif of the Woman in the Doorway and Related Imagery in Traditional Chinese Funerary Art." *Journal of the American Oriental Society*, 121/4 (2001): 539–48.

Graff, David Andrew. *Medieval Chinese Warfare*. New York: Routledge, 2002.

Greenfeld, Liah. *Nationalism: Five Roads to Modernity*. Cambridge, MA: Harvard University Press, 1992.

Gu Jiegang. "Qin Han tongyi de youlai he Zhanguo ren duiyu shijie de xiangxiang." In *Gushi bian*, 2:1–16. Beiping: Pushe, 1930.

Guanshan Liao mu. Beijing: Wenwu chubanshe, 2011.

Guo Maoyu and Zhao Zhenhua. "Tang Shi Xiaozhang muzhi yanjiu." *Zhongguo bianjiang shidi yanjiu*, 17/4 (2007): 115–21.

Hall, Jonathan M. *Ethnic Identity in Greek Antiquity*. Cambridge University Press, 1997.

Hansen, Valerie. *Changing Gods in Medieval China, 1127–1276*. Princeton University Press, 1989.

"Introduction: Turfan as a Silk Road Community." *Asia Major*, 3rd ser., 11/2 (1998): 1–11.

Harrell, Stevan. "The History of the History of the Yi." In *Cultural Encounters on China's Ethnic Frontiers*, ed. Stevan Harrell, 63–91. Seattle: University of Washington Press, 1994.

Hartwell, Robert M. "Demographic, Political, and Social Transformations of China, 750–1550." *Harvard Journal of Asiatic Studies*, 42/2 (1982): 365–442.

Hastings, Adrian. *The Construction of Nationhood: Ethnicity, Religion, and Nationalism*. Cambridge and New York: Cambridge University Press, 1997.

"Hebei Ding xian faxian liang zuo Song dai taji." *Wenwu*, 8/1972: 39–51.

"Hebei Quyang xian Jiancicun Ding yao yizhi diaocha yu shijue." *Kaogu*, 8/1965: 394–412.

"Hebei Xuanhua xin faxian liang chu Liao Jin bihua mu." *Zhongguo zhongyao kaogu faxian*, 1998: 105–10.

"Henan Xin'an xian Song cun Bei Song diaozhuan bihua mu." *Kaogu yu wenwu*, 3/1998: 22–28.

Henderson, John B. "Chinese Cosmographical Thought: The High Intellectual Tradition." In *The History of Cartography*, ed. J. B. Harley and David Woodward, vol. 2, Book 2: *Cartography in the Traditional East and Southeast Asian Societies*, 203–16. University of Chicago Press, 1994.

The Development and Decline of Chinese Cosmology. New York: Columbia University Press, 1984.

Herman, John E. *Amid the Clouds and Mist: China's Colonization of Guizhou, 1200–1700*. Cambridge, MA: Harvard University Asia Center, 2007.

Hesse, Carla and Thomas Laqueur. "Introduction" to *Representations*, Special Issue: *National Cultures before Nationalism*, 47 (1994): 1–12.

Hobsbawm, E. J. *Nations and Nationalism since 1780: Programme, Myth, Reality*. 2nd edn. Cambridge and New York: Cambridge University Press, 1992.

Hodder, Ian. "Social Structure and Cemeteries: A Critical Appraisal." In *Anglo-Saxon Cemeteries, 1979*, ed. Philip A. Rahtz et al., 161–69. Oxford: British Archaeological Reports, 1980.

Holcombe, Charles. "Immigrants and Strangers: From Cosmopolitanism to Confucian Universalism in Tang China." *Tang Studies*, 20–21 (2002–03): 71–112.

"Re-Imagining China: The Chinese Identity Crisis at the Start of the Southern Dynasties Period." *Journal of the American Oriental Society*, 115/1 (1995): 1–14.

Holmgren, Jennifer. "Northern Wei as a Conquest Dynasty: Current Perceptions; Past Scholarship." *Papers on Far Eastern History*, 40 (1989): 1–50.

Hon, Tze-ki. *Revolution as Restoration: Guocui xuebao and China's Path to Modernity, 1905–1911*. Leiden and Boston, MA: Brill, 2013.

Huang Gang. *Biansai shi lungao*. Hefei: Huangshan sheshu, 1996.

Hymes, Robert P. *Statesmen and Gentlemen: The Elite of Fu-chou, Chiang-hsi, in Northern and Southern Sung*. Cambridge University Press, 1986.

"Sung Society and Social Change." In *Cambridge History of China*, vol. 5, Part 2: *Sung China, 960–1279*, ed. John W. Chaffee and Denis Twitchett, 526–664. Cambridge University Press, 2015.

Idema, Wilt L. *Meng Jiangnü Brings Down the Great Wall*. Seattle: University of Washington Press, 2008.

Iwai Shigeki. "China's Frontier Society in the Sixteenth and Seventeenth Centuries." *Acta Asiatica*, 88 (2005): 1–20.

Jay, Jennifer W. *A Change in Dynasties: Loyalism in Thirteenth-Century China*. Bellingham, WA: Western Washington University, 1991.

"Memoirs and Official Accounts: The Historiography of the Song Loyalists." *Harvard Journal of Asiatic Studies*, 50/2 (1990): 589–612.

Ji Chengzhang. "Haoqianying di liu hao Liao mu ruogan wenti de yanjiu." *Wenwu*, 9/1983: 9–14.

Jia Jingyan. "Hu Qiao xian Liao ji shuzheng." *Shixue jikan*, 4/1983: 5–17.

"Lu Zhen Chengyao lu shuzheng gao." *Lishi dili*, 4/1986: 190–209.

"Xining shi Qidan tuchao shuzheng gao." *Wenshi*, 22 (1984): 121–52.

Jiang Sheng and Yu Jinfang. "Hubei Xiangfan Liujia geng Tang Song muzang qingli jianbao." *Jiang Han kaogu*, 2/1999: 30–36, 40.

Jie Xigong. "Taiyuan Xiaojingyu Song Ming mu diyi ci fajue ji." *Kaogu*, 5/1963: 250–58.

"Jilin Shuangliao xian Gaolige Liao mu qun." *Kaogu*, 2/1986: 138–46.

Jin Fengyi. "Liaoning Chaoyang Qianchuanghu cun Liao mu." *Wenwu*, 12/1980: 17–29.

Jin Yongtian. "Liao Shangjing chengzhi fujin fosi yizhi ji huozang mu." *Neimenggu wenwu kaogu*, 3 (1984): 94–97.

"Shangjing fujin faxian de xiaoxing muzang." In *Linhuang shiji*, 45–47. Bairin Zuoqi: Bairin zuoqi yinshuachang, 1988.

"Jinan shi Song Jin zhuandiao bihua mu." *Wenwu*, 8/2008: 33–54.

Johnson, David. "The Last Years of a Great Clan: The Li Family of Chao chün in Late T'ang and Early Sung." *Harvard Journal of Asiatic Studies*, 37/1 (1977): 5–102.

The Medieval Chinese Oligarchy. Boulder, CO: Westview Press, 1977.

Kane, Daniel A. *The Kitan Language and Script*. Leiden and Boston, MA: Brill, 2009.

Karlgren, Bernhard. "The Book of Documents." *Bulletin of the Museum of Far Eastern Antiquities*, 22 (1950): 1–81.

Kervyn, L. "Le tombeau de l'empereur Tao-tsong des Leao, et les premières inscriptions connues en écriture 'K'itan'." *T'oung pao*, 22 (1923): 292–301.

Keyes, Charles F. "The Dialectics of Ethnic Change." In *Ethnic Change*, ed. Charles F. Keyes, 4–30. Seattle: University of Washington Press, 1981.

"Keyou zhong qi Daiqintala Liao mu qingli jianbao." In *Neimenggu wenwu kaogu wenji*, 2:651–67. Beijing: Zhongguo dabaike quanshu chubanshe, 1997.

Kim Sŏnggyu. *Sōdai no seihoku mondai to iminzoku seisaku*. Tokyo: Kyūko Shoin, 2000.

Knapp, Ronald G. *China's Traditional Rural Architecture: A Cultural Geography of the Common House*. Honolulu: University of Hawai'i Press, 1986.

Kuhn, Dieter. "Decoding Tombs of the Song Elite." In *Burial in Song China*, ed. Dieter Kuhn, 11–159. Heidelberg: Edition Forum, 1994.

   A Place for the Dead: An Archaeological Documentary on Graves and Tombs of the Song Dynasty. Heidelberg: Edition Forum, 1996.

"Kulun qi di wu, liu hao Liao mu." *Neimenggu wenwu kaogu*, 2 (1982): 35–46, 28.

Kurz, Johannes L. "The Yangzi in the Negotiations between the Southern Tang and its Northern Neighbours." In *China and Her Neighbours*, ed. Sabine Dabringhaus and Roderich Ptak, 29–48. Wiesbaden: Harrassowitz, 1997.

Lamouroux, Christian. "De l'étrangeté à la différence: Les récits des émissaires Song en pays Liao (XIè s.)." In *Récits de voyages asiatiques: Genres, mentalités, conception de l'espace*, ed. Claudine Salmon, 101–26. Paris: École française d'Extrême-Orient, 1996.

   "From the Yellow River to the Huai: New Representations of a River Network and the Hydraulic Crisis of 1128." In *Sediments of Time: Environment and Society in Chinese History*, ed. Mark Elvin and Liu Ts'ui-jung, 545–84. Cambridge University Press, 1998.

   "Geography and Politics: The Song–Liao Border Dispute of 1074/75." In *China and Her Neighbours*, ed. Sabine Dabringhaus and Roderich Ptak, 1–28. Wiesbaden: Harrassowitz, 1997.

   "Militaires et bureaucrates aux confins du Gansu-Qinghai à la fin du XIe siècle." *Extrême-Orient Extrême-Occident*, 28 (2006): 95–125.

Lane, George. *Daily Life in the Mongol Empire*. Westport, CT: Greenwood Press, 2006.

Lattimore, Owen. "The Frontier in History." In *Studies in Frontier History: Collected Papers*, 469–91. Paris: Mouton & Co., 1962.

Lau Nap-yin and Huang K'uan-chung. "Founding and Consolidation of the Sung Dynasty under T'ai-tsu (960–976), T'ai-tsung (976–997), and Chen-tsung (997–1022)." In *Cambridge History of China*, vol. 5, Part 1: *The Sung Dynasty and its Precursors, 907–1279*, ed. Denis Twitchett and Paul Jakov Smith, 206–78. Cambridge University Press, 2009.

Lee, Peter H. *Sourcebook of Korean Civilization*. New York: Columbia University Press, 1993–96.

Leung, Irene S. "'Felt Yurts Neatly Arrayed, Large Tents Huddle Close': Visualizing the Frontier in the Northern Song Dynasty." In *Political Frontiers, Ethnic Boundaries, and Human Geographies in Chinese History*, ed. Nicola di Cosmo and Don J. Wyatt, 192–219. New York: RoutledgeCurzon, 2003.

Levenson, Joseph R. *Confucian China and its Modern Fate: A Trilogy*. Berkeley: University of California Press, 1968.

Levine, Ari Daniel. "Che-tsung's Reign (1085–1100) and the Age of Faction." In *Cambridge History of China*, vol. 5, Part 1: *The Sung Dynasty and its Precursors, 907–1279*, ed. Denis Twitchett and Paul Jakov Smith, 484–555. Cambridge University Press, 2009.

"Welcome to the Occupation: Collective Memory, Displaced Nostalgia, and Dislocated Knowledge in Southern Song Ambassadors' Travel Records of Jin-dynasty Kaifeng." *T'oung Pao*, 99/4–5 (2013): 379–444.

Lewis, Mark Edward. *The Construction of Space in Early China*. Albany: State University of New York Press, 2006.

Li Feng. *Landscape and Power in Early China: The Crisis and Fall of the Western Zhou*. Cambridge University Press, 2006.

Li Huarui. *Song Xia guanxi shi*. Shijiazhuang: Hebei renmin chubanshe, 1998.

Li Mingde and Guo Yitian. "Anyang Xiaonanhai Songdai bihua mu." *Zhongyuan wenwu*, 2/1993: 74–79.

Li Qingfa. "Jianping Xiyaocun Liao mu." *Liaohai wenwu xuekan*, 1/1991: 120–23.

Li, Wai-yee. "Full-Length Vernacular Fiction." In *Columbia History of Chinese Literature*, ed. Victor H. Mair, 620–58. New York: Columbia University Press, 2001.

Li Zhongyi. "Handan shiqu faxian Songdai muzang." *Wenwu chunqiu*, 3/1994: 19–23, 35.

Liang Zhangju. *Langji congtan*. Beijing: Zhonghua shuju, 1981.

Liao Chenguo gongzhu mu. Beijing: Wenwu chubanshe, 1993.

Lin Ruihan. "Bei Song zhi bianfang." *Songshi yanjiu ji*, 13 (1981): 199–229.

Lindner, Rudi Paul. "What Was a Nomadic Tribe?" *Comparative Studies in Society and History*, 24/4 (1982): 689–711.

Liu Deqing. *Ouyang Xiu jinian lu*. Shanghai guji chubanshe, 2006.

Liu Fengzhu et al. (eds.). *Liao Shangjing diqu chutu de Liaodai beike huiji*. Beijing: Shehui kexue wenxian chubanshe, 2009.

Liu, James T. C. "Polo and Cultural Change: From T'ang to Sung China." *Harvard Journal of Asiatic Studies*, 45 (1985): 203–24.

Liu Jianzhong and He Yong. "Hebei Zhuolu xian Liaodai bihua mu fajue jianbao." *Kaogu*, 3/1987: 242–45.

Liu Jingwen and Wang Xiulan. "Liao Jin bingqi yanjiu." *Beifang wenwu*, 1/2004: 49–54.

Liu, Lydia. *The Clash of Empires: The Invention of China in Modern World Making*. Cambridge, MA: Harvard University Press, 2004.

Lorge, Peter. *The Reunification of China: Peace Through War under the Song Dynasty*. Cambridge University Press, 2015.

Louis, François. "Iconic Ancestors: Wire Mesh, Metal Masks, and Kitan Image Worship." *Journal of Song-Yuan Studies*, 43 (2013): 91–115.

"Luoyang Mangshan Songdai bihua mu." *Wenwu*, 12/1992: 37–51.

Luttwak, Edward. *The Grand Strategy of the Roman Empire: From the First Century CE to the Third*. Rev. and updated edn. Baltimore, MD: Johns Hopkins University Press, 2016.

Major, John S. "The Five Phases, Magic Squares, and Schematic Cosmography." In *Explorations in Early Chinese Cosmology*, ed. Henry Rosemont, Jr., 133–66. Chico, CA: Scholars Press, 1984.

Mao Yangguang. "Xinjian si fang Tangdai Luoyang Mite ren muzhi kao." *Zhongyuan wenwu*, 6/2009: 74–80.

McDermott, Joseph P. *A Social History of the Chinese Book*. Hong Kong University Press, 2006.

McGrath, Michael. "Military and Regional Administration in Northern Sung China (960–1126)." PhD Thesis. Princeton University, 1982.

"The Reigns of Jen-tsung (1022–1063) and Ying-tsung (1063–1067)." In *Cambridge History of China*, vol. 5, Part 1: *The Sung Dynasty and its Precursors, 907–1279*, ed. Denis Twitchett and Paul Jakov Smith, 279–346. Cambridge University Press, 2009.

Meskill, Johanna Menzel. *A Chinese Pioneer Family: The Lins of Wu-feng, Taiwan (1729–1895)*. Princeton University Press, 1979.

Miyake Soetsu. "Keikanko o shutsudo seru saisho no kofun ni tsuite." *Kokuritsu chūō hakubutsukan jihō*, 5 (1940): 1–6.

Miyashita Saburō. "Su Sung." In *Sung Biographies*, ed. Herbert Franke, 3:969–70. Wiesbaden: Franz Steiner Verlag, 1976.

Mollier, Christine. *Buddhism and Taoism Face to Face: Scripture, Ritual, and Iconographic Exchange in Medieval China*. Honolulu: University of Hawai'i Press, 2008.

Mosca, Matthew W. *From Frontier Policy to Foreign Policy: The Question of India and the Transformation of Geopolitics in Qing China*. Stanford University Press, 2013.

Mu Qing. "Zaoqi Dingci chutan." *Wenwu chunqiu*, 3/1995: 30–42, 91.

Mullaney, Thomas S. *Coming to Terms with the Nation: Ethnic Classification in Modern China*. Berkeley: University of California Press, 2011.

Needham, Joseph and Wang Ling. *Mathematics and the Sciences of the Heavens and the Earth*. Vol. 3 of *Science and Civilisation in China*. Cambridge University Press, 1959.

"Neimeng Huolinguoleshi Liao mu qingli jian bao," *Beifang wenwu*, 2/1988: 39–40.

"Neimeng Tuquan xian faxian Liaodai wenwu." *Kaogu*, 4/1959: 210–11.

"Neimenggu Aohanqi Shazigou, Dahengou Liao mu." *Kaogu*, 10/1987: 889–904.

"Neimenggu Jiefang yingzi Liao mu fajue jianbao." *Kaogu*, 4/1979: 330–34.

Nguyen Dinh-Hoa. "Graphemic Borrowings from Chinese: The Case of Chu Nom – Vietnam's Demotic Script." *Zhongyang yanjiuyuan lishi yuyan yanjiusuo jikan*, 61/2 (1990): 383–432.

Nie Chongqi. "Song Liao jiaopin kao." *Yanjing xuebao*, 27 (1940): 1–51.

Nordman, Daniel. *Frontières de France: De l'espace au territoire (XVIe-XIXe siècle)*. Paris: Éditions Gallimard, 1998.

Nylan, Michael. *The Five "Confucian" Classics*. New Haven, CT: Yale University Press, 2001.

"The Rhetoric of 'Empire' in the Classical Era in China." In *Conceiving the Empire: China and Rome Compared*, ed. Fritz-Heiner Mutschler and Achim Mittag, 39–64. Oxford University Press, 2008.

Pan Yihong. "Marriage Alliances and Chinese Princesses in International Politics from Han through T'ang." *Asia Major*, 3rd ser., 10/1–2 (1997): 95–131.

"The Sino-Tibetan Treaties in the Tang Dynasty." *T'oung Pao*, 78 (1992): 116–61.

Parker Pearson, Michael. *The Archaeology of Death and Burial*. College Station: Texas A&M University Press, 2000.

"Mortuary Practices, Society and Ideology: An Ethnoarchaeological Study." In *Symbolic and Structural Archaeology*, ed. Ian Hodder, 99–113. Cambridge University Press, 1982.

Perdue, Peter C. "Boundaries, Maps, and Movement: Chinese, Russian, and Mongolian Empires in Early Modern Central Eurasia." *International History Review*, 20/2 (1998): 263–86.

China Marches West: The Qing Conquest of Central Asia. Cambridge, MA: Belknap Press, 2005.

Peterson, Charles A. "Court and Province in Mid- and Late T'ang." *Cambridge History of China*, vol. 3: *Sui and T'ang China*, ed. Denis Twitchett, 464–560. Cambridge University Press, 1979.

Phan, John. "Chu Nom and the Taming of the South: A Bilingual Defense for Vernacular Writing in the *Chi Nam Ngoc Am Giai Nghia*." *Journal of Vietnamese Studies*, 8/1 (2013): 1–33.

Pines, Yuri. "Beasts or Humans: Pre-Imperial Origins of the 'Sino-Barbarian' Dichotomy." In *Mongols, Turks, and Others: Eurasian Nomads and the Sedentary World*, ed. Reuven Amitai and Michal Biran, 59–102. Leiden: Brill, 2005.

The Everlasting Empire: The Political Culture of Ancient China and its Imperial Legacy. Princeton University Press, 2012.

Prescott, J. R. V. *Political Frontiers and Boundaries*. London and Boston, MA: Allen & Unwin, 1987.

Pulleyblank, Edwin G. *The Background of the Rebellion of An Lu-shan*. London and New York: Oxford University Press, 1955.

Qian Zheng and Yao Shiying. "*Dili tu bei*." In *Zhongguo gudai ditu ji: Zhanguo-Yuan*, ed. Cao Wanru et al., 46–49. Beijing: Wenwu chubanshe, 1990.

Reischauer, Edwin O. (trans.). *Ennin's Diary: The Record of a Pilgrimage to China in Search of the Law*. New York: Ronald Press, 1955.

Reynolds, Susan. "The Idea of the Nation as a Political Community." In *Power and the Nation in European History*, ed. Len Scales and Oliver Zimmer, 54–66. Cambridge University Press, 2005.

Rogers, J. Daniel et al. "Urban Centres and the Emergence of Empires in Eastern Inner Asia." *Antiquity*, 79 (2005): 801–18.

Rong Xinjiang. *Zhonggu Zhongguo yu wailai wenming*. Beijing: Sanlian shudian, 2001.

Rorex, Robert A. *Eighteen Songs of a Nomad Flute*. New York: Metropolitan Museum of Art, 1974.

"Some Liao Tomb Murals and Images of Nomads in Chinese Paintings of the Wen-Chi Story." *Artibus Asiae*, 45/2–3 (1984): 174–98.

Rosenwein, Barbara H. "Worrying about Emotions in History." *American Historical Review*, 107/3 (2002): 821–45.

Rossabi, Morris (ed.). *China Among Equals: The Middle Kingdom and its Neighbors, 10th–14th Centuries.* Berkeley: University of California Press, 1983.

Rubiés, Joan-Pau. *Travel and Ethnology in the Renaissance: South India through European Eyes, 1250–1625.* Cambridge and New York: Cambridge University Press, 2002.

Sahlins, Peter. *Boundaries: The Making of France and Spain in the Pyrenees.* Berkeley: University of California Press, 1989.

"Natural Frontiers Revisited: France's Boundaries since the Seventeenth Century." *American Historical Review*, 95/2 (1990): 1423–51.

Unnaturally French: Foreign Citizens in the Old Regime and After. Ithaca, NY: Cornell University Press, 2004.

Santos Alves, Jorge M. dos. "La voix de la prophétie: Informations portugaises de la 1e moitié du XVIe s. sur les voyages de Zheng He." In *Zheng He: Images & Perceptions*, ed. Claudine Salmon and Roderich Ptak, 39–55. Wiesbaden: Harrassowitz, 2005.

Schafer, Edward H. *Pacing the Void: T'ang Approaches to the Stars.* Berkeley: University of California Press, 1977.

Schirokauer, Conrad and Robert P. Hymes. "Introduction" to *Ordering the World: Approaches to State and Society in Sung Dynasty China*, ed. Robert P. Hymes and Conrad Schirokauer, 1–58. Berkeley: University of California Press, 1993.

Schottenhammer, Angela. "A Buried Past: The Tomb Inscription and Official Biographies of Wang Chuzhi." *Journal of the Economic and Social History of the Orient*, 52 (2009): 14–56.

Scott, James C. *The Art of Not Being Governed: An Anarchist History of Upland Southeast Asia.* New Haven, CT: Yale University Press, 2009.

Seed, Patricia. *Ceremonies of Possession in Europe's Conquest of the New World, 1492–1640.* Cambridge and New York: Cambridge University Press, 1995.

Seo Tatsuhiko. "Toshi no seikatsu to bunka." In *Gi Shin Nanbokuchō Zui Tō jidaishi no kihon mondai*, ed. Tanigawa Michio et al., 365–442. Tokyo: Kyūko shoin, 1997.

"Shanxi Datong jiaoqu wu zuo Liao bihua mu." *Kaogu*, 10/1960: 37–42.

Shao Guotian. "Aohan qi Baitazi Liao mu." *Kaogu*, 2/1978: 119–21.

Aohan wenwu jinghua. Chifeng: Neimenggu wenhua chubanshe, 2004.

Shaughnessy, Edward L. *Sources of Western Zhou History: Inscribed Bronze Vessels.* Berkeley: University of California Press, 1991.

"Writing of a Late Western Zhou Bronze Inscription." *Asiatische Studien*, 61/3 (2007): 845–77.

Shen, Hsueh-man. "Body Matters: Manikin Burials in the Liao Tombs of Xuanhua, Hebei Province." *Artibus Asiae*, 65/1 (2005): 99–141.

Shiba Yoshinobu. *Commerce and Society in Sung China*, trans. Mark Elvin. Ann Arbor, MI: Center for Chinese Studies, 1992.

"Urbanization and the Development of Markets in the Lower Yangtze Valley." In *Crisis and Prosperity in Sung China*, ed. John Winthrop Haeger, 13–48. Tucson: University of Arizona Press, 1975.

Skaff, Jonathan Karam. "The Sogdian Trade Diaspora in East Turkestan during the Seventh and Eighth Centuries." *Journal of the Economic and Social History of the Orient*, 46/4 (2003): 475–524.

"Straddling Steppe and Sown: Tang China's Relations with the Nomads of Inner Asia (640–756)." PhD Thesis. University of Michigan, 1998.

Sui-Tang China and its Turko-Mongol Neighbors: Culture, Power, and Connections, 580–800. Oxford and New York: Oxford University Press, 2012.

"Survival in the Frontier Zone: Comparative Perspectives on Identity and Political Allegiance in China's Inner Asian Borderlands during the Sui-Tang Dynastic Transition (617–630)." *Journal of World History*, 15/2 (2004): 117–53.

Skinner, G. William. "Introduction: Urban Development in Imperial China." In *The City in Late Imperial China*, ed. G. William Skinner, 3–31. Stanford University Press, 1977.

Smith, Anthony D. *The Ethnic Origins of Nations*. Malden, MA: Blackwell, 1988.

The Nation in History: Historiographical Debates about Ethnicity and Nationalism. Hanover: University Press of New England, 2000.

Smith, Paul Jakov. "A Crisis in the Literati State: The Sino-Tangut War and the Qingli-Era Reforms of Fan Zhongyan, 1040–1045." *Journal of Song-Yuan Studies*, 45 (2015): 59–137.

"Irredentism as Political Capital: The New Policies and the Annexation of Tibetan Domains in Hehuang (the Qinghai-Gansu Highlands) under Shenzong and his Sons, 1068–1126." In *Emperor Huizong and Late Northern Song China*, ed. Patricia Buckley Ebrey and Maggie Bickford, 78–130. Cambridge, MA: Harvard University Asia Center, 2006.

"Shen-tsung's Reign and the New Policies of Wang An-shih, 1067–1085." In *Cambridge History of China*, vol. 5, Part 1: *The Sung Dynasty and its Precursors, 907–1279*, ed. Denis Twitchett and Paul Jakov Smith, 347–483. Cambridge University Press, 2009.

"Shuihu zhuan and the Military Subculture of the Northern Song, 960–1127." *Harvard Journal of Asiatic Studies*, 66/2 (2006): 363–422.

"State Power and Economic Activism during the New Policies, 1068–1085." In *Ordering the World: Approaches to State and Society in Sung Dynasty China*, ed. Robert P. Hymes and Conrad Schirokauer, 76–127. Berkeley: University of California Press, 1993.

Taxing Heaven's Storehouse: Horses, Bureaucrats, and the Destruction of the Sichuan Tea Industry, 1074–1224. Cambridge, MA: Council on East Asian Studies, 1991.

So, Billy K. L. "Negotiating Chinese Identity in Five Dynasties Narratives: From the *Old History* to the *New History*." In *Power and Identity in the Chinese*

World Order, ed. Billy K. L. So et al., 223–38. Hong Kong University Press, 2003.

Standen, Naomi. "Alien Regimes and Mental States." *Journal of the Economic and Social History of the Orient*, 40/1 (1997): 73–89.

"(Re)Constructing the Frontiers of Tenth-Century North China." In *Frontiers in Question: Eurasian Borderlands, 700–1700*, ed. Daniel Power and Naomi Standen, 55–79. New York: St. Martin's Press, 1999.

Unbounded Loyalty: Frontier Crossings in Liao China. Honolulu: University of Hawai'i Press, 2007.

Steinhardt, Nancy Shatzman. "The Architectural Landscape of the Liao and Underground Resonances." In *Gilded Splendor: Treasures of China's Liao Empire*, ed. Hsueh-man Shen, 40–53. New York: Asia Society, 2006.

"Liao: An Architectural Tradition in the Making." *Artibus Asiae*, 54/1–2 (1994): 5–39.

Liao Architecture. Honolulu: University of Hawai'i Press, 1997.

"Liao Pagodas: Sources and Legacy." Paper presented in Chaoyang, Liaoning Province, on July 31, 2009.

Su Bai. *Baisha Song mu*. Beijing: Wenwu chubanshe, 2002.

Su Ritai. "Keyou zhongqi Bazhalaga Liao mu." *Neimenggu wenwu kaogu*, 2 (1982): 64–68.

Su Tianjun. "Shunyi xian Liao Jingguang sheli taji qingli jianbao." *Wenwu*, 8/1964: 49–54.

Subrenat, Jean-Jacques. "Shen Kua." In *Sung Biographies*, ed. Herbert Franke, 2:857–63. Wiesbaden: Franz Steiner Verlag, 1976.

Sullivan, Michael. *The Night Entertainments of Han Xizai: A Scroll by Gu Hongzhong*. Berkeley: University of California Press, 2008.

Sun Jianhua. *Neimenggu Liaodai bihua*. Beijing: Wenwu chubanshe, 2009.

Sutton, Donald S. "Ethnicity and the Miao Frontier in the Eighteenth Century." In *Empire at the Margins: Culture, Ethnicity, and Frontier in Early Modern China*, ed. Pamela Kyle Crossley et al., 190–228. Berkeley: University of California Press, 2006.

"Violence and Ethnicity on a Qing Colonial Frontier: Customary and Statutory Law in the Eighteenth-Century Miao Pale." *Modern Asian Studies*, 37/1 (2003): 41–80.

Tackett, Nicolas. *The Destruction of the Medieval Chinese Aristocracy*. Cambridge, MA: Harvard University Asia Center, 2014.

"The Great Wall and Conceptualizations of the Border under the Northern Song." *Journal of Song-Yuan Studies*, 38 (2008): 99–138.

"Imperial Elites, Bureaucracy, and the Transformation of the Geography of Power in Tang-Song China." Forthcoming in *Die Interaktion von Herrschern und Eliten in imperialen Ordnungen des Mittelalters*, ed. Wolfram Drews. Berlin: De Gruyter.

"The 'Qin Script Reform.'" Unpublished paper.

"The Story of Xu Xuan: Survival and Transformation of the South Chinese Elite during the Tenth Century." MA Thesis. Columbia University, 2002.

"The Transformation of Medieval Chinese Elites." PhD Thesis. Columbia University, 2006. Available at www.ntackett.com.

(Tan Kai). "Wan Tang Hebei ren dui Song chu wenhua de yingxiang." *Tang yanjiu*, 19 (2013): 251–81.

Tackett, Timothy. *The Coming of the Terror in the French Revolution*. Cambridge, MA: Belknap Press, 2015.

Tan Qixiang. *Zhongguo lishi ditu ji*. Beijing: Zhongguo ditu chubanshe, 1982.

Tao Jing-shen. "Barbarians or Northerners: Northern Sung Images of the Khitans." In *China Among Equals: The Middle Kingdom and its Neighbors, 10th–14th Centuries*, ed. Morris Rossabi, 66–81. Berkeley: University of California Press, 1983.

Song Liao guanxi shi yanjiu. Taipei: Lianjing, 1984.

Two Sons of Heaven: Studies in Sung-Liao Relations. Tucson: University of Arizona Press, 1988.

Tao Zongyi (ed.). *Shuofu*. Shanghai: Shangwu yinshuguan, 1927.

Thongchai Winichakul. *Siam Mapped: A History of the Geo-Body of a Nation*. Honolulu: University of Hawai'i Press, 1994.

Tian Xiaofei. *Beacon Fire and Shooting Star: The Literary Culture of the Liang*. Cambridge, MA: Harvard University Asia Center, 2007.

"From the Eastern Jin through the Early Tang." In *Cambridge History of Chinese Literature*, ed. Kang-i Sun Chang and Stephen Owen, 1:199–285. Cambridge University Press, 2010.

Tietze, Klaus. "The Liao-Sung Border Conflict of 1074–1076." In *Studia Sino-Mongolica: Festschrift für Herbert Franke*, ed. Wolfgang Bauer, 127–51. Wiesbaden: Franz Steiner Verlag, 1979.

Tillman, Hoyt Cleveland. "Proto-Nationalism in Twelfth-Century China? The Case of Ch'en Liang." *Harvard Journal of Asiatic Studies*, 39/2 (1979): 403–28.

Utilitarian Confucianism: Ch'en Liang's Challenge to Chu Hsi. Cambridge, MA: Council on East Asian Studies, 1982.

Torii Ryūzō. *Sculptured Stone Tombs of the Liao Dynasty*. Cambridge, MA: Harvard-Yenching Institute, 1942.

Trauzettel, Rolf. "Sung Patriotism as a First Step toward Chinese Nationalism." In *Crisis and Prosperity in Sung China*, 199–213. Tucson: University of Arizona Press, 1975.

Twitchett, Denis. "Introduction" to *The Cambridge History of China*, vol. 3, Part 1: *Sui and T'ang China*, ed. Denis Twitchett, 1–47. Cambridge University Press, 1979.

"Merchant, Trade, and Government in Late Tang." *Asia Major*, new ser., 14/1 (1968): 63–95.

"The T'ang Market System." *Asia Major*, new ser., 12/2 (1966): 202–48.

"Tibet in Tang's Grand Strategy." In *Warfare in Chinese History*, ed. Hans van den Ven, 106–79. Leiden and Boston, MA: Brill, 2000.

Twitchett, Denis and Klaus-Peter Tietze. "The Liao." In *Cambridge History of China*, vol. 6: *Alien Regimes and Border States, 907–1368*, ed. Herbert Franke and Denis Twitchett, 43–153. Cambridge University Press, 1994.

Vick, Brian E. *The Congress of Vienna: Power and Politics after Napoleon.* Cambridge, MA: Harvard University Press, 2014.

Von Glahn, Richard. "The Conquest of Hunan." Chapter Seven of "The Country of Streams and Grottoes: Geography, Settlement, and the Civilizing of China's Southwestern Frontier, 1000–1250." PhD Thesis. Yale University, 1983.

The Country of Streams and Grottoes: Expansion, Settlement, and the Civilizing of the Sichuan Frontier in Song Times. Cambridge, MA: Council on East Asian Studies, 1987.

Wakeman, Frederic, Jr. *The Great Enterprise: The Manchu Reconstruction of Imperial Order in Seventeenth-Century China.* Berkeley: University of California Press, 1985.

"*Hanjian* (Traitor)! Collaboration and Retribution in Wartime Shanghai." In *Becoming Chinese: Passages to Modernity and Beyond*, ed. Wen-hsin Yeh, 298–341. Berkeley: University of California Press, 2000.

Strangers at the Gate: Social Disorder in South China, 1839–1861. Berkeley: University of California Press, 1966.

Waldron, Arthur. *The Great Wall of China: From History to Myth.* Cambridge University Press, 1990.

Wang Ce and Zhu Zhigang. "Fengtai lukou nan chutu Liao mu qingli baogao." In *Beijing Liao Jin wenwu yanjiu*, 316–20. Beijing: Beijing Yanshan chubanshe, 2005.

Wang Gung-wu. "Feng Tao: An Essay on Confucian Loyalty." In *Confucian Personalities*, ed. Arthur F. Wright and Denis Twitchett, 123–45. Stanford University Press, 1962.

"The Rhetoric of a Lesser Empire: Early Sung Relations with its Neighbors." In *China Among Equals: The Middle Kingdom and its Neighbors, 10th–14th Centuries*, ed. Morris Rossabi, 47–65. Berkeley: University of California Press, 1983.

The Structure of Power in North China During the Five Dynasties. Stanford University Press, 1967.

Wang, Hongjie. *Power and Politics in Tenth-Century China: The Former Shu Regime.* Amherst, NY: Cambria Press, 2011.

Wang Jianqun and Chen Xiangwei. *Kulun Liaodai bihua mu.* Beijing: Wenwu chubanshe, 1989.

Wang Jilin. "Qidan yu Nan Tang waijiao guanxi zhi tantao." *Youshi xuezhi*, 5/1 (1966): 1–16.

Wang Jinxian and Wang Yonggen. "Shanxi Huguan Nancun Song dai zhuandiao mu." *Wenwu*, 2/1997: 44–54.

Wang Qiuhua. "Liaodai muzang fenqu yu fenqi de chutan." *Liaoning daxue xuebao*, 3/1982: 43–46.

Wang Yintian et al. "Shanxi Datong shi Liao mu de fajue." *Kaogu*, 8/2007: 34–44.

et al. "Shanxi Datong shi Liaodai junjiedushi Xu Congyun fufu bihua mu." *Kaogu*, 8/2005: 34–47.

Wang Yong. *Zhongguo dili xueshi*. Shanghai: Shangwu yinshuguan, 1938.

Wang Zhenping. *Tang China in Multi-Polar Asia: A History of Diplomacy and War*. Honolulu: University of Hawai'i Press, 2013.

Watson, Burton (trans.). *Records of the Grand Historian: Qin Dynasty*. New York: Columbia University Press, 1993.

Wechsler, Howard J. "T'ai-tsung the Consolidator." In *Cambridge History of China*, vol. 3, Part 1: *Sui and T'ang China*, ed. Denis Twitchett, 188–241. Cambridge University Press, 1979.

Weinstein, Stanley. *Buddhism under the T'ang*. Cambridge University Press, 1987.

Wen Yu. "Qionglu shi guhui guan." In *Linhuang shiji*, 97–98. Bairin Zuoqi: Bairin zuoqi yinshuachang, 1988.

Wittfogel, Karl A. and Feng Chia-Sheng. *History of Chinese Society: Liao (907–1125)*. Published as *Transactions of the American Philosophical Society*, new ser., 36 (1946). Available at JSTOR.

Woolley, Nathan. "From Restoration to Unification: Legitimacy and Loyalty in the Writings of Xu Xuan (917–992)." *Bulletin of the School of Oriental and African Studies*, 77/3 (2014): 547–67.

Worthy, Edmund H., Jr. "Diplomacy for Survival: Domestic and Foreign Relations of Wu Yüeh, 907–978." In *China Among Equals: The Middle Kingdom and its Neighbors, 10th–14th Centuries*, ed. Morris Rossabi, 17–44. Berkeley: University of California Press, 1983.

Wright, Arthur F. "The Sui Dynasty." In *Cambridge History of China*, vol. 3, Part 1: *Sui and T'ang China*, ed. Denis Twitchett, 48–149. Cambridge University Press, 1979.

The Sui Dynasty: The Unification of China. New York: Knopf, 1978.

Wright, David Curtis. *The Ambassadors Records: Eleventh-Century Reports of Sung Embassies to Liao*. Bloomington, IN: Research Institute for Inner Asian Studies, 1998.

From War to Diplomatic Parity in Eleventh-Century China: Sung's Foreign Relations with Kitan Liao. Leiden: Brill, 2005.

Wu Dongfeng. "Hebei Wuyi Longdian Song mu fajue baogao." In *Hebei sheng kaogu wenji*, 1 (1998): 323–29.

Wu Hung. *The Art of the Yellow Springs: Understanding Chinese Tombs*. Honolulu: University of Hawai'i Press, 2010.

Wu Qingjun and Liu Debiao. "Tangdai Yuan Yun muzhi qianshuo." *Wenwu chunqiu*, 6/2010: 73–75.

Wu Tingxie. *Bei Song jingfu nianbiao*. Beijing: Zhonghua shuju, 2004.

Wyatt, Don J. *Battlefronts Real and Imagined: War, Border, and Identity in the Chinese Middle Period*. New York: Palgrave Macmillan, 2008.

Xiang Chunsong. "Liaoning Zhaowuda diqu faxian de Liao mu huihua ziliao." *Wenwu*, 6/1979: 22–32.

"Zhaomeng diqu de Liaodai muzang." *Neimenggu wenwu kaogu*, 1981: 73–79.

Xin Yan. "Fuxin Nanzaoli yingzi yihao Liao mu." *Liaohai wenwu xuekan*, 1/1992: 54–63.

Xu Pingfang. "The Archaeology of the Great Wall of the Qin and Han Dynasties." *Journal of East Asian Archaeology*, 3/1–2 (2002): 259–81.

Xu Yulin. "Liaoning Anshan shi Wangjia yu Liao huaxiang shimu." *Kaogu*, 3/1981: 239–42.

"Liaoning Beipiao Shuiquan yihao Liao mu fajue baogao." *Wenwu*, 12/1977: 44–51.

Xuanhua Liao mu: 1974–1993 nian kaogu fajue baogao. Beijing: Wenwu chubanshe, 2001.

Xuanhua Xiabali er qu Liao bihuamu kaogu fajue baogao. Beijing: Wenwu chubanshe, 2008.

Yan Qinheng. "Bei Song dui Liao tangdai sheshi zhi yanjiu." *Guoli zhengzhi daxue xuebao*, 8 (1963): 247–57.

Yang Bin. *Between Winds and Clouds: The Making of Yunan, Second Century BCE to Twentieth Century CE.* New York: Columbia University Press, 2008. www.gutenberg-e.org/yang/index.html.

Yang Jing. "Liaodai Han ren muzang gaishu." *Wenwu chunqiu*, 2/1995: 53–56.

"Luelun jiguan hu." *Kaogu*, 7/1995: 632–37.

Yang Rui. *Xi Xia dili yanjiu: Bianjiang lishi dilixue de tansuo.* Beijing: Renmin chubanshe, 2008.

Yang, Shao-yun. "Becoming *Zhongguo*, Becoming Han: Tracing and Re-Conceptualizing Ethnicity in Ancient North China, 770 BC - AD 581." MA Thesis. National University of Singapore, 2007. Available at www.scholarbank.nus.edu.sg.

"*Fan* and *Han*: The Origins and Uses of a Conceptual Dichotomy in Mid-Imperial China, ca. 500–1200." In *Political Strategies of Identity Building in Non-Han Empires in China*, ed. Francesca Fiaschetti and Julia Schneider, 9–35. Wiesbaden: Harrassowitz, 2014.

"Reinventing the Barbarian: Rhetorical and Philosophical Uses of the *Yi-Di* in Mid-Imperial China." PhD Thesis. University of California, Berkeley, 2014.

Yang Xiaoneng (ed.). *New Perspectives on China's Past: Chinese Archaeology in the Twentieth Century.* New Haven, CT: Yale University Press, 2004.

Yang Yubin. "Shangcai Song mu." *Henan wenbo tongxun*, 4/1978: 34–35.

Ye Wa. "Mortuary Practice in Medieval China: A Study of the Xingyuan Tang Cemetery." PhD Thesis. University of California, Los Angeles, 2005.

Yü Ying-Shih. "Han Foreign Relations." In *Cambridge History of China*, vol. 1: *The Ch'in and Han Empires*, ed. Denis Twitchett and Michael Loewe, 377–462. Cambridge University Press, 1986.

Zelin, Madeleine. "The Rise and Fall of the Fu-Rong Salt-Yard Elite." In *Chinese Local Elites and Patterns of Dominance*, ed. Joseph W. Esherick and Mary Backus Rankin, 82–109. Berkeley: University of California Press, 1990.

Zhang Bozhong. "Kezuo houqi Husinao Qidan mu." *Wenwu*, 9/1983: 18–22.

Zhang Cong, Ellen. *Transformative Journeys: Travel and Culture in Song China.* Honolulu: University of Hawai'i Press, 2011.

Zhang Diyun. "Guanyu Wang Anshi shi Liao yu shi Liao shi de kaobian." *Wenxue yichan*, 1/2006: 73–82.

Zhang Jian and Wang Kai. "Luoyang Jianxi san zuo Song dai fangmugou zhuan-shimu." *Wenwu*, 8/1983: 13–24.

Zhang Songbo. "Guanyu jiguan hu yanjiu zhong de ji ge wenti." In *Neimenggu wenwu kaogu wenji*, 2:584–91. Beijing: Zhongguo dabaike quanshu chu-banshe, 1997.

Zhang Xiande. "Beijing shi Daxing xian Liaodai Ma Zhiwen fuqi hezang mu." *Wenwu*, 12/1980: 30–37.

Zhang Xiqing. *Songchao dianzhang zhidu*. Changchun: Jilin wenshi chubanshe, 2001.

Zhang Zengwu. "Henan Linxian chengguan Song mu qingli jianbao." *Kaogu yu wenwu*, 5/1982: 39–42.

Zhao Hong and Gao Ming. "Jiyuan shi Dongshilutou cun Songdai bihua mu." *Zhongyuan wenwu*, 2/2008: 19–21, 54.

Zhongguo wenwu ditu ji: Neimenggu zizhiqu fence. Xi'an ditu chubanshe, 2003.

Zhongguo wenwu ditu ji: Ningxia Huizu zizhiqu fence. Beijing: Wenwu chu-banshe, 2010.

Zhu Zifang and Xu Ji. "Liaoning Chaoyang Guyingzi Liao Geng shi mu fajue baogao." *Kaoguxue jikan*, 3 (1983): 168–95.

Index

319